A Note on the Author

BEN MACINTYRE is a columnist and Associate Editor on *The Times*. He has worked as the newspaper's correspondent in New York, Paris and Washington. He is the author of ten previous books including *Agent Zigzag*, shortlisted for the Costa Biography Award and the Galaxy British Book Award for Biography of the Year 2008, and the *Sunday Times* bestsellers *Double Cross* and *A Spy Among Friends*. His most recent book is *SAS Rogue Heroes*, the first authorised biography of the SAS.

benmacintyre.com

BY THE SAME AUTHOR

Forgotten Fatherland

The Napoleon of Crime

A Foreign Field

Josiah the Great

Agent Zigzag

For Your Eyes Only

The Last Word

Double Cross

A Spy Among Friends

SAS Rogue Heroes

OPERATION MINCEMEAT

The True Spy Story that Changed the Course of World War II

Ben Macintyre

B L O O M S B U R Y

LONDON · OXFORD · NEW YORK · NEW DELHI · SYDNEY

BLOOMSBURY PAPERBACKS
Bloomsbury Publishing Plc
50 Bedford Square, London, WC1B 3DP, UK
29 Earlsfort Terrace, Dublin 2, Ireland

BLOOMSBURY, BLOOMSBURY PAPERBACKS and the
Diana logo are trademarks of Bloomsbury Publishing Plc

First published in Great Britain 2010
This paperback edition first published in 2016

Map by Duncan Stewart

British Library Cataloguing-in-Publication Data
A catalogue record for this book is available from the British Library.

ISBN: PB: 978-1-4088-8539-0
ePub: 978-1-4088-0854-2

15

Typeset by Newgen Knowledge Works (P) Ltd., Chennai, India
Printed and bound in Great Britain by CPI Group (UK) Ltd, Croydon CR0 4YY

To find out more about our authors and books visit www.bloomsbury.com. Here you will find extracts, author interviews, details of forthcoming events and the option to sign up for our newsletters.

For
Kate & Melita
and
Magnus & Lucie

‘Who in war will not have his laugh amid the skulls?’

– Winston Churchill, *Closing the Ring*

CONTENTS

Preface

In the early hours of 10 July 1943, British, Commonwealth and American troops stormed ashore on the coast of Sicily in the first assault against Hitler's 'Fortress Europe'. With hindsight, the invasion of the Italian island was a triumph, a pivotal moment in the war, and a vital stepping stone on the way to victory in Europe. The offensive – then the largest amphibious landing ever attempted – had been months in the planning, and although the fighting was fierce, the casualty rate among the Allies was limited. Of the 160,000 soldiers who took part in the invasion and conquest of Sicily, more than 153,000 were still alive at the end. That so many survived was due, in no small measure, to a man who had died seven months earlier. The success of the Sicilian invasion depended on overwhelming strength, logistics, secrecy and surprise. But it also relied on a wide web of deception, and one deceit in particular: a spectacular con trick dreamed up by a team of spies led by an English lawyer.

I first came across the remarkable Ewen Montagu while researching an earlier book, *Agent Zigzag*, about the wartime double agent Eddie Chapman. A barrister in civilian life, Montagu was a Naval Intelligence officer who had been one of Chapman's handlers, but he was better known as the author, in 1953, of *The Man Who Never Was*, an account of the deception plan he had masterminded in 1943 codenamed 'Operation Mincemeat'. In a later book, *Beyond Top Secret Ultra*, written in

1977, Montagu referred to 'some memoranda which, in very special circumstances and for a very particular reason, I was allowed to keep'.

That odd aside stuck in my memory. The 'special circumstances', I assumed, must refer to the writing of *The Man Who Never Was*, which was authorised and vetted by the Joint Intelligence Committee. But I could think of no other case in which a former intelligence officer had been 'allowed to keep' classified documents. Indeed, retaining top-secret material is exactly what intelligence officers are supposed not to do. And if Ewen Montagu had kept them for so many years after the war, where were they now?

Montagu died in 1985. None of the obituaries referred to his papers. I went to see his son, Jeremy Montagu, a distinguished authority on musical instruments at Oxford University. With an unmistakable twinkle, Jeremy led me to an upstairs room in his rambling home in Oxford, and pulled a large and dusty wooden trunk from under a bed. Inside were bundles of files from MI5, MI6 and the Naval Intelligence Department, some tied up with string and many of them stamped 'Top Secret'. Jeremy explained that some of his father's papers had been transferred after his death to the Imperial War Museum, where they had yet to be catalogued, but the rest were just as he had left them in the trunk: letters, memos, photographs and operational notes relating to the 1943 deception plan, as well as the original, uncensored manuscripts of his books. Here, too, was Ewen Montagu's unpublished 200-page autobiography and, perhaps most importantly, a copy of the official, classified report on 'Operation Mincemeat' – the boldest, strangest and most successful deception of the war.

If my discovery of these papers reads like something out of a spy film, that may be no accident: Montagu himself had a rich sense of the dramatic. He must have known they would be found one day.

More than half a century after publication, *The Man Who*

Never Was has lost none of the flavour of wartime intrigue, but it is, and was always intended to be, incomplete. The book was written at the behest of the Government in order to conceal certain facts; in parts, it is deliberately misleading. Now, with the relaxation of government rules surrounding official secrecy, the recently declassified files in the National Archives, and the contents of Ewen Montagu's ancient trunk, the full story of Operation Mincemeat can be told for the first time.

The plan was born in the mind of a novelist, and took shape through a most unlikely cast of characters: a brilliant barrister, a family of undertakers, a forensic pathologist, a gold prospector, an inventor, a submarine captain, a transvestite English spy master, a rally driver, a pretty secretary, a credulous Nazi, and a grumpy admiral who loved fly-fishing.

This deception operation – which underpinned the invasion of Sicily and helped to win the war – was framed around a man who never was. But the people who invented him, and those who believed in him, and those who owed their lives to him, most certainly were.

This is their story.

Ben Macintyre
London, October 2009

1

The Sardine Spotter

José Antonio Rey María had no intention of making history when he rowed out into the Atlantic from the coast of Andalucia in southwest Spain on 30 April 1943. He was merely looking for sardines.

José was proud of his reputation as the best fish-spotter in Punta Umbria. On a clear day, he could pick out the telltale iridescent flash of sardines several fathoms deep. When he saw a shoal, José would mark the place with a buoy, and then signal to Pepe Cordero and the other fishermen in the larger boat, *La Calina*, to row over swiftly with the horseshoe net.

But the weather today was bad for fish-spotting. The sky was overcast, and an onshore wind ruffled the water's surface. The fishermen of Punta Umbria had set out before dawn, but so far they had caught only anchovies and a few bream. Rowing *Ana*, his little skiff, in a wide arc, José scanned the water again, the rising sun warming his back. On the shore, he could see the little cluster of fishing huts beneath the dunes on Playa del Portil, his home. Beyond that, past the estuary where the rivers Odiel and Tinto flowed into the sea, lay the port of Huelva.

The war, now in its fourth year, had hardly touched this part of Spain. Sometimes José would come across strange flotsam in the water, fragments of charred wood, pools of oil, and other debris that told of battles somewhere out at sea. Earlier that morning, he had heard gunfire in the distance, and a loud explosion. Pepe said that the war was ruining the fishing business; no one had any money, and he might have to sell *La Calina* and *Ana*. It was rumoured that the captains on some of the larger fishing boats spied for the Germans or the British. But in most ways the hard lives of the fishermen continued as they had always done.

José had been born on the beach, in a hut made from driftwood, twenty-three years earlier. He had never travelled beyond Huelva and its waters. He had never been to school, or learned to read and write. But no one in Punta Umbria was better at spotting fish.

It was mid-morning when José noticed a 'lump' above the surface of the water. At first he thought it must be a dead porpoise, but as he rowed closer the shape grew clearer, and then unmistakable. It was a body, floating, face down, buoyed up by a yellow life jacket, the lower part of its torso invisible. It seemed to be dressed in uniform.

As he reached over the gunwale to grab the body, José caught a gust of putrefaction and found himself looking into the face of a man, or, rather, what had been the face of a man. The chin was entirely covered in green mould, while the upper part of the face was dark, as if tanned by the sun. José wondered if the dead man had been burned in some accident at sea. The skin on the nose and chin had begun to rot away.

José waved and shouted to the other fishermen. As *La Calina* drew alongside, Pepe and the crew clustered by the gunwale. José called for them to throw down a rope and haul the body aboard, but 'no one wanted to touch it'. Annoyed, José realised he would have to bring it ashore himself. Seizing a handful of sodden uniform, he hauled the corpse on to the stern, the legs trailing in the water, and rowed back to shore, trying not to breathe in the smell.

At the part of the beach called La Bota – the boot – José and Pepe dragged the body up to the dunes. A black briefcase, attached to the man by a chain, trailed in the sand behind them. They laid out the corpse in the shade of a pine tree. Children streamed out of the huts and gathered around the gruesome spectacle. The man was tall, at least six foot, dressed in a khaki tunic and trench coat, with large army boots. Seventeen-year-old Obdulia Serrano spotted a small silver chain with a cross around the dead man's neck: he must have been a Roman Catholic, she thought.

Obdulia was sent to summon the officer from the defence unit guarding that part of the coast. A dozen men of Spain's 72nd Infantry Regiment had been marching up and down the beach earlier that morning, as they did, rather pointlessly, most mornings. The soldiers were now taking a siesta under the trees. The officer ordered two of his men to stand guard over the body in case someone tried to go through the dead man's pockets, and trudged off up the beach to find his commanding officer.

The scent of the wild rosemary and jacaranda growing among the dunes could not mask the stench of decomposition. Flies buzzed around the body. The soldiers moved upwind. Somebody went to fetch a donkey to carry the body to the village of Punta Umbria four miles away. From there, it could be taken by boat across the estuary to Huelva.

José Antonio Rey María, unaware of the events he had just set in train, pushed the skiff back into the sea, and resumed his search for sardines.

Two months earlier, in a tiny, tobacco-stained basement room beneath the Admiralty building in Whitehall, two men had sat puzzling over a conundrum of their own devising: how to create a person from nothing, a man who had never been.

The younger man was tall and thin, with thick spectacles and an elaborate Air Force moustache, which he twiddled in rapt concentration. The other, elegant and languid, was dressed in naval uniform and sucked on a curved pipe that fizzed and crackled evilly. The stuffy underground cavern lacked windows, natural light and ventilation. The walls were covered in large maps, and the ceiling stained a greasy nicotine-yellow. It had once been a wine cellar. Now it was home to a section of the British Secret Service made up of four intelligence officers, seven secretaries and typists, six typewriters, a bank of locked filing cabinets, a dozen ashtrays and two scrambler telephones. Section 17M was so secret that barely twenty people outside the room even knew of its existence.

Room 13 of the Admiralty was a clearing house of secrets, lies and whispers. Every day the most lethal and valuable intelligence – decoded messages, deception plans, enemy troop movements, coded spy reports and other mysteries – poured into this little basement room, where they were analysed, assessed, and despatched to distant parts of the world – the armour and ammunition of a secret war.

The two officers – Pipe and Moustache – were also responsible for running agents and double agents, espionage and counterespionage, intelligence, fakery and fraud: they passed lies to the enemy that were damaging, as well as information that was true but harmless; they ran willing spies, reluctant spies pressed into service, and spies who did not exist at all. Now, with the war at its height, they set about creating a spy who was different from all the others and all that had come before: a secret agent who was not only fictional, but dead.

The defining feature of this spy would be his falsity. He was a pure figment of imagination, a weapon in a war far removed from the traditional battle of bombs and bullets. At its most visible, war is fought with leadership, courage, tactics and brute force; this is the conventional war of attack and counterattack, lines on a map, numbers and luck. This war is usually painted in black, white and blood red, with winners, losers and casualties: the good, the bad and the dead. Then there is the other, less visible, species of conflict, played out in shades of grey, a battle of deception, seduction and bad faith, of tricks and mirrors, in which the truth is protected, as Churchill put it, by a 'bodyguard of lies'. The combatants in this war of the imagination were seldom what they seemed, for the covert world, in which fiction and reality are sometimes enemies and sometimes allies, attracts minds that are subtle, supple, and often extremely strange.

The man lying in the dunes at Punta Umbria was a fraud. The lies he carried would fly from London to Madrid to Berlin, travelling from a freezing Scottish loch to the shores of Sicily, from fiction to reality, and from Room 13 of the Admiralty all the way to Hitler's desk.

2

Corkscrew Minds

Deceiving the enemy in wartime, thought Admiral John Godfrey, Director of Naval Intelligence, was just like fishing: specifically fly-fishing for trout. 'The Trout Fisher,' he wrote, in a top-secret memo, 'casts patiently all day. He frequently changes his venue and his lures. If he has frightened a fish he may "give the water a rest for half-an-hour", but his main endeavour, viz. to attract fish by something he sends out from his boat, is incessant.'

Godfrey's 'Trout Memo' was distributed to the other chiefs of wartime intelligence on 29 September 1939, when the war was barely three weeks old. It was issued under Godfrey's name, but it bore all the hallmarks of his personal assistant, Lieutenant Commander Ian Fleming, who would go on to write the James Bond novels. Fleming had, in Godfrey's words, a 'marked flair' for intelligence planning, and was particularly skilled, as one might expect, at dreaming up what he called 'plots' to outfox the enemy. Fleming called these plans 'romantic Red Indian daydreams', but they were deadly serious. The memo laid out numerous ideas for bamboozling the Germans at sea, the many ways that the fish might be trapped through 'deception, ruses de guerre, passing on false information and so on'. The ideas were extraordinarily imaginative and, like most of Fleming's writing, barely credible. The memo admitted as much. 'At first sight, many of these appear somewhat fantastic, but nevertheless they contain germs of some good ideas; and the more you examine them, the less fantastic they seem to appear.'

Godfrey was himself a most literal man: hard-driving, irascible and indefatigable, he was the model for 'M' in Fleming's Bond stories. There was no one in naval intelligence with a keener appreciation of the peculiar mentality needed for espionage and counterespionage. 'The business of deception, handling double agents, deliberate leakages and building up in the minds of the enemy confidence in a double agent, needed the sort of corkscrew mind which I did not possess,' he reflected. Gathering intelligence, and distributing false intelligence, was, he said, like 'pushing quicksilver through a gorse bush with a long-handled spoon'.

The Trout Memo was a masterpiece of corkscrew thinking, with fifty-one suggestions for 'introducing ideas into the heads of the Germans', ranging from the possible to the wacky. These included dropping footballs painted with luminous paint to attract submarines; distributing messages cursing Hitler's Reich in bottles from a fictitious U-boat captain; a fake 'treasure ship' packed with commandos; and sending out false information through bogus copies of *The Times* ('an unimpeachable and immaculate medium'). One of the nastier ideas envisaged setting adrift tins of explosives disguised as food, 'with instructions on the outside in many languages', in the hope that hungry enemy sailors or submariners would pick them up, try to heat the tins, and blow themselves up.

Though none of these plans ever came to fruition, buried deep in the memo was the kernel of another idea: Number 28 on the list was fantastic in every sense. Under the heading 'A Suggestion (not a very nice one)' Godfrey and Fleming wrote: 'The following suggestion is used in a book by Basil Thomson: a corpse dressed as an airman, with despatches in his pockets, could be dropped on the coast, supposedly from a parachute that had failed. I understand there is no difficulty in obtaining corpses at the Naval Hospital, but, of course, it would have to be a fresh one.'

Basil Thomson, former assistant premier of Tonga, tutor to the King of Siam, ex-governor of Dartmoor prison, policeman and novelist, had made his name as a spy catcher during the First World War. As head of Scotland Yard's Criminal Investigation Division and the Metropolitan Police Special Branch, he took credit (only partly deserved) for tracking down German spies in Britain, many of whom were caught and executed. He interviewed Mata Hari (and concluded she was innocent), and distributed the 'Black Diaries' of the Irish nationalist and revolutionary Sir Roger Casement, detailing his homosexual affairs: Casement was subsequently tried and executed for treason. Thomson was an early master of deception, and not just in his professional life. In 1925 the worthy police chief was convicted of an act of indecency with 'Miss Thelma de Lava' on a London park bench, and fined £5.

In between catching spies, carrying out surveillance of union leaders and consorting with prostitutes (for the purposes of 'research', as he explained to the court), Thomson found time to write twelve detective novels. The hero of these, Inspector Richardson, inhabits a world peopled by fragrant damsels in distress, stiff upper lips and excitable foreigners in need of British colonisation. Most of Thomson's novels, with titles such as *Death in the Bathroom* and *Richardson Scores Again*, were instantly forgettable. But in *The Milliner's Hat Mystery*, published in 1937, he planted a seed. The novel opens on a stormy night with the discovery of a dead man in a barn, carrying papers that identify him as 'John Whitaker'. By dint of some distinctly plodding detective work, Inspector Richardson discovers that every document in the pockets of the dead man has been ingeniously forged: his visiting cards, his bills, and even his passport, on which the real name has been erased using a special ink remover, and a fake one substituted. 'I know the stuff they use; they employed it a lot during the war,' says Inspector Richardson. 'It will take out ink from any document without leaving a trace.' The remainder of the novel is spent unravelling the identity of the body in the barn. 'However improbable a story sounds we are trained to investigate it,' says Inspector Richardson. 'Only that way can we arrive at the truth.' Inspector Richardson is always saying things like that.

The idea of creating a false identity for a dead body lodged in the mind of Ian Fleming, a confirmed bibliophile who owned several of Thomson's novels. From one spy and novelist it passed into the mind of another future spy-novelist and in 1939, the year that Basil Thomson died, it formally entered the thinking of Britain's spy chiefs as they embarked on a ferocious intelligence battle with the Nazis.

The trout-fishing Admiral Godfrey later wrote that the Second World War 'offers us far more interesting, amusing and subtle examples of intelligence work than any writer of spy stories can devise'. For almost four years, this 'not very nice' idea, as he called it, would lie dormant, a bright lure cast by a fisherman-spy, waiting for someone to bite.

In late September 1942, a frisson of alarm ran through British and American intelligence circles, when it seemed that the date of the planned invasion of French North Africa might have fallen into German hands. On 25 September, an RAF Catalina FP119 seaplane, flying from Plymouth to Gibraltar, crashed in a violent electrical storm off Cadiz on Spain's Atlantic coast, killing all three passengers and seven crew. Among these was Paymaster Lieutenant James Hadden Turner, a Royal Navy courier, carrying a letter to the Governor of Gibraltar informing him that the American General Dwight Eisenhower would be arriving on the rock immediately before the offensive, and that 'the target date has now been set as 4th November'. A second letter, dated 21 September, contained additional information on the forthcoming invasion of North Africa.

The bodies had washed ashore at La Barrosa, south of Cadiz, and were recovered by the Spanish authorities. After twenty-four hours Turner's body, with the letter still in his pocket, was turned over to the local British consul by the Spanish admiral in command at Cadiz. As the war raged, Spain had maintained a neutrality of sorts, with the Allies haunted by the fear that General Francisco Franco might throw in his lot with Hitler. Spanish official opinion was broadly in favour of the Axis powers; many Spanish officials were in contact with German intelligence, and the area around Cadiz, in particular, was known to be a hotbed of German spies. Was it possible that the letter, revealing the date of the Allied attack, had been passed into enemy hands? Eisenhower was said to be 'extremely worried'.

The invasion of North Africa, 'Operation Torch', had been in preparation for months. Major General George Patton was due to sail from Virginia on 23 October with the Western Task Force of 35,000 men, heading for Casablanca in French Morocco. At the same time, British forces would attack Oran in French Algeria, while a joint Allied force invaded Algiers. The Germans were certainly aware that a major offensive was being planned. If the letter had been intercepted and passed on, they would now also know the date of the assault, and that Gibraltar, the gateway to the Mediterranean and North Africa, would play a key role in it.

The Spanish authorities assured Britain that Turner's corpse had 'not been tampered with'. Scientists were flown out to Gibraltar, and the body and letter were subjected to minute examination. The four seals holding down the envelope flap had been opened, apparently by the effect of the sea water, and the writing was still 'quite legible' despite being immersed for at least twelve hours. But some forensic spycraft suggested the Allies could relax. On opening Turner's coat to take out the letter in his breast pocket, the scientists noticed that sand fell out of the eyes in the buttons and the button holes, having been rubbed into the coat when the body washed up on the beach. 'It was highly unlikely,' the British concluded, 'that any agent would have replaced the sand when rebuttoning the jacket.' The German spies operating in Spain were good, but not that good. The secret was safe.

Yet British suspicions were not without foundation. Another victim of the Catalina air crash was Louis Daniélou, an intelligence officer with the Free French forces, travelling under the name Charles Marcil, who was on a mission for the Special Operations Executive (SOE), the covert British organisation operating behind enemy lines. Daniélou had been carrying his notebook and a document, written in French and dated 22 September, which referred, albeit vaguely, to British attacks on targets in North Africa. Intercepted and decoded wireless messages indicated that this information had indeed been passed on to the Germans: 'All the documents, which included a list of prominent personalities [i.e. agents] in North Africa and possibly information with regard to our organisations there, together with a notebook, have been photostatted and come into the hands of the enemy.' An unnamed Italian agent had obtained the copied documents and handed them to the Germans, who mistakenly accorded the information 'no greater importance than any other bit of intelligence'. The Germans may also have suspected the 'documents had likely been planted as a deception'.

An important item of military intelligence had washed into the Germans' hands from the Atlantic; luckily, its significance had eluded them. 'This suggested that the Spanish could be relied on to pass on what they found, and that this unneutral habit might be turned to account.' Here was evidence of a most ingenious avenue into German thinking, an alluring fly to cast on the water.

The incident had rattled the wartime intelligence chiefs, but in the corkscrew mind of one intelligence officer it had lodged, and remained. That mind belonged to one Charles Christopher Cholmondeley, a twenty-five-year-old flight lieutenant in the Royal Air Force, seconded to MI5, the Security Service. Cholmondeley (pronounced 'Chumly') was one of nature's more notable eccentrics, but a most effective warrior in this strange and complicated war. Cholmondeley gazed at the world through thick pebble spectacles, from behind a remarkable moustache six inches long and waxed into magnificent points. Over six feet three inches tall, with size 12 feet, he never quite seemed to fit his uniform, and walked with a strange, lolloping gait, 'lifting his toes as he walked'.

Cholmondeley longed for adventure. As a schoolboy at Canford School in Dorset, he had joined the Public Schools Exploring Society on expeditions to Finland and Newfoundland, to map as yet uncharted territory. Living under canvas, he had survived on Kendal Mint Cake, discovered a new species of shrew after it died inside his sleeping bag, and enjoyed every moment. He studied geography at Oxford, joined the Officers' Training Corps, and in 1938 applied, unsuccessfully, to the Sudan Service. He briefly worked as a King's Messenger, the corps of couriers carrying messages to embassies and consulates around the world that was often seen as a stepping stone to an intelligence career. The most distinguished of Cholmondeley's ancestors was his maternal grandfather, Charles Leyland, whose gift to the world was the Leyland Cyprus, or Leylandii, cause of countless suburban hedge disputes. Cholmondeley had a more glamorous future in mind: he dreamed of becoming a spy, a soldier, or at least a colonial official in some far-flung and exotic land. One brother, Richard, died fighting at Dunkirk, further firing Charles's determination to find action, excitement and, if necessary, a hero's death.

Cholmondeley may have had the mind of an adventurer, but he had neither the body nor the luck. He was commissioned pilot officer in November 1939, but his poor eyesight meant he would never fly a plane, even if a cockpit could have been found to accommodate his ungainly shape. 'This was a terrible blow,' according to his sister. So, far from soaring heroically into the heights, as he had hoped, Cholmondeley was grounded for the duration of the war, his long legs cramped under a desk. This might have blunted the ambitions of a lesser man, but Cholmondeley instead poured his imagination and energies into covert work.

By 1942 he had risen to the rank of flight lieutenant (temporary) in the RAF's Intelligence and Security Department, seconded to MI5. Tommy Argyll Robertson (universally known as 'Tar' on account of his initials), the MI5 chief who headed the B1A section of British intelligence, which ran captured enemy spies as double agents, recruited Cholmondeley as an 'ideas man', describing him as 'extraordinary and delightful'. When off duty, Cholmondeley restored antique cars, studied the mating habits of insects, and hunted partridge with a revolver. He was courtly and correct, and almost pathologically shy and secretive. He cut a distinctive figure around Whitehall, his arms flapping when animated, hopping along the pavements like a huge, flightless, myopic bird. But, for all his peculiarities, Cholmondeley was a most remarkable espionage thinker.

Some of Cholmondeley's ideas were madcap in the extreme. He had, in the words of a fellow intelligence officer, 'one of those subtle and ingenious minds which is forever throwing up fantastic ideas – mostly so ingenious as either to be impossible of implementation or so intricate as to render their efficacy problematical, but every now and again quite brilliant in their simplicity'. Cholmondeley's role, like that of Ian Fleming at Naval Intelligence, was to imagine the unimaginable, and try to lure the truth towards it. More formally, he was secretary of the top-secret XX Committee, or Twenty Committee, the group in charge of overseeing the exploitation of double agents, so-called because the two roman numerals formed a pleasing pun as a double-cross. (The name may also have been an ironic tribute to Charlie Chaplin, whose *Great Dictator*, a film released in 1940, operates under a XX flag, mimicking a swastika.) Under the chairmanship of John Masterman, a dry and ascetic Oxford don, the Twenty Committee met every Thursday in the MI5 offices at 58 St James's Street, to discuss the double-agent system run by 'Tar' Robertson, explore new deception plans, and plot how to pass the most usefully damaging information to the enemy. Its members included representatives of Navy, Army and Air

Intelligence, as well as MI5 (the Security Service, responsible for counterespionage) and MI6 (the Secret Intelligence Service, SIS, responsible for gathering intelligence outside Britain). As secretary and MI5 representative at this weekly gathering of high-powered spooks, Cholmondeley was privy to some of the most secret plans of the war. He had read the 1939 memo from Godfrey and Fleming containing the 'not very nice' suggestion of using a dead body to convey false information. And the Catalina crash off Cadiz had demonstrated that such a plan could work.

On 31 October 1942, just one month after the retrieval of Lieutenant Turner's body from the Spanish beach, Cholmondeley presented the Twenty Committee with his own idea, under the codename 'Trojan Horse', which he described as 'a plan for introducing documents of a highly secret nature into the hands of the enemy'. It was, in essence, an expanded version of the plan outlined in the Trout Memo.

> A body is obtained from one of the London hospitals (normal peacetime price £10), it is then dressed in Army, Naval or Air Force uniform of suitable rank. The lungs are filled with water and the documents are disposed in an inside pocket. The body is then dropped by a Coastal Command aircraft at a suitable position where the set of the currents will probably carry the body ashore in enemy territory. On being found, the supposition in the enemy's mind may well be that one of our aircraft has either been shot or forced down and that this is one of the passengers. Whilst the courier cannot be sure to get through, if he does succeed, information in the form of the documents can be of a far more secret nature than it would be possible to introduce through any normal B1A channel.

Human agents or double agents can be tortured or turned, forced to reveal the falsity of the information they carry. A dead body would never talk.

Like most of Cholmondeley's ideas, this one was both exquisitely simple and fiendishly problematical. Having outlined his blueprint for building a latter-day Trojan Horse, Cholmondeley now set about picking holes in it. An autopsy might reveal that the corpse had not died from drowning, and the plane carrying out 'the drop' might be intercepted. Even if a suitable body could be found, this would have to be made to 'double for an actual officer'. One member of the Twenty Committee pointed out that if a corpse was dropped out of a plane at any height, it would undoubtedly be damaged, 'and injuries inflicted after death can always be detected'. If the body was placed in a location where it would wash into enemy or enemy-occupied territory, such as Norway or France, there was every possibility of 'a full and capable postmortem' by German scientists. 'Neutral' Spain and Portugal were both leaning towards the Axis: 'Of these, Spain was clearly the country where the probability of documents being handed, or at the very least shown, to the Germans was greater.'

Cholmondeley's plan was both new, and very old. Indeed, the unsubtle choice of codename, Trojan Horse, shows how far back in history this ruse runs. Odysseus may have been the first to offer an attractive gift to the enemy containing a most unpleasant surprise, but he had many imitators. In intelligence jargon, the technique of planting misleading information by means of a faked accident even has a formal name: the 'haversack ruse'.

The haversack ruse was the brainchild of Richard Meinertzhagen, ornithologist, anti-semitic Zionist, big-game hunter, fraud and British spy. In *Seven Pillars of Wisdom*, T. E. Lawrence (of Arabia) offered a pen portrait of his contemporary Meinertzhagen as an extraordinary, and extraordinarily nasty, man. 'Meinertzhagen knew no half measures. He was logical, an idealist of the deepest, and so possessed by his convictions that he was willing to harness evil to the chariot of good. He was a strategist, a geographer, and a silent laughing masterful man;

who took as blithe a pleasure in deceiving his enemy (or his friend) by some unscrupulous jest, as in spattering the brains of a cornered mob of Germans one by one with his African knobkerri. His instincts were abetted by an immensely powerful body and a savage brain.'

In 1917, the British Army, under General Sir Edmund Allenby, twice attacked the Turks at Gaza, but found the way to Jerusalem blocked by a strong enemy force. Allenby decided that the next offensive should come at Beersheba in the east, while hoping to fool the Turks into expecting another attack on Gaza (which was the most logical target). The officer on Allenby's intelligence staff in control of the deception was Major Richard Meinertzhagen.

Meinertzhagen knew that the key to an effective deceit is not merely to conceal what you are doing, but to persuade the other side that what you are doing is the reverse of what you are actually doing. He stuffed a haversack with false documents, personal letters, a diary and £20 in cash, and smeared it with his horse's blood. He then rode out into no-man's land until shot at by a Turkish mounted patrol, upon which he slumped in the saddle as if wounded, dropped his haversack, binoculars and rifle, and galloped back to the British lines. One of the letters (written by Meinertzhagen's sister, Mary) purported to be from the haversack owner's wife, reporting the birth of their son. It was pure Edwardian schmaltz: 'Good-bye, my darling! Nurse says I must not tire myself by writing too much . . . Baby sends a kiss to Daddy!'

Meinertzhagen now launched an operation to make it seem as if a feverish search was underway for the missing bag. A sandwich, wrapped in a daily order referring to the missing documents, was planted near enemy lines, as if dropped by a careless patrol. Meinertzhagen was ordered to appear before a (non-existent) court of inquiry to explain the lost haversack.

The Turks duly concentrated their forces at Gaza, and redeployed two divisions away from Beersheba. On 31

October 1917, the British attacked again, rolling back the thin Turkish line at Beersheba. By December, the British had taken Jerusalem. Meinertzhagen crowed that his haversack ruse had been 'easy, reliable and inexpensive'. But victory may also be attributed to another devious Meinertzhagen ploy: the dropping of hundreds of cigarettes laced with opium behind Turkish lines. Some historians have argued that the haversack ruse was not quite the success Meinertzhagen claimed. The Turks may have been fooled. Or they may just have been incredibly stoned.

The ruse was updated and deployed once more early in the Second World War. Before the Battle of Alam Halfa in 1942, a corpse clutching a map that appeared to show a 'fair going' route through the desert was placed in a blown-up scout car. It was hoped that Rommel's tanks would find the map, be misdirected into soft sand and get bogged down. In another variation on the theme, a fake defence plan of Cyprus was left with a woman in Cairo who was known to be in contact with Axis intelligence. But the most recent variant had been plotted, with pleasing symmetry, by Peter Fleming, Ian Fleming's older brother, an intelligence officer serving under General Archibald Wavell, then Supreme Allied Commander in the Far East. Peter, who shared his brother's vivid imagination and was already a successful writer, concocted his own haversack ruse, codenamed 'Error', aimed at convincing the Japanese that Wavell himself had been injured in the retreat from Burma and had left behind various important documents in an abandoned car. In April 1942, the fake documents, a photograph of Wavell's daughter, personal letters, novels and other items were placed in a green Ford sedan, and pushed over a slope at a bridge across the Irrawaddy River, just ahead of the advancing Japanese army. Operation Error may have been great fun, but 'there was never any evidence that the Japanese had paid any attention to the car, much less that they drew any conclusions from its contents'.

This was the central problem with the haversack ruse: it had become, over three decades, deeply embedded in intelligence folklore, and the source of many an after-dinner anecdote, but there was precious little proof that it had ever actually worked.

3

Room 13

John Masterman, the chairman of the Twenty Committee, wrote detective novels in his spare time. These featured an Oxford don, much like himself, and a sleuth in the Sherlock Holmes mould. The operation outlined by Charles Cholmondeley appealed strongly to Masterman's novelistic cast of mind, as a mystery to be constructed, scene by scene, with clues for the Germans to unravel. Despite some misgivings about its feasibility, the Twenty Committee instructed Cholmondeley to investigate the possibilities of utilising the Trojan Horse plan in one of the theatres of the Second World War.

Spies, like generals, tend to fight the last battle. Axis intelligence had failed to act on the genuine documents that had washed up with Lieutenant Turner, and so missed the opportunity to anticipate Operation Torch; they would be unlikely to make the same mistake twice. 'The Germans, having cause to regret the ease with which they had been taken by surprise by the North African landings, would not again easily dismiss strategic Allied documents if and when they came into their possession.'

Since, in Cholmondeley's outline plan, the corpse would be arriving by sea, the operation would fall principally under naval control, so the representative of the Naval Intelligence Department on the Twenty Committee, Lieutenant Commander Ewen Montagu, was assigned to help Cholmondeley flesh out the idea. Montagu had also read the Trout Memo. He 'strongly supported' the plan, and volunteered to 'go into the question of obtaining the necessary body, the medical problems and the formulation of a plan'.

The choice of Ewen Montagu as Cholmondeley's planning partner was largely accidental, but inspired. A barrister and workaholic, Montagu's organisational skills and mastery of detail perfectly complemented Cholmondeley's 'fertile brain'. Where Cholmondeley was awkward and charming, Montagu was smooth and sardonic, refined, romantic and luminously intelligent.

Ewen Edwin Samuel Montagu, aged forty-two, was the second of three sons of Baron Swaythling, the scion of a Jewish banking dynasty of quite dazzling wealth. The first half of his life had been almost uniformly pleasurable, materially and intellectually. 'My memory is of a continuous happy time,' he wrote, looking back on his early years. 'We were lucky in every way.'

Montagu's grandfather, founder of the family fortune, had changed his name from Samuel to the more aristocratic-sounding Montagu, prompting a cruel limerick by Hilaire Belloc:

Montagu, first Baron Swaythling he,
Thus is known to you and me.
But the Devil down in Hell
Knows the man as Samuel.
And though it may not sound the same
It is the blighter's proper name.

Ewen's father had taken over the bank, and made even more money. His uncle Edwin went into politics, becoming Secretary of State for India. The family home was a red-brick palace in the heart of Kensington, at 28 Kensington Court. The hall was panelled in old Spanish leather; the 'small dining room' seated twenty-four; for larger gatherings there was the Louis XVI drawing room, with silk-embroidered chairs, Art Deco mouldings and an 'exquisite chandelier' of unfeasible size. The Montagus entertained nightly, and lavishly: 'Statesmen (British and world), diplomats, generals, admirals etc.'. Presiding over these occasions were 'Father' (vast, bearded and stern), 'Mother' (petite, artistic and indefatigable), 'Granniemother', Dowager Lady Swaythling, who, in Ewen's estimation, looked 'like a very animated piece of Dresden China [and] like most women of her milieu never did a hand's turn for herself'.

Ewen and his brothers had been brought up surrounded by servants and treasures but, in a reflection of the ideological ferment of the time, each emerged from childhood utterly different from the others. The eldest son, Stuart, was pompous and unimaginative as only an English aristocratic heir can be; by contrast Ewen's younger brother, Ivor, rejected the family money and went on to become a committed communist, a pioneer of British table tennis, a collector of rare breeds of mice, and a radical film-maker.

The house was equipped with a hydraulic lift, which the Montagu children never entered: 'It was a *servants'* lift, to carry trays or washing baskets or themselves invisibly past the gentlemanly regions when untimely menial presence might offend convention.' There were at least twenty servants (although no one was counting), including a butler and two footmen, a cook and kitchen maids, two housemaids, Mother's personal maid, a nurse and nursemaid, a governess, a secretary, a cockney coachman, a groom, and two chauffeurs. 'Born as I was into a very rich family, the servants abounded, and made one's life entirely different,' wrote Ewen.

Ewen had attended Westminster School, where he was clad in top hat and tails, educated superbly, and beaten only infrequently. Before going on to Trinity College, Cambridge, he spent a year at Harvard, studying English composition, but mostly enjoying the Jazz Age in a way the Great Gatsby might have envied and living, in his own words, 'the sort of American social life one saw in the films'. The experience turned Montagu into a lifelong Americanophile: 'I felt a great debt of gratitude to Americans for all their kindness to me and felt that I should try to repay it in some small measure.' The war would provide that opportunity.

At Cambridge, Ewen had a personal valet and a 1910 Lancia two-seater sports car he called 'Steve'. He dabbled in Labour politics, but left the more extreme left-wing thinking to his brother Ivor, who followed him to Cambridge a year later and was already well on his way to becoming a committed Marxist. Despite their differing personalities and politics, Ewen and Ivor were close friends. 'The "spread" among us three brothers was amusing,' Ewen reflected. Stuart 'already had a banker's attitude to life', whereas Ewen and Ivor had no intention of following the family career path. 'He and I were much closer than either of us [was] with Stuart as we had many more interests in common.'

'We had nothing to do but enjoy ourselves,' Ewen reflected. 'And, from time to time, work.' They did, however, find time to 'invent' table tennis. Ivor was extremely good at 'ping pong'. The game had no real rules or regulations and so he founded the English Ping Pong Association. Jaques, the sports manufacturer, got wind of the fledgling club and stuffily pointed out that the company had copyrighted the name 'ping pong'. Ewen recalled: 'I advised him to choose another name for the game; as we bandied names at one another, one of us came up with table tennis.' Ivor would go on to found the International Table Tennis Federation in 1926, and served as its first president for the next forty-one years.

Another project initiated by the Montagu brothers at Cambridge was 'The Cheese Eaters' League'. Ivor and Ewen shared a passion for cheese, and set up a dining club to import and taste the most exotic specimens from around the world: camel's milk cheese, Middle Eastern goat cheese, cheese made from the milk of long-horned Afghan sheep. 'Our great ambition was to get whale's milk cheese,' Ewen wrote, and to this end he contacted a whaling company to arrange that 'if a mother whale was killed the milk should be "cheesed" and sent to us'.

Montagu made the most of his privileged time at Cambridge, but he was already honing the intellectual muscles that would stand him in good stead, first as a lawyer, then as an intelligence officer – most notably the ability 'to study something with little or no sleep intensively over a short period'. He was also physically tough. Once, when riding to hounds, his foot slipped out of a stirrup, which then swung up as the horse swerved, cutting a large gash in his chin and knocking out five teeth. Another huntsman picked up one of Ewen's smashed teeth. 'I put it in my pocket and rode on,' Ewen recalled. The accident left him with a lopsided smile, which he deployed charmingly, but sparingly, and a useful ledge on which to hang his pipe.

While still at university, Ewen became engaged to Iris Solomon. It was, in many ways, a perfect match. Iris was the daughter of Solomon J. Solomon, the portrait painter. She was vivacious, intelligent, and of just the right Anglo-Jewish stock. They married in 1923. A son soon arrived, followed by a daughter.

Through the 1920s and 1930s, the young lawyer and his wife lived a golden existence, in the interval between one devastating war and another. They socialised with the most powerful in the land; at weekends they repaired to Townhill, the Montagu estate near Southampton, where twenty-five gardeners tended exquisite gardens laid out by Gertrude Jekyll. Here they shot pheasants, hunted, and played table tennis. In summer they sailed Ewen's forty-five-foot yacht on the Solent; in winter they skied in Switzerland.

But most of all, Ewen (like his future boss, Admiral Godfrey) loved to fish, in the river and salmon pools at Townhill. In later life he would be described as 'one of the best fly-fishermen in the realm'; he modestly denied this, insisting he was 'never better than a mediocre if enthusiastic fisherman'. For Montagu, on the riverbank, in court and, soon, at war, there was no more satisfying experience than 'the thrill of the strike and the joy of playing the fish'.

Ivor Montagu, meanwhile, was pursuing a different career path. By the age of twenty-two he had founded the English Table Tennis Association, written a book entitled *Table Tennis Today*, created the Film Society (with Sidney Bernstein), and made two expeditions to the Soviet Union, where he perfected his Russian and searched for 'an exceedingly primitive vole' found only in the Caucasus. The experience led to a zoological monograph on *Prometheomys*, the 'Prometheus Mouse', and a lifelong faith in the Soviet machinery of state. In 1927 he had married Frances Hellstern, universally known as 'Hell' (and regarded as such by her mother-in-law) – an unmarried mother and the daughter of a bootmaker from south London. The marriage made tabloid headlines: 'Baron's Son Weds Secretary'. Queen Mary wrote to Lady Swaythling: 'Dear Gladys, I feel for you. May.' Ivor could not have cared less.

In 1929 Ivor linked up with the Soviet film director Sergey Eisenstein, and together they travelled to Hollywood, where Ivor became close friends with Charlie Chaplin, whom he taught to swear in Russian. The youngest Montagu brother would go on to work as a producer on five of Alfred Hitchcock's British films.

Ivor's politics, meanwhile, marched steadily leftward, from the Fabian Society to the British Socialist Party to the Communist Party of Great Britain. He visited Spain during the civil war, and made a series of pro-Republican documentaries. While Ewen hobnobbed with generals and ambassadors, Ivor mixed with the likes of George Bernard Shaw and H. G. Wells. While Ewen lived in Kensington, Ivor cut himself off from his father's money and moved with Hell to a terraced house in Brixton. Yet, for all their differences, the brothers remained close, and saw one another often.

After joining the bar in 1924, Ewen had developed into an exceptionally able lawyer. He learned to absorb detail, improvise, and mould the collective mind of a malleable jury. Ewen

Montagu was born to argue. He would dispute with anyone, at any hour of the day, on almost any subject, and devastatingly, since he possessed the rare ability to read an interlocutor's mind – the mark of the good lawyer, and the good liar. He became fascinated by the workings of the criminal mind, and confessed to feeling 'a certain sympathy with rogue characters'. He relished the cut and thrust of the courtroom, where victory depended on being able to 'see the point of view, and anticipate the reactions, of an equally astute opposing counsel'. Montagu was invariably kind to people below him in social status, and capable of the most 'gentle manners', but he liked to cut those in authority down to size. He could be fabulously rude. Like many defence lawyers, he enjoyed the challenge of defending the apparently defenceless, or indefensible. He had one client, a crooked solicitor, in whom he may have seen something of himself: 'If he could see a really artistic lie, a gleam would come into his eye and he would tell it.' In 1939, Montagu was made a King's Counsel.

Ewen was sailing his yacht off the coast of Brittany, six months after taking silk, when he learned that war had been declared. The sailing trip had been delightful, 'hard in the wind, in glorious weather and escorted by porpoises playing around our bow'. On hearing the prime minister's grim wireless statement that Britain was now at war, Ewen had swung the helm around and headed back to port, knowing that nothing in his gilded life would ever be as shiny again. He recalled 'looking out to sea and realising all had gone smash for me. All had been going so well, as a new Silk all looked promising, and in my family and private life all was so wonderful. And now full stop.'

Iris and the two children, Jeremy and Jennifer, would be packed off to the safety of America, away from the Luftwaffe bombs that would soon rain down on London. As one of the country's most prominent Jewish banking families, Ewen knew the Montagu clan faced special peril in the event of a Nazi invasion.

At thirty-eight, Ewen was too old for active service, but he had already volunteered for the Royal Naval Volunteer Reserve. With the outbreak of war, he was commissioned as acting lieutenant commander and swiftly came to the attention of Admiral John Godfrey, the head of Naval Intelligence. 'It is quite useless, and in fact dangerous to employ people of medium intelligence,' wrote Godfrey. 'Only men with first-class brains should be allowed to touch this stuff. If the right sort of people can't be found, better keep them out altogether.' In Montagu he knew he had the right sort of person.

Godfrey's Intelligence Department was an eclectic and unconventional body. In addition to Ian Fleming, his personal assistant, Godfrey employed 'two stockbrokers, a schoolmaster, a journalist, a collector of books on original thought, an Oxford classical don, a barrister's clerk, and an insurance agent'. This heterogeneous crew was crammed into Room 39 at the Admiralty, which was permanently wreathed in tobacco smoke and frequently echoed to the sounds of Admiral Godfrey, shouting and swearing. Fleming awarded Godfrey the heavily ironic nickname 'Uncle John', for seldom has there been a less avuncular boss. 'The permanent inhabitants who finally settled in this cave,' he wrote, 'were people of very different temperaments, ambitions, social status and home life, all with their particular irritabilities, hopes, fears, anguishes, loves, hates, animosities and blank spots.' Any and every item of intelligence relevant to the war at sea passed through Room 39 and though the atmosphere inside was often tense, Godfrey's team 'worked like ants, and their combined output was prodigious'. The ants under Godfrey were responsible not merely for gathering and disseminating secret intelligence, but for running agents and double agents, as well as developing deception and counterespionage operations.

Godfrey had identified Montagu as a natural for this sort of work, and he was swiftly promoted. Soon, he not only represented the Naval Intelligence Department on most of the important intelligence bodies, including the Twenty Committee, but ran his own subsection of the department: the top-secret Section 17M (for Montagu).

Housed in Room 13, a low-ceilinged cavern twenty feet square, Section 17M (later renamed Section 12) was responsible for dealing with all 'special intelligence' relating to naval matters, principally the so-called 'Ultra' intercepts, the enemy communications deciphered by the cryptanalysts at Bletchley Park following the breaking of the Enigma, the German cipher machine. In the early days of 17M, the Ultra signals came in dribs and drabs, but gradually the volume of secret information swelled to a torrent, with more than 200 messages arriving every day, some a few words long but others covering pages. The work of understanding, collating and disseminating this huge volume of information was like 'learning a new language' according to Montagu, whose task it was to decide which items of intelligence should pass to other intelligence agencies and which merited inclusion in the Special Intelligence Summaries, 'the cream of all intelligence', while coordinating with MI5, Bletchley Park, the intelligence departments of the other services, and the Prime Minister. Montagu became fluent at reading this traffic, which, even after decoding, could be impossibly opaque. 'The Germans have a passion for cross-references and for abbreviations, and they have an even greater passion (only equalled by their ineptitude in practice) for the use of codenames.'

Section 17M expanded. First came Joan Saunders, a young woman married to the librarian of the House of Commons, 'to do the detailed work of indexing, filing and research'. Joan – a tall, strapping, jolly-hockeysticks woman with a booming voice and a personality to match – was effectively Montagu's chief assistant. She had been a nurse in the early part of the war, and had run a nursing station during the retreat from France. She was practical, bossy, occasionally terrifying and wore a tiger-skin fur coat to work in winter. The other female staff called her

'Auntie', but never to her face. Her familiarity with dead bodies would prove most useful. 'She is extraordinarily good, very methodical but also frightfully alert,' Montagu told his wife. 'Very pleasant to work with, although not much to look at. I'm not lucky in assistants as regards looks.' Montagu was something of a connoisseur of female beauty.

By 1943, the section had swelled to fourteen people, including an artist, a yachting magazine journalist, and two 'watchkeepers' to monitor any night traffic. The working conditions were atrocious. Room 13 was 'far too small, far too cluttered with safes, steel filing cabinets, tables, chairs etc. and especially far too low, with steel girders making it even lower. There was no fresh air, only potted air [in] conditions which would have been condemned instantly by any factories inspector.' The only light came from fluorescent strips 'which made everyone look mauve'. In theory, the staff 'were not supposed to listen to what we said over the telephone or to each other'. In such a confined space, this was impossible: there were no secrets between the secret keepers of Room 13. Despite the rigours, Montagu's unit was highly effective: they were, in the words of Admiral Godfrey, 'a brilliant band of dedicated war winners'.

As he had in the courtroom, Montagu delighted in burrowing into the minds of his opponents in the field of espionage, the German saboteurs, spies, agents and spymasters whose daily wireless exchanges, eavesdropped, decoded and translated, poured into Room 13. He came to recognise individual German intelligence officers among the traffic and, like his former rivals in court, he 'began to regard some almost as friends': 'They were so kind to us unconsciously.'

In America, at Ewen's instigation, Iris had begun working for British Security Coordination, the intelligence organisation based in New York and run by William Stephenson, the spymaster who revelled in the codename 'Intrepid'. Behind a front as British Passport Control, Stephenson's team ran black propaganda against Nazi sympathisers in the US, organised espionage, and worked assiduously to prod America into the war, by fair means or foul. In a way, spying and concealment was already in Iris's blood, for her father, the painter Solomon J. Solomon, had played a part in the invention of military camouflage during the First World War. In 1916, he had built a fake nine-foot tree out of steel plates shrouded in real bark, for use as an observation post on the Western Front. This was a family that understood the pleasure and challenge of making something appear to be what it was not. Ewen was pleased that his wife was now, as he put it, 'in the racket' too. Ewen and Iris wrote to one another every day, although Montagu could never describe exactly what his day involved: 'If I am killed there are four or five people who will be able after the war to tell you the sort of things I have been doing.'

Montagu's role expanded once more when Godfrey placed him in charge of all naval deception through double agents – 'the most fascinating job in the war', in Montagu's words. By means of the Ultra intercepts and other intelligence sources, Britain captured every single spy sent to Britain by the Abwehr, the German military intelligence organisation. Many of these were used as double agents, feeding misinformation back to the enemy. Montagu found himself at the very heart of the 'Double Cross System', helping 'Tar' Robertson and John Masterman to deploy double agents wherever and whenever the Navy was involved. He worked with Eddie Chapman, the crook turned spy, codenamed 'Zigzag', to send false information about submarine weaponry; he investigated astrology to see if Hitler's apparent belief in such things could be used against him ('very entertaining but useless') and in November 1941 he travelled to the US to help establish a system for handling double agent 'Tricycle' (the Serbian playboy Dusko Popov), in the penetration of German spy rings operating in America. The Double Cross System also involved the creation of bogus spies. 'A great number who did not really exist at all in real life, but were imaginary people notionally recruited as sub-agents by double agents whom we were already working.' In order to convince the enemy that these invented characters were real, every aspect of the fake personality had to be conjured into existence.

Some of the material that crossed Montagu's desk was strange beyond belief. In October 1941, Godfrey ordered Montagu to investigate why the Germans had suddenly imported 1,000 Rhesus monkeys, as well as a troop of Barbary apes. Godfrey speculated that 'it might be an indication that the Germans intended to use gas or bacteriological warfare, or for experimental purposes'. Montagu consulted Lord Victor Rothschild, MI5's expert on explosives, booby traps, and other unconventional forms of warfare. His lordship was doubtful that the large monkey imports were sinister. 'Though I have kept a close eye on people applying for animals,' he wrote, 'those cases so far investigated have proved innocuous. For example, an advertisement in *The Times* for 500 hedgehogs proved to be in connection with the experiments being done by the foot and mouth disease research section.'

Montagu would never fight on the front line, but there was no doubting his personal bravery. When Britain was under threat of German invasion in 1940, he hit on the idea of trying to lead the invading force into a minefield, using himself as bait. The minefields off Britain's east coast had gaps in them, to allow the fishing boats in and out. The Germans knew the approximate, but not the precise, location of these channels. If a chart could be got into their hands showing channels close enough to the real gaps to be believable, yet slightly wrong, then the invading fleet might be persuaded to ram confidently up the wrong route, and, with any luck, sink. Popov – Agent Tricycle – would pass the false chart to the Germans, claiming he had obtained it from a Jewish officer in the Navy keen to curry favour with the Nazis. Popov would say that this man, a prominent lawyer in civilian life, 'had heard and believed the propaganda stories about the ill-treatment of Jews and did not want to face the risk of being handed over to the Gestapo'. The chart was his insurance policy, and he would only hand it over in return for a written guarantee that he would be safe in the event of a successful German invasion of Britain. Popov liked the plan, and asked what name he should give the Germans for this treacherous naval officer. 'I thought you had realised,' said Montagu. 'Lieutenant Commander Montagu. They can look me up in the Law List and any of the *Jewish Year Books*.'

There was considerable courage in this act, although Montagu later denied it. If the Germans had invaded, they would have swiftly realised that the chart was phoney, and Montagu would have been even more of a marked man than he was already. There was also the possibility that someone in British intelligence might hear of the chart, and the treacherous Jewish lawyer prepared to sell secrets to save his own skin: at the very least, he would have some complicated explaining to do. The plot made Montagu appear, to German eyes, to be 'an out and out traitor'. He was unconcerned: what mattered was telling a convincing story.

Before placing Montagu in charge of naval deception, Godfrey had passed him a copy of the 'Trout Memo' written with Ian Fleming. Montagu considered Fleming 'a four-letter man', and got on with him very well. ('Fleming is charming to be with, but would sell his own grandmother. I like him a lot.') Years later, when both men were long retired, Godfrey gently reminded Montagu of the debt, and the origins of the operation: 'The bare idea of the dead airman washed up on a beach was among those dozen or so notions which I gave you when 17M was formed,' he wrote. Montagu replied blandly: 'I quite honestly don't remember your passing on this suggestion to me. Of course, what you said may have been in my subconscious and may have formed the link – but I can assure you that it was not conscious which shows the strange workings of fate (or something!).'

The strange workings of fate had now thrown together, in Room 13, Montagu, the whip-smart lawyer, and Cholmondeley, the gentle, lanky, unpredictable ideas man, an ill-matched pair who would develop into the most remarkable double act in the history of deception. They had the backing of the Twenty Committee, they had plenty of precedents, and they had the outline of a plan: what they did not yet have was a clear idea of what to do with it.

4

Target Sicily

The plan of action agreed by Winston Churchill and Franklin Delano Roosevelt when they met in Casablanca in January 1943 was, in some respects, blindingly obvious: after the successful North Africa campaign, Operation Torch, the next target would be the island of Sicily.

The Nazi war machine was at last beginning to stutter and misfire. The British 8th Army under Montgomery had vanquished Rommel's invincible Afrika Korps at El Alamein. The Allied invasion of Morocco and Tunisia fatally weakened Germany's grip, and with the liberation of Tunis, the Allies would control the coast of North Africa, its ports and airfields, from Casablanca to Alexandria. The time had come to lay siege to Hitler's fortress. But where?

Sicily was the logical place from which to deliver the gut punch into what Churchill famously called the soft 'underbelly of the Axis'. The island at the toe of Italy's boot commanded the channel linking the two sides of the Mediterranean, just eighty miles from the Tunisian coast. If the combined British and American armies were to free Europe, prise Italy out of the Fascist embrace, and roll back the Nazi behemoth, they would first have to take Sicily. The British in Malta and Allied convoys had been pummelled by Luftwaffe bombers taking off from the island and, as Montagu remarked, 'no major operation could be launched, maintained, or supplied until the enemy airfields and other bases in Sicily had been obliterated so as to allow free passage through the Mediterranean'. An invasion of Sicily would open the road to Rome, draw German troops from the Eastern Front to relieve the Red Army, allow for preparations to invade France, and perhaps knock a tottering Italy out of the war. Breaking up the 'Pact of Steel' forged in 1939 by Hitler and Mussolini would shatter German morale, Churchill predicted, 'and might be the beginning of their doom'. The Americans were initially dubious, wondering if Britain harboured imperial ambitions in the Mediterranean, but eventually they compromised: Sicily would be the target, the precursor to the invasion of mainland Europe.

If the strategic importance of Sicily was clear to the Allies, it was surely equally obvious to Italy and Germany. Churchill was blunt about the choice of target: 'Everyone but a bloody fool would *know* it was Sicily.' And if the enemy was foolish enough not to see what was coming, he would surely cotton on when 160,000 British, American and Commonwealth troops and an armada of 3,200 ships began assembling for the invasion. Sicily's 500-mile coastline was already defended by seven or eight enemy divisions. If Hitler correctly anticipated the Allies' next move, then the island would be reinforced by thousands of German troops held in reserve in France. The soft underbelly would become a wall of muscle. The invasion could turn into a bloodbath.

But the logic of Sicily was immutable. On 22 January, Churchill and Roosevelt gave their joint blessing to 'Operation Husky', the invasion of Sicily, the next great set-piece offensive of the war. General Eisenhower was summoned to Casablanca, and given his orders.

All of which presented Allied intelligence chiefs with a fiendish conundrum: how to convince the enemy that the Allies were *not* going to do what anyone with an atlas could see they *ought* to do.

The previous June, Churchill had established the London Controlling Section (a deliberately vague title) under a

Controller of Deception, Lieutenant Colonel John H. Bevan, to 'prepare deception plans on a worldwide basis with the object of causing the enemy to waste his military resources'. Bevan was responsible for the overall planning, supervision, and coordination of strategic deception. Immediately after the Casablanca conference, he was instructed to draw up a new deception policy to disguise the impending invasion of Sicily. The result was 'Operation Barclay', a complex, many-layered plan that would try to convince the Germans that black was white or, at the very least, grey.

Johnnie Bevan was an Old Etonian stockbroker, an upright pillar of the Establishment whose convivial and modest temperament belied an exceedingly sharp mind. He had that rare English ability to achieve impressive feats while maintaining a permanent air of embarrassment, and he tackled the monumental task of wartime deception in the same way that he played cricket. 'When things were looking pretty bad for his side at cricket, he would shuffle in, about sixth wicket down, knock up 100 and shuffle out again looking rather ashamed of himself.' Bevan played with the straightest of straight bats, as honest and upright a team player as one could imagine: which was probably what made him such a superb deceiver.

While Bevan controlled the business of deception from within the Cabinet War Rooms, the fortified underground bunker beneath Whitehall, his counterpart in the Mediterranean was Lieutenant Colonel Dudley Wrangel Clarke, the chief of 'A' Force, the deception unit based in Cairo. Clarke was another master of strategic deception, but of a very different stamp. Unmarried, nocturnal and allergic to children, he was possessed of 'an ingenious imagination and a photographic memory', and a flair for the dramatic that invited trouble. For the Royal Tournament in 1925, he mounted a pageant depicting imperial artillery down the ages, which involved two elephants, thirty-seven guns and 'fourteen of the biggest Nigerians he could find'. He loved uniforms, disguises and dressing up. Most of one of his ears was lopped off by a German bullet when he took part in the first Commando raid on occupied France, and in 1940 he was summoned to Egypt, at the express command of General Sir Archibald Wavell, commander-in-chief in the Middle East, and ordered to set up a 'special section of intelligence for deception'.

Clarke and 'A' Force had spent the last two years baffling and bamboozling the enemy in a variety of complicated and flamboyant ways. Between them, Colonels Bevan and Clarke would construct the most elaborate wartime web of deception ever spun. Yet in its essence the aim of Operation Barclay was quite simple: to convince the Axis powers that instead of attacking Sicily in the middle of the Mediterranean, the Allies intended to invade Greece in the east, and the island of Sardinia, followed by southern France, in the west. The lie went as follows: the British 12th Army (which did not exist) would invade the Balkans in the summer of 1943, starting in Crete and the Peloponnese, bringing Turkey into the war against the Axis powers, moving against Bulgaria and Romania, linking up with the Yugoslav resistance and then finally uniting with the Soviet armies on the Eastern Front. The subsidiary lie was intended to convince the Germans that the British 8th Army planned to land on France's south coast, and then storm up the Rhône valley, once American troops under General Patton had attacked Corsica and Sardinia. Sicily would be bypassed.

If Operation Barclay succeeded, the Germans would reinforce the Balkans, Sardinia and southern France in preparation for invasions that would never materialise, while leaving Sicily only lightly defended. At the very least, enemy troops would be spread over a broad front and the German defensive shield would be weakened. By the time the real target became obvious, it would be too late to reinforce Sicily.

The deception plan played directly on Hitler's fears, for the Ultra intercepts had clearly revealed that the Führer, his staff and local commanders in Greece all feared that the Balkans represented a vulnerable point on the Nazis' southern flank.

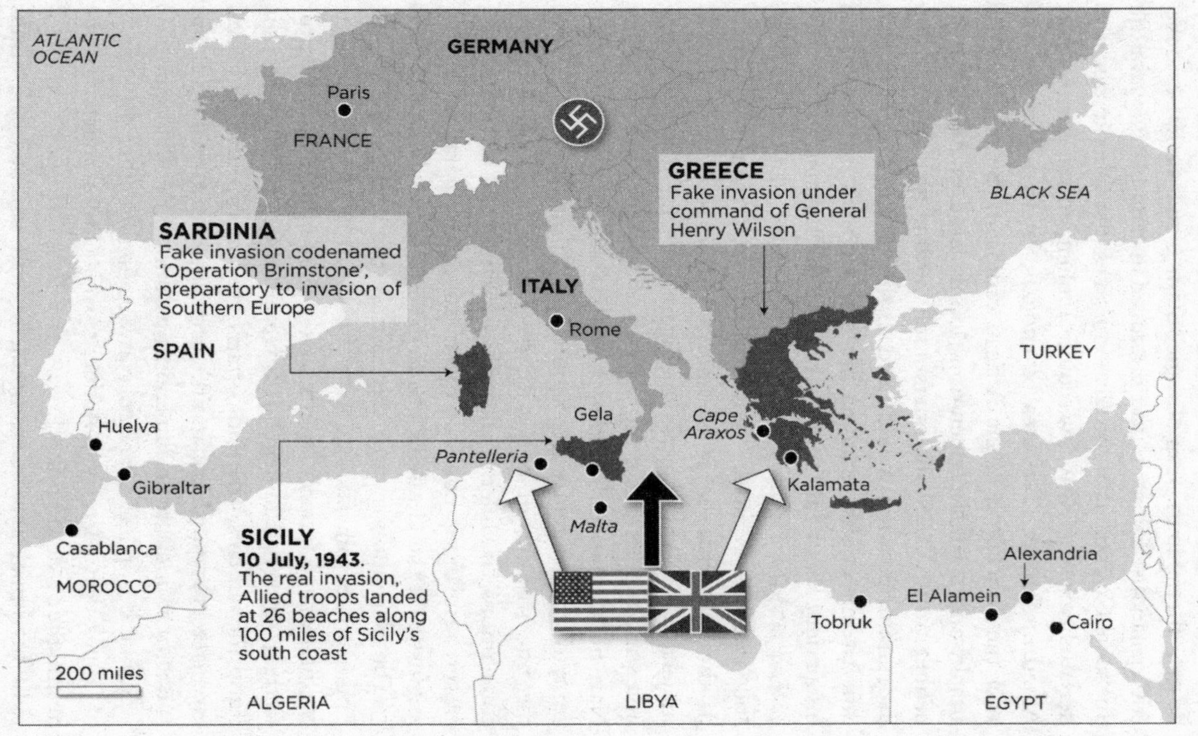
ATLANTIC OCEAN
GERMANY
Paris
FRANCE
GREECE
Fake invasion under command of General Henry Wilson
BLACK SEA
SARDINIA
Fake invasion codenamed 'Operation Brimstone', preparatory to invasion of Southern Europe
ITALY
Rome
SPAIN
TURKEY
Gela
Cape Araxos
Huelva
Pantelleria
Gibraltar
Kalamata
Malta
Casablanca
SICILY
10 July, 1943.
The real invasion, Allied troops landed at 26 beaches along 100 miles of Sicily's south coast
Alexandria
MOROCCO
El Alamein
Tobruk
Cairo
200 miles
ALGERIA
LIBYA
EGYPT

Even so, shifting German attention away from Sicily would not be easy, for the strategic importance of the island was self-evident. A German intelligence report produced in early February for the Supreme Command of the Armed Forces, the Oberkommando der Wehrmacht (OKW), was quite explicit, and accurate, about Allied intentions: 'The idea of knocking Italy out of the war after the conclusion of the African campaign, by means of air attacks and a landing operation, looms large in Anglo-Saxon deliberations . . . Sicily offers itself as the first target.' The deception operation would need to shift Hitler's mind in two different directions: reducing his fears for Sicily, while stoking his anxiety about Sardinia, Greece and the Balkans.

'Uncle' John Godfrey identified what he called 'wishfulness' and 'yesmanship' as the twin frailties of German intelligence: 'If the authorities were clamouring for reports on a certain subject, the German secret intelligence service was not above inventing reports based on what they thought probable.' The Nazi high command, at the same time, when presented with contradictory intelligence reports, was 'inclined to believe the one that fits in best with their own previously formed conceptions'. If Hitler's paranoid wishfulness and his underlings' craven yesmanship could be exploited, then Operation Barclay might work: the Germans would deceive themselves.

The deception swung into action on a range of fronts. Engineers began fabricating a bogus army in the Eastern Mediterranean; double agents started feeding false information to their Abwehr handlers; plans were drawn up for counterfeit troop movements, fake radio traffic, the recruitment of Greek interpreters and officers, and the acquisition of Greek maps and currency to indicate an impending assault on the Peloponnese.

While Bevan and Clarke began weaving together the strands of Operation Barclay, Montagu and Cholmondeley went hunting for a dead body.

In his initial plan, Cholmondeley had assumed one could simply pop into a military hospital and pick a bargain cadaver off the shelf for £10. The reality was rather different. The Second World War may have been responsible for the deaths of more people than any conflict in history, yet dead bodies of the right sort were surprisingly hard to find. People tended to be killed, or to kill themselves, in all the wrong ways. A bombing victim would never do. Suicides were more common than in peacetime, but these were usually by rope, gas or chemical means that could easily be detected in a postmortem examination. Moreover, the requirements were specific: the plan called for a fresh male body of military age, with no obvious injuries or infirmities, and cooperative next of kin who would not object when the corpse of their loved one was whisked away for unspecified purposes, to an unstipulated place, by complete strangers. Montagu turned for advice to someone who knew more about death than any man living.

Sir Bernard Spilsbury was the senior pathologist at the Home Office, an expert witness in many of the most famous trials of the age, and pioneer of the modern science of forensics. Sir Bernard collected deaths as other people collect stamps or books. For half a century, until his own mysterious demise in 1949, Spilsbury accumulated ordinary deaths and extraordinary deaths, carrying out some 25,000 autopsies: he studied death by asphyxiation, poisoning, accident and murder, and he jotted down the particulars of each case in his spidery handwriting on thousands of index cards, laying the foundations for modern crime scene investigation.

Spilsbury had come to public attention with the infamous Dr Crippen case of 1910. When Michigan-born Dr Hawley Harvey Crippen was captured attempting to flee to North America with his mistress, it was Spilsbury who identified the remains buried in his cellar in London as those of his missing wife, Cora, through distinctive scar tissue on a fragment of skin. Crippen was hanged in 1910. Over the next thirty years, Spilsbury would testify in courtrooms across the land, laying out the Crown's case in clear, precise, unarguable tones of moral rectitude. The newspapers adored him as an erect, handsome figure in the witness box, who combined scientific certainty with Edwardian upright character. As one contemporary observed, Spilsbury was a one-man instrument of retribution: 'He could achieve single-handed all the legal consequences of homicide – arrest, prosecution, conviction and final postmortem – requiring only the brief assistance of the hangman.' His courtroom manner was famously oracular and clipped, never using three words where one would suffice. 'He formed his opinion; expressed it in the clearest, most succinct manner possible; then stuck to it come hell or high water.'

Before Spilsbury, forensic pathology was widely discredited, regarded as inexact and medically dubious. However, by 1943, he had helped to transform the study of dead bodies – the 'Beastly Science' as it was known – into a branch of science both ghoulish and glamorous. Simultaneously, he acquired a reputation for experimenting on himself. Spilsbury inhaled carbon monoxide to test its effect on the body and made notes on his sensations (which were unpleasant). He climbed down a manhole in Redcross Street to check on gas that had killed a workman. When he accidentally ingested meningitis germs in a hospital laboratory, he 'just carried on'. It was said that Sir Bernard could identify the cause of death simply by smelling a corpse. In 1938, *The Washington Post* hailed him as 'England's modern Sherlock Holmes'.

But a lifetime of inhaling death, peering into cadavers, and familiarity with the darkest sides of human nature had affected the great scientist. Media attention had gone to his head. Sir Bernard was aloof, arrogant, and utterly convinced of his own infallibility. He saw the world bleakly, through a veil of cynicism and self-satisfaction, and seldom evinced a shred of sympathy for anyone, living or dead. With heavy-lidded eyes and a 'haughty, aristocratic bearing', he looked like a lizard in a lab coat, and smelled permanently of formaldehyde.

Ewen Montagu arranged to meet the famous pathologist

over a glass of lukewarm sherry at Spilsbury's club, the Junior Carlton. Spilsbury had already done macabre service for British intelligence. Captured enemy spies were offered a stark choice: either work as double agents, or face execution. Most agreed to cooperate, but a few resisted, or were deemed unusable. These, the 'unlucky sixteen' as they became known, were tried and executed. Spilsbury was brought in to carry out autopsies on these executed spies, including Josef Jakobs, shot by firing squad in the summer of 1941, the last person to be executed in the Tower of London.

Sir Bernard was sixty-six, but looked far older. Montagu was not in the habit of subservience, but he had seen Spilsbury perform in court and was deeply in awe of 'that extraordinary man'. Conscious of how odd the words sounded, the younger man explained that the Navy 'wanted the Germans and Spaniards to accept a floating body as that of a victim of an aircraft disaster'. What manner of death would fit in with the impression the Government wished to give? Spilsbury's heavy lids did not even blink at the question. Indeed, as Montagu later recorded, 'never once did he ask why I wanted to know, or what I was proposing to do'.

There was a long pause while the forensic scientist considered the question, and sipped his sherry. Finally, in his courtroom voice, 'clear, resonant, without any trace of uncertainty', he presented his verdict. The easiest way, of course, would be to find a drowned man and float him ashore in a life jacket. But failing that, any number of other causes of death would do, for the victims of air accidents at sea, Spilsbury explained, do not necessarily die from traumatic injury or drowning: 'Many die from exposure, or even from shock.'

Spilsbury returned to his laboratory at St Bartholomew's Hospital, and Montagu reported back to Cholmondeley that the hunt for a suitable corpse might be easier than they had anticipated. Even so, it was hardly possible to 'ask around' for a dead body, as gossip would undoubtedly spread and embarrassing questions would be asked. Briefly they considered whether grave robbery might be the answer, 'doing a Burke and Hare', but that idea was swiftly scotched. (In 1827, William Burke and William Hare stole the body of an army pensioner from its coffin, and sold it to the Edinburgh Medical College for £7. They went on to murder sixteen people, selling their bodies for medical dissection. Hare testified against Burke, who was hanged and publicly dissected.) It was not a happy comparison. Stealing corpses was unpleasant, immoral and illegal, and even if successful, a body that had lain in the ground for only a few days would be too decomposed for use. What was needed was a discreet and helpful individual with legal access to plenty of fresh corpses.

Montagu knew just such a man: the coroner of St Pancras in north-west London, who went by the delightfully Dickensian name of Bentley Purchase.

Under English law, the coroner, a post dating back to the eleventh century, is the government official responsible for investigating deaths, particularly those occurring under unusual circumstances, and determining their causes. When a death is unexpected, violent or unnatural, the coroner is responsible for deciding whether to hold a postmortem and, if necessary, an inquest.

Bentley Purchase was a friend and colleague of Spilsbury in the death business, but Purchase was as cheery as Sir Bernard was grim. Indeed, for a man who spent his life with the dead, Purchase was the life and soul of every occasion. He found death not only fascinating but extremely funny. No form of violent or mysterious mortality surprised or upset him. 'A depressing job?' he once said. 'Far from it. I can't imagine it getting me down.' He would offer slightly damp chocolates to guests in his private chambers, and joke: 'They were found in Auntie's bag when she was fished out of the Round Pond at Hampstead last night.' A farmer by birth, Purchase was 'rugged in appearance and character', with 'an impish sense of humour' and a finely calibrated sense of the ridiculous: he loved Gilbert and Sullivan operas, toy trains, boiled eggs, and the model piggery he ran near Ipswich. He never wore a hat, and laughed loudly and often.

Montagu knew Purchase as 'an old friend from my barrister days', and dropped him a note asking if they might meet to discuss a confidential matter. Purchase replied with directions to the St Pancras Coroner's Court, and a typically jovial postscript: 'An alternative means of getting here is, of course, to get run over.'

Purchase had fought in the First World War as a doctor attached to the Field Artillery, winning the Military Cross for 'conspicuous gallantry and devotion to duty'. He fought on until 1918, when a shell splinter removed most of his left hand. By the time war broke out again, he was nearly fifty, too old to wear uniform, but 'aching to get into the war'. Indeed, he had already demonstrated a willingness to help the intelligence services and, if necessary, 'distort the truth in the service of security'. When an Abwehr spy named William Rolph killed himself by putting his head in a gas oven in 1940, Purchase obliged with a verdict of 'heart attack'. In the same month that he received Montagu's note, Purchase had been called in to deliberate on the case of Paul Manoel, an agent of the Free French Intelligence Service who had been found hanging in a London basement following interrogation as a suspected enemy agent. Purchase's inquest was 'cursory in the extreme'.

The coroner was initially dubious when Montagu explained that he needed to find a male corpse for 'a warlike operation' but 'did not wish to disclose why a body was needed'.

'You can't get bodies just for the asking, you know,' Purchase told him. 'I should think bodies are the only commodities not in short supply at the moment [but] even with bodies all over the place, each one has to be accounted for.'

Montagu would say only that the scheme required a fresh cadaver that might appear to have drowned or died in an air accident. The matter, he added gravely, was 'of national importance'.

Still Purchase hesitated, pointing out that if word got out that the legal system for disposing of the dead was being circumvented, 'public confidence in coroners of the country would be shaken'.

'At what level has this scheme been given approval?' the coroner asked.

Montagu paused before replying, not entirely truthfully: 'The Prime Minister's.'

That was enough for Bentley Purchase, whose 'well developed sense of comedy' was now thoroughly aroused. Chortling, he explained that, as a coroner, he had 'absolute discretion' over the paperwork and that in certain circumstances a death could be concealed, and a body obtained, without getting official permission from anyone. 'A coroner,' he explained, 'could, in fact, always get rid of a corpse by a certificate that it was going to be buried outside the country – it would then be assumed that a relative was taking it home (i.e. to Ireland) for burial and the coroner could then do what he liked with it without let, hindrance or trace.'

Bodies were pouring into London morgues at an unprecedented rate: in the previous year Purchase had dealt with 1,855 cases, and held inquests into 726 sudden deaths. Many of the bodies 'remained unidentified and were in the end buried as unknowns'. One of these would surely fit the bill. The St Pancras mortuary was attached to the Coroner's Court, so Purchase offered to give Montagu a tour of the bodies currently in cold storage. 'After one or two possible corpses had been inspected and for various reasons rejected', the two men shook hands and parted, with Purchase promising to keep a lookout for a suitable candidate.

The St Pancras mortuary was without doubt the most unpleasant place Montagu had ever been: but then, his had been a life almost entirely free of unpleasant places and upsetting sights.

Ewen Montagu bemoaned 'the inevitable misery of separation' from his family. His letters to his wife Iris are filled with longing and loneliness. 'I miss you most frightfully, and life has just seemed one long, grey monotone since we have been separated.' But he had grown to enjoy his existence as a bachelor spy. 'The interest and pressure of my work managed to keep my morale up,' he wrote. 'In a way it was like a mixture of constructing a crossword puzzle and sawing a jigsaw puzzle and then waiting to see whether the recipient could and would solve the clues and place the bits together successfully.' The only drawback to living at Kensington Court was the presence of Lady Swaythling, with whom he argued constantly. He found time to get away for fishing trips on Exmoor. 'It was lovely to be far from the noise and the worry and just listening to the noise of the stream,' he told Iris. 'I haven't enjoyed anything as much since you left.' He relished the fishing most when it was hardest. 'The greatest fun is the very delicate casting into awkward places.'

Lord Swaythling had taken the Rolls-Royce with him to Townhill, so Montagu borrowed a bicycle to commute to work. In order to transport his 'super-secret papers', he bolted a large pannier on the front and chained his briefcase to it. The head of security at the Naval Intelligence Department questioned whether it was safe to cycle around with a briefcase full of secrets. What if the case was stolen? But after some argument, Montagu was given formal permission to continue with this unorthodox arrangement for transporting documents 'as long as I always wore a shoulder holster and an automatic pistol'.

On 24 January 1943, Montagu cycled as usual back to Kensington Court, where Ward the butler opened the massive front door to him. Nancy, 'one of the best cooks in London', had rustled up a fine dinner in spite of rationing, although the Dowager Lady Swaythling insisted that standards had slipped. 'Mother is too awful for words,' Ewen wrote to Iris. 'She complains that she can't get her nice chocolates "of decent quality" whereas everyone else is overjoyed at getting any at all.'

Ewen ate alone in the dining room panelled in oak from

the Place Vendôme, beneath the glowering portraits of his ancestors. There was always plenty of cheese. He then spent an hour in the great library, working on the 'crossword puzzles' in his briefcase. The Casablanca Conference had ended with the decision to invade Sicily. Cholmondeley's plan to foist a dead body on the Germans with false documents was still only on the drawing board, but the decision at Casablanca had sharply accelerated the timescale: unless Montagu found a suitable body, and fast, Trojan Horse would be, in a manner of speaking, dead in the water.

Finally, Montagu turned in, returned the papers to his briefcase, locked it, and headed to the basement bedroom where he now slept because of the air raids. Mabel the maid ('who had been in the family for more than thirty-five years') had turned down the crisp cotton sheets on the bed.

That same evening, in a grimy disused warehouse on the other side of London, a young Welshman swallowed a large dose of rat poison, ending a life which could not have been more different, in every conceivable way, from that of the Hon. Ewen Montagu.

5

The Man Who Was

Aberbargoed was a grim place a century ago, a brooding village of coal-dusted sadness and unremitting toil. The colliery opened in 1903. Before the coal was found, there was nothing at Aberbargoed, save the green valleys. With the coal came rows of pinched, terraced streets, housing hundreds of miners and their families. Without coal it was nothing. And when the coal ran out, as it eventually did, there was nothing much left. Even before the First World War, Aberbargoed was suffering, and struggling.

Into this bleak world Glyndwr Michael was born, on 4 January 1909, at 136 Commercial Street. His mother was Sarah Ann Chadwick, his father a colliery haulier named Thomas Michael. What few records have survived of this family give a flavour of their troubled lives. At the age of twenty, in 1888, Sarah had married another coalminer, George Cottrell. She signed their marriage certificate with a cross. Sarah never learned to read or write, or ever had any use for either skill. Although two daughters resulted from her marriage to Cottrell, the relationship did not last, and by 1904 she was living with Thomas Michael in a cramped house beside the railway line at Dinas. They never married. Like his father, who died of tuberculosis when Thomas was a child, Thomas Michael had been a coalminer all his life. A Welsh Baptist, born in Dinas, he worked deep in the pits, hauling coal trucks by hand through the bowels of the earth. At some point before meeting Sarah, Thomas Michael contracted syphilis, which he passed on to her, and which apparently went untreated. It is possible that when Glyndwr Michael was born, his parents bequeathed him congenital syphilis, which can cause damage to bones, eyes and brain.

When Glyn was an infant, the family moved twelve miles from Aberbargoed to Taff's Well, next to Rockwood Pit, where another child, Doris, was born two years later. Unable to pay the rent, the Michaels moved from one dingy house to another, each more decrepit than the last, first to 7 Garth Street, and then again, a few years later, to 28 Cornwall Road, Williamstown, Penygraig, in the Rhondda Valley, where Sarah gave birth to her third child by Thomas. There was little food. The children wore shoes once a week, to church. Thomas Michael drank.

Around 1919, when Glyn was nine or ten, his father's health began to decline, probably due to the delayed effects of syphilis, combined with the lung-rotting damage caused by working underground for over three decades. Soon after this, his grandmother died of 'senile decay'. Mental frailty would be a recurrent feature of the family's medical history. Thomas Michael began to cough horribly, and sweat at odd times of the day. The right side of his chest began to sink inwards.

Early in 1924, Michael was no longer able to work, and the family was forced to live on charity from the Pontypridd Union, the second largest Poor Law authority in Britain. For a time they were homeless and were forced to move into a single room at Llwynypia Homes, a charity hostel. The Pontypridd Union paid 23 shillings for a man and wife, and 2 shillings for each child. A family of five was now surviving, barely, on £1, 9 shillings a week. Thomas Michael became 'melancholic', according to a medical report which added that he was 'confused and very depressed', rapidly losing weight and had a racking, rattling cough.

Just before Christmas 1924, Thomas Michael stabbed himself in the throat with a carving knife. He was rushed to the county mental hospital in Bridgend, where the wound was cleaned and stitched up. Thomas Michael was a mental and physical wreck, coughing blood and in 'deep mental depression'. He was fifty-one years old, but looked eighty. Percy Hawkins, a nurse at the institution, described him: 'Hair is grey and thin. Pupils are somewhat irregular, they react to light and converge. Tongue has a dry white fur. Teeth very deficient and carious. He is thin and poorly nourished. Patient coughs and spits a good deal, and sweats heavily at night.' Both lungs were riddled with disease.

At first, Thomas seemed to be recovering. He began to speak quite rationally, and to notice his surroundings. But on 13 March 1925 he caught influenza, which developed into bronchial pneumonia, with 'a hectic temperature, copious and foul-smelling expectoration, very weak and depressed'. He stopped eating. On 31 March Thomas Michael died.

Glyndwr Michael, now sixteen years old, had witnessed his father turn from a vigorous coalminer into a diseased husk. He had seen him stab himself, and then watched him fall apart in a lunatic asylum. Glyn had been born poor. Now he was a pauper. He may already have been suffering from mental illness. When Thomas Michael was buried in a common grave in Trealaw cemetery, Reverend Overton presiding, Glyn Michael signed the burial register in a blotted, uncertain hand without using capital letters.

The widowed Sarah moved, with her three youngest children, into a minuscule flat in the back streets of Trealaw, now dependent entirely on alms for survival. The Pontypridd Union, however, was going bust, such was the demand for charity in the struggling South Wales coalfields. A year after Thomas Michael's death, Health Minister Neville Chamberlain told Parliament that the Pontypridd Union had run up an overdraft of £210,000, and further money would be advanced only 'on condition that the scale of relief was reduced'. As the Depression struck, the economic situation in South Wales turned from bad to catastrophic. Glyn found part-time employment as a gardener and labourer, but work was hard to come by.

At the outbreak of war in 1939, Sarah and Glyn Michael were still living at 135 Trealaw Road. Glyn's two half-sisters and his sister Doris had each married coalminers, and now had families of their own. His younger brother had left home. Glyndwr was not considered eligible for military service, which suggests that he was unfit, either physically or, more probably, mentally. On 15 January 1940, Glyn's mother died in her bed of a heart attack and an aortic aneurism. Sarah had been his only emotional support. On 16 January, Glyndwr Michael witnessed his mother's death certificate, buried her alongside his father in the Trealaw cemetery, and disappeared. A country at war had little attention to spare for a man who was homeless, destitute and most likely mentally ill.

Bentley Purchase often wondered why people came to the capital to die. More than a quarter of all the cases he examined were suicides, but many of these were not Londoners. What impulse, he mused, 'led men and women to London to end their lives? Was it because the dead from the provinces hoped that in the vastness of the capital one more tragedy would pass unnoticed? Or did they wish to spare relatives and friends the distress that would arise inevitably if they ended their lives on their own doorsteps?' Purchase was puzzled, in a detached and scientific way: 'It still surprised him how many people seemed to be utterly friendless and unwanted when they arrived in his mortuary.'

It is not clear how or when Glyndwr Michael got to London. In the winter of 1942 he was staying in 'a common lodging house' in west London, although he also appears to have been sleeping rough in disused buildings and undergoing some sort of treatment at a lunatic asylum. He was clean shaven, which suggests he owned a razor, and was living somewhere where he could use it.

On 26 January 1943, Michael was found in an abandoned warehouse near King's Cross and was taken to St Pancras

Hospital, suffering from acute chemical poisoning. As Sir Bernard Spilsbury's case notes attest, suicides in wartime Britain found an extraordinary variety of ways to poison themselves: with Lysol disinfectant, camphor, opium, carbolic, hydrochloric acid, alcohol, chloroform and coal gas. Michael ingested rat poison, probably 'Battle's Vermin Killer', a paste laced with highly toxic white phosphorus. It was assumed that Michael had killed himself intentionally. His father had attempted suicide, and self-destruction, tragically, often runs in families. But it is also possible that the poisoning was accidental. Rat poison was usually spread on stale bread and other scraps: the phosphorus made it glow in the dark, so the rodents would be attracted by both the light and smell. It is entirely possible that Michael ate rotting leftover food laced with poison because he was hungry.

Phosphorus poisoning is a horrific way to die, as acid in the digestive system reacts with the phosphide to generate the toxic gas phosphine. The pathology follows three distinct phases. Often within minutes, the victim suffers nausea and vomiting, as the phosphorus affects the gastric tract, followed by delirium, cramps, restlessness, convulsions, extreme thirst, and two particularly unpleasant symptoms peculiar to phosphorus poisoning: 'smoking stool' and 'garlic breath'. The second phase, some twenty-four hours after the initial poisoning, is one of relative calm when the symptoms appear to subside. In the third phase, the victim suffers breakdown of the central nervous system, jaundice, coma, kidney, heart and liver failure, and finally death. It took poor Glyndwr Michael more than two days to die, but he appears to have been sufficiently lucid in the second phase to tell the nurses at St Pancras who he was, and what he had eaten. He was pronounced dead on 28 January 1943.

At the age of thirty-four, Glyndwr Michael had simply slipped through the cracks of a wartime society with other concerns: a single man, illegitimate and probably illiterate, without money, friends or family, he had died unloved and unlamented, but not unnoticed.

As soon as the body of Glyndwr Michael reached St Pancras morgue, Bentley Purchase informed Ewen Montagu that a candidate for the project had arrived in his jurisdiction and would be 'kept in suitable cold storage until we were ready for it'.

Purchase carried out a swift inquest, with a foregone conclusion. In a suspected poisoning, the coroner would normally have held an autopsy, but none was ordered in this case, for obvious reasons. Purchase listed Michael as 'lunatic', which suggests that he had been certified insane and was undergoing treatment. The death certificate, based on the coroner's inquest, described him as 'labourer, no fixed abode', and gives the cause of death as 'phosphorus poisoning. Took rat poison [in a] bid [to] kill himself while of unsound mind.' Purchase informed the registrar that the body was being 'removed out of England' for burial.

In private, the coroner gave Montagu a more detailed account. The dead man, he explained, had taken 'a minimal dose' of rat poison. 'This dose was not sufficient to kill him outright, and its only effect was so to impair the functioning of the liver that he died a little time afterwards.' The human body normally contains traces of phosphorus, the coroner explained, and 'phosphorus is not one of the poisons readily traceable after long periods, such as arsenic which invades the roots of the hair, etc., or strychnine'. The rat poison would leave few clues to the cause of death, 'except possibly faint traces of chemical action in the liver'. Determining how the man had died after immersion in water would require 'a highly skilled medico-criminal chemist who would have to weigh all the chemical compositions of every organ before he could come to any conclusion'. Purchase liked a flutter, and he was willing to 'bet heavily against anyone being able to determine the cause of death with sufficient certainty to deny the presumption that the man had been drowned or killed by shock through an aeroplane crash and then been immersed in water'.

For a second, even weightier, opinion Montagu turned once more to Sir Bernard Spilsbury, the world's foremost medico-criminal chemist. They met again at the Junior Carlton Club. Sir Bernard's verdict was as dry as his sherry: 'You have nothing to fear from a Spanish postmortem; to detect that this young man had not died after an aircraft had been lost at sea would need a pathologist of my experience – and there aren't any in Spain.'

Spilsbury's answer was typical of the man. Typically self-assured, typically laconic, but also (and this was increasingly true of Sir Bernard's lofty pronouncements) typically open to question. For Sir Bernard Spilsbury was not the forensic oracle he had once been; far from infallible, he had started to make some terrible mistakes. Today, even his evidence in the Crippen case is open to doubt. Utterly convinced of his own rectitude and adamant in his prejudices, Spilsbury helped to send 110 men to the gallows. Some, with hindsight, were plainly innocent. His theories and opinions had increasingly taken precedence over the facts, most notably in the case of Norman Thorne, sentenced to death for killing his girlfriend. The woman had almost certainly committed suicide, and the evidence was at best contradictory, but Spilsbury's testimony had been unwavering, despite a rising tide of protest at the way one man's 'expertise' was sending a possibly innocent man to the gallows. 'I am a martyr to Spilsburyism,' said Thorne, shortly before his execution.

By the 1940s, Spilsbury's reputation had begun to fade; his marriage was collapsing, and his mind had started to fail. His fabled sense of smell had deserted him. He was overworked and in 1940 he suffered a small stroke. The death of a son in the Blitz affected him deeply. His answers to Montagu's questions bore all the hallmarks of the last days of Sir Bernard Spilsbury: emphatic but questionable, and potentially extremely dangerous.

Identifying whether an individual has drowned, or died by some other means, is one of the oldest and most difficult medical dilemmas. In the thirteenth century, a book by Chinese physicians entitled *The Washing Away of Wrongs* addressed the thorny issue of suspicious death by drowning. Even today, the medical community has no universally agreed diagnostic tests for drowning. Spilsbury himself had closely studied the pathology of drowning in the spectacular 'Brides in the Bath' case of 1915, when George Joseph Smith, a swindler and bigamist, was accused of killing at least three of his wives. In each case, the victim had been found in the bath. Spilsbury exhumed the bodies, and set about proving that they could not have died by natural causes. In court, it took him just twenty minutes to convince the jury that it is possible to murder someone, and leave no marks of violence, by suddenly submerging them in water while bathing. Smith was hanged.

In the course of that case, Spilsbury had become intimately acquainted with the symptoms of drowning: the fine white froth, known as *champagne de mousse*, in the lungs and on the lips; the marbled and swollen appearance of the lungs, inflated by the inhalation of water; water in the stomach; foreign material, such as vomit or sand, in the lungs; and haemorrhages in the middle ear. A drowning person dies violently, struggling, often bruising or rupturing the muscles in the neck or shoulder as he grasps and gasps for air. None of these symptoms would be present in the body of Glyndwr Michael, who had not died in water, but in a hospital bed, heavily sedated. On the other side of the coin, anyone killed by phosphorus, however small the dosage, would have yellowed skin and probably gastric burns, as well as significant traces of the chemical in the body, easily detectable with the science of 1943.

The renowned forensic scientist did not examine the body of Glyndwr Michael. Instead, Sir Bernard offered his opinion, as was his habit, *de haut en bas*, and stuck to it, come hell or high water.

Spilsbury was also wrong in his complacent avowal that Spain contained no able pathologists. If the body was examined by a country doctor, the deception might pass unnoticed; but it was intended that the body and its documents should pass into German hands: there was at least one highly trained pathologist in Spain working for German intelligence who would be able to spot the imposture as fast as Spilsbury himself, and probably faster. So far from offering certainty, Sir Bernard's opinion, accepted by Montagu, represented an enormous gamble. If it failed, then the victims of Spilsburyism could number in their thousands.

Montagu would later claim that the body used in the deception had 'died from pneumonia after exposure'; that his relatives had been contacted and told that the body was needed for a 'really worthwhile purpose'; and that permission was duly obtained 'on condition that I should never let it be known whose corpse it was'. None of this was true. Montagu and Cholmondeley certainly made 'feverish enquiries into his past and about his relatives', but only to ensure that Glyndwr Michael had no past to speak of, and no relatives likely to cause problems by asking questions. Sarah was dead. Michael had two siblings, and two half-siblings, all still living in the Welsh valleys. Apparently they had not looked after him in life; there was little chance they would care more for him after death. Anyway, they were not consulted. Indeed, they were not even located. In a draft, unpublished manuscript, Montagu wrote: 'The most careful possible enquiries, made even more carefully than usual in view of our proposals, failed to reveal any relative.' Montagu never did reveal Glyndwr Michael's identity. However, he could not remove his name from the official record, and he left personal papers which also identify him. In one letter, Montagu referred to Glyndwr Michael as 'a ne'er do well, and his relatives were not much better . . . the actual person did nothing for anyone ever – only his body did good after he was dead.' It was true that Michael's life had been a short and unhappy one: he had never done well, but then, he had never had much of an opportunity. Posthumously, the ne'er do well was about to do very well indeed.

Bentley Purchase warned that time was of the essence. The corpse could not be frozen solid to arrest decay entirely, since fluids in the body expand as they turn to ice, damaging fragile soft tissue, which would be only too evident once the body was defrosted. The mortuary at St Pancras had one 'extra-cold refrigerator' which could be set at four degrees centigrade, cold enough to retard decomposition substantially, but not so cold as to prevent it entirely. The body of Glyndwr Michael was already beginning to rot. If the corpse was to be of any use, warned Purchase, it 'would have to be used within three months'.

Before the operation could be formally launched, it needed a new codename. Trojan Horse had been acceptable as the initial title, but if any German agent were to stumble across it, the implication of some sort of hoax would be glaringly obvious. Codenames were compiled by the Inter-Services Security Board, covering almost every aspect of the war: nations, cities, plans, locations, military units, military operations, diplomatic meetings, places, individuals and spies were all disguised under false names. In theory these codewords were neutral and indecipherable, a shorthand for those in the picture, and deliberately meaningless to those outside it. Random lists of codenames were issued in alphabetical blocks of ten words, and then selected by chance as needed; six months after it became defunct, a codeword could be reassigned and reused, a deliberate ploy to muddy the waters.

Churchill had a clearly defined policy on choosing codewords for major operations: 'They ought not to be given names of a frivolous character such as "Bunnyhug" and "Ballyhoo",' the Prime Minister decreed. 'Intelligent thought will already supply an unlimited number of well-sounding names that do not suggest the character of the operation and do not enable some widow or mother to say that her son was killed in an operation called "Bunnyhug" or "Ballyhoo".'

However, the rule requiring that codewords be devoid of meaning was routinely ignored, by all sides, throughout the war, for spies found the temptation to invent joking and hinting titles for their most secret projects almost irresistible. Agent 'Tate' was so-called because he looked like the music-hall performer Harry Tate; the criminal Eddie Chapman was named 'Zigzag', since no one could be certain which way he might turn; Stalin, meaning 'man of steel', was awarded the codename 'Glyptic', meaning 'an image carved from stone'. The Germans were even more culpable in this respect. The Nazis' long-range radar system was named 'Heimdall' after the Norse god with the power to see great distances; the planned invasion of Britain was codenamed 'Sealion' – a most unsubtle reference to the lions on the royal coats of arms, and the planned seaborne attack.

Montagu was particularly scathing of the Abwehr's 'stupidity' in selecting such revealing codewords: the codename for Britain, he pointed out, was 'Golfplatz', meaning golf course, while America was 'Samland', a reference to Uncle Sam. Montagu now broke his own rule that codenames be chosen so that 'no deductions could be made from them', and selected a name that had been used for a mine-laying operation in 1941, and was now up for grabs.

Plan Trojan Horse became 'Operation Mincemeat'. There was nothing haphazard about the choice. All the talk of corpses was having an effect, and Montagu's 'sense of humour having by this time become somewhat macabre', a codeword that signified dead meat seemed only too apt, and a 'good omen'. There was no danger of any grieving mother complaining that her dead son had been deployed under a frivolous and tasteless codeword because, as the planners knew very well, in the case of Glyndwr Michael, there was no one to grieve.

Even before Bentley Purchase had completed his inquest, Cholmondeley and Montagu set to work, drawing up a formal proposal to put to the intelligence chiefs. On 4 February, a week after the death of Michael and on the very day Purchase completed his inquest, they presented a draft of Operation Mincemeat to the Twenty Committee: 'This operation is proposed in view of the fact that the enemy will almost certainly get information of the preparation of any assault mounted in North Africa and will try to find out its target.'

The plan envisaged dropping the dead body, with fake documents, from a plane, to give the impression that 'a courier carrying important "hand of officer" documents was en route for Algiers in an aircraft which crashed'. The overall scheme should not only divert the Germans from the real target, but portray the real target as a 'cover target', a mere decoy. This was a brilliant piece of double bluff, for it would ensure that when the Germans found out about genuine preparations to attack Sicily, as they must, they would assume this was part of the deception plan. Sicily could not be left out of the equation altogether, for as Cholmondeley and Montagu pointed out, if 'the real target is omitted from both the "operation plan" and the "cover plan" the Germans will almost certainly suspect, as not only is Sicily a very possible target, but the Germans are believed already to anticipate it as a possible target'. Since 'the Germans will be looking with care for our cover plan as well as our real plan', Operation Mincemeat would feed them both a false real plan, and a false cover plan – which would actually be the real plan.

The outline did not go into specifics as to how this misinformation would be put across, nor where the body would be dropped, and warned that, once launched, it could not be delayed: 'The body must be dropped within twenty-four hours of its being removed from its present place in London. The flight, once laid on, must not be cancelled or postponed.' The Twenty Committee pondered only briefly, before issuing a flurry of requests to the representatives of the different services. The Air Ministry should investigate finding a suitable plane, preferably one used by SOE; the draft plan should be shown to the intelligence chiefs of the Army, Navy and RAF; Colonel Johnnie Bevan of the London Controlling Section should be asked for his approval; the Admiralty should 'find out a suitable position for dropping the body'; and the War Office should look 'into the question of providing the body with a name and necessary papers'. The naval attaché in Madrid, Captain Alan Hillgarth, should be informed of the plan so that 'he will be able to cope with any unforeseen circumstances'.

Montagu and Cholmondeley were instructed to 'continue with preparations to give MINCEMEAT his necessary clothes, papers, letters, etc. etc.'. Out of the officially nameless corpse in the mortuary they must conjure up a living person, with a new name, a personality, and a past. Operation Mincemeat began as fiction, a plot twist in a long-forgotten novel, picked up by another novelist, and approved by a committee presided over by yet another novelist. Now it was the turn of the spies to take the reality of a dead Welsh tramp, make him into a fiction, and so change reality.

6

A Novel Approach

Montagu and Cholmondeley had spent much of the previous three years nurturing, moulding and deploying spies who did not exist. The Twenty Committee and Section B1A of MI5 had turned the playing of double agents into an art form, but as the Double Cross System developed and expanded, more and more of the agents reporting back to Germany were purely fictional: Agent A (real) would notionally employ Agent B (unreal), who would in turn recruit other agents, C to Z (all equally imaginary). Juan Pujol García, Agent 'Garbo', the most famous double agent of them all, was eventually equipped with no fewer than twenty-seven sub-agents, each with a distinct character, friends, jobs, tastes, homes and lovers. Garbo's 'active and well-distributed team of imaginary assistants' were a motley lot, including a Welsh Aryan supremacist, a communist, a Greek waiter, a wealthy Venezuelan student, a disaffected South African serviceman and several crooks. In the words of John Masterman, the thriller-writing chairman of the Twenty Committee, 'The one-man band of Lisbon developed into an orchestra, and an orchestra which played a more and more ambitious programme.' Graham Greene, a wartime intelligence officer in West Africa, based his novel *Our Man in Havana*, about a spy who invents an entire network of bogus informants, on the Garbo story.

Masterman, writing after the war, declared that 'for deception, "notional" or imaginary agents were on the whole preferable' to living ones. Real agents tended to become truculent and demanding; they needed feeding, pampering, and paying. An imaginary agent, however, was infinitely pliable, and willing to do the bidding of his German handlers at once, and without question: 'The Germans could seldom resist such a fly if it was accurately and skilfully cast,' wrote Masterman, himself a dab hand with a fly-fishing rod.

Maintaining a small army of fake people needed concerted attention to detail. 'How difficult it was,' wrote Montagu, 'to remember the characteristics and life pattern of each one of a mass of completely non-existent notional sub-agents.' These imaginary individuals had to suffer all the vagaries of normal life, such as getting ill, celebrating birthdays, and running out of money. They had to remain perfectly consistent in their behaviour, attitudes and emotions. As Montagu put it, the imaginary agent 'must *never* step out of character'. The network of fake agents enabled British intelligence to supply the Germans with a steady stream of untruths and half-truths, and it lulled the Abwehr into believing it had a large and efficient espionage network in Britain, when it had nothing of the sort.

Creating a personality to go with the corpse in the St Pancras morgue would require imaginative effort on an even greater scale. In his novel *The Case of the Four Friends*, Masterman's sleuth, Ernest Brendel, observes that the key to detective work is anticipating the actions of the criminal: 'To work out the crime before it is committed, to foresee how it will be arranged, and then to prevent it! That's a triumph indeed.' With Masterman's help, Cholmondeley and Montagu would lay out the clues to a life that had never happened, and frame a new death for a dead man.

The fictitious agents so far invented by the Double Cross Team all spoke for themselves, or rather through others, in wireless messages and letters to their handlers, but they were never seen. In the case of Operation Mincemeat, the fraudulent individual could communicate only through the clothes on his back, the contents of his pockets and, most importantly, the letters in his possession. He would carry official typed letters to convey the core deception, but also handwritten personal letters, to put across his personality. 'The more real he appeared, the more convincing the whole affair would be,' reflected Montagu, since 'every little detail would be studied by the Germans'.

The information he carried would have to be credible, but also legible. 'Would the ink of the manuscript letters, and the signatures on the others, not run so as to make the documents illegible?' Montagu wondered. Waterproof ink might be used, but that would 'give the game away'. They turned to MI5's scientists, and numerous tests were carried out using different inks and typewriters, and then immersing the letters in sea water for varying periods to test the effects. The results were encouraging: 'Many inks on a freshly written letter will run at once if the surface is wetted. On the other hand, a lot of quite usual inks, if thoroughly dried, will stand a fair amount of wetting even if exposed directly to the water. When a document is inside an envelope, or inside a wallet which is itself inside a pocket, well dried inks of some quite normal types will often remain legible for a surprising length of time – quite long enough for our purpose.'

The precise form of the deception would be decided in time: first they needed to create a credible courier.

It is no accident that both Montagu and Cholmondeley were both enthusiastic novel-readers. The greatest writers of spy fiction have, in almost every case, worked in intelligence before turning to writing. Somerset Maugham, John Buchan, Ian Fleming, Graham Greene, John le Carré: all had experienced the world of espionage at first hand. For the task of the spy is not so very different from that of the novelist: to create an imaginary, credible world, and then lure others into it, by words and artifice.

As if constructing a character in a novel, Montagu and

Cholmondeley, with the help of Joan Saunders in Section 17M, set about creating a personality with which to clothe their dead body. Hour after hour, in the Admiralty basement, they discussed and refined this imaginary person, his likes and dislikes, his habits and hobbies, his talents and weaknesses. In the evening, they repaired to the Gargoyle, a glamorous Soho club of which Montagu was a member, to continue the odd process of creating a man from scratch. The project reflected all the possibilities and pitfalls of fiction: if they painted his personality too brightly, or were inconsistent in the portrait, then the Germans would surely detect a hoax. But if the enemy could be made to believe in this British officer, then they were that much more likely to credit the documents he carried. Eventually, they came to believe in him themselves. 'We talked about him until we did feel that he was an old friend,' wrote Montagu. 'He became completely real to us.' They gave him a middle name, a nicotine habit, and a place of birth. They gave him a hometown, a rank, a regiment and a love of fishing. He would be furnished with a watch, a bank manager, a solicitor and cufflinks. They gave him all the things that Glyndwr Michael had lacked in his luckless life, including a supportive family, money, friends, and love.

But first he needed a name and, more importantly, a uniform. It was originally intended that the dropped body should appear to be that of an army officer ferrying important messages to the top brass in North Africa. An army officer could wear battledress, normal combat uniform, rather than a formal fitted uniform. Army officers did not carry identity cards with photographs when travelling outside England, which obviated the need to obtain a mugshot of Glyndwr Michael for a fake card. The Director of Military Intelligence, however, pointed out that if the courier were an army officer, then the discovery of the body would have to be reported to the military attaché in Madrid, and the information passed from there to London, increasing the number of people in the know, and the danger of a leak.

Since the idea had originated in Naval Intelligence, it was more sensible to make him a naval officer, thus keeping the secret within naval circles. A naval officer, however, would be unlikely to carry documents relating to the planned invasion, and such officers always travelled in full naval 'display' uniform, complete with braid and badges of rank on the sleeve. The idea of getting the corpse measured up by a tailor was too ghoulish (and too dangerous) to contemplate. The Secret Service contained men of varied talents and occupations, but no gentlemen's outfitters with experience of dressing the dead.

After much discussion, it was decided that the body would be dressed as a Royal Marine, the corps which forms the amphibious infantry of the Royal Navy. Marines always travelled in battledress, made up of beret or cap, khaki blouse and trousers, gaiters and boots. This uniform came in standard sizes.

Since the Marines, unlike the Army, travelled with photographic identity cards, one of these would have to be faked. This raised an additional problem. Although there were thousands of British Army officers currently serving, the number of Royal Marines officers was comparatively small, and their names appeared on the Navy List, of which German intelligence undoubtedly possessed a copy. One of these would need to 'lend' his name to the dead body.

Casting his eye down the list of serving naval officers, Montagu noticed a large block of men with the surname Martin. No fewer than nine of these were Royal Marines, eight lieutenants, and one captain, who had been promoted to acting major in 1941. The ferrying of important documents would be entrusted to a fairly senior officer, so Captain William Hynd Norrie Martin was unknowingly pressganged into the job. The real Norrie Martin was commissioned in 1927, becoming one of the Fleet Air Arm's best pilots. In 1943 he was instructing British aircrew at Quonset Point, Rhode Island, and thus unlikely to get wind of what was being done with his name. By pure coincidence, the real Martin had served aboard the aircraft carrier *Hermes*, which was sunk by the Japanese in April 1942, with the loss of more than 300 men. A death notice for the fake William Martin would need to be posted in the British press: the Germans would believe this referred to the body carrying the documents, but the real Major Martin's friends and colleagues would probably assume he had died in the sinking of the *Hermes*, with his death only belatedly confirmed.

Captain William 'Bill' Martin was duly issued with identity card number 148228 by the Admiralty. He was made four years younger than Glyndwr Michael, but Cardiff was chosen as his place of birth, just ten miles from Michael's birthplace in Aberbargoed. The card assigned Martin to 'Combined Operations', the force set up to harass the Germans by combined Navy and Army operations, and directed by Lord Louis Mountbatten. The identity card was suspiciously shiny, so as an added precaution it was endorsed 'issued in lieu of No. 09650 lost'. This was Montagu's own identity card number, to ensure that anyone investigating this non-existent officer with the fake identity card would eventually come to him. Losing an identity card was a serious lapse in wartime Britain, but as well as explaining its newness, the replacement card provided the first plank in the personality of Bill Martin: he was accident-prone. Montagu signed the card, the first of many occasions when he would stand in for Bill Martin.

All that was needed to complete the card was a photograph. Glyndwr Michael had never had a passport or any other form of photographic identity card, and trying to obtain a recent photograph, if such a thing existed, would have involved contacting the Michael family. Montagu and Cholmondeley repaired to the St Pancras mortuary with a camera and tape measure. While Cholmondeley measured Glyndwr for the Royal Marines battledress and boots, Montagu prepared him for his photograph. It was the first time they had seen the body: the face seemed thin and sickly, rather different from the strapping young warrior they had already framed in their minds. Still, as

Montagu remarked: 'He does not have to look like an officer – only like a staff officer', and these were seldom the most impressive physical specimens.

This was possibly the first time Glyndwr Michael had ever been photographed. But the morbid modelling session was a 'complete failure'. After only a few days, the eyes of a corpse in cold storage begin to sink into the skull, and the facial muscles start to sag. It is simply impossible to take a photograph of the face of a dead person that looks anything other than entirely, unmistakably dead. Michael had been emaciated before he died. Every day he spent in the St Pancras mortuary, he looked slightly deader. No matter at what angle he was photographed, and under what light, the newly named William Martin resolutely refused to come alive for the camera.

Back in the office, and in the street, Montagu and Cholmondeley surreptitiously scanned the faces of friends and strangers alike, in the hope of spotting someone who might stand in as Bill Martin's double. Glyndwr Michael's face was unremarkable, with greying hair, thinning in front. It was not, thought Montagu, an 'appearance that would have singled him out in a crowd'. Yet finding someone who even vaguely resembled him was proving extraordinarily difficult.

While Montagu searched for the right face, 'rudely staring at anyone with whom we came into contact', Cholmondeley went clothes shopping. Glyndwr Michael had been tall and thin, 'almost the same build' as Cholmondeley himself. Cholmondeley first bought braces, gaiters, and standard issue military boots, size 12. Then, having obtained permission from Colonel Neville of the Royal Marines, he presented himself at Gieves, the military tailors in Piccadilly, to be fitted for a Royal Marines battledress, complete with appropriate badges of rank, Royal Marines flashes and the badge flashes of Combined Operations. The uniform was finished off with a trench coat and beret. The clothes would need the patina of wear, so Cholmondeley climbed into the uniform, and wore it every day for the next three months.

Underwear was a more ticklish problem. Cholmondeley, understandably, was unwilling to surrender his own, since good underwear was hard to come by in rationed, wartime Britain. They consulted John Masterman, Oxford academic and chairman of the Twenty Committee, who came up with a scholarly solution that was also personally satisfying. 'The difficulty of obtaining underclothes, owing to the system of coupon rationing,' wrote Masterman, 'was overcome by the acceptance of a gift of thick underwear from the wardrobe of the late Warden of New College, Oxford.' Major Martin would be kitted out with the flannel vest and underpants of none other than H. A. L. Fisher, the distinguished Oxford historian and former President of the Board of Education in Lloyd George's Cabinet. John Masterman and Herbert Fisher had both taught history at Oxford in the 1920s, and had long enjoyed a fierce academic rivalry. Fisher was a figure of ponderous grandeur and gravity who ran New College, according to one colleague, as 'one enormous mausoleum'. Masterman considered him long-winded and pompous. Fisher had been run over and killed by a lorry after attending a tribunal examining the appeals of conscientious objectors, of which he was chairman. The obituaries paid resounding tribute to his intellectual and academic stature, which nettled Masterman. Putting the great man's underclothes on a dead body and floating it into German hands was just the sort of joke that appealed to his odd sense of humour. Masterman described the underwear as a 'gift'; it seems far more likely that he simply arranged for the dead don's drawers to be pressed into war service.

Montagu and Cholmondeley were both, in different ways, adapting themselves to the part of Bill Martin. Montagu had forged his signature. Cholmondeley was wearing his clothes. Slowly, the personality of Major Martin was coming into focus, a character who would have to be revealed by whatever was in his wallet, pockets and briefcase. Martin, it was decided, was the adored son of an upper-middle-class family from Wales. (His Welshness was virtually the only concession to Glyndwr Michael's real identity.)

He was a Roman Catholic. Catholic countries were believed to be averse to surgical autopsies for religious reasons, and this traditional reluctance would presumably be compounded if the body was thought to be that of a co-religionist.

The William Martin they conjured up was clever, even 'brilliant', industrious but forgetful, and inclined to the grand gesture. He liked a good time, enjoyed the theatre and dancing, and spent more than he had, relying on his father to bail him out. His mother Antonia had died some years earlier. They began to ink in his past. He had been educated, they decided, at public school and university. He was a secret writer of considerable promise, though he had never published anything. After university, he had retired to the country to write, listen to music, and to fish. He was something of a loner. With the outbreak of war, he had signed up with the Royal Marines, but found himself consigned to an office, which he disliked. 'Keen for more active and dangerous work,' he had escaped by switching to the Commandos, and had distinguished himself by his aptitude for technical matters, notably the mechanics of landing craft. He had predicted that the Dieppe raid would be a disaster, and he had been right. Martin was, they concluded, 'a thoroughly good chap', romantic and dashing, but also somewhat feckless, unpunctual, and extravagant.

The first witness to Martin's fictional character was his bank manager. Montagu approached Ernest Whitley Jones, joint general manager of Lloyds Bank, and asked him if he would be prepared to write an angry letter about an overdraft that did not exist, to a client who was also imaginary – a request that is surely unique in the annals of British banking. Whitley Jones was, perhaps predictably, a cautious man. It was not, he pointed out, normal practice for the general manager of the bank's head office to perform such a mundane task. But when Montagu explained that he would rather not 'bring in' anyone else, the manager relented. Such a letter 'could sometimes come from head office', he said, 'especially when the general manager was the personal friend of the father of a young customer whose extravagance needs some check and the father does not want to nag his son'.

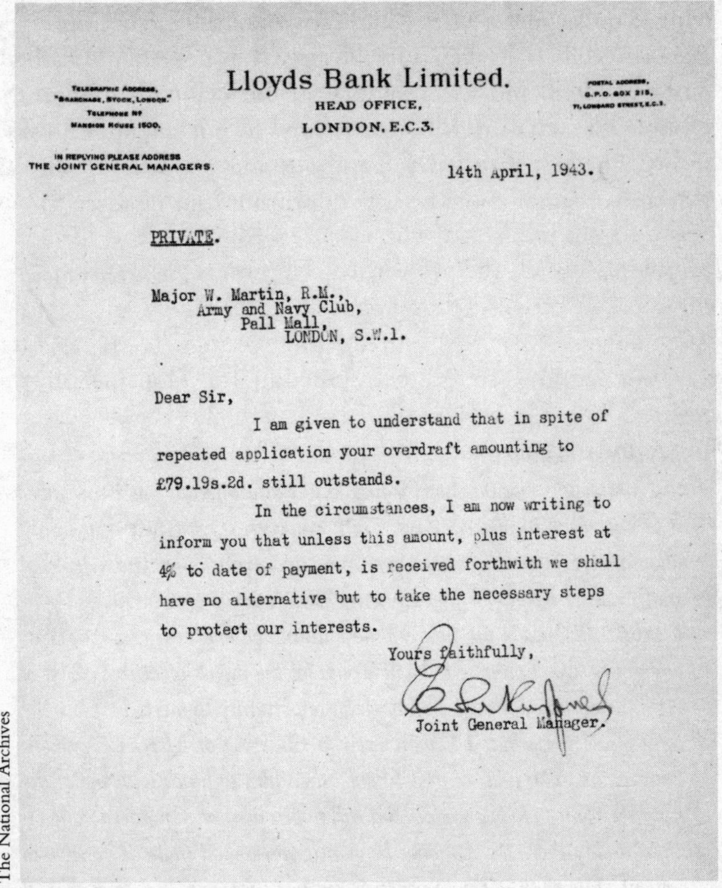

Lloyds Bank Limited.
HEAD OFFICE,
LONDON, E.C.3.

TELEGRAPHIC ADDRESS,
"BRANCHAGE, STOCK, LONDON."
TELEPHONE Nº
MANSION HOUSE 1500.

POSTAL ADDRESS,
G.P.O. BOX 215,
71, LOMBARD STREET, E.C.3.

IN REPLYING PLEASE ADDRESS
THE JOINT GENERAL MANAGERS.

14th April, 1943.

PRIVATE.

Major W. Martin, R.M.,
Army and Navy Club,
Pall Mall,
LONDON, S.W.1.

Dear Sir,

I am given to understand that in spite of repeated application your overdraft amounting to £79.19s.2d. still outstands.

In the circumstances, I am now writing to inform you that unless this amount, plus interest at 4% to date of payment, is received forthwith we shall have no alternative but to take the necessary steps to protect our interests.

Yours faithfully,

Joint General Manager.

The National Archives

The dunning letter was addressed to Major Martin at the Army and Navy Club, in Pall Mall. This, it was decided, would be Martin's home when in 'town'. Cholmondeley obtained a bill from the club, made out to Major Martin.

Having imagined Martin's father, Montagu and Cholmondeley now decided this anxious parent deserved a larger part in the unfolding drama. Enter John G. Martin, paterfamilias, 'a father of the old school' in Montagu's words, who may well have been modelled on his own father: affectionate, but formal and controlling. The letter itself was probably written by Cyril Mills, a colleague in MI5. Mills, the son of the circus impresario Bertram Mills, had taken over the circus business after his father's death in 1938, and was now one of the key operatives in the Double Cross Team. Mills knew how to put on an impressive show. The resulting letter, pompous and pedantic as only an Edwardian father could be, was 'a brilliant tour de force'.

Tel. No. 98 — *Black Lion Hotel*
Mold
N. Wales
13th April 1943

My Dear William,

I cannot say that this hotel is any longer as comfortable as I remember it to have been in pre-war days. I am, however, staying here as the only alternative to imposing myself once more upon your aunt whose depleted staff & strict regard for fuel economy (which I agree to be necessary in wartime) has made the house almost uninhabitable to a guest, at least one of my age. I propose to be in Town for the nights of 20th & 21st of April when no doubt we shall have an opportunity to meet. I enclose the copy of a letter which I have written to Gwatkin of McKenna's about your affairs. You will see that I have asked him to lunch with me at the Carlton Grill (which I understand still to be open) at a quarter to one on Wednesday the 21st. I should be glad if you would make it possible to join us. We shall not however wait luncheon for you, so I trust that, if you are able to come, you will make a point of being punctual.

Your cousin Priscilla has asked to be remembered to you. She has grown into a sensible girl though I cannot say that her work for the Land Army has done much to improve her looks. In that respect I am afraid that she will take after her father's side of the family.

Your affectionate
Father

Cholmondeley and Montagu were now enjoying themselves, warming to the task of invention, the depth of detail, the odd plot twists: the exasperated father sorting out his son's financial affairs, resentful of his sister-in-law's rule over the family house and having to stay in a second-class hotel; niece Priscilla, sensible but chunky, with, it was implied, a slight crush on her older cousin Bill; the hints of wartime deprivation and rationing; the artful ink splodge on the first page. Montagu's acidulous sense of humour ran through every word of the forgeries.

While the larger themes of Martin's life were being sketched out, Cholmondeley also began to gather the smaller items that a wartime officer might carry in his pockets and wallet, individually unimportant but vital corroborative detail. In modern spy parlance, this is known as 'wallet litter', the little things everyone accumulates that describe who we are, and where we have been. Martin's pocket litter would include a book of stamps, two used; a silver cross on a neck chain and a St Christopher's medallion, a pencil stub, keys, a packet of Player's Navy Cut cigarettes (the traditional Navy smoke), matches, and a used twopenny bus ticket. In his wallet they inserted a pass for Combined Operations HQ which had expired, as further evidence of his lackadaisical attitude to security. The members of Section 17M, all of whom were party to the secret, added their own refinements. There was much discussion over exactly which wartime nightclub Bill might favour. Margery Boxall, Montagu's secretary, obtained an invitation to the Cabaret Club, a swinging London nightclub, as proof of Martin's taste for the high life. To this was added a small fragment of a torn letter, written to Bill from an address in Perthshire, relaying some snippet of romantic gossip: '. . . at the last moment – which was the more to be regretted since he had scarcely ever seen her before. Still, as I told him at the time . . .' The handwriting is that of John Masterman.

Two identity discs, stamped 'Major W. Martin, R.M., R/C'

(Roman Catholic), were attached to the braces that would hold the dead man's trousers up. A bill for shirts from Gieves, paid in cash, was crumpled up in preparation for stuffing into a pocket. Bill Martin would be carrying cash on his final journey: one £5 note, three £1 notes, and some loose change. The banknote numbers were carefully noted. As with all money that might be passed to, or received from, the enemy, the currency was carefully tracked in case it might reappear somewhere significant. If the money disappeared after the body arrived in Spain, it would at least prove that the clothes had been searched.

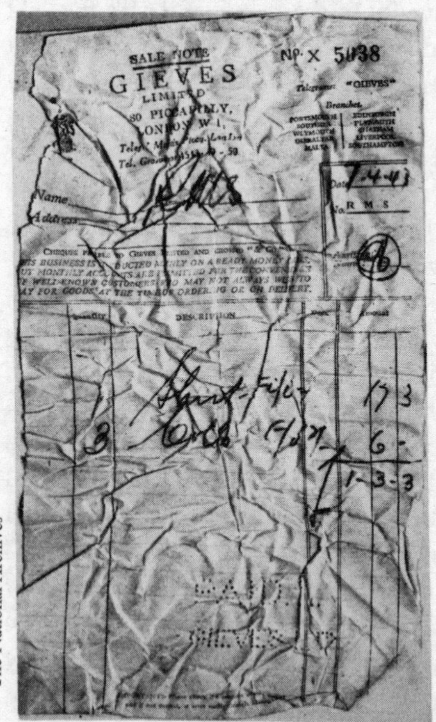
SALE NOTE
GIEVES
LIMITED
Telegrams: "GIEVES"
Date 7-4-43
Name
Address
DESCRIPTION
1-3-3

The National Archives

Nothing was left to chance. Everything the body wore or carried was minutely inspected to ensure that it added to the story, on the assumption that the Germans would make every 'effort to find a flaw in Major Martin's make-up'. And yet something was missing from Martin's life. It was Joan Saunders who pointed it out: he had no love life. Bill Martin must be made to fall in love. 'We decided that a "marriage would be arranged" between Bill Martin and some girl just before he was sent abroad,' wrote Montagu. Though he referred nonchalantly to 'some girl', Montagu already had a girl firmly in mind.

7

Pam

Jean Leslie was just eighteen in 1941 when she joined the counterintelligence and double-agent section of MI5. Jean was beautiful, in a most English way, with alabaster skin and wavy chestnut hair. She had left school at seventeen, and then been educated by her upper-class parents in the traditional ladylike skills of typing, secretarial work and attending debutante parties. But she was far cleverer than this might suggest. She was too clever, from her widowed mother's point of view. 'What on earth are we going to do with Jean?' she worried. A family friend suggested that there might be a suitable job in the War Office. A few weeks later, Jean had found herself signing the Official Secrets Act, and then plunged into the byzantine business of MI5's top-secret paperwork. Initially, she worked in the section B1B, which gathered, filed and analysed Ultra decrypts, Abwehr messages and other intelligence to be used in running the double agents of the Double Cross System. She loved it.

The secretarial unit was headed by a sharp-tongued dragon named Hester Leggett, who demanded absolute obedience and perfect efficiency among her 'girls'. Jean's job was to sort through the 'yellow perils', yellow carbon copies of interrogations from Camp 020, the wartime internment centre in Richmond, near London, where all enemy spies were grilled. She would read the accounts given by the captured spies, and try to spot anything that required the attention of her senior (male) colleagues. It was Jean Leslie who identified the 'glaring inconsistencies' in the confession of one Johannes de Graaf, a Belgian agent. De Graaf was subsequently found to be playing a triple game. Jean was delighted with herself; and then distraught, when it appeared that De Graaf would face execution.

The all-female secretarial team was known as 'The Beavers', and the most eager beaver of all was young Jean Leslie. 'I was frightfully willing to help, always. I ran everywhere. I was so keen to please.' Hester Leggett, rather cruelly nicknamed 'The Spin', for spinster, repeatedly reprimanded her for sprinting through the hushed offices in St James's Street. 'Don't run, Miss Leslie!'

This beautiful young woman who ran everywhere had caught the eye of Ewen Montagu. Jean could not fail to notice how the friendly and undoubtedly handsome older officer seemed to pay her special attention. 'In fact, he was trailing me a bit. He was rather smitten.' Indeed he was: Montagu's writings, official and unofficial, describe her variously as 'charming', 'very attractive', and other admiring adjectives.

In mid-February, the hunt began for a suitable mate for Major Martin. 'The more attractive girls in our various offices' were asked to supply photographs for use in an identity parade. Montagu made a point of asking Miss Leslie if she would oblige. 'I think he had every intention of getting one off me somehow.' That evening, Jean, keen as ever and rather flattered by the attention, ransacked her dressing-room drawer for a recent photograph. With the bombing of London, Mrs Leslie had moved out of the capital, to a borrowed house on the Thames near Dorchester in Oxfordshire, where her daughter spent weekends. A few weeks earlier, she had gone swimming in the river at Wittenham Clumps with Tony, a Grenadier Guard on leave who, like Montagu, was smitten, and about to return to the war. 'The swimming there was horrible', but the occasion had been a happy one. Tony had taken a photograph, which he sent to her afterwards. In it, Jean has just emerged from the water in a patterned one-piece swimsuit, with towel held demurely, hair windswept, and a sweet grin on her face. In 1940s England, the image was not just attractive, but very nearly saucy, and both Jean Leslie and Ewen Montagu knew it.

The National Archives

The request for photographs had garnered 'quite a collection'. It was no accident that the Naval Intelligence Department contained a high ratio of particularly attractive women. 'Uncle John gave specific orders that only the prettiest girls should be employed, on the theory that then they would be less likely to boast to their boyfriends about the secret work they were doing.' Some of Montagu's female colleagues in Room 13 were distinctly put out when he selected a photograph of a woman from another department: 'We were all rather jealous,' recalled Patricia Trehearne, one of his assistants. But there was never any doubt who would win this particular beauty contest. Jean's photograph was added to the growing pile of Martin's possessions, and a new and central character was worked into the unfolding plot: this was 'Pam', his new fiancée, a vivacious young woman working in a government office, who was excitable, pretty, gentle and really quite dim. It was decided that Bill had met Pam just five weeks earlier, and had proposed to her after a whirlwind romance, buying a large and expensive diamond ring for the purpose. John Martin, his father, did not approve, suspecting Pam might be something of a gold digger. No date for the wedding had been set. Here was a typical wartime romance: sudden, thrilling and, as matters would shortly turn out, doomed.

Jean Leslie had sufficient security clearance to be partially inducted into the secret. Montagu told her that the photograph depicted a fictitious fiancée, as part of a deception plan. 'I knew it was going to be planted on a body, but I didn't know where.' Charles Cholmondeley later took Jean aside and asked her in serious tones: 'Has anybody else got that photograph? If so, you should ask for it back. If you gave it to someone and they were going out on the second front and were captured and this photograph was discovered in his possession, the consequences could be very serious.' Jean contacted Tony, the Grenadier Guard, and told him to destroy any other copies of the photograph. Hurt, Tony complied. Montagu also took Jean aside, and impressed upon her the need for absolute secrecy. Then he asked her out to dinner. She accepted.

Montagu adored his wife, Iris. 'I never realised how lonely and really empty life could be just because you weren't there,' he wrote once. His wartime letters are passionate, peppered with rude jokes, poems and stories, and haunted by the fear that they might be parted for ever: 'How ultra-happy our life was before this bloody business started . . . Bugger Hitler.' Whenever Iris's letters were delayed from New York, he would half-joke: 'You must have gone off with an American.' But he longed for female company. 'I am always the gooseberry,' he complained. He declined an invitation to a dance, although he longed to go: 'It was a question of whether there was a girl I could take, I literally couldn't think of anyone, not even anyone to try.' Jean Leslie was single, extremely pretty, and good company. Ewen did not try to conceal his first date with Jean from his wife, but he did not dwell on it either. 'I took a girl from the office to Hungaria [a restaurant] and had dinner and danced. She is an attractive child.'

Bill would need love letters to go with his photograph of Pam. The job of drafting these fell to Hester Leggett, 'The Spin', the most senior woman in the department. Jean remembered her as 'skinny and embittered'. Hester Leggett was certainly fierce and demanding. She never married, and she devoted herself utterly to the job of marshalling a huge quantity of secret paperwork. But into Pam's love letters, she poured every ounce of pathos and emotion she could muster. These letters may have been the closest Hester Leggett ever came to romance: chattering pastiches of a young woman madly in love, and with little time for grammar.

The Manor House
Ogbourne St George
Marlborough, Wiltshire
Telephone Ogbourne St George 242 *Sunday 18th*

I do think dearest that seeing people like you off at railway stations is one of the poorer forms of sport. A train going out can leave a howling great gap in ones [sic] life & one had to try madly - & quite in vain – to fill it with all the things one used to enjoy a short five weeks ago. That lovely golden day we spent together oh! I know it has been said before, but if <u>only</u> time could stand still for just a minute – But that line of thought is too pointless. Pull your socks up Pam & don't be a silly little fool.

Your letter made me feel slightly better – but I shall get horribly conceited if you go on saying things like that about me – they're utterly unlike ME, as I'm afraid you'll soon find out. Here I am for the weekend in this divine place with Mummy & Jane being too sweet and understanding the whole time, bored beyond words & panting for Monday so that I can get back to the old grindstone again. What an idiotic waste!

Bill darling, do let me know as soon as you get fixed & can make some more plans, & don't please let them send you off into the blue the horrible way they do nowadays – now that we've found each other out of the whole world, I don't think I could bear it.

All my love, Pam

The headed notepaper (obtained from Montagu's brother-in-law) was used on the basis that 'no German could resist the "Englishness"' of such an address. The next letter, notionally dated three days later, was on plain paper, written by 'Pam' in a frantic rush as her boss, 'The Bloodhound', threatened to return from lunch at any moment. As the official report on Operation Mincemeat acknowledged, Hester Leggett's effort 'achieved the thrill and pathos of a war engagement with great success'.

Office
Wednesday 21st

The Bloodhound has left his kennel for half an hour so here I am scribbling nonsense to you again. Your letter came this morning just as I was dashing out – madly late as usual! You do write such heavenly ones. But what are these horrible dark hints you're throwing out about being sent off somewhere – of course I won't say a word to anyone – I never do when you tell me things, but it's not abroad is it? Because I won't have it, I WON'T, tell them so from me. Darling, why did we go and meet in the middle of a war, such a silly thing for anybody to do – if it weren't for the war we might have been nearly married by now, going round together choosing curtains etc. And I wouldn't be sitting in a dreary Government office typing idiotic minutes all day long – I know the futile work I do doesn't make the war one minute shorter –

Dearest Bill, I'm so thrilled with my ring – scandalously extravagant – you know how I adore diamonds – I simply can't stop looking at it.

I'm going to a rather dreary dance tonight with Jock & Hazel, I think they've got some other man coming. You know what their friends always turn out to be like, he'll have the sweetest little Adam's apple & the shiniest bald head! How beastly and ungrateful of me, but it isn't really that – you know – don't you?

Look darling, I've got next Sunday & Monday off for Easter. I shall go home for it, of course, <u>do</u> come too if you possibly can, or even if you can't get away from London I'll dash up and we'll have an evening of gaiety – (by the way Aunt Marian said to bring you to dinner next time I was up, but I think that might wait?)

Here comes the Bloodhound, masses of love & a kiss from

Pam

Hester Leggett ended the second letter with a flourish, as Pam's looping, girlish handwriting collapses into a hasty scrawl.

For good measure, Montagu and Cholmondeley added to Martin's wallet a bill for an engagement ring from S. J. Phillips of New Bond Street, for a whopping £53 0s. 6d. The ring was engraved 'P. L. from W. M. 14.4.43'.

TELEPHONE Nº MAYFAIR 6261 (2 LINES)
TELEGRAMS EUCLASE WESDO LONDON

113 New Bond Street
London W.1. 19th April 1943.

Major W. Martin, R.M.,
Naval + Military Club,
94, Piccadilly – W.1.

To S. J. Phillips.
Silversmith.
Jewels, Antique Plate, Bijouterie.

15th April, 1943.	Single diamond ring small diad shoulders plat. (pre purchase tax)	52 10 –
	Engraving "P.L. from W.M. 14.4.43"	10 6
		£53 – 6

The National Archives

Two more letters rounded off Martin's personal cache. The first was from his solicitor, F. A. S. Gwatkin, of McKenna & Co., referring to his will and tax affairs: 'We will insert the legacy of £50 to your batman,' wrote Mr Gwatkin, who regretted that he could not yet complete Martin's tax return for 1941/42: 'We cannot find that we have ever had these particulars and shall, therefore, be grateful if you will let us have them.' On top of everything else, Major Martin's tax return was overdue. Finally there was another letter from John Martin, this time a copy of a letter to the family solicitor, discussing the terms of his son's marriage settlement and insisting that 'since the wife's family will not be contributing to the settlement I do not think it proper that they should preserve, after William's death, a life interest in the funds which I am providing. I should agree to this course only were there children of the marriage.'

Montagu and Cholmondeley were delighted with the plot they had created, with its looming premonition of disaster, a dashing but flawed hero, a sexy, faintly dippy, heroine and a rich cast of comic supporting characters: The Bloodhound, Father, Fat Priscilla, and Whitley Jones the Bank Manager. But from a distance of nearly seventy years, the plot seems almost hackneyed. The sense of impending doom, and Pam's 'foreboding', are thumpingly melodramatic. 'Bill darling, don't please let them send you off into the blue the horrible way they do . . .'

Admiral John Godfrey was strict on the danger of 'overcooking' an espionage ruse. 'The nearer the approach to the "thriller" type of intelligence the more must both the giver, and the recipient, be on their guard. Elegant trimmings should have no place in the intelligence officer's vocabulary. On the other hand the man who cannot tell a good story is a dull dog.'

By this time, Godfrey was no longer on hand to offer his sage judgement, for in the midst of Operation Mincemeat, Montagu and Cholmondeley had lost their mentor. The admiral's sandpaper personality had finally proven too much for his superiors: he was removed from the Naval Intelligence Department, despatched to naval command in India, and replaced by Commodore (later Rear Admiral) Edmund Rushbrooke, an able administrator but an officer with little of Godfrey's fire and flair. 'He is very old and lacking in energy after that human dynamo,' wrote Montagu, whose assessment of Godfrey was equally blunt: 'He was the world's prize shit, but a genius . . . I had enormous admiration for him as an intelligence brain and organiser – the more sincere as I loathed him as a man.' The good news about Godfrey's departure was that Montagu and Cholmondeley now had 'the unhoped for benefit of an entirely free hand'. But it also meant that the 'preparation and devising of Mincemeat', in Montagu's words, 'was entirely unsupervised and unchecked'.

Godfrey was one of the few senior officers who could – and probably would – have pointed out that the story contained a surfeit of elegant trimmings. The characters seem closer to caricatures: the beastly bank manager, the bullying boss, the cheerful gal about to be socked in the eye by fate. The doomed love affair, the stiff-upper-lipped marine heading to death: these were the staples of popular culture in 1943. The Bill Martin story was the product of minds that had read too many romantic novels, and seen too many films in which the hero pulls away in the train, never to be seen again. That may have been partly intentional, for this was not supposed to be a genuine collection of people and events, aimed at convincing a British audience, but a story that a German might believe to be British. The task of the barrister, and the intelligence officer, in Montagu's estimation, was to ask: '"How will that argument or bit of evidence appeal to the hearer?" And not "How does it appeal to me?"'

In one sense, the story of Bill Martin was too perfect. There were no loose ends. A person's pockets and wallet will usually contain at least something that makes no obvious or immediate sense: an unidentified photo, an illegible note-to-self, paperclips, a button. In Martin's pockets there was nothing stray or inexplicable, nothing unlikely or meaningless. The personal letters contain no obscure allusions to third persons, or in-jokes, or spelling mistakes: none of the qualities that distinguish real, as opposed to manufactured, correspondence. Everything tied together, everything added up. There was excessive detail. Would 'Pam' really bother to identify that she worked in a 'Government office'? Bill would surely know this. In the same way, would a jeweller trouble to replicate the words engraved on a ring when sending in a bill? In the warped intelligence mentality, something that looks perfect is probably a fake.

But then, the plot was not perfect. Indeed, it contained some potentially catastrophic mistakes. Major Martin left money to his 'batman': an officer in the Royal Marines would never have referred to a batman, but rather to his Marine Officer's Attendant, or MOA. Why did he pay cash for his shirts (at a military tailor that extended the most generous credit to serving officers) when he was deeply overdrawn and owed £53 for an engagement ring?

Far more dangerously, the plot would never have stood up to scrutiny if German spies in Britain had made even the most cursory checks on it. A single telephone call to Ogbourne St George 242 would have established that no one by the name of Pam was known there. A glance at the hotel register for the Black Lion Hotel would have showed that no Mr J. C. Martin had stayed on the night of 13 April. Even a moderately competent agent could have called S. J. Phillips of New Bond Street to check when payment for the ring was due, and discovered that no such ring had been sold.

Montagu and Cholmondeley were blasé about the danger of being rumbled by an enemy agent in Britain, for the simple reason that they did not believe there were any. 'There was almost complete security,' wrote Montagu. 'We were able to put over what we liked to the enemy.' True, of the several hundred enemy spies dropped, floated or smuggled into Britain, all but one was picked up and arrested: the exception was found dead in a bunker after committing suicide. The Germans simply did not have an intelligence operation in Britain. By March 1943 there were so many double agents in the Double Cross System that 'Masterman raised the question whether we ought not to "liquidate" some of our agents, both for greater efficiency and for plausibility'. An 'execution subcommittee was formed' to bump off a fake agent 'every few months'.

Montagu would cycle home every evening, his briefcase full of secrets, complacent that he was 'the only deceptioneer in daily contact with the whole of special intelligence', and that his secrets were perfectly safe. Yet there were numerous spies living in London from supposedly neutral countries happy to furnish information to the Axis powers. Ewen Montagu never knew it, but there was one spy operating under his nose, a man with whom he shared a taste for exotic cheese and table tennis, and both parents.

Ivor Montagu was addicted to founding, and joining, different clubs. From the Cheese Eaters' League and the English Table Tennis Association, he had graduated to the Association of Cine Technicians, the Zoological Society, Marylebone Cricket Club, the editorial board of *Labour Monthly*, the World Council of Peace, the Friends of the Soviet Union, Southampton United Football Club, the Society for Cultural Relations with Soviet Russia, and Chairmanship of the Woolwich-Plumstead Branch of the Anti-War Congress.

He had also joined a less public and even more exclusive club, as an agent for Soviet military intelligence.

In part to antagonise his patrician parents, Ivor Montagu had from an early age displayed a keen 'enthusiasm for all things Russian', and a penchant for radical politics. In 1927, the twenty-three-year-old Ivor was contacted by Bob Stewart, a founder member of the British Communist Party and a recruiter of Soviet agents in Britain. Stewart told Montagu: 'We have had a request from the Communist International for you to go at once to Moscow. How soon can you leave?' In Moscow, Ivor was fêted and flattered: he played table tennis in the Comintern building with 'the keenest players in Moscow', went to the Bolshoi, and watched the revolutionary parade from a VIP stand in Red Square. Someone in the upper reaches of the Soviet state was taking good care of Ivor Montagu.

Back in Europe, Ivor's film career blossomed, as did his interests in table tennis, small rodents and Soviet movies. At the same time, his commitment to communism deepened. In 1929, he began to correspond with Leon Trotsky, the Bolshevik revolutionary expelled from the Communist Party and now living in exile on the Turkish island of Prinkipio.

'Dear Comrade Trotsky,' Ivor wrote on 1 July. 'Allow me to volunteer to be of service . . . I should be glad to be of assistance in any way possible.'

Trotsky replied, in friendly vein, and a most unlikely correspondence ensued. Ivor made plans to meet the exiled Soviet revolutionary in person. He would frame his trip to Prinkipio as the innocent journey of a young idealist studying the splits in Russian communism. It seems more likely that he was sent by Moscow to gain Trotsky's confidence, and report back on his activities. Ivor arrived in Istanbul in the pouring rain, 'like Edinburgh at its worst', and hired a boat to take him to the island. 'Two Turkish policemen were guarding the villa. Mrs Trotsky, a short motherly woman with an air of distress, made me welcome. Trotsky appeared and we settled down to talk.'

They talked deep into the night, about Trotsky's frustrations, his friends exiled to Siberia and his desire to make contact with Christian Rakovsky, the Bulgarian Bolshevik who would eventually perish at the hands of Stalin's executioners. At the end of the evening Ivor was handed a loaded pistol 'to put under my pillow as a precaution against assassins'. (Trotsky would be assassinated in Mexico in 1940.) Ivor could not sleep. 'I did not know what precautions to take against the revolver, and was terrified.'

The next morning, Trotsky and Ivor went fishing in the

Sea of Marmara. The Turkish bodyguards rowed. The political conversation continued. The weather was atrocious. They caught nothing. 'The memory I shall always retain of him,' wrote Ivor, 'is of our little boat, perilously poised at the top of a wave, ready to crash down on top of a monstrous rock, Trotsky himself perched aquiline in the stern and in a voice and with an authority that might have commanded an army, repeating the Turkish equivalent of "in-out in-out" as the policemen rowed for dear life.'

The meeting with Trotsky marked a turning point. Ivor Montagu was attracted to this 'fascinating and commanding personality' but 'repelled by his self-admiration', the raw ambition of the revolutionary in exile: 'I felt I understood now why he was impossible in a party, that his personality swamped his judgement.' Ivor was not yet thirty, but he was already a party disciplinarian, and a fully committed Stalinist. Trotsky knew that Ivor was a willing tool of the Soviet regime. In 1932, he wrote: 'Ivor Montagu has, or had, some personal sympathy for me, but now he is even on that small scale paralysed by his adherence to the party.'

That adherence was now absolute, and permanent: he gave speeches, wrote pamphlets and made films in support of communism. The more covert, and more dangerous, manifestations of that party obedience remained secret for the rest of his life.

MI5 had started to take an interest in the Hon. Ivor Montagu back in 1926, after intercepting a letter he had written to a member of a visiting Soviet trade delegation requesting permission to visit Moscow. The snoopers immediately began to open Ivor's mail and follow his movements, reporting that 'Montagu has for some time been known to associate with the inner ring of the Communist Party'. His behaviour was distinctly suspicious: he attended radical meetings, played table tennis, translated French plays, mixed with left-wing film actors and directors, wore a long Mongolian leather coat, and distributed Soviet films. The correspondence with Trotsky was copied, and added to Ivor's growing MI5 files. A report by Special Branch in 1931 was tinged with anti-semitism: 'Montagu has dark curly hair and is of distinctly Jewish appearance. His eyes are dark brown and his complexion is pale. He is generally rather dirty and untidy.'

By the outbreak of war, Ivor Montagu had all but severed contact with his family, with the exception of Ewen. While his older brother continued to enjoy the services of the family butler at Kensington Court, Ivor lived in Brixton, sharing a grotty flat with a mongrel from Battersea Dogs Home called Betsy, his wife Hell, her daughter Rowna, and his mother-in-law, who was addicted to cheese and pickles even though these gave her chronic indigestion. 'What is the use of living if you cannot eat cheese and pickles?' she asked. As co-founder of the Cheese Eaters' League, Ivor thought she had a point.The brothers Montagu could not have been more different personalities, nor have entertained more opposed political views, yet they continued to meet throughout the war.

Ewen Montagu sent Iris regular bulletins on Ivor's activities, mocking but affectionate. 'Last night Ivor came to dinner after the Prom at the Albert Hall,' he wrote in June 1942. 'He is simply enormous, almost all tummy. Hell is well and digging for victory, which she hasn't found yet.' He regarded Ivor's politics as a harmless obsession. 'Ivor is really bad on this war,' he told his wife. 'He is busy working for the Russian government on Russian propaganda [and] writing anti-war or Communist letters to the papers.'

MI5 was well aware that one of the country's most senior intelligence officers – a man who, by his own account, 'knew in advance practically every secret of the war, including the atom bomb' – was in regular contact with a brother who was a known Soviet sympathiser, corresponded with Russian revolutionaries and opposed the war. By 1939, MI5 had started referring to 'that particularly unpleasant communist, the Hon. Ivor'. Ivor represented a major security risk. Ewen knew that there was an

MI5 dossier on Ivor, but had no idea that, by 1943, it extended to three volumes and hundreds of pages.

In Ivor Montagu's MI5 files, any explicit reference to Ewen has been weeded out, but as the older brother's intelligence career developed and his responsibilities grew, so surveillance of the younger brother intensified. MI5 questioned Ivor's neighbours, infiltrated the meetings he addressed, and analysed his writings and speeches, yet they could find no hard evidence against him. That would take another two decades.

Between 1940 and 1948, American cryptanalysts intercepted copies of thousands of telegrams passing between Moscow and its diplomatic missions abroad, written in a code that was theoretically unbreakable. Over the next forty years, Allied codebreakers struggled to unpick the Soviet code in an operation initially known as 'the Russian problem' and later codenamed 'Venona', a project so secret that the CIA remained unaware of its existence until 1952. Large swaths of the correspondence were, and are still, unreadable, but finally some 2,900 messages were translated, a tiny fraction of the whole but an astonishing glimpse into Soviet espionage.

These decrypted intercepts included 178 sent to and from the London office of the GRU, the military branch of Soviet intelligence, between March 1940 and April 1942.

The messages are partial and fragmentary, and many are missing, but they revealed something quite remarkable: for at least two years, the Soviet Union had run an undetected British spy ring codenamed 'X Group' (*Gruppa iks*) under the leadership of an individual codenamed 'Intelligentsia'.

Soviet spies, like their British and German counterparts, seemed to take perverse delight in selecting codenames containing the most unsubtle hints. The Venona code for France was 'Gastronomica'; the Germans were 'Sausage Dealers' (*Kolbasniki*). The codename chosen for the spy in control of X Group was no exception. Agent Intelligentsia was the intellectually inclined Ivor Montagu.

On 25 July 1940, Simon Davidovitch Kremer, secretary to the Soviet military attaché in London and a GRU spy handler, sent a message under the codename 'Barch' to 'Director' in Moscow:

> I have met representatives of the X GROUP. This is IVOR MONTAGU (brother of Lord Montagu), the well-known local communist, journalist and lecturer. He has [*unintelligible*] contacts through his influential relatives. He reported that he had been detailed to organise work with me, but that he had not yet obtained a single contact. I came to an agreement with him about the work and pointed out the importance of speed.

The report went on to relay Ivor's analysis of Hitler's 'Last Appeal to Reason', his 'peace offer' to Britain. Ivor, correctly, thought a peace deal unlikely: 'Intelligentsia considers there is an anti-Sausage Dealer mood in the army.' The reference to Ivor's 'influential relatives' suggests that the GRU knew of Ewen Montagu's senior status within British intelligence.

Ewen and Ivor Montagu were now, in effect, spying for opposite sides in the war. Since 1939, under the Molotov-Ribbentrop pact, the Soviet Union and Nazi Germany had been bound together in a formal non-aggression agreement, and until Hitler ruptured the pact in June 1941, information passed to Soviet intelligence could find its way into the hands of the Gestapo.

Initially, Ivor Montagu's Soviet spymasters were unimpressed:

> Intelligentsia has not yet found the people in the military finance department. He has promised to deliver documentary material from Professor Haldane who is working on an admiralty assignment concerned with submarines and their operation. We need a man of a different calibre and one who is bolder than INTELLIGENTSIA.

Professor J. B. S. Haldane was one of the most celebrated scientists in Britain. A pioneering and broad-ranging thinker, he developed a mathematical theory of population genetics, predicted that hydrogen-producing windmills would replace fossil fuel, explained nuclear fission, and suffered a perforated eardrum while testing a homemade decompression chamber: 'Although one is somewhat deaf, one can blow tobacco smoke out of the ear in question, which is a social accomplishment.' Haldane was a dedicated atheist and communist: 'I think that Marxism is true,' he declared in 1938.

Ivor Montagu and Jack Haldane had become friends at Cambridge, and soon after the outbreak of war, Ivor recruited the scientist into X Group. In 1940, Haldane was working at the Navy's underwater research establishment at Gosport, and in July he submitted a secret paper to the Admiralty entitled *Report on Effects of High Pressure, Carbon Dioxide and Cold*, a study of long-term submersion in submarines. Two months later, Kremer reported: 'Intelligentsia has handed over a copy of Professor Haldane's report to the Admiralty on his experiments relating to the length of time a man can stay underwater.'

Under Kremer's nagging guidance, Ivor Montagu's X Group slowly expanded, and the quality of intelligence improved. By the autumn of 1940, Ivor had recruited 'three military sources', and an agent codenamed 'Baron', probably a senior officer in the secret service of the Czechoslovakian government in exile, who furnished copious information on German forces in Czechoslovakia. MI5 later speculated that another of Ivor's recruits, codenamed 'Bob', was the future trade union leader Jack Jones. In October 1940, Ivor 'reported that a girl working in a government establishment noticed in one document that the British had broken some Soviet code or other'. Kremer told Ivor 'that this was a matter of exceptional importance and he should put to the [X] Group the business of developing this report'.

By the end of 1940, X Group had become so productive that

the handling of Ivor Montagu was taken over by the top GRU officer in London, Colonel Ivan Sklyarov, the Soviet military and air attaché, codenamed 'Brion'. The surviving X Group messages reveal a steady stream of military intelligence passing to Moscow, including troop movements, air raid damage, technical information obtained from 'an officer of the air ministry', tank production and weapons, and reports on British preparations for a possible German invasion. 'The coastal defence is based on a network of blockhouses that are weak in design with no allowance made for the manoeuvrability of strong artillery and tank equipment of the Sausage Dealers.' Such information was of great interest to Moscow, but it would have been of even greater importance to the Germans, then actively planning Operation Sealion, the invasion of Britain.

Ivor Montagu's most valuable information was passed to Moscow on 16 October 1940, following an air raid on an aircraft factory near Bristol: '30 Sausage Dealer bombers and 30 fighters used a radio beam to fly from Northern France'.

The aim of the Luftwaffe bombers had been steadily improving in recent months, prompting suspicion that the Germans had developed some sort of sophisticated guiding apparatus using radio beams. This was the so-called 'Knickebein' system: the German bombers followed a radio beam broadcast from France until the beam was intersected by another over the target, at which point the bombs were released. Churchill had formed a secret committee to try to discover how the system worked, and how it might be countered. The problem was codenamed 'Headache'; the countermeasures, inevitably, were codenamed 'Aspirin'. In time, the RAF developed a technique for 'bending' the radio beams to redirect the Luftwaffe's bombs away from the intended targets: Headache was cured. But in October 1940, Headache was a highly classified secret, known only to a handful of intelligence chiefs, senior RAF officers and government scientists. X Group was now gathering intelligence from the very highest levels.

Ivor Montagu was an idealist, but his actions were treasonable.

He was not merely passing important military secrets to a foreign power, but to one that was bound in a friendly pact with the enemy. Ivor was a committed anti-fascist, and would have been appalled at the accusation that he was aiding Nazism, but his commitment to the cause of communism was absolute, though naïve. If caught, he would certainly have been arrested and prosecuted under the Treason Act.

Some of Ivor's information may have come, inadvertently, from his older brother. Ewen Montagu was aware of his brother's politics ('he still seems to be going on with his meetings', he told his wife) but was entirely in the dark about his espionage activities. He had no idea how closely his sibling was being monitored by his own colleagues in MI5. Ivor, on the other hand, was aware that his brother worked in Naval Intelligence at a senior level, and was undoubtedly interested in the contents of his locked briefcase. Did Ivor's slavish adherence to the party, as noted by Trotsky, outweigh his brotherly affection?

We will probably never know whether Ivor spied on his brother, because at the end of 1942 the Venona intercepts come to an abrupt halt. The traffic between the London *rezidentura* and Moscow continued unabated, but was henceforth unreadable. The last translated report from Brion reads: 'Intelligentsia has reported that his friend, a serviceman in a Liverpool regiment has handed over [*unintellgible*] German exercise, with dive bombers taking part [*unintelligible*] between Liverpool and Manchester everything – industry . . .' This was the last decipherable word from Agent Intelligentsia.

By 1943, Nazi Germany and the Soviet Union were locked in mortal conflict, and there was now little danger that information from X Group would be passed on to Berlin. But Ivor undoubtedly remained immersed in the spying game. Germany had spies operating within Soviet intelligence. Ewen had spent months planning the most elaborate deception of the war. The person most likely to blow Operation Mincemeat, if he should ever discover it, was his own brother.

8

The Butterfly Collector

Cholmondeley and Montagu were convinced that they had created a fully credible character in William Martin. 'We felt that we knew him just as one knows one's best friend,' wrote Montagu. 'We had come to feel that we had known Bill Martin from his earliest childhood, his every thought and his probable reaction to any event that might occur in his life.'

It is hardly surprising that Montagu and Cholmondeley felt they knew Bill Martin as well as they knew themselves, for in a way the personality they had created was their combined alter ego, the person they would have liked to be. One contemporary described Cholmondeley as 'an incurable romantic of the old cloak and dagger school'. In Bill Martin, he found an imaginary figure who could wear the cloak and wield the dagger on his behalf. Where Cholmondeley was earthbound by his eyesight and deskbound by his job, Bill Martin was a young officer on the front line, heading to war with a girl waiting for him at home. Montagu once wrote that he 'joined up to go to sea, to use my seamanship experience, and to fight'. Bill Martin was the active naval officer that he was not. But Montagu took the identification with Bill Martin a stage further.

'Ewen *lived* the part,' according to Jean Leslie. 'He *was* Willie Martin and I was Pam. He had the sort of mind that worked that way.' Ewen (as Bill) began to pay court to Jean (as Pam) in earnest. He took her to clubs, films and out to dinner. He gave her presents, jewellery, and a Royal Marines shirt collar, as a memento of 'Bill'.

'He wrote me endless letters, *from Bill.*' Jean kept some of these letters from her imaginary fiancé. They are an extraordinary testament to one of the oddest love affairs imaginable, to the way that fiction was eliding into fact in an entirely unexpected way. Jean Leslie was not, it seems, averse to Montagu's advances or, perhaps more accurately, to those of Bill Martin. She had a copy of the bathing photograph enlarged, and wrote on it: 'Till death us do part, Your loving Pam', and gave it to Montagu.

Montagu wrote back:

Pam dearest,

I just loved the photograph – so much so that I couldn't bear the idea of anything happening to it and I have left it in the care of my best friend – I know you'll like him a lot – he has done everything for me and made me what I am today.

This sounds as if I have a foreboding – I have, and from your inscription on the photo I think you have the same fear.

In case I don't come back you may not like to wear the ring I gave you so I hope you will like this brooch. You can still wear that even if, as I hope you will, you meet someone worthier than me – I know he will understand if he is the sort of man you'll like.

Ever yours,

Bill

P.S. Try the RNVR next time.

Ewen Montagu, of course, was in the RNVR, the Royal Naval Volunteer Reserve. He placed Pam's photograph on his dressing table at Kensington Court.

Montagu had been apart from his wife since 1940, with only one, brief, reunion in America in 1941, when he was sent out to liaise with the FBI. In letters to his wife, Ewen referred openly to his dates with a young woman with lodgings in the Elms in Hampstead, although he never identified Jean Leslie by name.

'The girl from the Elms is one of Tar Robertson's secretaries and is a very nice, very intelligent girl (22-24?),' he told Iris. 'One of her appealing virtues [is] she is such a good listener.' He added: 'She has been much connected with one side of my doings.' Iris had already broached the subject of whether she and the children should return to Britain. On 15 March 1943, Ewen wrote to her: 'I took the girl from the Elms to dinner and we went to see "Desert Victory" at the Astoria.' In the very same letter he observed: 'I feel definitely that you ought not to come back yet.'

If Iris was suspicious of Ewen's relationship with this unnamed woman connected with her husband's 'doings', she was not alone. Montagu later claimed he had placed 'Pam's' photograph, with its loving inscription, on his dressing table at Kensington Court to see whether his inquisitive mother would react to it, or even remove it. 'If Mother did touch my things it would be the last straw. It is the only irritating thing she doesn't do so far.' Lady Swaythling duly spotted the picture, and demanded an explanation. 'I told her truthfully that it was a souvenir of something I had been doing . . . I'm not entirely sure what she thought I meant by that!!'

Montagu's mother began sending coded warnings to her daughter-in-law in New York, 'writing in her letters that she felt that [Iris] should come home as soon as [her] job allowed it'.

The relationship between Ewen Montagu and Jean Leslie may have been mere romantic play-acting, nothing more than flirtatious, joking banter. But when Iris later saw the photograph with its passionate dedication, Montagu insisted that it was a joke, part of a wartime operation, and that nothing had gone on between him (and his alter ego) and Jean (and hers). His wife may have believed him. He may have been telling the truth.

Forging the character of Major William Martin, and flirting with his fiancée, had been a most pleasurable challenge. Far more taxing – and more important – was the task of creating documentary evidence to be planted on the body. If the faked intelligence was too obvious, the Germans would spot the hoax; if it was too subtle, they might miss the clues altogether. At what level should the disinformation be pitched? Major Martin was supposed to be a serving officer whose plane had crashed en route from Britain to Gibraltar. He could not simply carry operational orders or battle plans, since these would never have been entrusted to a single messenger, but instead sent by diplomatic bag. Moreover, if a message contained highly classified information, it would tend to be transmitted by encrypted wireless message. The false information, it was decided, would have to be conveyed in the form of private letters between individual officers, of sufficiently elevated rank to ensure the enemy took the information seriously. These had to be names the Germans would recognise. A communication from some minor member of the planning staff in London to a counterpart in Algiers 'would not carry enough weight'. The job, as Montagu saw it, was 'to fake documents of a sufficiently high level to have strategic effect, even after prolonged study and consideration by suspicious and highly trained minds which would be reluctant to believe them'. Even more problematic was the question of how, exactly, to phrase the disinformation. If Sicily was identified as the cover target but the Germans somehow rumbled the trick, then that would reveal Sicily as the real target. Instead of the enemy being misled, he would be tipped off.

Montagu approached the forging of the letters as if he was in court, briefing his opposing counsel with selective, invented evidence. It was, he later reflected, 'a crooked lawyer's dream of heaven'. He set out three basic principles on which the letter or letters should be drafted:

1. That the planted target [i.e. Greece, Sardinia, or both] should be casually but definitively identified.

2. That two other places should be identified as cover, that one of these should be Sicily itself and the other thrown in so that, if the Germans grasped that the document was a plant, Sicily should not be pinpointed.

3. That the letter should be 'off the record' and of the type that would go by the hand of an officer but not in an official bag; it would have to have personal remarks and evidence of a personal discussion or arrangement which would prevent the message being sent by signal.

Montagu knocked out a first draft: a letter from General Sir Archibald 'Archie' Nye, Vice Chief of the Imperial General Staff (VCIGS), to General Sir Harold Alexander in Tunisia. Nye was privy to all military operations. Alexander was in command of an army under General Dwight Eisenhower at 18th Army Group Headquarters. The two British generals knew one another fairly well, and were senior enough to be fully apprised of the battle plans. Harold Alexander had fought with distinction in the First World War, but was widely perceived as not too bright. Indeed, one colleague unfairly described him as 'bone from the neck up'. Still, he was the epitome of British martial uprightness, ramrod stiff, and always looking 'as if he had just had a steam bath, a massage, a good breakfast and a letter from home'. More importantly, he was probably Britain's most famous soldier after Montgomery, and destined to become Eisenhower's commander of ground forces in Sicily. The Germans would know instantly who, and how important, he was.

Montagu's rough draft was a chatty, chummy letter between two members of the top brass, making no obvious reference to Allied intentions but dropping clues that no careful reader could miss. It implied a debate over whether Sicily or Marseilles should be the cover target; it referred to a choice of landing spots in Sardinia; it contained some apparently idle chat about the American allies ('Will Eisenhower go ahead at his own speed?'), salutations from a mutual friend ('So and so [naming a general] sends his best') and some light-hearted ribbing of Montgomery, the victor of El Alamein, for his big-headedness.

Montagu thought his draft hit the perfect note, with just the right mix of 'personal and "off the record"' information. He was very pleased with it. His immediate bosses, however, were not. The planners at the London Controlling Section (LCS), the committee in overall command of deception, suggested a less ambitious plan, arguing that 'the contents of such a letter should be of the nuts-and-bolts variety and not on a high level'. On 11 March, Johnnie Bevan, the head of the LCS, flew to Algiers for a meeting with Dudley Wrangel Clarke, the officer in command of deception for Operation Husky, the assault on Sicily. Clarke also believed that Operation Mincemeat was aiming too high. He suggested that the letter should merely give a false indication of the date of a planned invasion, without pin-pointing where this would take place.

Over the next month, the letter would be repeatedly revised, redrafted and rewritten, as senior intelligence officers, the Chiefs of Staff and others, added their pennyworth to the plan. One of the hazards of having a good idea is that intelligent people tend to realise it is a good idea, and seek to play a part. Like most novelists, Montagu did not like the editing process. He did not like the way Operation Mincemeat was being watered down. He did not like senior officers pulling rank and tinkering with a project in which he had invested so much of his time, energy and personality. But most of all, he did not like Johnnie Bevan.

Montagu had once been a supporter of Bevan, the smooth, patrician chief of the London Controlling Section. But tensions rose quickly in the cramped and strained atmosphere of wartime deception planning. Soon after Bevan was appointed, they began to spar, which led to disagreements, and culminated in a titanic personality clash. Bevan took malicious pleasure in ordering Montagu about; Montagu responded with withering contempt. Early in March, in the midst of discussions over the form of Operation Mincemeat, Montagu mounted a full-scale assault on Bevan, accusing him of being incompetent, mendacious, inefficient, and 'almost completely ignorant of the German Intelligence Service, how they work and what they are likely to believe'.

When Montagu got the bit between his teeth, he was not easily reined in. Bevan, he protested, 'is almost completely inexperienced in any form of deception work. He has a pleasant and likeable personality and can "sell himself" well. He has not got a first-grade brain. He can expound imposing platitudes such as "we want to contain the Germans in the West" with great impressiveness . . . I am sure he will not improve with experience. The remainder of the staff of the London Controlling Section are either unsuited to this sort of work (in which they are all wholly inexperienced) or are third-rate brains.'

The rant continued for several more pages. Montagu's character assassination of Bevan was completely over the top. It was also wrong, because Bevan possessed a brain quite as supple as that of Ewen Montagu. The memo attacking Bevan was internally circulated to the chiefs of Naval Intelligence, but Montagu's colleagues seem to have realised he was merely blowing off steam, and the document did not leave NID – which was just as well, for if Montagu's complaints had reached the ears of Churchill, who had complete faith in Bevan, then he might well have been sacked. Some saw Montagu's attitude towards Bevan as evidence of thwarted ambition and backstabbing. More likely, it was the overreaction of an obsessive perfectionist, frustrated at the way his pièce de résistance was being tampered with, and deeply alarmed by what he saw as the leaden response to developments in the Mediterranean.

At the end of February, Bletchley Park deciphered a message from the Nazi high command to the German command in Tunisia, assessing the situation in the Mediterranean. 'From reports coming out about Anglo-American landing intentions it is apparent that the enemy is practising deception on a large scale. In spite of this, a landing on a fairly large scale can be expected in March. It is thought the Mediterranean is the most probable theatre of operations and the first operation to be an attack against one of the large islands, the order of probability being Sicily first, Crete second, and Sardinia or Corsica third.'

The Germans not only anticipated a deception operation, but had correctly divined the intended target, and time was running out to change their minds. 'Sicily has now been allowed to become our most probable target and will be hard to remove from the enemy's minds,' warned Montagu. 'It is much easier to persuade the Germans that we will attack X than it is to dissuade them from an appreciation already formed by them that we will attack Y.' Bevan seemed to be doing nothing: 'He still has no deception plan for Husky . . . why, even now, weeks after HUSKY has been laid on, have we got no deception plan drafted, much less approved and started?' Mincemeat was pushing ahead, but if it did not work, there would be a 'complete failure to deceive the Germans by any action of ours'. The Allies were on the verge of attacking a target that the Germans expected to be attacked. Britain and her allies, Montagu warned, were 'now in a highly dangerous situation'.

He wrote another letter to 'Tar' Robertson, more temperate this time but flatly rejecting Bevan's idea that a 'nuts-and-bolts' letter would be sufficient: 'It would be a very great pity if we used a letter on a low level. I do not feel that such a letter would impress either the Abwehr or the operational authorities.'

While Montagu fought it out with Bevan, and the wrangling continued over the contents of the letters, a separate debate was underway to determine where the body should be floated ashore. After briefly toying with Portugal, or the south coast of France, the planners had settled once more on Spain. Both Britain and Germany maintained embassies in Madrid, but pro-German and anti-British sentiment was rife, particularly within the armed forces and Spanish bureaucracy. As one MI5 officer observed, parts of the Spanish state were effectively in German employ: 'Spanish police records and officers of the Seguridad [the Spanish Security Service] were instructed to facilitate the Germans in all they required, passports to Spanish nationals were issued on German recommendation, or refused on their instructions. The Spanish press and radio services were under German control. The Spanish general staff was collaborating to the maximum. The use of Spanish diplomatic bags was theirs for the asking.' If the misleading documents could be put into the right Spanish hands, then they would almost certainly be passed on to the Germans. But Spain was unpredictable, and there were plenty of Spaniards fundamentally opposed to the Nazis. The worst outcome would be if the body and its papers ended up with a British sympathiser, and were then handed back intact and unread. Where, then, was the most pro-German part of the Spanish coast?

A cable was sent to Captain Alan Hillgarth, the naval attaché at the Madrid embassy and Churchill's intelligence chief in Spain, asking him to send a trusted lieutenant to London for an urgent conference. Salvador Augustus Gómez-Beare, assistant naval attaché at the British Embassy in Madrid, duly presented himself at the Admiralty, fresh off the plane from Madrid, and was ushered into Room 13.

Gómez-Beare, universally known by his nickname 'Don', was an Anglo-Spaniard from Gibraltar who perfectly straddled the two cultures. He was a British citizen, enjoyed a large private income, spoke pure upper-class English, and displayed impeccable English manners and habits as only someone who is not English can. He played bridge with Ian Fleming at the Portland Club, and golf all year round. But in Spain, he was Spanish, brown-skinned, speaking with a southern accent, and invisible. In 1914, as a medical student in Philadelphia, he had volunteered to join the British Army, and spend two years in the trenches before joining the Royal Flying Corps. During the Spanish civil war he had 'worked in military intelligence for

Franco's army'. Gómez-Beare could reach places no Englishman could penetrate, 'a Spaniard to Spaniards and an Englishman to the English, who served England with an intensity and thoroughness that no mere Anglo-Saxon could attain'. Hillgarth had recruited him in 1939, initially suggesting that he be given the rank of captain in the Royal Marines, 'because of his enormous RAF moustache'. He was given the rank of lieutenant commander in the RNVR on condition he shaved and despite having 'no more than a smattering of sea experience'. From the start of the war, Gómez-Beare could be found 'padding about Madrid, driving up to San Sebastian, flitting over to Barcelona, hovering about Gibraltar, and smuggling British airmen out of France'. When Airey Neave escaped from Colditz in 1942, it was Gómez-Beare who smuggled him across the border to Gibraltar. He had a villa in Seville, a flat in Madrid, and spies in every corner of the Spanish establishment, society, and the underworld. Gómez-Beare was Hillgarth's primary recruiter and runner of secret agents.

Alan Hillgarth, as a senior member of the embassy staff in a neutral country, could not be seen to engage directly in espionage or recruit spies, but Gómez-Beare was under no such constraints. In Hillgarth's words, he was 'exceptionally favoured by character and linguistic attainments to cultivate such people, and in the majority of cases his contacts would not have agreed to work with anyone else'. Gómez-Beare's spies ran through the Spanish bureaucracy like veins through marble: he had agents in the Spanish police, the Security Service, the Ministry of the Interior, the Spanish general staff and every branch of the military. He had informants in high society and low, from the salons of Madrid to the docks of Cadiz. These spies never met one another, and only ever made contact through Gómez-Beare himself. 'He was invaluable,' said Hillgarth. 'It was he who handled our special contacts. His loyalty and discretion are unequalled and the Spaniards, particularly the Spanish Navy, love him.'

The Germans, by contrast, did not love Don Gómez-Beare. Britain's assistant naval attaché narrowly escaped being blown up by a car bomb during a clandestine visit to Lisbon. His chauffeur, in German pay, loosened the wheels on his car before his boss went driving in the mountains of Despeñaperros. Gómez-Beare spotted the assassination attempt just in time. Madrid was a festering nest of espionage and counterespionage, and for four years a fierce war had raged between British spies and German spies in Spain, undeclared, unofficial and unrelenting. Both sides deployed bribery and corruption on a lavish scale. Abwehr agents spied on the British counterparts, who responded in kind; the Spaniards spied on both sides, rather inefficiently. At first, the odds seemed stacked against the British. The Germans simply had too many advantages, with numerous 'privileges and facilities (of course unofficially)' provided by willing Spanish collaborators. The Abwehr infiltrated all branches of the civil service, police, government and even business. But with time, the contest had levelled out, as Hillgarth and Gómez-Beare extended their web of informants through a combination of charm, bribery and skulduggery. 'Spain contained a large number of German agents and plenty of Spaniards in German pay,' wrote Hillgarth. 'They had some ingenious ideas. We did our best to learn their plans, and to some extent succeeded.' In this febrile atmosphere, it was impossible to be sure who was spying for whom. 'Madrid was full of spies,' wrote Hillgarth, 'no one is watched all the time, but everyone is watched some of the time.'

And no one was watched more closely, or better at watching, than Don Gómez-Beare.

Once tea had been served in Room 13, Cholmondeley and Montagu laid out their plans before the Gibraltarian. Where, they asked, would be the best place to launch a dead body with false information into German hands? Gómez-Beare considered the problem. If the body washed up close to Cadiz, then it might simply be handed over to the British authorities in Gibraltar, which would scupper the plan at the outset. There was also, he explained, a 'danger of the body being recovered and/or dealt with by the Spanish Navy who might not cooperate with the Germans'. The navy, owing in part to the efforts of Gómez-Beare, was far more sympathetic to Britain than other branches of the military, so if possible the body and its contents should be kept out of naval hands.

The ideal place, Gómez-Beare finally declared, would be somewhere near Huelva, the fishing port on Spain's coast where the River Tinto flows into the Atlantic. 'German influence in Huelva is very strong,' explained Gómez-Beare; the town was home to a large and patriotic German community. The British consul in Huelva, Francis Haselden, was 'a reliable and helpful man', whose assistance would be needed for the ruse to succeed. Huelva also had a 'very pro-German chief of police [who] would give the Germans access to anything of interest found on the body'.

But most importantly Huelva was the home turf of a particular – and particularly troublesome – German spy. The agent in question was 'active and influential' across the region, as well as highly efficient, well connected and perfectly ruthless. It would not merely be desirable to stitch this man up, Gómez-Beare observed, but a positive pleasure.

Adolf Clauss collected butterflies. The walls of his large home were covered with cases of butterflies, each one carefully pinned and identified. He spent his days with butterfly net, binoculars and camera on the cliffs at Rabida, where the Odiel and the Tinto meet and flow into the sea, the spot from which Christopher Columbus prepared to set sail for the New World. Clauss owned a large farm at Rabida, where he grew enormous tomatoes and beetroots. He painted, played tennis in the evenings, and smoked filterless cigarettes whenever he was awake. He constructed elaborate wooden chairs which fell apart when you sat on them. Adolf was an extraordinary-looking man. A bout of malaria picked up while travelling in the Congo had rendered him cadaverously thin, and as the disease recurred, he grew ever more emaciated. His large ears stuck out at right angles; he looked like a corpse with two saucers attached. His tendency to appear at your shoulder, silently and without warning, had earned him the nickname 'The Shadow'. At forty-six, Clauss was said to have retired, although quite what he had retired from was a mystery.

The Clauss family was the richest in Huelva. Adolf's father, Ludwig, was an industrialist and entrepreneur who had moved from Leipzig to Spain at the end of the nineteenth century. With his partner, Bruno Wetzig, Ludwig set up a company processing agricultural products, selling fish to the Madrid markets, and supplying food and other material to the workers in the British-owned Rio Tinto mines. Clauss and Wetzig made a fortune. With this, Ludwig purchased land outside Huelva, built himself a large walled compound, and became Germany's honorary consul.

The German community was matched by the equally large, and even richer British community. If the Clauss family ruled over the Germans of Huelva, then the Rio Tinto Company ruled everyone else, employing more than 10,000 workers and running the town like a corporate fiefdom. The mines were 100 kilometres inland, and the copper and pyrite were brought to the dock at Huelva by a specially constructed railway. The company bosses rode around on horseback, and were referred to as 'the viceroys', so arrogant and regal was their bearing. The richer Spaniards aped British colonial manners, taking tea at five and playing bridge. Privately, the British were loathed, and resented for extracting so much money from Spanish soil: 'First the Romans mined it, then the British, then the Spanish, by which time there was nothing left.'

Like many colonists, the British and Germans tended to exaggerate their cultural distinctiveness. The British built a reproduction English village, which they called Queen Victoria

Barrio, with gabled cottages and a village green. The Germans sent their children to be educated in Germany, and maintained German traditions: Spain was home, but Germany was the Fatherland. Before the war, the two communities had mixed on terms of social equality, playing golf and tennis together and attending one another's functions. With the outbreak of war, all social contact ceased.

Spanish opinion in Huelva was divided on Adolf Clauss, Ludwig's younger son. Some said he was 'the black sheep', because he never seemed to do any work. Others reckoned he was 'the only clever one in the family', again because he never seemed to do any work. Clauss was very clever indeed, and he was also probably working harder than anyone else in Huelva, spying for Hitler's Reich.

Adolf Clauss had trained as an architect and industrial engineer in Germany, and at the age of seventeen, with the outbreak of the First World War, he joined the army, and volunteered for secret service work. Speaking impeccable Spanish, he was sent on a mission by submarine to blow up British factories in Cartagena. The rubber dinghy he set off in had sunk, owing to the weight of explosives on board, and Clauss was finally picked up by the Spanish navy after treading water for eight hours. He was briefly imprisoned, and then sent back to Germany. The incident, oddly, seemed only to increase Clauss's appetite for cloak and dagger work, and by 1920, although theoretically working as an agricultural technician, he was already the chief Abwehr agent in Huelva.

His marriage, during the 1930s, to the daughter of a senior Spanish army officer gave Clauss an entrée into the fascist Falange movement. When civil war erupted, he immediately enlisted as a captain in the Condor Legion, the German volunteer unit fighting for the Nationalists under General Franco. Most infamously, pilots of the Condor Legion carried out the bombing of the Basque town of Guernica on 26 April 1937, an act of brutality immortalised in Pablo Picasso's painting of that name. For most of the conflict, Clauss acted as the personal interpreter for Colonel Wilhelm von Thoma, commander of the Condor Legion's ground contingent. When Madrid fell to the Nationalists, Captain Clauss proudly rode into the captured capital on his tank. He was awarded the Red Cross for Military Merit by a grateful Franco regime, to add to the Iron Cross already awarded for his service to Germany in the First World War. He later earned another Iron Cross from Hitler's Third Reich. Clauss would later claim, as many did, that he had fought for Germany, not for Hitler. But there is no evidence he ever questioned Nazi policy. A number of Abwehr officers shrank from Hitler's barbarism. Clauss was not one of these. When war broke out he was happy to offer his well-honed espionage talents, his high-level Spanish contacts and his almost limitless energies to the Nazi cause.

By 1943, Adolf Clauss was running the largest and most efficient spy ring on the Spanish coast. Huelva, situated between the Portuguese frontier and Gibraltar, was of vital strategic importance in the war. From here, British merchant ships headed into the Atlantic, heavily laden with raw materials from the mines. From his farm, ideally situated on the coast, Clauss monitored every ship leaving port, and every ship coming in. His informants up and down the coast completed the picture. Sometimes he would take photographs using a Minox camera and a long-distance lens. The information was then relayed to Berlin by a team of Abwehr wireless operators, working out of the German consulate at 51 Avenida de Italia. Adolf's older brother, Luis, was an equally enthusiastic supporter of Nazism. Since their father Ludwig Clauss, the honorary German consul, was now in his eighties and almost stone deaf, consular duties were delegated to Luis. Both sons were named as vice consuls, and the consulate was placed at the disposal of the Abwehr. Luis had a fleet of fishing vessels with onboard radios to relay shipping movements.

The other main function of the Abwehr chief in Huelva,

in addition to sabotage and target-spotting for U-boats, was bribery. Every evening, thin-faced Adolf Clauss could be found at the Café del Palma, a bar near the port, buying drinks but drinking little, meeting and massaging his contacts, and discreetly distributing large quantities of cash. Clauss bribed everyone who mattered, and many who did not. He bribed the harbour master and the stevedores, the officers of the Guardìa Civil and the police chief. Word soon got out that Don Adolfo was prepared to pay handsomely for information on the movement of shipping, the activities of the British in Huelva, and the comings and goings of Spanish officials. Nothing could be said, nothing could be whispered in Huelva, without news eventually reaching the preternaturally large ears of Adolf Clauss, who faithfully relayed everything he heard back to his Abwehr bosses in Madrid.

Gaunt, introverted, and unsociable, Adolf Clauss nonetheless possessed the spy's essential talent for listening. 'He didn't dispute; if you thought you had the right argument, he always let you have the last word.' But even his family found him 'cold, distant and silent'. He started work at six in the morning and never took a siesta. He seldom drank alcohol. He almost never smiled. His was the mind of the collector, the perfectionist. He liked to collate the different sorts of information from his intelligence network, and then to pin it down, in different compartments, like butterflies.

The British authorities in Huelva knew what the odd-looking German lepidopterist was up to, for the British had their own spies and informers. In Huelva's peaceful, orange-tree-lined streets, another spy contest was underway, a smaller but no less intense echo of the espionage battle taking place in Madrid. The Clauss spy network was a menace to British shipping. Countless lives had already been forfeited on account of his activities, yet Clauss was an elusive adversary. As one British intelligence officer put it: 'He was an active and intelligent person. It was impossible for any of our agents to watch him and keep tabs on him. He was sharper and gave the slip to anyone who followed him.'

Don Gómez-Beare described the Clauss network to Montagu and Cholmondeley. Some of what he said was familiar. The decoding of Abwehr messages had revealed, early in the war, the existence in Huelva of this 'very efficient German agent who had the majority of Spanish officials there working for him, either for pay or for fascist ideology'. For more than three years, Montagu had monitored the steady build-up of German espionage activity in southern Spain, the use of Spanish territorial waters by German U-boats, and the activities of what he called this 'super-super efficient agent' in Huelva with 'first-rate' sources, who seemed to own the town: 'No ship can move without being seen, named and reported by W/T [wireless telegraphy]. The Germans get reports from lighthouse keepers, fishing boats, pilots and navy vessels, and agents in neutral fishing boats.' When the Germans began building an infrared spotting system to track ships passing through the Strait of Gibraltar at night, Churchill briefly considered launching a commando raid against the installation. Only the most vigorous diplomatic objections from the British government persuaded the Spanish to intervene and have it removed. For the most part, the Spanish government quietly tolerated, or actively condoned, the German espionage and sabotage of British and Allied ships.

Gibraltar, just fifty miles south of Huelva, was Britain's key to the Mediterranean, 'one of the most difficult and complicated places on the map', in John Masterman's words. The Rock guarded the gateway to the sea, a pivotal British outpost on the Spanish coast, and a magnet for spies. As MI5's senior officer on the island wrote, in a burst of lyricism: Gibraltar was 'the tiniest jewel in the imperial crown . . . this strategic dot on the world's map is not only a colony: it is also a garrison town, a naval base, a commercial port, a civil and military aerodrome, and a shop window for Britain in Europe'. The Abwehr funnelled money to willing Spanish saboteurs in Gibraltar and the surrounding region through one Colonel Rubio Sánchez, codenamed 'Burma', the chief of military intelligence in the Algeciras region. Sánchez was distributing 5,000 pesetas a month to saboteurs in and around Gibraltar. So far, the damage was limited since, as the MI5 chief in Gibraltar pointed out, the saboteurs' 'mercenary instincts were more outstanding than either their efficiency or their enthusiasm'. Montagu believed that special intelligence had successfully foiled several sabotage attempts, but the threat from German espionage in southern Spain was growing. In the month that Operation Mincemeat was born, Montagu warned that German sabotage had 'increased and spread' and was now being actively pursued by the Nazis and their collaborators 'in all Spanish and Spanish-owned ports'.

Adolf Clauss had, so far, enjoyed a most pleasant and productive war. In Madrid and Berlin he was held in high esteem, as 'one of the most important, active and intelligent German agents in the South of Europe'. Even NID and MI6 had a healthy respect for his manipulative skills. His network of spies and informers extended from Valencia to Seville. If anything of importance or interest washed up within fifty miles of the Café del Palma, let alone a body carrying documents, then Clauss would surely hear of it. The German spy's industriousness would be used against him. Later, if the operation worked, the proof of Clauss's espionage activities would be so blatant that it could be used to ignite a diplomatic row, and, with luck, 'sufficient evidence can be obtained to get the Spaniards to eject him'. It was agreed: Huelva was the target, and if the unpleasant Clauss could be undermined, made to look a fool and thrown out of Spain as a result, then so much the better.

A memo was sent to the Royal Navy's hydrographer, the official repository of technical maritime information, with a veiled enquiry: if an object was dropped off the Spanish coast near Huelva, would the tides and prevailing winds bring it ashore? At the same time, Gómez-Beare was instructed to fly to

Gibraltar and inform the flag officer there, and his staff officer in charge of intelligence, of the plan's broad outlines. 'They would have to be in the picture,' Montagu explained, 'in case the body or documents should by any chance find their way to Gibraltar.' Before returning to Madrid, Gómez-Beare should visit the British consuls at Seville, Cadiz and Huelva and instruct them that 'the washing ashore of any body in their area was to be reported only to NA Madrid [naval attaché Alan Hillgarth] and to no other British authority'. Francis Haselden, the consul in Huelva, 'was to be told the outline of the plan without, of course, any description of its object'. Gómez-Beare should then return to Madrid and fully brief his boss.

Captain Alan Hillgarth would stage-manage the Spanish end of the operation, and there was no one better suited to the task.

9

My Dear Alex

Even Charles Cholmondeley's elastic mind was having trouble wrapping itself around the problem of how to transport a corpse from London to Spain, and then drop it in the sea, without being spotted, in such a way that it would appear to be the victim of an air crash. There were, he reckoned, four possible methods of shipping Major Martin to his destination. The body could be transported aboard a surface ship, most easily on one of the naval escorts accompanying merchant vessels in and out of Huelva port. This option was rejected, 'owing to the need for placing the body close inshore'; nothing was more likely to attract the attention of Adolf Clauss and his spies than a Royal Navy ship lingering in shallow waters. An alternative would be to take the body by plane, and simply open the door and throw it out at the right spot. The problem, however, was that 'if the body were dropped in this way it might be smashed to pieces on landing', particularly if it had already started to decompose. A seaplane, such as a Catalina, might be able to land if the conditions were right, and slip the body into the water more gently. Cholmondeley drew up a possible scenario: the seaplane and its cargo would 'come in from out at sea simulating engine trouble, drop a bomb to simulate the crash, go out to sea as quickly as possible, return (as if it were a second flying boat) and drop a flare as if searching down the first aircraft, land, and then while ostensibly searching for survivors, drop the body etc., and then take off again'. On examination, this plan seemed far too elaborate. Any number of things could go wrong, including a real plane crash.

A submarine would be better. The drop could be carried out at night, and if there was insufficient depth of water, then a rubber dinghy could be used to take the body closer inshore. The submarine captain could monitor the winds and tides in order to surface and drop the body at the optimum moment. 'After the body has been planted it would help the illusion if a "set piece" giving a flare and explosion with delayed action fuse could be left to give the impression of an aircraft crash.' The only problem, as Cholmondeley delicately put it, was the 'technical difficulties in keeping the body fresh during the passage'. Submariners were a notoriously hardy bunch, able to withstand long periods underwater in the most foetid and cramped conditions. But even submariners would surely object to having a rotting corpse as a shipmate. Moreover, the operation was top secret: the presence of a dead body on a submarine would not remain secret very long. 'Of these methods,' Cholmondeley concluded, 'a submarine is the best (if the necessary preservation of the body can be achieved).'

There is no easy way to smuggle a dead body aboard a submarine, let alone prevent it from rotting in the warm, fuggy atmosphere of a submarine hold. For help, Cholmondeley turned to Charles Fraser-Smith of 'Q-Branch', chief supplier of gadgets to the Secret Service. A former missionary in Morocco, Fraser-Smith was officially a bureaucrat in the Ministry of Supply's Clothing and Textile Unit; his real job was to furnish secret agents, saboteurs, and prisoners of war with an array of wartime gizmos, such as miniature cameras, invisible ink, hidden weaponry and concealed compasses. (Fraser-Smith provided Ian Fleming with equipment for some of his more outlandish plans, and he doubtless helped to inform the character of 'Q', the eccentric inventor in the James Bond films.)

Fraser-Smith possessed a wildly ingenious but supremely practical mind. He invented garlic-flavoured chocolate to be

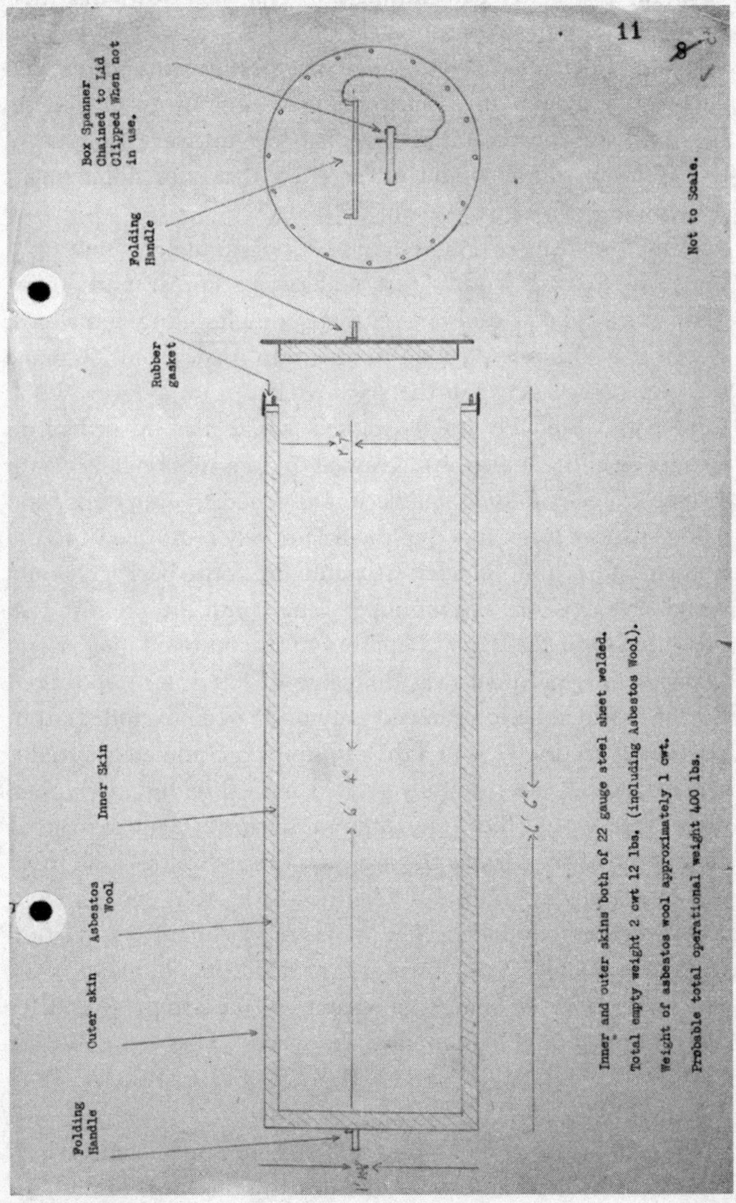

The National Archives

consumed by agents parachuting into France in order that their breath should smell appropriately Gallic as soon as they landed; he made shoelaces containing a vicious steel garrotte; he created a compass hidden in a button which unscrewed clockwise, based on the impeccable theory that the 'unswerving logic of the German mind' would never guess that something might unscrew the wrong way.

With the help of Fraser-Smith, Cholmondeley drew up a blueprint for the world's first underwater corpse transporter. This was a tubular canister, six feet six inches long and almost two feet in diameter, with a double skin made from 22-gauge steel, the space between the skins packed with asbestos wool. One end would be welded closed, while the other had an airtight steel lid, which was screwed on to a rubber gasket with sixteen bolts. A folding handle was attached to either end, and a box spanner was clipped to the lid for easy removal. With the body inside, Cholmondeley estimated the entire package would weigh about 400lb, and would fit snugly into the pressure hull of a submarine. Sir Bernard Spilsbury was consulted once more. Oxygen, he explained, was the cause of rapid decomposition. But 'if most of the oxygen had previously been excluded' from the tube with dry ice, and if the canister was completely airtight, and if the body was carefully packed around with dry ice, then the corpse would 'keep perfectly satisfactorily', and remain as cold as it had been inside the morgue. Fraser-Smith's task, then, was to design 'an enormous Thermos flask', thin enough to fit down the torpedo hatch. The Ministry of Aircraft Production was given the plans, and instructed to build this container as fast as possible, without being told what it was for. On the outside of the canister should be stencilled the words: 'HANDLE WITH CARE – OPTICAL INSTRUMENTS – FOR SPECIAL FOS SHIPMENT.'

Montagu, meanwhile, contacted Admiral Sir Claude Barry, the Flag Officer in command of Submarines (FOS), to find out which submarine might best be used for the mission. Barry replied that British submarines passed Huelva frequently, en route to Malta; indeed, HM Submarine *Seraph* was currently in Scotland, docked at Holy Loch on the Clyde and preparing to return to the Mediterranean in April. The *Seraph* was commanded by Lieutenant Bill Jewell, a young captain who had already carried out several secret assignments and who could be relied on for complete discretion. Montagu drew up some draft operational orders for Jewell, and arranged to meet the submarine officer in London and give him a full briefing on his new mission.

The hydrographer at the Admiralty submitted his report on the winds and tides off the coast at Huelva. As befits a man immersed in the vagaries of marine conditions, he was distinctly non-committal, pointing out that 'the Spaniards and Portuguese publish practically nothing about tides, tidal streams and currents off their coasts'. Moreover, 'the tides in that area run mainly up and down the coast'. If the object was dropped in the right place, in the right conditions, 'wind between S[outh] and W[est] might set it towards the head of the bight near P. Huelva'. However, if the body did wash up on the shore, there was no guarantee it would stay there because 'if it did not strand, it would be carried out again on the ebb'. This was less than perfect, but not discouraging enough to call off the operation. In any case, Montagu reflected, the 'object' in question was a man in a life jacket, rather larger than the object the hydrographer had been asked to speculate about, and might be expected to catch an onshore wind and drift landwards. He concluded: 'The currents on the coast are unhelpful at any point but the prevailing southwest wind will bring the body ashore if Jewell can ditch it near enough to the coast.'

In the last week of March, Montagu drew up a seven-point progress report for Johnnie Bevan, who had just returned from North Africa, where he had coordinated plans for Operation Barclay with Lieutenant Colonel Dudley Clarke. Relations between Montagu and Bevan remained tense. 'I am not quite clear as to who is in sole charge of administrative arrangements in connection with this operation,' Bevan wrote to Montagu, in a note calculated to rile him. 'I think we all agree that there are quite a number of things that might go wrong.' Montagu was fully aware of the dangers and in no doubt whatever that he was in sole charge of the operation, even if Bevan did not see it that way. Privately, Montagu accused Bevan of 'thinking it couldn't come off and disclaiming all responsibility'.

Montagu's report laid out the state of play: the body was almost ready, with Major Martin's uniform and accoutrements selected; the canister was under construction; Gómez-Beare and Hillgarth were standing by in Spain. And there was now a deadline. 'Mincemeat will be taken out as an inside passenger in HMS *Seraph* leaving the northwest coast of this country probably on the 10th April.' That left just two weeks to complete preparations. Montagu and Cholmondeley had deliberately sought to arrange everything before obtaining final approval for the operation, on the assumption that senior officers were far less likely to meddle when presented with a *fait* very nearly *accompli*. But there was now little time to finalise the last, and by far the most important, piece of the puzzle. Montagu's letter to Bevan ended on a note of exasperation: 'All the details are now "buttoned up",' he wrote. 'All that is required are the official documents.'

The debate about what should, or should not, be contained in Major Martin's official letters had already taken up more than a month. It is doubtful whether any documents in the war were subjected to closer scrutiny, or more revisions. Draft after draft was proposed by Montagu and Cholmondeley, revised by more senior officers and committees, scrawled over, retyped, sent off for approval, and then modified, amended, rejected, and rewritten all over again. There was general agreement that, as Montagu had originally envisaged, the main plank of the deception should be a personal letter from General Nye to General Alexander. It was also agreed that the letter should identify Greece as the target of the next Allied assault, and Sicily as the cover target. Beyond this, there was very little agreement about anything at all.

Almost everyone who read the letter thought it could do with 'alteration and improvement'. Everyone, and every official body concerned, from the Twenty Committee to the Chiefs of Staff, had a different idea about how this should be achieved. The Admiralty thought it needed to be 'more personal'. The Air Ministry insisted the letter should clearly indicate the bombing of Sicilian airfields was in preparation for invading Greece, and not a prelude to an attack on Sicily itself. The Chief of the Imperial General Staff and Chairman of the Chiefs of Staff, General Sir Alan Brooke, wanted 'a letter in answer to one from General Alexander'. The Director of Plans thought the operation was premature, and 'should not be undertaken earlier than two months before the real operation', in case the real plans changed. Bevan wondered whether the draft letter sounded 'rather too official', and insisted 'we must get Dudley Clarke's approval as it's his theatre'. Clarke himself, in a flurry of cables from Algiers, warned of the 'danger of overloading this communication', and stuck to the view that it was 'a mistake to play for high deception stakes'.

Bevan remained anxious: 'If anything miscarries and the Germans appreciate that the letter is a plant they would no doubt realise that we intend to attack Sicily.' Clarke framed his own draft, further enraging Montagu, who regarded this effort as 'merely a lowish grade innuendo at the target of the type that has often been, and could always be, put over by a double agent'. The Director of Plans agreed that 'Mincemeat should be capable of much greater things'. Bevan then also tried his hand at a letter, which again Montagu dismissed as 'of a type which could have been sent by signal and would not have appeared genuine to the Germans if carried in the way this document would be'. There was even a brief but fierce debate over how to spell the Greek city 'Kalamata'. The operation seemed to be running into a swamp of detail.

Typically, Montagu tried to insert some tongue-in-cheek

jokes into the letter. He wanted Nye to write: 'If it isn't too much trouble, I wonder whether you could ask one of your ADCs to send me a case of oranges or lemons. One misses fresh fruit terribly, especially this time of year when there is really nothing to buy.' The Chiefs of Staff excised this: General Nye could not be made to look like a scrounger. Even to the Germans. Especially to the Germans. So Montagu tried another line: 'How are you getting on with Eisenhower? I gather he is not bad to work with . . .' That was also removed: too flippant for a general. Next Montagu attempted a quip at the expense of the notoriously big-headed General Montgomery: 'Do you still take the same size in hats, or do you need a couple of sizes larger like Monty?' That, too, was censored. Finally, Montagu managed to squeeze a tiny half-joke in at the end, relating to Montgomery's much-mocked habit of issuing orders every day. 'What is wrong with Monty? He hasn't issued an order of the day for at least forty-eight hours.' That stayed in, for now.

Montagu's temper, never slow to ignite, began smouldering dangerously as the deadline neared and the key letter was tweaked and poked, polished and moulded. And then scrapped, and restarted. Page after page of drafts went into the files, covered with Montagu's increasingly enraged squiggles and remarks.

Finally, the Chiefs of Staff came up with a good suggestion: why not have General Nye draft the letter himself since this would be 'the best way of giving it an authentic touch'? Archie Nye was no wordsmith, but he knew General Alexander fairly well, and he knew the sound of his own voice. Nye read all the earlier drafts, and then put the letter into his own words. The key passage referred to General Sir Henry 'Jumbo' Wilson, then Commander-in-Chief of the Middle East, making it appear that he would be spearheading an attack on Greece; it indicated, falsely, that Sicily was being set up as a cover target for a simultaneous assault in another part of the Mediterranean; it referred to some run-of-the-mill army matters, which also happened to be authentic, such as the appointment of a new commander of the Guards Brigade and an offer from the Americans to award Purple Hearts to British soldiers serving alongside American troops. Above all, it sounded right. Montagu, after so many weeks spent trying to pull off the forgery himself, admitted that Nye's letter was 'ideally suited to the purpose'. The false targets were 'not blatantly mentioned although very clearly indicated', allowing the enemy to put two and two together, making at least six.

Bevan wrote to Nye, asking him to have the letter typed up, and then to sign it in non-waterproof ink, since a waterproof signature might raise suspicions. 'Your signature in ink might become illegible owing to contact with sea water and consequently it would be advisable to type your full title and name underneath the actual signature.'

Bevan had one final tweak. 'General Wilson is referred to three times, as "Jumbo", "Jumbo Wilson" and "Wilson". I wonder whether it would not be more plausible to refer to him on the first occasion as "Jumbo Wilson" and "Jumbo" thereafter.'

Nye replied: 'I referred to him variously intentionally (and committed a couple of – almost – grammatical errors) so as not to be guilty of too meticulous a letter. In fact, in dictating letters, which one normally does, these things occur and I think to leave them in makes it more realistic.' At the last moment, Nye dropped the joke about Monty. 'I would never have written such a thing . . . it wouldn't be me. It might have struck a false note and, if so, did one really gain anything by taking such a risk?' The general toyed with a joke of his own: 'P.S. We saw you on the cinema the other night and Colleen thought you looked uncommonly like Haile Selassie!' General Alexander *did* look a little like the Ethiopian Emperor, and Nye thought this remark 'might help to strike the right note of informality'. On the other hand, General Nye had no sense of humour, and was enough of a realist to know it. His final letter was entirely joke-free. He sent it back with a note and a flourish: 'Now I hope your friends will ensure delivery.' It was, in Montagu's words, 'a truly magnificent letter'.

Telephone: Whitehall 9400
Chief of the Imperial General Staff
War Office
Whitehall
London S.W.1.

23rd April 1943

<u>Personal and Most Secret</u>

My Dear Alex,

I am taking advantage of sending you a personal letter by hand of one of Mountbatten's officers, to give you the inside history of our recent exchanges of cables about Mediterranean operations and their attendant cover plans. You may have felt our decisions were somewhat arbitrary, but I can assure you that the C.O.S. Committee gave the most careful consideration both to your recommendation and to Jumbo's.

We have had recent information that the Boche have been reinforcing and strengthening their defences in Greece and Crete, and C.I.G.S. felt that our forces for the assault were insufficient. It was agreed by the Chiefs of Staff that the 5th Division should be reinforced by one Brigade Group for the assault on the beach south of CAPE ARAXOS and that a similar reinforcement should be made for 56th Division at KALAMATA. We are earmarking the necessary forces and shipping.

Jumbo Wilson had proposed to select SICILY as the cover target for 'HUSKY', but we had already chosen it as cover for operation 'BRIMSTONE'. The C.O.S. Committee went into the whole question exhaustively again and came to the conclusion that in view of the preparations in Algeria, the amphibious training which will be taking place on the Tunisian coast and the heavy bombardment which will be put down to neutralise the Sicilian airfields, we should stick to our plan for making it the cover for 'BRIMSTONE' – indeed, we stand a very good chance of making him think we will go for Sicily – it is an obvious objective and one about which he must be nervous. On the other hand, they felt there wasn't much hope of persuading the Boche that the extensive preparations in the Eastern Mediterranean were also directed at Sicily. For this reason they have told Wilson his cover plan should be something nearer the spot i.e. the Dodecanese. Since our relations with Turkey are now so obviously closer, the Italians must be pretty apprehensive about these islands.

I imagine you will agree with these arguments. I know you will have your hands more than full at the moment and you haven't much chance of discussing future operations with Eisenhower. But if, by any chance, you do want to support Wilson's proposal, I hope you will let us know soon, because we can't delay much longer.

I am very sorry we weren't able to meet your wishes about the new commander of the Guards Brigade. Your own nominee was down with a bad attack of the 'flu and not likely to be really fit for another few weeks. No doubt, however, you know Forster personally; he has done extremely well in command of a brigade at home, and is, I think, the best fellow available.

You must be about as fed up as we are with the whole question of war medals and 'Purple Hearts'. We all agree with you that we don't want to offend our American friends, but there is a good deal more to it than that. If our troops who happen to be serving in one particular theatre are to get extra decorations merely because the Americans happen to be serving there too, we will be faced with a good deal of discontent among those troops fighting elsewhere perhaps just as bitterly – perhaps more so. My own feeling is that we should thank the Americans for their kind offer, but say firmly it would cause too many anomalies and we are sorry we can't accept. But it is on the agenda for the next Military Members Meeting, and I hope you will have a decision very soon.

Best of Luck
Yours ever,
Archie Nye

General the Hon Sir Harold R.L.G. Alexander, G.C.B., C.S.I, D.S.O., M.C.
Headquarters, 18th Army Group

The letter twanged every chord. It indicated that there was not one assault planned, but two: General Wilson's army under Montgomery would attack two points in Greece under the codename 'Husky'; General Alexander, under Eisenhower's command, was preparing to launch a separate attack in the western Mediterranean, codenamed 'Brimstone'. The cover target for this latter operation was Sicily. The letter openly stated the intention to deceive the Germans into believing an attack on Sicily was imminent, pointing out that amphibious training in North Africa and the bombardment of Sicilian airfields would tend to support that impression. The training and bombing were, of course, preparations for the real attack on Sicily. Husky was the genuine codename for that invasion; if the Germans came across any allusion to Husky in the future, having read Nye's letter, they would, with luck, assume that this referred to the attack on Greece.

Nye's letter hinted at a second assault in the western Mediterranean, but did not say where the fictional Operation Brimstone would be aimed. Nor did it explain why such an important letter was being carried by this particular officer. There was nothing to explain what Major Martin was doing in North Africa, on the eve of a major invasion. A second letter was called for. Since Martin was on the staff of Combined Operations, Colonel Neville of the Royal Marines, who had been consulted on Major Martin's uniform, drafted a letter to be signed by Lord Louis Mountbatten, Chief of Combined Operations, and addressed it to Admiral Sir Andrew Cunningham, commander-in-chief in the Mediterranean. Cunningham was Eisenhower's naval deputy, a hard-grained Scot with red-rimmed eyes who had been in uniform ever since the Boer War. Like Alexander, his name and seniority would be well known to the Germans; unlike Alexander, there was nothing smooth and refined about Admiral Cunningham, who preferred the cut and thrust of battle to the comforts and trappings of high rank. His favourite expression, when things seemed to be going too well, was: 'It's too velvety-arsed and Rolls-Royce for me.'

The letter clearly indicated that Martin, a trusted expert on landing craft, was coming out to help Admiral Cunningham with preparations for the next amphibious assault.

In reply quote: S.R. 1924/43
Combined Operations Headquarters
1A Richmond Terrace
Whitehall, S.W.1

21st April

Dear Admiral of the Fleet,

I promised VCIGS that Major Martin would arrange with you for the onward transmission of the letter he has with him for General Alexander. It is very urgent and very 'hot' and as there are some remarks in it that could not be seen by others in the War Office, it could not go by signal. I feel sure that you will see that it goes on safely and without delay.

I think you will find Martin the man you want. He is quiet and shy at first, but he really knows his stuff. He was more accurate than some of us about the probable run of events at Dieppe and he has been well in on the experiments with the latest barges and equipment which took place in Scotland.

Let me have him back, please, as soon as the assault is over. He might bring some sardines with him – they are 'on points' here!

Yours sincerely,
Louis Mountbatten

Admiral of the Fleet Sir A.B. Cunningham G.C.B., D.S.O.
Commander-in-Chief Mediterranean
Allied Forces HQ
Algiers

The most crucial element of the letter was the last paragraph, clearly indicating that the assault on which Martin would advise was to be on the home of the sardine. Operation Brimstone, therefore, must be aimed at Sardinia. It was, Montagu admitted, a 'laboured' witticism. Like many Britons, Montagu found the German sense of humour somewhat leaden. 'I thought that that sort of joke would appeal to the Germans.'

The Germans might or might not be amused, but would they be taken in? This second letter contained some dangerous flaws. It appeared to indicate that Mountbatten knew the contents of Nye's letter, which, in reality, was exceedingly unlikely. Would the Chief of Combined Operations have needed to explain why the information was not being sent by cable? The sardines joke smelled fishy. Louis Mountbatten was a member of the royal family, and hardly constrained by rationing. If anyone could get sardines whenever he wanted them, it was surely Lord Louis. The reference looked dangerously like an artificial attempt to crowbar the word 'sardines' into the letter.

There was one final letter to add to the cache. This had no military significance whatever, and was included to literally make weight. If Martin was carrying only two letters, he would most probably have put them in an inside pocket for safety. But in that case, they might be overlooked by the Spanish or Germans, as had happened with the body of Lieutenant Turner in 1942. 'Papers actually on the body would run a grave risk of never being found at all due to the Roman Catholic prejudice against tampering with corpses.' A briefcase would be much harder to miss, but if Martin were to carry a briefcase, then he would need something bulkier than a couple of letters to put in it. Hilary Saunders, the House of Commons librarian and the husband of Montagu's colleague Joan Saunders, had just written a pamphlet on the history of the Commandos, a tub-thumping story of derring-do to boost public morale. It was decided that in addition to the other letters, Martin's briefcase would contain proofs of this worthy book, together with another letter from Mountbatten, asking General Eisenhower to write a puff for the American edition.

In reply quote: S.R. 1989/43
Combined Operations Headquarters
1A Richmond Terrace
Whitehall, S.W.1
22nd April

Dear General,

I am sending you herewith two copies of the pamphlet which has been prepared describing the activities of my Command; I have also enclosed copies of the photographs which are to be included in the pamphlet.

The book has been written by Hilary St. George Saunders, the English author of Battle of Britain, Bomber Command, and other pamphlets which have had a great success both in this country and in yours.

The edition which is to be published in the States has already enjoyed pre-publication sales of nearly a million and a half, and I understand the American authorities will distribute the book widely throughout the U.S. Army.

I understand from the British Information Service in Washington that they would like a 'message' from you for use in the advertising for the pamphlet, and that they have asked you direct, through Washington, for such a message.

I am sending the proofs by hand of my Staff Officer, Major W. Martin of the Royal Marines. I need not say how honoured we shall all be if you will give such a message. I fully realise what a lot is being asked of you at a time when you are so fully occupied with infinitely more important matters. But I hope you may find a few minutes' time to provide the pamphlet with an expression of your invaluable approval so that it will be read widely and given every chance to bring its message of co-operation to our two peoples.

We are watching your splendid progress with admiration and pleasure and all wish we could be with you.

You may speak freely to Major Martin in this as well as any other matters since he has my entire confidence.

Yours sincerely,

Louis Mountbatten

General Dwight Eisenhower
Allied Forces H.Q.
Algiers

Both letters were written on the same typewriter, and signed by Mountbatten himself, who was told the letters were needed for a secret mission. The only element now missing was the seal of approval from on high.

At 10.30 in the morning on 13 April, the Chiefs of Staff Committee gathered for its seventy-sixth meeting. Presided over by the Chief of the Imperial General Staff, the First Sea Lord and the Chief of the Air Staff, the committee included eight other senior officers from the different services. Item 10 on the agenda was Operation Mincemeat. The letters were approved, and Lieutenant General Sir Hastings 'Pug' Ismay was told to inform Johnnie Bevan of the decision, with instructions to make an appointment with the Prime Minister in order to obtain final approval for the operation to commence. Ismay dropped Churchill a note, advising him that 'the Chiefs of Staff have approved, subject to your consent, a somewhat startling cover plan in connection with HUSKY. May the Controlling Officer see you for five minutes within the next day or two, to explain what is proposed?' The note came back with 'yes', scrawled in Churchill's hand. '10.15 on Thursday.'

Two days later, Bevan found himself sitting on Winston Churchill's bed, and explaining Operation Mincemeat to a Prime Minister wearing his pyjamas and dressing gown, and puffing on a large cigar. Large wine cellars that had once served a stately home opposite St James's Park had been transformed into a fortified network of chambers, tunnels, offices, and dormitories known as the Cabinet War Rooms, the operational nerve centre. Above the war rooms was the Number Ten

Annexe, including the private flat where Churchill usually slept. Britain's wartime Prime Minister tended to work late, whisky in hand, and rise at a commensurate hour.

Bevan had arrived for the meeting in full uniform, at ten o'clock sharp. 'To my surprise I was ushered into his bedroom in the annexe where I found him in bed smoking a cigar. He was surrounded with papers and black and red cabinet boxes.' Churchill loved deception plans, the more startling the better, and relished the seamy, glamorous trade of espionage. 'In the higher ranges of Secret Service work, the actual facts of many cases were in every respect equal to the most fantastic inventions of romance and melodrama,' Churchill wrote after the war.

Bevan handed over a single sheet of foolscap paper, outlining the plan, and Churchill read it through. Bevan felt he had better say something: 'Of course there's a possibility that the Spaniards might find out this dead man was in fact not drowned at all from a crashed aircraft, but was a gardener in Wales who's killed himself with weedkiller.' Bevan had left the details to Montagu and Cholmondeley, and now found himself trying to explain the pathology of chemical poisoning to a Prime Minister in his nightwear, and scrambling the facts in the process. 'Weedkiller goes into the lungs and is very difficult to diagnose,' he bluffed. 'Apparently it would take you three weeks to a month just to find out what it was.'

Churchill 'took much interest' in the scheme, so much so that Bevan felt obliged to warn him that it could go spectacularly wrong. 'I pointed out that there was of course a chance that the plan might miscarry and that we would be found out. Furthermore that the body might never get washed up or that if it did, the Spaniards might hand it over to the local British authority without having taken the crucial papers.'

The Prime Minister's response was characteristically pithy. 'In that case, we shall have to get the body back and give it another swim.'

Churchill was on board. But he had one stipulation: before Operation Mincemeat could go ahead, agreement must be obtained from General Eisenhower, whose invasion of Sicily would be profoundly affected by its success or failure. Leaving Churchill to finish his cigar in bed, Bevan returned to the London Controlling Section offices and dashed off a Most Secret Cypher Telegram, under the codename 'Chaucer', to Eisenhower at Advance Headquarters in Algiers. The response arrived within hours: 'General Eisenhower gives full approval MINCEMEAT.'

10

Table Tennis Traitor

There was discreet rejoicing among the handful of people privy to the secret. Montagu's dark mood lifted: 'I get more and more optimistic,' he told Iris. 'We ought, by the time you get this, to have exposed Hitler's weak spot (Italy) to attack and the Ities ought not to last too much longer.' Astonishingly, this overt reference to war plans passed the censor. 'Mincemeat is in the making,' Guy Liddell, MI5's head of counterespionage, wrote in his secret diary. 'Plan Mincemeat has been approved by the Prime Minister. The documents are extremely well faked.'

Liddell was in overall command of 'B' Section, that branch of the Security Service dedicated to rooting out enemy spies and suspected agents: he monitored defectors, suspect refugees, Nazi agents, double agents, Soviet sympathisers and, among many others, Ivor Montagu. For while the Hon. Ewen was about to launch a most elaborate feat of espionage, concern about the behaviour of the Hon. Ivor had been steadily growing within both MI5 and MI6.

In May 1942 MI5 noted that Ivor was 'in close touch with many Russians in this country, including members of the embassy, the Trade Delegation and the TASS [news] agency'. Agents introduced into the audience during anti-war rallies, at which Ivor was a regular speaker, reported that he was 'an incurable anti-nationalist'. One P. Wimsey (possibly his real name) filed a report stating that on 16 December 1942, Ivor Montagu addressed a meeting of the Friends of the Soviet Union and stated that 'facilities for sport were far greater in Russia than in England'. Ivor was spotted having lunch with Constantine Zinchenko, Second Secretary at the Soviet Embassy, and consorting with 'men of decidedly foreign appearance, possibly Russian'. A minor scare was set off when he was seen hanging around a secret Royal Observer Corps installation in Watford, but the informant added that he 'did not think Montagu would get anything secret unless he got inside the station'. Given 'his association with the Russians in this country', MI5 concluded, 'any information of importance that came into his possession would undoubtedly be passed on'. Mr Aiken Sneath (again, surely, a name too implausible not to be real) informed MI5, without producing any evidence, that Montagu was 'an active Fifth Columnist'. His neighbours were encouraged to spy on him. They reported that 'he is always very keen to listen to the foreign news' on the radio, and 'has a wooden hut at the bottom of the garden and it is well stocked with books'. Ivor's wife Hell shared his politics, and was also viewed as a potential subversive. It is probable that Hell knew of Ivor's covert activities, and may have contributed to them. If so, MI5 could find no proof.

In 1940 Ivor had applied for a travel permit to visit the USSR as a journalist accredited to the *Daily Worker*. The application was turned down at the urging of MI5. 'It does not seem desirable to allow the Communist Party to have a courier travelling from this country to Moscow. . . a Communist Party member of his standing should not be allowed to leave the country. It is one thing to allow the *Daily Worker* to conduct its war propaganda in this country, but it is another thing to give such a newspaper special facilities for sending correspondents abroad for the purpose of facilitating propaganda.' Ivor complained about his failed application to a left-wing MP, who raised the matter in Parliament, demanding to know 'whether this refusal is personal to Mr Montagu, whether I should be allowed to go, or whether it indicates hostility to Russia?'

Courtesy of Jeremy Montagu

Ewen Montagu, naval intelligence officer, lawyer, angler, and the principal organiser of Operation Mincemeat.

Courtesy of Tom Cholmondeley

Charles Cholmondeley, the RAF officer seconded to MI5 whose 'corkscrew mind' first alighted on the idea of using a dead body to deceive the Germans.

Topical Press Agency / Getty Images

Sir Bernard Spilsbury, the senior pathologist at the Home Office and pioneer of forensics who knew more about death than any man alive.

Universal Picture Press and Agency

Bentley Purchase, the cheerful coroner of St Pancras.

Courtesy of Jeremy Montagu

Iris Montagu, wife of Ewen.

Harris Picture Library

Admiral John Godfrey, the irascible Director of Naval Intelligence and model for 'M' in the Bond novels, whose 'Trout Memo' written in 1939 inspired the deception plan.

The Times

Ian Fleming, wartime naval officer and the creator of James Bond, seen here in Room 39 of the Admiralty, the nerve centre of British naval intelligence.

Lawrence and Wishart

Ivor Montagu, film-maker, communist, table tennis pioneer and Soviet spy, with his wife Hell.

Courtesy of Fiona Mason

Ewen Montagu at work in Room 13, c. 1943.

Courtesy of Jeremy Montagu

Cartoon by Robert Bartlett depicting Ewen Montagu in Room 13. Montagu tended to shout on the scrambler telephone; the telephonist is telling him to hush.

Courtesy of Jean Gerard Leigh

Jean Leslie, the attractive MI5 secretary whose photograph would be used to depict 'Pam', the fictional fiancée of 'William Martin'.

Courtesy of Fiona Mason

The staff of Section 17M in Room 13 in the Admiralty basement: Ewen Montagu, front row, seated second right; Joan Saunders, back row third right; Juliette Ponsonby to her right; Patricia Trehearne to her left.

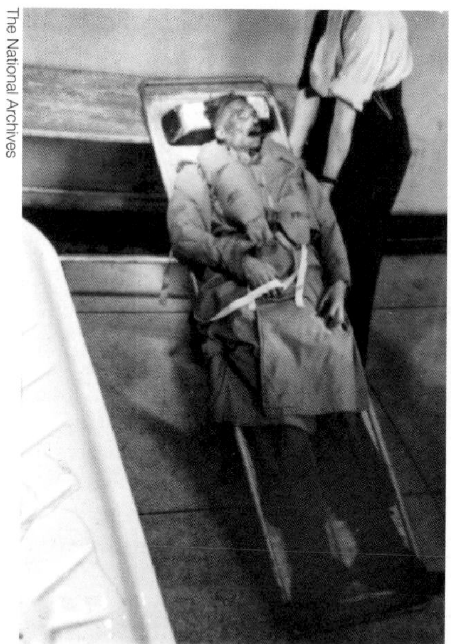

The National Archives

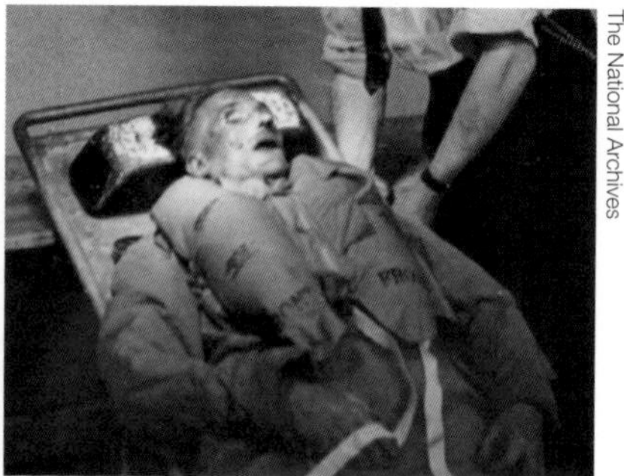

The National Archives

Glyndwr Michael, dressed as Major William Martin, on the Hackney mortuary gurney. His clenched hand and discoloured upper face are evidence of phosphorus poisoning. The figure on the right is PC Glyndon May, the coroner's officer.

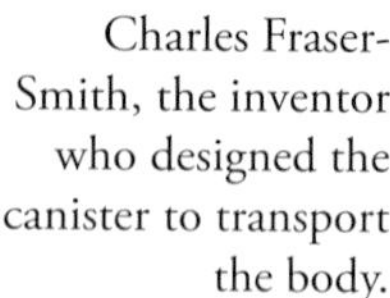

Charles Fraser-Smith, the inventor who designed the canister to transport the body.

Mail on Sunday

Courtesy of Jeremy Montagu

Cholmondeley and Montagu posing outside the van at Langbank on the River Clyde, at dawn on Sunday, 18 April 1943, a few hours before delivering the body to the submarine.

Courtesy of Jeremy Montagu

The racing driver Jock Horsfall, enjoying a cup of tea in the back of the van taking the body to Scotland. 'William Martin' is inside the canister.

Courtesy of Yvette Bourguignon

Courtesy of Yvette Bourguignon

Salvador Augustus 'Don' Gómez-Beare, Assistant Naval Attaché, First World War flying ace and agent-runner.

Imperial War Museum

The crew of HM Submarine *Seraph* posing in the conning tower. Lieutenant Bill Jewell is at the helm (*left*); his second-in-command, First Lieutenant David Scott, is standing, centre.

Ivor had openly and vehemently opposed the war, but once the Soviet Union became locked in battle with Germany he had declared his willingness to fight. 'I myself have registered and am ready to join up and I hope if I get in shall make a ruddy good soldier,' he told the Woolwich-Plumstead Branch of the Anti-War Congress, words that were immediately channelled back to MI5. Ivor was called up in 1941, but his call-up papers were immediately rescinded, it being 'most undesirable that he should be allowed to serve in HM armed forces'.

'I expect they've checked up on you,' one of his communist friends joked, and was overheard by the MI5 phone-tapper. Ivor had, by this time, moved with his family to the village of Bucks Hill in Hertfordshire, much to the annoyance of his Soviet handler: 'INTELLIGENTSIA lives in the provinces and it is difficult to contact him.'

Ivor Montagu was overdrawn and dishevelled. He once met Sylvia Pankhurst, the suffragette; he listened to the foreign news, denigrated British sporting facilities, promoted Soviet films, mixed with left-wing actors and directors, and read books. He had a German woman living in his house, Elfriede Stoecker, a Jewish refugee. From MI5's point of view, this was all most suspicious. Britain's counterespionage officers saw signs of treachery in everything Ivor Montagu did: they saw it in his friends, his appearance, his opinions, and his behaviour. But above all, they saw it in his passionate, and dubious, love of table tennis.

Suspicion that Ivor's interest in ping pong must disguise some darker purpose was the legacy of Colonel Valentine Vivian, the foremost communist spy hunter in the British Secret Service. Vivian headed Section V, MI6's counterintelligence unit, before going on to become Deputy Chief of SIS in charge of MI6's war station at Bletchley Park. Throughout his long intelligence career most of Vivian's energies, and those of Section V, were directed against British communists and the Comintern, which he regarded 'as a criminal conspiracy rather than a clandestine political movement'. He had become deeply, even fanatically, obsessed with the activities of Ivor Montagu, suspecting, quite rightly, that this son of privilege was more than merely a fellow traveller. But years of intense surveillance – opening Ivor's letters, eavesdropping on his conversations, trailing and photographing him – had so far produced only circumstantial evidence of skulduggery. Colonel Vivian had convinced himself that Ivor Montagu's enthusiasm for ping pong was a cover for something very much more sinister.

Many of Ivor's intercepted letters – a suspiciously large number, in the eyes of the interceptors – referred to the supply of table-tennis equipment from foreign parts. Two Bulgarians, Zoltan Mechlovitz and Igor Bodanszky, wrote to him repeatedly, ostensibly about arcane aspects of the game, the spin potential of different types of ball, and the optimal weight of bat. Vivian gave instructions that the Bulgarians should be investigated to find out if they are 'known to be queer in any other way'. (The word 'other' is most telling.) To the MI6 man in Sofia, Vivian wrote: 'The reason for our tentative interest in these people will appear to you rather quaint. They write interminably to Ivor Montagu about table tennis and the trying out of table-tennis balls. Montagu is, of course, known as a Ping Pong enthusiast well at the heart of the Table Tennis International, but even in England, which is not noted for sanity in this respect, we find it hard to believe that a gentleman can spend weeks upon weeks testing tennis balls.'

The reply from Bulgaria was disappointing: 'Bulgarian police authorities have nothing on their records . . . in a superficial way one would judge that Mechlovitz and Bodanszky are perfectly solid individuals who spend their time testing table-tennis balls.' Even more worrying was Ivor's correspondence, before the war, with Fritz Zinn, treasurer of the German Table Tennis Association. The letters went back and forth, discussing something called the 'Hanno-ball' and 'certain net-stretchers'. There were also hints that Zinn was getting a divorce, and 'suspected of running an illegal gaming club'. Was the 'Hanno-ball' code for some secret weapon? Was Ivor Montagu sending secret messages to his Bulgarian and German contacts under the seemingly innocent guise of sport? Could Montagu and these shadowy foreigners 'be using the channel of international table tennis for this curious piece of domestic espionage'? Vivian was determined to break up the mysterious table-tennis conspiracy. 'I know this all seems very trivial,' he wrote, 'but when one looks at it closely it is also puzzling.'

Vivian was not alone in thinking that a man who spent so much time discussing table tennis was probably a spy. When he was first inducted into the inner circle of British intelligence, Ewen Montagu had expected that MI5 would make a thorough check of his background, and thus would know about Ivor and his communist politics. 'I had no great faith in the records of MI5. I felt that they were likely to confuse me with my younger and communist brother.' He was half-right. One day, apparently apropos of nothing, John Masterman leaned across the table during a Twenty Committee meeting and asked Montagu in an offhand way: 'How is the table tennis going?' Masterman had clearly been making his own enquiries into the Montagu brothers, and had read up on Colonel Vivian's investigation into the international table-tennis fraternity. 'That's my communist younger brother,' Montagu replied. 'He's the progenitor of table tennis, not me.' Montagu assumed Masterman had simply made a mistake, mixing up the two brothers. But the precise Oxford don did not make mistakes: he was probing, to see if his colleague on the Twenty Committee might just be part of this sinister table-tennis connection.

Vivian was right, of course, but also profoundly wrong. Ivor Montagu *was* spying for the Soviet Union, as Agent Intelligentsia, and would continue to do so for the rest for the war, undetected and unrepentant. On the other hand, his interest in table tennis was neither puzzling nor malign. He just liked table tennis. Sometimes even MI5 officers can go slightly mad looking at the same spot, and imagine shadows where none exist. As Freud once said, when asked about the significance of his ever-present pipe: 'Sometimes a pipe is just a pipe.' And sometimes a table-tennis ball is just a table-tennis ball.

As the launch date for Operation Mincemeat approached, Cholmondeley and Montagu raced around London, attempting to tie up loose ends. The Prime Minister had approved the plan, and HMS *Seraph* was waiting, so the operation was now unstoppable, yet a number of serious problems remained: solutions would be found for all of them, though none was entirely satisfactory.

Nye was instructed to fold the key letter once, but only once. The 'special examiners' at the Censor's Department, responsible for investigating wartime postal communication, then took close-up photographs of the fold using a camera with a microscopic lens. That way, it might be possible to determine whether the letter had been opened and replaced in the envelope. In a final, rather melodramatic demonstration of spycraft, a single dark eyelash was placed in the fold of the paper. If this was still in place if and when the letter was retrieved, it would suggest the letters had not been read, but 'if the eyelash was gone, it would be a simple way of knowing whether the letter had been opened'. Montagu was somewhat coy about the measures taken to detect whether the letters had been tampered with. To his lawyerly mind, the presence or absence of a single eyelash was not the sort of evidence that would stand up in court.

The key letter was placed in an envelope, and then sealed, twice, with the formal wax seal of the VCIGS, depicting the heraldic arms of the War Office. Once again the Censor's Department photographed the ragged edges of the wax seals, to ensure that any tampering could be traced. Mountbatten's letters were also sealed, and the seals photographed in close-up. Once the letters were in his hands, Montagu ensured that he, and only he, handled them. The same went for Martin's other possessions. Montagu kept Pam's letters in his own wallet, unfolding and folding them repeatedly, as a newly engaged man might. The Germans, if they were suspicious and had the opportunity, might well dust the letters for fingerprints: 'Mine were used for Major Martin's throughout,' he wrote. This was a sensible precaution, but hardly a foolproof one. If the Germans compared the fingerprints on the letters to those of the dead man, they would easily spot the difference.

The letters and proofs of the Commandos pamphlet would be placed inside 'an ordinary black Government briefcase with the Royal cipher' embossed on the flap. The key to the lock was placed on Major Martin's key chain. But here arose another issue. The Spaniards would be more likely to notice, and pass to the Germans, an official-looking briefcase, but how to ensure that the briefcase and body arrived in Spain together? The case might be placed in the dead man's hand, but it was highly unlikely that rigor mortis alone would ensure that the body drifted ashore still clutching the case. The man was supposed to have died in an air crash, so the most realistic alternative would simply be to put the body and case into the water simultaneously but separately, and hope both floated ashore. But as the Hydrographer's Department had made clear, the winds and tides off Huelva were highly unpredictable. A body held up by a life jacket would behave quite differently from a soggy leather briefcase filled with paper. The case might sink, or wash up in Portugal. The solution, it was agreed, would be to attach the briefcase to Major Martin using a leather-covered chain of the sort used by bank messengers, passing up the right sleeve and fastened to the belt by a dog-lead clip, with a similar clip at the other end attached to the case handle. The case and corpse would then float ashore chained together. This might serve to underline the value and importance of the contents in the case. The only snag was that British military officers never used this method to transport and safeguard documents.

The chain seemed 'horribly phoney' to Montagu's mind. Cholmondeley was equally dubious. After a meeting with the other planners, he wrote, 'the use of a chain to the bag from the body [is] too doubtful and might endanger the whole operation'. But there seemed little alternative.

From the Air Ministry, Cholmondeley requisitioned a rubber dinghy and oars, of the type used on Catalinas. The original plan had been to distribute debris out at sea and have this float ashore with the body, but further research revealed that 'little or no wreckage floated from a normal aircraft' after a crash, so it was agreed that 'for simplification and for security with the submarine crew, nothing should be released except the rubber dinghy'.

Most frustrating was the apparent impossibility of finding a lookalike to pose for Bill Martin's identity card. Two fellow officers had agreed to be photographed. Neither closely resembled Glyndwr Michael, but time was running out. In late March, Montagu attended a meeting at B1A to discuss the case of Eddie Chapman, the double agent 'Zigzag'. Chapman, a career criminal, had been parachuted into Britain after being trained as a saboteur in a secret spy camp in occupied France, and Montagu was on the committee debating what to do with him. Sitting across the table was Chapman's case officer, Ronnie Reed, a former BBC technician and radio expert. Reed's resemblance to the man in the morgue was striking. Montagu would later assert that he 'might have been the twin brother' of the dead man. He certainly had the same sharp chin and narrow face as Glyndwr Michael, though his hair was thicker and darker. Reed was four years older than the dead man, and wore a small moustache. But he would do. Reed was duly photographed, the epaulettes of the Royal Marines battledress clearly showing on his shoulders. Montagu believed Major Martin's identity card looked 'far more like [him] even after his death than mine was like me'. The only official photograph of William Martin shows a thin-faced man wearing a small, sly smile.

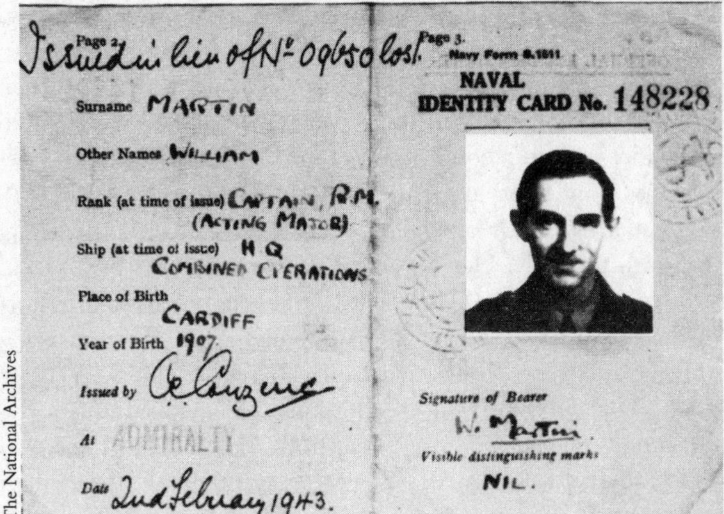

Page 2. Issued in lieu of No. 09650 lost.

Surname MARTIN

Other Names WILLIAM

Rank (at time of issue) CAPTAIN, R.M. (ACTING MAJOR)

Ship (at time of issue) H Q COMBINED OPERATIONS

Place of Birth CARDIFF

Year of Birth 1907

Issued by [signature]

At ADMIRALTY

Date 2nd February 1943.

Page 3. Navy Form S.1511

NAVAL IDENTITY CARD No. 148228

Signature of Bearer W. Martin.

Visible distinguishing marks NIL.

The National Archives

Bill Martin now had a face that fitted, and a uniform, which might not. They decided to return to St Pancras mortuary and try on the clothes Cholmondeley had broken in. A last-minute discovery that the trousers were too short, or that the shirt did not fit, would be disastrous. Stripping and then dressing the dead body – starting with the late Warden Fisher's underwear and ending with the trench coat – was a task they 'heartily disliked'. Montagu suffered an 'odd psychological reaction' on seeing the corpse lying stiff on the mortuary slab, gradually being transformed into someone he almost knew by the clothes, and the personality, they had fashioned for it. The uniform fitted well. It was decided to leave him in battledress inside the refrigerator, and put the boots on later.

Courtesy of Nicholas Reed

Ronnie Reed, the MI5 case officer who 'might have been the twin brother' of Glyndwr Michael.

HMS *Seraph* had spent five months in the Mediterranean in close underwater combat with the enemy, before returning to Britain for repairs at Blyth dockyard. The submarine had then sailed around Scotland to the River Clyde, where she worked up under realistic conditions, preparing for her next sortie. She was now lying alongside the submarine depot ship HMS *Forth* at Holy Loch on the west coast of Scotland, and ready to return to battle. Her departure date was delayed by a week, and her commander, Lieutenant Bill Jewell, was 'told to report to the intelligence side of the Admiralty' while the remaining officers and crew continued 'normal final training' at Holy Loch. The delay offered an additional week to complete the finishing touches, and ensure that both Alan Hillgarth in Spain and Dudley Clarke in Algiers were fully prepared. Bevan sent a coded telegram to Clarke: 'Mincemeat sails 19th April and operation probably takes place 28th April.'

The later date would also 'enable the operation to be carried out with a waning moon in a reasonably dark period (approximately 28th–29th April)'. Jewell arrived at Submarine Headquarters, a block of flats requisitioned in Swiss Cottage, north London, where Rear Admiral Barry told him to go to an address in St James's. There he was greeted by Montagu, Cholmondeley, Captain Raw, Chief Staff Officer to Admiral Submarines, and a set of operational orders laying out his mission.

Lieutenant Norman Limbury Auchinleck Jewell was thirty years old, with a cheerful grin and bright blue eyes. Understated and charming, Bill Jewell, as he was known, was also tough as teak, ruthless, occasionally reckless, and entirely fearless. He had seen fierce action in the Mediterranean and Atlantic. His submarine had been depth-charged, torpedoed, machine-gunned and mistakenly shot at by the RAF; he had spent seventy-eight hours, slowly suffocating with his crew, in a half-crippled submarine at the bottom of the sea; he had taken part in several clandestine operations which, had they been intercepted, might have led to espionage charges and, possibly, a German firing squad. In four years of watery war, Jewell had seen so much secrecy, strangeness and violence that the request to deposit a dead body in the sea off Spain did not remotely faze him. 'In wartime, any plan that saved lives was worth trying,' he reflected.

Jewell was never informed of the identity of the body, or the exact nature of the papers he was carrying, and he hardly needed to be told of 'the vital need for secrecy'. The tall man with the extravagant moustache was introduced as 'a squadron leader for RAF intelligence'. The body, Cholmondeley explained, would be brought to him in Scotland, 'packed, fully clothed and ready', inside a large steel tube. This canister could be lifted by two men, but should on no account be dragged by a single handle, 'as the steel is made of light gauge to keep the weight as low as possible', and it might give way if roughly handled. The possibility of the container breaking and the body falling out was too awful to contemplate. The canister would fit down the torpedo hatch, and could then be hidden below decks. Jewell would also receive a rubber dinghy in a separate package, a locked briefcase with chain attached, and three separate identity cards for William Martin, with three different photographs. In idle moments, Montagu had taken to rubbing Martin's fake identity cards on his trouser leg to give them the patina of use.

What, Jewell asked, should he tell the men under his command about this large object on his small ship? Montagu explained that the lieutenant could take his officers into his confidence once underway, but that the rest of the crew should be told only that the container 'held a super-secret automatic meteorological reporting apparatus, and that it was essential that its existence and position should not be given away or it would be removed by the Spaniards and the Germans would learn of its construction'.

Jewell pointed out that if the weather was rough, the officers might need the help of the crew to get the canister up on deck. If a member of the crew spotted the body, he should be told that 'we suspected the Germans of getting at papers on bodies washed ashore and therefore this body was going to be watched: if our suspicions were right the Spaniards would be asked to remove the Germans concerned'. This cover story could also be told to the officers, but 'Lt Jewell was to impress on [them] that they would never hear the result and that if anything leaked out about this operation not only would the dangerous German agents not be removed, but the lives of those watching what occurred would be endangered'.

Upon reaching a position 'between Portil Pillar and Punta Umbria just west of the mouth of the Rio Tinto River', Jewell should assess the weather conditions. 'Every effort should be made to choose a period with an onshore wind.' Jewell studied the charts and estimated 'the submarine could probably bring the body close enough inshore to obviate the need to use a rubber dinghy'. Cholmondeley had originally envisaged setting off an explosion out at sea to simulate an air crash, but after some discussion 'the proposed use of a flare was dropped'. There was no point in attracting any unnecessary attention.

Under cover of darkness, the canister should be brought up through the torpedo hatch 'on specially prepared slides and lashed to the rail of the gun platform'. Any crew members should then be sent below, leaving only the officers on deck. 'The container should then be opened on deck as the "dry-ice" will give off carbon dioxide.' It would also smell terrible.

Montagu and Cholmondeley had given a great deal of thought to exactly how the briefcase should be attached to Major Martin. No one, even the most assiduous officer, would sit on a long flight with an uncomfortable chain running down his arm. 'When the body is removed from the container all that will be necessary will be to fasten the chain attached to the briefcase through the belt of the trench coat which will be the outer garment of the body . . . as if the officer has slipped the chain off for comfort in the aircraft, but has nevertheless kept it attached to him so that the bag should not either be forgotten or slide away from him in the aircraft.' Jewell should decide which of the three identity cards most closely resembled the dead man in his current state, and put this in his pocket. The body, with life jacket fully inflated, should then be slipped over the side. The inflated dinghy should also be dropped, and perhaps an oar, 'near the body but not too near if that is possible'. Jewell's final task would be to reseal the canister, sail into deep water, and then sink it.

If, for any reason, the operation had to be abandoned, then 'the body and container should be sunk in deep water', and if it was necessary to open the canister to let water in, 'care must be taken that the body does not escape'. A signal should be sent with the words: 'Cancel Mincemeat'. If the drop was successful, then another message should be sent: 'Mincemeat completed'.

Jewell noted that the two intelligence officers seemed utterly absorbed by the project, and had obviously had 'a pleasant time building up a character'. Before the meeting broke up, Montagu asked the young submariner if he would like to contribute, in a small way, to 'making a life for the Major of Marines'. A nightclub ticket was needed for the dead man's wallet. Would Lieutenant Jewell care to spend a night on the town, and then send over the documentary evidence? 'I had the enjoyment of going around London nightclubs on his ticket,' said Jewell. 'It was an enjoyable period.'

While Jewell returned north with his new operational orders and a slight hangover, another telegram was despatched to General Eisenhower in Algiers. 'Mincemeat sails 19th April and operation probably takes place 28th April but could if necessary be cancelled on any day up to and including 26th April.'

If all went according to plan, Major Martin would wash up in Spain on or soon after 28 April, where an extraordinary reception was being prepared for him by Captain Alan Hugh Hillgarth: naval attaché in Madrid, spy, former gold prospector and, perhaps inevitably, successful novelist.

11

Gold Prospector

In his six novels, Alan Hillgarth hankered for a lost age of personal valour, chivalry and self-reliance. 'Adventure was once a noble appellation borne proudly by men such as Raleigh and Drake,' he wrote in *The War Maker*, but it is now 'reserved for the better-dressed members of the criminal classes'. Hillgarth's own life read like something out of the *Boy's Own Paper*, or the pages of Rider Haggard.

The son of a Harley Street ear, nose and throat surgeon, Hillgarth had entered the Royal Naval College at the age of thirteen, fought in the First World War as a fourteen-year-old midshipman (his first task was to assist the ship's doctor during the Battle of Heligoland Bight by throwing amputated limbs overboard) and skewered his first Turk, with a bayonet, before his sixteenth birthday. At Gallipoli he found himself in charge of landing craft, as all the other officers had been killed. He was shot in the head and leg, and spent the recovery time learning languages and cultivating a passion for literature. Hillgarth was small and fiery, with dense bushy eyebrows and an inexhaustible supply of energy. He was also an arborphile: he loved trees, and was never happier than in forest or jungle.

In 1927, Evelyn Waugh recalled his first meeting with 'a young man called Alan Hillgarth, very sure of himself, writes shockers, ex-sailor'. By this time, Hillgarth had embarked on a second career as a novelist, a third, as adviser to the Spanish Foreign

Legion during the uprising of the Rif tribes in Morocco, and a fourth, as a 'King's Messenger', carrying confidential messages on behalf of the government. But it was Hillgarth's fifth career, as a treasure hunter, that defined the rest of his life, and the next stage of Operation Mincemeat.

In 1928, Hillgarth met Dr Edgar Sanders, a Swiss adventurer born in Russia and living in London, who told him a most intriguing story. Sanders had travelled to the interior of Bolivia in 1924, lured by legends of a vast hoard of gold, the treasure of Sacambaya, mined by the Jesuits, and hidden before they were expelled from South America in the eighteenth century. Sanders showed Hillgarth a document, given to him by a Boer War veteran and rubber tapper, who claimed to have obtained it from the family of an elderly Jesuit priest. The document identified the hiding place of the gold in a network of underground caverns 'that took five hundred men two and one half years to hollow out'.

Sanders claimed to have found the site amid the ruins of a once-great Jesuit colony deep in the remote Quimsa Cruz range of the eastern Andes.

A 'squarish man with conspicuously high cheekbones and hard slate eyes', Sanders was fanatical in his quest, and utterly convincing. He believed the Jesuits had created the underground cavern by tunnelling from the river bank but the water table had since risen: getting to the entrance would require large pumps, digging equipment, a lot of money, and a great deal of sweat. Sanders invited Hillgarth to join him in what promised to be the greatest treasure hunt of all time. The twenty-eight-year-old accepted without hesitation.

The Sacambaya Exploration Company was duly formed. On the eve of the Great Crash, money could be minted from dreams, and investors flocked to a project promising returns of 48,000 per cent.

Hillgarth and Sanders set about recruiting 'men who had had considerable experience of harsh conditions', which were described in detail. 'Sacambaya is a poisonous place, a dark, dirty valley, shut in by hills that rise almost immediately to 4,000 feet. It is either very dry or you are flooded out. It is generally very hot by day and pretty near freezing at night. It abounds in bugs, fleas, flies, ants, mosquitoes, sand flies, rattlesnakes and other kinds of snakes. It is famous among Indians as a plague spot of Malaria. There are also skunks.' There were also bandits, no certainty of success, and a high probability of death. But this was an age that revered Shackleton and Scott. Some twenty-three men were chosen on the basis of expertise, resilience and amusement value, including a photographer, a doctor, a Serbian miner and an American engineer named Julius Nolte.

On 1 March 1928, the expedition set sail from Liverpool on the first stage of the 9,000-mile journey from England to Sacambaya. The 40 tons of equipment stashed in the hold included two Morris six-wheel tractors, four vast compressors to drive the pneumatic hoists, picks, spades and drills, two pumps, six cranes, a petrol motor, winches, electric light plants, forges, tents, mosquito nets, and a circular saw to cut wood for the railway that would have to be built at the other end. Dr P. B. P. Mellows, of St Bartholomew's Hospital, brought, in addition to the usual medical supplies, 28,000 quinine tablets to fight malaria and 5,000 aspirin. Hillgarth purchased twenty rifles and twenty automatic pistols, four shotguns, two automatic rifles and enough ammunition to start a small war.

From the port of Arica in Chile, the expedition chartered a train to take them the 330 miles to La Paz, then south, as far as a station called Eucalyptus, where the line stopped. From here the road, such as it was, went as far as Pongo, a one-eyed mining town built to service the Guggenheim mines and presided over by a formidable American woman named Alicia O'Reardon Overbeck, whom the team nicknamed 'Mrs Starbird'. Sacambaya was still forty-five miles distant, along a track partly washed away by rains. Now the hard work began.

The smaller machinery was packed into loads of up to 500lb, and strapped on to reluctant mules, while the largest items, including the compressors each weighing 1½ tons, had to be dragged along the mountain tracks using manpower and oxen.

'This,' said Hillgarth, with echoing understatement, 'was quite an undertaking.' In some places the track had to be rebuilt, cut out of the solid rock. In others, the heavy machinery had to be lowered with a block and tackle. One compressor, two oxen and several men hurtled over the edge, and were saved only by becoming entangled in trees thirty feet below. Hillgarth, five other white men, and twenty Indians, successfully transferred all the equipment to Sacambaya in five weeks and four days. Total losses en route amounted to 'one case containing 200lb of macaroni'.

That was the last piece of good news.

Armed with modern technology and an ancient document, the Sacambaya Exploration Company now set about picking, drilling, pumping and blasting its way '100 feet into the hillside' in pursuit of Jesuit gold. For ten hours a day, six days a week, from June to October, the men hacked into the mountain. Some 37,000 tons of rock were removed to create an enormous hole.

Conditions at Sacambaya were quite as nasty as advertised. Within weeks, three-quarters of the men had jiggers – small worms that burrow into the feet. 'A complete absence of fresh fruit and vegetables from our dietary [sic] has brought on chronic constipation, but a great range of purges varying in propulsive powers have catered for all tastes,' Dr Mellows reported cheerily. The mules and oxen came under attack from vampire bats, which were also partial to human gore if they could get it. 'One of our party awakened the other night and was startled to find a vampire bat tearing at his mosquito net.' Mellows identified a new ailment, which he named *Sacambayaitis*: 'Claustrophobia brought on by being shut up in an unhealthy valley between high mountains for month after month, working hard, living on a monotonous diet, with no diversions, subject to constant fear of possible attack by bandits.'

The only member of the team immune to Sacambayaitis was Alan Hillgarth. The photographs of the expedition show him fresh-faced and happy: digging, grinning, never without a tie, even when helping to perform a rustic appendectomy on a colleague.

It was not the jiggers, the claustrophobia, the constipation, bats, or bandits that finally did for the Sacambaya Exploration Company, but water. It poured from the sky in sheets, and bubbled up from the ground in gouts, filling every hole as soon as it was dug, despite the panting efforts of the pumps. Finally, even Hillgarth had to admit defeat, despite believing that the cave wall might be just fifteen feet away.

The expedition had been an unmitigated, magnificent disaster. The company went spectacularly bust. Two of the team headed into the interior and were never seen again. The chief engineer was left behind in Pongo. 'He has fallen seriously in love with Mrs Starbird, and apparently does not intend to leave.' The Serbian miner was poisoned in La Paz, 'either by the hotel people or the police'.

Sanders was flung into a Bolivian jail. Some months earlier, he realised the Bolivian police were intercepting his mail, so he had planted a fake letter referring to a shipment of mustard gas, to see if this would flush them out. The Bolivian authorities took the letter at face value: Sanders was accused of planning a coup against the Bolivian government, and charged with smuggling arms into the country, including fifty machine guns and 100 tons of poison gas.

Hillgarth returned to Britain to face the wrath of his investors, and the realisation that he had been thoroughly and comprehensively duped. Sanders's documents, it transpired, were fakes. The words on them had not even been written by a Spanish speaker, since they contained numerous grammatical errors and modern English idioms directly translated into Spanish.

The Sacambaya debacle had been a salutary experience. A very large hole in the Bolivian jungle was testament to the heroic pointlessness of that achievement, but it was also a lesson that Hillgarth would never forget: otherwise entirely sensible people could be persuaded to believe, passionately, what they already wanted to believe. All it required was a few, carefully forged documents, and some profoundly wishful thinking on the part of the reader. The Sacambaya trip formed the basis for Hillgarth's fifth and most successful novel, *The Black Mountain*, published in 1933 to acclaim from, among others, Graham Greene.

By then, Hillgarth had settled in Majorca with his wife Mary and three children, becoming honorary British vice consul, and then consul, in Palma. At the same time, 'he doubled up as a spy'. On the eve of the Spanish Civil War, Winston Churchill met Hillgarth in Majorca, on his way to a holiday in Marrakesh. They got on famously. When Clementine Churchill complained about the smell of the drains at their hotel, Hillgarth invited the Churchills to stay at his picturesque villa, Son Torella.

Hillgarth played a pivotal role as a go-between during the Spanish Civil War, helping to arrange prisoner swaps between the two sides, and successfully ensuring the bloodless handover of Minorca to Franco's forces in 1939. The commander of Nationalist forces in the Balearic Islands was Rear Admiral Salvador Moreno Fernández, and it was through him that Hillgarth arranged for the Republican forces to leave the island, thus averting, in Hillgarth's words, 'an intense bombardment which could have caused some 20,000 deaths'. Hillgarth's prolonged negotiations with Moreno, a convivial and subtle politician, marked the start of a most fruitful partnership. When Captain John Godfrey of HMS *Repulse* wanted to dock in Barcelona, it was Hillgarth who ensured, through his navy contacts with Franco's regime, that the British ship did not come under air attack.

As the newly appointed Director of Naval Intelligence at the start of the war, Godfrey remembered Hillgarth, and recommended his promotion to naval attaché in Madrid. It was an inspired appointment, to a most difficult and sensitive job. Spain was pivotal to British interests, the key to the Mediterranean and Gibraltar. With the fall of France, there were German troops on Spain's border. Franco was in debt to both Italy and Germany for arms. Would he side with the Axis powers, and if he did not, and Spain remained non-belligerent, would Hitler invade? Hillgarth's role would be to combat Nazi influence, stymie German sabotage efforts, prevent U-boats refuelling and resupplying at Spanish ports, and countering the pro-Axis Falange within Franco's government. With Ian Fleming, he helped to plan the campaign of sabotage and guerrilla war that would erupt if Spain was invaded, codenamed 'Operation Goldeneye' (the name that Fleming would eventually bestow on his Caribbean home). British policy required a nuanced approach, and Hillgarth's reports showed how well he understood that delicate balance: Franco was anxious to preserve his neutrality and freedom of action, Hillgarth reported, but 'a decisive German victory over Russia might enable the Falange to take complete control [and] Spain would probably throw in her lot with Germany'.

Sir Samuel Hoare, a former Chamberlain loyalist appointed ambassador in Madrid by Churchill, played this tricky game at the diplomatic level. Hillgarth did so at a subterranean level, while simultaneously coordinating the operations of MI6, SOE and his own network of agents. In all of this, Hillgarth had the personal backing of Winston Churchill (they were distinctly similar characters), who regarded him as a 'very good' man 'equipped with a profound knowledge of Spanish affairs'. The Prime Minister instructed Hillgarth to write to him 'privately about anything interesting'. Ian Fleming shared Churchill's high opinion of Hillgarth, describing him as a 'useful petard and a good war-winner'. Despite contrasting personalities, Hoare and Hillgarth got on well, and cooperated closely. The ambassador called him 'the embodiment of drive'. By contrast

Kim Philby, who ran counterintelligence on the Iberian desk at MI6 and was later revealed as a Soviet spy, disliked Hillgarth intensely, believing that Churchill's support, the 'secret funds that were made available to him for undercover activity', and his direct access to 'C', Stewart Menzies, the head of MI6, had all 'helped to feed the gallant officer's illusions of grandeur'. Philby was particularly irked by Hillgarth's choice of 'Armada' as a codename, which he considered self-inflating.

It is hard to say which reflected better on Hillgarth: the admiration of Fleming and Churchill, or Philby's animosity. Philby would have been even angrier had he known the extent of funds available to Hillgarth, for the purposes of bribery, on a staggering scale. Adolf Clauss bribed policemen and dock workers; Gómez-Beare paid off 'local police, dock watchmen and stevedores'. But Hillgarth bribed generals.

The Spanish armed forces contained many patriotic monarchists opposed to the fascist Falange, who had no desire to become 'expendable parts of Hitler's war machine'. Such officers, Hillgarth calculated, needed only a little financial encouragement to lobby Franco against an alliance with Hitler, and keep Spain out of the war. The money was channelled to the generals through Juan March, a Majorcan businessman whom Hillgarth had known for many years. March had made a fortune in tobacco, worked for British intelligence in the First World War, helped to finance Franco's rebellion in 1936, and purchased twelve bombers for Mussolini. He was small, thin, greedy, clever, morally void and monstrously bent. March 'took corruption for granted, and used it casually and openly'. He had been imprisoned for bribery, escaped to France, and by 1939 he was the richest, and dodgiest, man in Spain, nicknamed 'the last pirate of the Mediterranean', with a fortune that extended to shipping, oil, banks and newspapers. 'It would be a mistake to trust him an inch,' Hillgarth reported cheerfully. But March was also prepared to back Britain and that, as far as Hillgarth was concerned, was all that mattered: 'He has already had two

German agents shot in Iviza [Ibiza], though I did not ask him to do so . . .' March was the ideal conduit for bribing the generals. The money would have no British fingerprints on it, and if word ever leaked that March was involved, no one would be remotely surprised.

In the first phase of the scheme, with Churchill's approval, $10 million was released by the Treasury, and deposited in a Swiss bank in New York. From this, selected Spanish generals were invited to make withdrawals, in pesetas, with the balance to be paid after the war. Some $2 million is thought to have been funnelled to General Antonio Aranda Mata, who was expected to take over the army if Franco should fall. Another happy beneficiary was General Luis Orgaz y Yaldi, the commander of Spanish Morocco. (Orgaz was being rewarded by both sides: the Abwehr promised him 'an amphibious car'.) It is probable that Admiral Moreno, the man who had negotiated the surrender of Minorca with Hillgarth and had since been promoted to Navy Minister in Franco's government, was also on the payroll. The admiral had long opposed Spanish involvement in the war: he kept Hillgarth abreast of the mood in Francoist government circles, reassuring him that if Germany ever invaded Spain there would be a general uprising: 'There was not a Spaniard who would not wish to fight if the Germans came in,' he told Hillgarth.

Hillgarth poured money into the pockets of sympathetic officers. 'The Cavalry of St George have been charging,' noted Hugh Dalton, head of SOE and Minister for Economic Warfare. This was an oblique reference to the image of St George slaying the dragon on the British gold sovereign. In September 1941, the scheme hit a snag. The Swiss account in New York was locked, as part of the American freeze on European assets, but Hillgarth urgently needed reinforcements from St George's cavalry. 'We must not lose them now, after all we have spent – and gained,' wrote Churchill, who sent an urgent appeal, via Henry Morgenthau, the US Treasury Secretary, to Roosevelt, urging him to unfreeze the New York account. The sluice gates reopened. There is no documentary evidence that Roosevelt backed this campaign of corruption and subversion but, as the historian David Stafford notes, 'his approval can safely be assumed'.

The bribery scheme continued up to 1943, but whether the 'Cavalry of St George' achieved anything is open to question. Many Spanish officers were already disinclined to become entangled in the war and naturally opposed to the fascists, fearing that 'German victory would mean servitude for Spain, and an end to the individual freedom which is as necessary as air to most Spaniards'. Even Hillgarth acknowledged, with the sort of generalisation beloved of certain Englishmen, that 'the Spaniard is xenophobic and suspicious and wants to keep clear of other peoples' quarrels'. The money may simply have made the generals rich – and Juan March even richer – but it certainly reaffirmed Churchill's faith in his Madrid spymaster, and paymaster: 'I am finding Hillgarth a great prop,' he said.

Hillgarth possessed, by his own account, 'a natural sympathy' for Spain. 'Handling Spaniards is a special technique,' he wrote. 'Everything in Spain is on a personal basis.' He cultivated his contacts like an expert forester planting trees, propagating and nourishing them, metaphorically and literally, with large and lavish dinners. An intelligence officer, he once remarked, 'will be at a very definite disadvantage if he is a teetotaller. A good digestion is also important.' Charming, polished, and speaking perfect Spanish, Hillgarth moved effortlessly through the Madrid elite, making contacts with generals, admirals, diplomats, and foreign newspaper correspondents. 'Even during the worst of the war, I had little difficulty in maintaining old friendships and making new ones.'

Hillgarth could call in (or buy in) favours from every level of Spanish officialdom. But perhaps his most useful agent, whom he ran in tandem with MI6, was 'Agent Andros', a senior officer in the Spanish navy. Andros has never been identified. More than sixty years later, MI6 will not divulge the name of the 'very reliable and well-placed straight agent called ANDROS who obtained information of great value'. Andros would also demonstrate his value as a double agent. In 1943 he was approached in Madrid by a senior officer of the SD, the Sicherheitsdienst, the feared intelligence service of the SS, named Eugene Messig, who asked him 'to supply intelligence which he would send straight to Berlin (i.e. not through the German intelligence HQ in Madrid)'. The SD and the Abwehr were mutually suspicious rivals. 'C' was initially dubious, fearing that this 'might compromise a very valuable agent', but Hillgarth was keen to open a channel of disinformation into the SS. Andros accepted Messig's invitation, and began feeding him nuggets of false information, selected by Hillgarth: 'The items were so chosen that the Germans would be bound to draw the deductions that we wanted.' Andros, who also went by the codename 'Blind', proved a brilliant double agent, successfully passing on information indicating that the Spanish navy had learned, through its own sources, that U-boats were liable to attack from British planes and submarines in Spanish waters: 'Messig swallowed the stories whole, was extremely pleased, and continually pressed for more.'

In order to mislead Messig, Andros must have had genuine access to top-grade Spanish intelligence. 'It was a delicate job. However, Andros was in a particularly good position to inform Messig.' The admission that Andros was in 'a particularly good position' to misinform the Germans suggests that he may have been highly placed within Spanish naval intelligence. Whoever Andros was, Hillgarth trusted him completely.

The British and German spies circled one another, spitting like cats. Hillgarth knew that 'copies of all our telegrams were given to the Germans', and that his telephone was tapped: 'It seemed the listening in was done by an Abwehr member, but it might have been done by a Spanish telephone operator.' 'Only by naval ciphers can really safe messages be sent,' he reported.

One of the guards at the British Embassy was 'suborned by a woman in German pay', but was intercepted before he could do much damage. Even so, he knew that the Germans 'kept lists of everyone who went in and out of the British embassy'.

Hillgarth relished the contest – 'the Germans would have someone following him, and he would have someone following the Germans' – and found the constant surveillance, by both Spanish and German spies, quite amusing since these were usually 'very amateurish and inefficient'. Occasionally he would bump into Abwehr officers at official functions. 'Our deportment towards the German diplomats was to behave as if they did not exist. If we met them at a party, we ignored them. They did exactly the same to us.'

Madrid was the crucible of European espionage, and as the chief among the British spies, Hillgarth found himself fielding some odd customers from the intelligence world.

Dudley Wrangel Clarke was the master of 'A' Force, based in Cairo, the unit devoted to deception operations in the Mediterranean. As the intelligence officer in overall command of deception for Operation Husky, Clarke had been involved at every stage in the build-up to Operation Mincemeat. But Hillgarth had already come across him in a very different guise. In October 1941 he had bailed Dudley Clarke out of a Spanish jail. There was nothing so odd in that: Hillgarth was often bailing people out of jail. What made the occasion special, and acutely embarrassing, was Colonel Clarke's outfit: he was dressed as a woman. A Spanish police photograph shows this master of deception in high heels, lipstick, pearls, and a chic cloche hat, his hands, in long opera gloves, demurely folded on his lap. He was not supposed to even be in Spain, but in Egypt. In spite of the colonel's predicament, in the photo he seems thoroughly comfortable, even insouciant.

His fellow spy chiefs were not. Guy Liddell of MI5 noted: 'The circumstances of his release were to say the least of it peculiar. At the time he was dressed as a woman complete with brassiere, etc.' It is the 'brassiere etc.' that gives it away. What on earth was the blighter thinking of? A chap might go in disguise, if needed, but in a brassiere? The Spanish authorities seemed to find the incident equally amusing, and put out a propaganda leaflet announcing that a man named 'Wrangal Craker' who claimed to be *The Times*'s correspondent in Madrid had been arrested, dressed as a woman.

Having helped to get Clarke out of prison, Hillgarth obtained the photographs of his colleague, both in and out of drag, and gleefully sent them to Churchill's personal assistant, Charles 'Tommy' Thompson, who showed them to the Prime Minister. Hillgarth attached a deadpan note: 'Herewith some photographs of Mr Dudley Wrangel Clarke as he was when arrested and after he had been allowed to change.' The 'after' photograph showed Clarke in his more usual bow tie and jacket. 'PM has seen,' said a note scrawled on Hillgarth's letter. Sadly, history does not relate Churchill's reaction to what he had seen. Word of the photographs spread around Whitehall: some wondered whether Clarke was 'sound in mind', while the more sympathetic explanation was that 'he is just the type who imagines himself as the super secret service agent'. It did his career no long-term damage, but Dudley Clarke's strange episode of cross-dressing remains an enduring mystery.

By the spring of 1943, following the successful North African campaign, the danger than Spain might join the Axis had receded, and after more than three years of playing cat and mouse with the Germans, Hillgarth was keen to counterattack. In February 1943 he sent a letter to the Director of Naval Intelligence, declaring: 'It is time to pass from the defensive to the offensive. It is time to get tough.' Axis submarines were still using Spanish waters; Spanish fishing vessels were being used to spot U-boat targets; German and German-paid saboteurs were preying on British shipping, and the Spanish port authorities were supplying the Abwehr with 'more or less any naval intelligence they obtain'. All of this was in direct violation of

Spanish neutrality. Despite repeated British protests, Hillgarth pointed out, the Axis was 'allowed with little or no interference from the Spanish authorities, and in spite of constant British representations, to establish and maintain observation and reporting stations at vantage points along the Spanish coast'. Hillgarth specifically cited the activities of Adolf Clauss's older brother Luis in Huelva.

The solution Hillgarth proposed was simple and dramatic: 'I have found a good man prepared to stick a limpet bomb on one of the larger German ships from a fishing boat, on a dark night with rain.' The cost of the operation would be 50,000 pesetas, 5,000 before and 45,000 on completion. The bomb would be timed to go off after the enemy ship left harbour. The Foreign Office should not be involved. 'All operations are, if I may say so, better left to me,' wrote Hillgarth. 'If anything goes wrong there is a perfectly good comeback by referring to German sabotage in Spain, and I could always be disowned and officially sacrificed. I am happy to stand the rub, as I feel so strongly that the situation now warrants action of this kind.' All Hillgarth wanted was a nod of approval, and a bomb.

The request was turned down flat. If the Spaniards got wind that the British naval attaché was sticking limpet mines to boats, there would be a diplomatic explosion, possibly undoing all Hillgarth's good work to date. 'You and your staff have shown that you are quite able to take care of yourselves, but I am not prepared to take the chance of anything going wrong,' wrote Commodore Rushbrooke, the new Director of Naval Intelligence, adding that an attack on German shipping in Spanish waters was both 'undesirable and unnecessary'. Kim Philby, looking back, reckoned that a campaign of British sabotage would have sparked a 'James Bond style free-for-all in Spain'.

Hillgarth was deeply frustrated, itching to land a blow on his German adversaries, but held in check. The Cavalry of St George had disbanded. He was getting bored. At the very moment Hillgarth's sabotage plan was scuppered, Gómez-Beare reappeared in Madrid, fresh from his briefing on Operation Mincemeat and with new instructions for his boss: once the body was delivered by HMS *Seraph*, it would be up to Hillgarth to coordinate its reception in Spain, find out where and when it landed, and what happened to the documents, and maintain the essential fiction that a crucial batch of secrets had gone missing.

Hillgarth the naval novelist would now write the second chapter of Operation Mincemeat. He would take the role of hero; Gómez-Beare would play second lead; Adolf Clauss in Huelva would, with luck, act as the helpful receptionist.

And in Madrid, at the very centre of the web of German intelligence, was a man who might have been typecast as the leading villain of the piece.

12

The Spy Who Baked Cakes

The Abwehr's agents and informants in Spain came not as single spies, but in battalions; Spanish collaboration with the Germans, as one MI5 officer put it, was 'ubiquitous'. Of the 391 people employed in the German Embassy in Madrid, 220 were Abwehr officers, divided into sections for espionage, sabotage and counterespionage, deploying some 1,500 agents throughout Spain, many of them German émigrés. These, in turn, recruited their own subagents in a vast and sprawling network: 'All classes were represented from Cabinet Ministers to unnamed stewards of cargo ships', according to a wartime intelligence assessment. 'In the higher ranks there was undoubtedly a genuine ideological sympathy but at a lower level the transaction was mainly financial and in a country where so many live at starvation level, recruiting was fairly easy.' The quantity of intelligence pouring into the Abwehr's Madrid headquarters, which adjoined the embassy, was so enormous that it required thirty-four radio operators, ten secretaries (including Adolf Clauss's cousin, Elsa) and maintained a direct teletype link with Berlin, via Paris.

Thanks to one of his agents, a senior officer in the Dirección General de Seguridad, the Spanish security service, Alan Hillgarth knew the name, rank, role and in most cases the codename, of virtually every Abwehr agent of importance. At Hillgarth's behest, this agent had set up a special section to monitor German espionage. Ostensibly this was to ensure that the Spanish Ministry of the Interior was kept informed of covert German activities. 'Indeed, the reports went to the Ministry of the Interior,' wrote Hillgarth, 'but they also came to us.' This same informer provided Hillgarth with a complete list of Abwehr personnel in Spain, with 'particulars on each'. Menzies, the head of MI6, authorised Hillgarth to buy the list 'for a very large sum'. Back in London, Philby carped that the price paid by 'Armada' to this 'precious source' was 'very high indeed'; 'I had to fight to get an extra £5 a month for agents who produced regular, if less spectacular, intelligence!' he complained. But it was worth every peseta, providing British intelligence with a detailed picture of the Abwehr power structure in Spain: know thine enemy, and then work out how to deceive him.

At the head of the Abwehr station in Spain stood Wilhelm Leissner, honorary attaché at the German Embassy, who used the codenames 'Heidelberg' and 'Juan'. A small, soft-voiced figure and Condor Legion veteran, Leissner had stayed on in Spain, where he ran an import-export firm under the pseudonym Gustav Lenz. Beneath Leissner were Hans Gude, in charge of naval intelligence, Fritz Knappe-Ratey, an agent runner codenamed 'Federico', and George Helmut Lang, known as 'Emilio'. Since the autumn of 1942, the Abwehr's ranks in Spain had also included Major Fritz Baumann, a former policeman seconded by the German army to the sabotage branch of the Abwehr. Baumann was in charge of coordinating attacks on Allied shipping, but he was also an experienced pathologist who had studied forensic medicine at Hamburg Police Academy before the war. An expert in determining 'the cause of death and the extent of injuries', Baumann had 'examined hundreds of corpses' both before and during the war.

But the Abwehr officer who most intrigued Hillgarth was Major Karl-Erich Kuhlenthal. The MI5 file on this man is three inches thick; more was known about him than any other German spy in Spain. Kuhlenthal's father had been a distinguished soldier, rising to the rank of general and serving as Germany's military attaché in Paris and Madrid. The Kuhlenthal family was wealthy and well connected. Admiral Wilhelm Canaris, the head of the Abwehr, was a relative, which helped to explain Kuhlenthal's rapid rise through the ranks of the intelligence service. Like Clauss, Kuhlenthal had served in the Condor Legion, as secretary to Joachim Rohleder, the unit's chief of intelligence. After the civil war, he returned to Germany for a while, working for an uncle in the wine trade, and then for his father-in-law in the Dienz clothing firm. He travelled to London, Paris and Barcelona; he spoke good English and perfect Spanish. By 1938 he was back in Spain, ostensibly running a radio business while continuing his undercover work. At the outbreak of war, he was appointed adjutant general to Leissner, but soon distinguished himself by his raw ambition and drive.

In 1943, at the age of thirty-seven, Kuhlenthal was head of the Abwehr's espionage section in Madrid, coordinating political and military intelligence and operating under the codename 'Carlos' or, more usually, 'Felipe'. In the bars and cafés of Madrid, he was known as 'Don Pablo'. Kuhlenthal's spy network extended to every corner of the country, but his speciality was recruiting agents in neutral Spain to work overseas, in North Africa, Portugal, Gibraltar and, most importantly, Britain and America. In Britain alone, the so-called 'Felipe network' included dozens of undercover agents, sending back huge volumes of top-grade information. 'Nothing happened in the Abwehr station without him knowing about it,' said a fellow officer. Kuhlenthal cut a dandyish figure in the streets of Madrid. Tall and aristocratic, he wore his hair swept back, had 'fleshy, boneless cheeks', a 'curved hawk-like' nose and 'blue piercing eyes'. He wore elegant double-breasted suits, and drove 'a dark brown French four-seater coupé, using different number plates'. His fingernails were always 'carefully manicured'. He played tennis beautifully. MI5 assessed him as 'a very efficient, ambitious and dangerous man with an enormous capacity for work'. He was promoted, awarded the War Service Cross, and gradually 'contrived to push Leissner out of all positions of authority' until the nominal head of the Abwehr 'became a mere figurehead'.

By 1943, Kuhlenthal was in charge: 'He was an extremely able man and carried in his head all that went on in the office and became so essential that he became virtually the head of the office.' Inevitably, his Abwehr colleagues were envious of 'the esteem and reputation which Kuhlenthal seems to enjoy with the High Chiefs'. As the protégé of Canaris, he could do no wrong. A confidential file from 1943 described him as 'by far the best man in Group I [espionage] in Spain and very reliable from the political point of view'. Himmler himself 'sent a personal message of appreciation to Felipe in Madrid for the work achieved by his network in England'. In the eyes of the German high command, Kuhlenthal was the golden boy of the Madrid Abwehr.

The reality was rather different. So far from being a master spy, Kuhlenthal was a one-man espionage disaster area who had already fallen victim to one of the most elaborate hoaxes ever mounted. Instead of winning the spy war, Kuhlenthal was helping Germany to lose it in the most dramatic fashion.

In May 1941 a Spaniard named Juan Pujol García presented himself to the Abwehr in Madrid and explained that he intended to travel to Britain, and wished to spy for the Germans when he got there. Kuhlenthal was initially unenthusiastic, telling Pujol he was 'extremely busy and that his visit was inconvenient'. Pujol was bald, bearded, short-sighted and distinctly odd. But the Spaniard seemed to nurse a genuine hatred of the British, and a profound admiration for Hitler. He told Kuhlenthal he had good contacts within the Spanish security service and Foreign Office. Eventually, Kuhlenthal agreed to take him on. Pujol was instructed on writing in secret ink, and told to forward information through the Spanish military attaché in London. The Spaniard was sent off with a wad of English money, a number of cover addresses in Britain, and some advice from Kuhlenthal, who told his new recruit to be 'careful not to underestimate the

British as they were a formidable enemy'. Pujol could expect to stay in Britain indefinitely since this, Kuhlenthal predicted, 'would be a very long war'.

On 19 July, Kuhlenthal received a letter from Pujol, written in the secret ink, informing him that he had arrived safely in England, and had recruited a courier working for a civilian airline, who had agreed to carry his letters at £1 a time and post them in Lisbon, thus circumventing the British censor.

In fact, Pujol had not reached Britain and was still in Portugal: this was the first of a long and fantastic stream of lies he would feed to Kuhlenthal. Pujol was no Nazi-sympathiser. Born in 1912 to a liberal middle-class Catalan family, he had somehow contrived to fight for both sides in the Spanish Civil War, though he never fired a gun, deserted, and emerged with a ferocious hatred of fascism. By 1941 he had resolved to fight the war in his own way. Three times he approached the British authorities in Madrid, offering to spy for Britain. Repeatedly rejected, he offered himself instead to the Abwehr, intent on betraying them.

From Lisbon, Pujol began sending fictitious reports to the Germans, pretending to be in Britain. His information was culled from guide books and magazines borrowed at the public library, an old map of Britain, newsreels, a Portuguese publication entitled *The British Fleet* and a vocabulary of English military terms. Pujol had never set foot in Britain, and it showed. His reports were full of elementary mistakes. He could never get his head around the pre-decimal currency. He confidently asserted that: 'There are people in Glasgow who will do anything for a litre of wine', whereas most Glaswegians, at the time, would never have consented to drink wine, even if it had been served in litres.

Kuhlenthal, however, believed every word.

Meanwhile, Pujol's messages were being deciphered by Britain's codebreakers, to the consternation of MI5. Who was this German agent, operating undetected in Britain, who seemed to know nothing about the place?

Finally, early in 1942, after Pujol's wife approached the US legation in Lisbon, the self-made spy was identified and Allied intelligence realised, belatedly, that they had an espionage gem in their hands. Pujol was whisked to Britain, installed in a safehouse in Hendon, north London, and put to work as a double agent. His first codename, 'Bovril', was soon changed to the more respectful 'Garbo', in recognition of his astonishing acting talents.

Over the next three years, Agent Garbo sent 1,399 messages and 423 letters to his handlers in Spain. Three full-time MI5 case officers were needed to handle his traffic, and the twenty-seven fictional characters in the Garbo network. Garbo's subagents were British, Greek, American, South African, Portuguese, Venezuelan and Spanish; some were officials, such as his mole in the Spanish Ministry of Information, some were disgruntled soldiers or pilots, and at least five were seamen recruited from different ports around Britain. Other recruits included a commercial traveller, housewives, office workers, a wireless mechanic, and an Indian poet named Rags who was part of a strange Aryan organisation operating in Wales. Garbo's agents had nothing in common except for the fact that they did not exist. The information they sent to Madrid was a careful concoction of non-dangerous truths, half-truths and untruths, and Kuhlenthal happily passed it all on to Berlin, never once suspecting that he was being duped. 'We have absolute trust in you,' he told his star spy, massaging the ego of the agent whose success was ensuring his own rapid promotion: 'Your last efforts are all magnificent . . .'

Pujol's messages to his Nazi handler were flights of pompous poetry. He never used one word where eight, very long ones, would do, and he showered Kuhlenthal with a combination of flattery and Nazi bombast. 'My dear friend and comrade,' Pujol wrote in a typical effusion, 'we are two friends who share the same ideals and are fighting for the same ends. I have always had a very strong feeling of respect and admiration for your advice, full of good sense and calm . . . These things can only be dealt with between men of spirit and tenacity, and by people who follow a doctrine, by fighting men and bold combatants. The unfolding of confidences can only be made between comrades. Thus the great Germany has become what it is. Thus it has been able to deposit such great confidence in the man who governs it, knowing that he is not a democratic despot but a man of low birth who has only followed an ideal . . .'

For page after page, Garbo railed against 'the democratic-Jewish-Masonic ideology', urged the Germans to attack Britain ('England must be taken by arms, she must be fallen upon, destroyed, dominated . . .'), his letters peppered with Nazi jingoism: 'With a raised arm I end this letter with a pious remembrance for all our dead.'

Kuhlenthal swallowed the lot. 'His characteristic German lack of sense of humour, in such serious circumstances as these, blinded him to the absurdities of the story we were unfolding.' The Abwehr officer openly boasted of his talented spy, codenamed 'Arabel', who was sending top-secret information from the heart of Britain. When Canaris, the Abwehr chief, visited Spain, Kuhlenthal was 'the star turn', and amused his boss with one story in particular. In March 1943, Agent Arabel had obtained a valuable handbook on RAF planes, which he had wrapped inside greaseproof paper, and baked into a cake. On the top, in chocolate icing, he had inscribed: 'With good wishes to Odette'. Enclosed with the cake was a letter to make it seem that the gift came from a British seaman to a girlfriend in Lisbon. Kuhlenthal explained to Canaris that the cake had been dropped off at a safehouse in Lisbon, along with a covering note from Pujol which he read to his delighted audience: 'I did the lettering myself. I had to use several rationed products which I have given in a good cause . . . Good Appetite.' Kuhlenthal ended his performance with a lumbering joke, pointing out that although his agent 'made cakes which were unpleasant in taste, their contents were excellent'.

Canaris was impressed. Kuhlenthal's reputation went up another notch. (The cake, in fact, had been baked by Garbo's wife, sent to Lisbon by diplomatic bag, and dropped off by an MI6 agent. The RAF pamphlet was out of date, and British intelligence knew the Abwehr had it already.)

The high point of Garbo's career would come with the Allied invasion of Normandy in 1944. The deception plan covering the invasion was codenamed 'Fortitude'; its aim was to persuade the Nazis that instead of attacking Normandy, the main thrust would come in the Pas de Calais. To this end, a vast fake US army was 'assembled' in Kent, wireless traffic was confected, and hints were dropped to less than reliable 'neutral' diplomats. Many strands of deception were woven into Operation Fortitude, but none was more important than the double-agent system, and of these agents none was more vital than Garbo. From the safehouse in Crespigny Road, Hendon, Pujol fired off more than 500 radio messages between January 1944 and D-Day, a fantastic web of deceit from his posse of bogus 'agents', tiny elements in a jigsaw which would only make sense once completed by the Germans. The deception was astonishingly successful. Six weeks after D-Day, Pujol was awarded the Iron Cross by order of the Führer for 'extraordinary services' to the Third Reich. He was also appointed MBE, in secret.

By 1943, Karl-Erich Kuhlenthal, the star of the Madrid Abwehr, was eating out of Garbo's hand, and was voracious for more. A separate office was set up to handle the 'vast information' coming in, and running the 'Felipe network' had become his principal job: 'As a keen and efficient officer he did everything in his power to supply Garbo with ciphers, secret inks, and addresses of the highest grade to ensure his greater security. He was also forthcoming with considerable funds.' Through radio interceptions, the British watched with pleasure as Kuhlenthal grew steadily more dependent on Garbo, and his stock rose in Berlin. 'We had the satisfaction of knowing through MSS [Most Secret Sources, principally Ultra material] that all GARBO material was being given priority and that every military report which reached Madrid from the GARBO network was immediately retransmitted to Berlin.' Garbo's British handlers were amazed how readily Kuhlenthal believed 'the many incredible things we ask them to believe'. Indeed, 'the more sensational the reports, the more certain could we be of Madrid retransmitting them to headquarters'. Sometimes Kuhlenthal seemed to pass on Garbo's information without even reading, let alone questioning it. 'In some cases where messages appeared to be of extreme urgency they were retransmitted to Berlin with approximately one hour's delay in Madrid.' Through Garbo and Kuhlenthal, British intelligence was speaking directly to Berlin: 'Felipe had become our mouthpiece.' Here, then, was 'an invaluable channel through which we would be able to deceive the enemy'.

As they combed through Kuhlenthal's messages to Berlin, the British codebreakers noticed something rather odd. Garbo's intelligence was already sensational enough, but Kuhlenthal was spicing it up still further, to lend extra weight. He was not above inventing his own subagents, and adding them to the pot. Many of his elaborations were either wrong, or meaningless. He also made some hilarious mistakes, including his 'conviction that the Isle of Man is in the North of Ireland'. The added extras, MI5 concluded, were 'invented by Felipe himself'. Kuhlenthal was deceiving his Abwehr bosses, by passing on invented intelligence, along with the information he fervently believed to be true, which was not. 'The information provided by his organisation up to date has been either untrue, useless, or provided by MI5 through the double agents under its control.' Guy Liddell of MI5 considered Kuhlenthal to be 'one of the people who make up most of their information'. He may also have been embezzling. Some within the Abwehr certainly thought so. According to one intercepted message, Kuhlenthal was said to be running a very expensive agent in London, a Yugoslav diplomat, who had cost the Abwehr £400 over two years. 'There are officers in Spain who are convinced that K is making half-part business, i.e. splitting the monthly allowances between his and the Diplomat's pocket.'

There was one other factor that made Garbo's German spymaster ideally suited to receive the Mincemeat hoax: Karl-Erich Kuhlenthal was Jewish.

The Abwehr officer had a Jewish grandmother, though Kuhlenthal did not consider himself Jewish. Marriage to a half-Jewish woman had not impeded his father's military career. But that was before the rise of the Nazis. Under Hitler's brutal racial policies, the one quarter of Jewish blood in Kuhlenthal was enough to mark him out for discrimination, persecution, or worse. Kuhlenthal would later claim that anti-semitism had forced him to flee Germany, 'leaving a good job as manager of a large champagne and wine cellar owned by his uncle'. His brother, an army officer, had left Germany for the same reason, winding up in Chile. It was Canaris who had intervened on behalf of his relative (the Abwehr chief had a record of helping Jews), and arranged for him to take up the post in Spain, since 'he could not serve in the Army being a half-blood Jew'. In Madrid, he was farther from Gestapo persecution, though hardly safe.

In 1941, Canaris had his protégé 'Aryanised', and formally declared to be of good German stock. Leissner, the chief of the Abwehr station, confirmed that Kuhlenthal was now officially racially pure. In the minds of hard-line Nazis, however, either a person had Jewish blood, and was thereby corrupt and dangerous, or they did not. The attempt to tinker with Hitler's race laws provoked a rebuke from Berlin: 'He has been created an Aryan at the instigation of his station. A formulation of this nature is out of touch of all reality. Can JUAN [Leissner] state the legal foundation for such acts of state?' The Spanish branch of the SD, the SS intelligence organisation, also questioned how Kuhlenthal could simply be declared Aryan, 'since there appeared to be no authority for such an act'. Canaris again intervened, and the SD in Madrid was instructed 'to let the matter drop'. Kuhlenthal's colleagues in Spain knew of his Jewish ancestry, and the attempt to expunge it. For some, this was prima facie evidence of treachery. Major Helm, the head of counterespionage in Spain, sent a confidential report to Canaris accusing Kuhlenthal of being 'in the pay of the British Secret Service'. The Abwehr chief 'refused to take the report seriously'. Helm was transferred to another Abwehr station.

The British spies tracking Kuhlenthal had noted that he seemed 'cold and reserved', but also deeply uneasy. 'Appearance: nervous, uncertain. Peculiarity: shifty eyes,' read one surveillance report. Kuhlenthal had every reason to be anxious. His stock in Berlin was high, thanks to Pujol and the Felipe network, but if Canaris should fall from power or cease to defend him, or if something went wrong with his organisation, then his anti-semitic enemies would pounce. Kuhlenthal was deeply, and understandably, paranoid. Failure might well prove fatal. As one informer told British intelligence: 'Kuhlenthal is trembling to keep his position so as not to have to return to Germany and he is doing his utmost to please his superiors.'

Kuhlenthal had already fallen for the elaborate con trick that was Agent Garbo. He was the ideal target for Operation Mincemeat: deeply gullible, but admired and trusted by his bosses, including Himmler and Canaris; ambitious and determined, but also frantically eager to please, ready to pass on anything that might consolidate his reputation, and save him from the fate suffered by others of Jewish blood; he was also vain, possibly corrupt, and prepared to deceive those of higher rank to enhance his own standing. Kuhlenthal perfectly exemplified the qualities that John Godfrey had identified as the two most dangerous flaws in a spy: 'wishfulness' and 'yesmanship'. He would believe anything he was fed, and he would do whatever he could to suck up to the boss and preserve his own skin.

To succeed, Operation Mincemeat needed to reach Hitler himself. The best way of doing that, Alan Hillgarth knew, was to get the information to Adolf Clauss in Huelva, from whom it was certain to pass into the hands of Karl-Erich Kuhlenthal, and then, with the blessing of that favoured but gullible officer, up the German chain of command. Clauss was the perfect recipient, because he was such an efficient spy. Kuhlenthal was the ideal spy to pass the information on, because he was worse than useless.

13

Mincemeat Sets Sail

Leverton & Sons, undertakers and funeral directors, began making coffins in the St Pancras area of London around the time of the French Revolution. For two hundred years the business was passed from father to son, along with the severe and formal cast of countenance required of officials in the death business.

By 1943 the custodian of this long tradition, six generations on, was Ivor Leverton. His older brother Derrick was serving as a major with the Royal Artillery in North Africa, and about to take part in the invasion of Europe everyone knew was coming. Ivor had breathing difficulties and was declared medically unfit for military service, and therefore was left to run the family business. Although only twenty-nine, Ivor took the traditions of the firm very seriously, ensuring that all clients, rich or poor, were treated with the same solemnity and dignity. But beneath that decorous exterior, like most undertakers, Ivor Leverton was a man of unflappable temperament, and a bone-dry sense of humour. He felt a lingering guilt over being unable to fight on the front line. The closest he had come to seeing action was in 1941 when he went to collect a dead body from the Temperance Hospital in Euston and a Luftwaffe bomb came down the chimney, blasting shards of glass through his black 'Anthony Eden' hat. Ivor longed to play his part. He was only too pleased, therefore, to be asked to transport a body, in the middle of the night, in deadly secrecy, as a task of 'national importance'.

The request came from PC Glyndon May, an officer working for Bentley Purchase, the St Pancras coroner. Leverton & Sons did regular business with the coroner, but had never been presented with a job quite like this. 'I was not to divulge what I was told, under the Official Secrets Act, not even to my own family,' Ivor wrote in his diary. 'No record would be made, and we would not be paid a penny.' May's request arrived on April Fool's Day, and for a moment Ivor Leverton wondered whether the 'phone call from St Pancras Coroner's Court might be dismissed as a hoax'. But Constable May was entirely serious: Ivor should get a coffin, and take it to the mortuary behind the coroner's office, where May would meet him at 1.00 a.m. on the morning of Saturday, 17 April. He should act entirely alone, and carry the coffin himself. 'I was still in fairly good shape,' grumbled Ivor, 'but this was really asking a bit much.'

Soon after midnight, Ivor Leverton tiptoed downstairs from the flat above the funeral parlour in Eversholt Street, taking care not to wake his wife, and retrieved a hearse from the company garage in Crawley Mews. He then drove to the front of the parlour, and manhandled one of the firm's wood and zinc-lined 'removal coffins' into the back, hoping Pat, their most inquisitive neighbour, would not wake up and spot him wrestling with a heavy coffin in the dark. Glyn May was waiting at the coroner's court. Together, with some difficulty, they heaved the body into the coffin. The dead man was wearing a khaki military uniform, but no shoes. Leverton was struck by his height. Leverton & Sons' standard coffins measured six foot two inside, but the dead man 'must have stood six foot four inches tall' and could not be made to lie flat. 'By adjustment to the knees and setting the very large feet at an angle, we were just able to manage.'

After an uneventful drive through the deserted city streets to Hackney, Leverton helped May unload the coffin, 'left our passenger' in one of the mortuary refrigerators, and returned home. His wife, pregnant with one of the next generation of Leverton undertakers, was still asleep.

Hackney had been selected by Bentley Purchase because it was run by 'a mortuary-keeper on whom he could rely not to talk'. Later that day, at six in the evening, Purchase met Cholmondeley and Montagu at the mortuary, with Glyn May. The body of Glyndwr Michael was removed from the refrigerator and placed on a mortuary gurney. Nearly three months had now elapsed since Michael's death, and during the long period of refrigeration his eyes had sunk into their sockets; the skin was yellow from the poison-induced jaundice, otherwise the body appeared to be in a reasonable state of preservation. A 'Mae West' military life jacket was put over his head and tied around his waist (Mae West being rhyming slang for 'breasts': when fully inflated, the rubber jacket gave the wearer a distinctly busty look – reminiscent, if you happened to be a sex-starved soldier, of the curvaceous film star). The chain was looped around his shoulder, outside the coat and under the Mae West, and securely tied to the belt of the trench coat. It had been assumed that the briefcase would be given to Lieutenant Jewell to clip to the chain at the last moment, but it was found that the canister could accommodate both case and body. The handle of the case was fastened to the end of the chain, and the case placed on top of the body. Jewell would now only have to insert the documents and tip the body into the water, thus ensuring it would arrive on shore in a way that 'made it as easy as possible for the Spaniards or the Germans to remove the bag and chain without trace'. The watch, with the winder run down, was set to 2.59, and fastened to the left wrist: with luck, the Germans should assume that the watch had stopped when the imagined Catalina crashed into the sea.

All Major Martin now needed to complete his outfit was footwear. But getting him into his boots proved to be the most difficult aspect of the entire dressing operation. In the extra-cold refrigerator, the feet had frozen solid, with the ankles at right angles to the leg. Even when the laces were fully undone, the boots refused to go on. Bentley Purchase came up with a solution. 'I've got it,' said the coroner. 'We'll get an electric fire and thaw out the feet only. As soon as the boots are on we'll pop him back in the refrigerator again and refreeze him.'

PC May went to fetch the single-bar electric heater from the lodge of the coroner's office. There then followed a truly macabre scene, as Montagu attempted to defrost the dead man's feet, and Cholmondeley tried to lever on the boots. Finally, the ankles defrosted sufficiently, and the boots went on, followed by gaiters. Thawing and refreezing was certain to hasten decomposition, but with the gaiters securely buckled, his feet would probably not fall off. It was, said Montagu with feeling, 'the least pleasant part of our work'.

Major Martin's wallet, containing the letters from Pam and Father, were slipped into his inside breast pocket. His remaining pockets were filled with all the 'litter' that made up a complete personality: pencil, loose change, keys and, in an inspired last-minute addition, two ticket stubs for *Strike A New Note*, a variety show at the Prince of Wales Theatre starring the music-hall comedian Sid Field. This was another of Cholmondeley's brainwaves. HMS *Seraph* would depart from Holy Loch on Monday, 19 April, and take ten or eleven days to reach Huelva. The Germans, however, needed to be persuaded that the body had washed up after no more than a week at sea, following an air crash. If the body was found on, say, 28 April, then there must be something in his pockets indicating that he was still in London on 24 April. This was where Sid Field could play his part. Cholmondeley purchased four tickets for his new show at the Prince of Wales Theatre on 22 April, tore off the dated counterfoils of the two in the middle, and put them in the pocket of Major Martin's trench coat. 'We decided Bill Martin and Pam should have a farewell party before he left.' This would be their last evening together, before the young officer headed to North Africa, and certain death. The stubs would offer incontrovertible 'proof' that the only way he could have reached Spain by the 28th was by aircraft.

Close examination of the letters and pocket litter would offer a detailed itinerary of Major Martin's last, poignant days in London:

18 April – Check in to the Naval and Military Club
19 April – Receive bill from S. J. Phillips of New Bond Street for diamond ring
21 April – Lunch with Father and Gwatkin, the solicitor, at the Carlton Grill; Pam attends dance with Jock and Hazel
22 April – To the theatre with Pam, followed by a nightclub
24 April – Check out of Naval and Military Club, pay bill in cash (£1. 10s); collect letters from Combined Operations HQ and War Office; board flight to Gibraltar; 1459 hours, crash in the Gulf of Cadiz.

The body was photographed twice on the mortuary gurney. Only the torso of the man holding the trolley is visible, but this was almost certainly PC May, the coroner's officer. The mouth of the corpse has fallen open. The skin around the nose has sunk, and the upper part of the face is discoloured. The fingers of the left hand are bent, as if clawing in pain. These are the only known pictures of Glyndwr Michael, a man whom no one bothered to photograph when he was alive.

The already visible decomposition of the face raised another potential complication. The body would now have to be driven 400 miles to Scotland, then loaded into a cramped submarine and taken on a ten-day sea voyage

SECRETARY'S OFFICE.
TEL. NO. GROSVENOR 2103.

94, PICCADILLY.
W. 1.

24th April 1943

Major W. Martin
Temporary Member

DR. TO NAVAL & MILITARY CLUB

1943
Bedroom 18th to 23rd April
6 nights @ 5/- £ 1 10

Received the sum of One pound ten shillings
(£1.10.0)
24/4/1943

PAID
Cash
24/4/43

The National Archives

that might encounter rough weather. If the canister was jolted about, the face would surely suffer further damage from chafing against the sides of the canister. Again, Bentley Purchase came up with a solution: 'Get an army blanket. Wrap the face and neck in it, and there will be no friction.' The body was rolled up in a blanket, and 'lightly tied with tape'. Following Bernard Spilsbury's instructions, 21lb of dry ice had already been placed in the canister to expel the oxygen. The body was now 'reverently' inserted into the homemade carrying case, and packed around with more dry ice before the lid was screwed tightly in place. The body now needed to get to Scotland, fast.

Waiting in the Hackney mortuary car park was a Fordson BBE van, with two seats in front, fitted with a customised V8 engine. At the wheel was a small man with a neat moustache, wearing civilian clothes. His name was St John 'Jock' Horsfall, an MI5 chauffeur who also happened to be one of the most famous racing drivers in the country.

St John Ratcliffe Stewart Horsfall, born in 1910 into a family of car fanatics, acquired his first Aston Martin at the age of twenty-three. Between 1933 and the outbreak of war, he won trophy after trophy on the racing circuit, including the Dunlop Outer Circuit Handicap at over 100 mph. Horsfall was short-sighted and astigmatic, but declined to use spectacles. He seldom wore racing leathers or a crash helmet, preferring to race in 'a shirt and tie, with either a bomber jacket or a sleeveless sweater'. He drove at staggering speed, and suffered a number of serious accidents, including a trial run at Brooklands when his car 'went berserk [and] tried to hurl itself over the top of the banking'. On another occasion, the throttle stuck open, forcing the engine up to 10,000 rpm until the clutch exploded, sending 'potentially lethal pieces of metal' bursting through the bell housing at his feet.

At the start of the war Horsfall had been recruited into the Security Service by Eric Holt-Wilson, the deputy director of MI5, who had employed the racing driver's mother as a staff car driver during the First World War. Horsfall's primary job was driving MI5 and MI6 officers and agents, double agents, and captured enemy spies from one place to another, very fast. He was also involved in testing the security of naval sites and airfields, and privy to a good deal of highly classified information.

Horsfall knew only that he was to transport to the west of Scotland a canister containing a dead body, which would be used to play a humiliating trick on the Germans. Horsfall was fond of practical jokes. He once wired up a loo seat to a battery and waited for a girlfriend to use it. 'The scream that Kath gave when the magneto was turned on was most satisfying.' He even wrote a poem to commemorate the occasion.

I gave her time to start her piddle
Then gave the thing a violent twiddle
Before I could complete a turn
She closed the circuit with her stern,
And shooting off the wooden seat
Emitted a most piercing shriek.

Though the idea of carrying a dead body through the night in order to bamboozle the Germans appealed strongly to Jock Horsfall's sense of humour, he never told anyone of this, perhaps the most significant drive of his life. Reckless behind the wheel, outside a motorised vehicle Jock Horsfall was discretion personified. MI5 had a fleet of cars and vans, but for this operation Horsfall had selected one of his own, a six-year-old 30cwt Fordson van, customised to accommodate an Aston Martin in the back, with a souped-up engine in which 'he claimed to have done 100 mph in the Mall'. It was past midnight when Ewen Montagu, Charles Cholmondeley and Jock Horsfall loaded the canister into the back.

The trio paused for a brief pit stop at Cholmondeley's mews flat off the Cromwell Road, where they ate a light meal, with 'one of us sitting in the window to make sure that no one stole Major Martin from the van (even if he was not worth much to the thief, he was valuable to us)'. It was, Cholmondeley later said, the first time he had ever 'had supper with a corpse parked in his garage'. Cholmondeley's sister, Victoria, prepared some cheese sandwiches and a vacuum flask of hot tea, and at around two in the morning, the party set off, heading north. Jewell had requested that the additional passenger be brought aboard HMS *Seraph* no later than midday on 18 April. Horsfall was racing against the clock, his second favourite occupation.

Operation Mincemeat almost came to a premature and embarrassing end before they had left London. On passing a local cinema, where a spy film was showing, Jock Horsfall remarked on the 'much better story' they were currently engaged in, became paralysed with giggles, and nearly drove into a tram stop. A little later, the myopic racing driver failed to see a roundabout until too late and shot over the grass circle in the middle. This is what driving with Jock Horsfall was like; an experience rendered yet more alarming by the need to drive with masked headlights during the blackout. Luckily there were few other cars about. Montagu and Cholmondeley took it in turns to lie in the back and try to sleep. This was the closest either came to death in action during the war.

South of the village of Langbank, on the road between Glasgow and Greenock along the west side of the River Clyde, they stopped to stretch, and eat Dottie's sandwiches. In the pallid dawn light of the Highlands, they posed for photographs beside the van. Jock Horsfall climbed into the back, and was photographed drinking a cup of tea perched on the canister.

At Greenock Dock a launch waited to meet them. With the help of half a dozen seamen and some rope, the 400lb canister was carefully lowered into the boat, followed by the dinghy and the oars. It took only a few minutes to motor to HMS *Forth*, the depot ship with the submarine lying alongside. The officers of the ship were 'partially "in the know"', but the arrival of the canister provoked no suspicion or comment among the crew, 'being accepted as merely being a more than usually urgent and breakable FOS shipment'. Montagu and Cholmondeley were greeted warmly by Jewell, who gave orders for the special shipment to be lowered on to the submarine the following morning, along with a large supply of gin, sherry and whisky he was transporting to refresh the 8th Flotilla in Algiers. This cargo was also kept secret from the crew.

Jewell now received his final instructions from Montagu and Cholmondeley, and a large buff envelope containing the documents. This would be securely stashed in the submarine safe until the body was ready to be launched. In the ship's log, the operation was referred to as '191435B', the code number of Jewell's secret operational orders. At the last moment, Montagu decided to keep one of the dinghy oars as a souvenir. If the forty-four-man crew of the *Seraph* thought it strange to be taking on a dinghy with only one oar, no one said so.

After three months in the imaginary company of Bill Martin, Montagu and Cholmondeley headed for home. There was something oddly touching in the leave-taking. 'By this time Major Martin had become a completely living person to us,' wrote Montagu, who would never have come across a man like Glyndwr Michael in his normal life. The fictional creation had taken on a form of reality. 'We felt that we knew him just as one knows one's best friend . . . we had come to feel that we had known Bill Martin from his early childhood and were taking a genuine and personal interest in the progress of his courtship and financial troubles.'

Montagu wrote in excitement to Iris, relaying his 'news such as can be written': 'I had to go up to Scotland last weekend. It was great fun as I and another couple had to drive up in a lorry. It was a lovely moonlit night, so wasn't too bad even with wartime headlights and it was quite like old times to go for a long drive. I had two days on board a ship (stationary . . . I haven't been to sea yet!!). It was great fun as they were a grand lot on board. When I got back things were very hectic as I had to button up the job I had been on.'

On board the *Seraph*, First Lieutenant David Scott, second-in-command, was instructed by Jewell to take extra care when bringing aboard the canister marked 'Optical Instruments'. 'I was to see that this package was treated with every precaution to ensure that it was not bumped while being embarked through the torpedo loading hatch.' One torpedo was left behind, to make room for the canister in the reload rack. Like most wartime submarines, the *Seraph* did not have enough bunks to accommodate all the crew, and so they took turns to sleep in the forward torpedo room. For the next ten days, they would be sleeping alongside Bill Martin.

At 1600 hours on 19 April, HMS *Seraph* slipped her moorings, and sailed out of Holy Loch into the Clyde. Montagu sent word to the Admiralty that Operation Mincemeat was underway. 'It was a real thrill,' he reflected. Yet the excitement was tinged with real anxiety. 'Would it work?'

The *Seraph* ploughed towards the sea in the gloaming. 'Spring was on the way,' wrote Scott, 'but there was little sign of it in the wooded slopes of the hills on our port side. To starboard lay Dunoon, its outlines softened by a light mist and the smoke from wood and coal fires rising from the chimneys of its dour, grey houses.' Out in the broad Clyde, the *Seraph* linked up with her escort, a minesweeper, whose principal task was to ward off possible attacks from British aircraft, which tended to assume submarines were hostile unless there was clear evidence otherwise.

Abreast of the Isle of Arran, the *Seraph* performed a 'trim dive' to ensure that the submarine was correctly balanced, and then headed into the Irish Sea. South of the Scilly Isles, the minesweeper departed, having taken aboard a canvas bag of the crew's last letters. 'A final exchange of "Good Luck" signals passed by light and we headed out into the Atlantic swell, diving shortly afterwards.' The *Seraph* was alone. The weather was fine, and with only a light sea running, the ship settled into the strange, half-lit world of a long submarine journey, compounded in equal parts of boredom, anticipation and fear. By day, the submarine would travel submerged; at night she would resurface and continue by diesel, to recharge her batteries, and then dive again as dawn broke. If they were not attacked or otherwise diverted, covering 130 miles a day, the passage to Huelva should take ten days.

It was stuffy below decks. The crew and officers were on watch for two hours, and then off for four, twenty-four hours a day, seven days a week. 'Monotony never really set in, because at the back of our minds was the determination to survive, which demanded constant alertness.' By wartime standards, the food on the *Seraph* was excellent and plentiful. 'We were never short of meat, butter, sugar or eggs. We even had luxuries like chocolate biscuits and honey . . . we were lucky enough to have a chef who could bake good bread.' No one shaved, and everyone slept in their clothes. A few days out of Holy Loch, and the smell of unwashed bodies and engine oil suffused the ship.

Lieutenant Scott lay on his bunk, attempting to read *War and Peace*, and trying not to think about death. He admired Jewell, considering him the 'epitome of what a submarine captain should be: quite fearless, he was invariably cool and calculating'. Yet however brave and astute his commanding officer, Scott knew that he was quite likely to die before his twenty-third birthday. 'At that time, the chances of returning home from a Mediterranean-based submarine were 50/50.' Before joining the *Seraph,* Scott had spent a week in London. On the last day of his leave, his Uncle Jack and recently widowed mother took him to lunch in an expensive restaurant. When the time came to say goodbye, both mother and uncle had tears in their eyes. 'I realised with a bit of a shock that they were thinking they might not see me again.'

A few feet away, in his own bunk, the commander of the *Seraph*, Lieutenant Jewell, was not thinking about death. Indeed, in more than three years of the most ferocious submarine combat and several irregular and exceptionally dangerous missions, the thought of dying seems never to have crossed his mind.

Jewell had been born in the Seychelles, where his father, a doctor, was in the Colonial Service. He volunteered for submarine work in 1936. The war was already two years old when the young lieutenant qualified for command of the newly launched *Seraph*, an S-class submarine. Shortly after taking command, Jewell fell down the hatch. In 1946, a doctor pointed out that Jewell had broken two vertebrae: he fought the entire war with a broken neck.

His first patrol, in July 1942, had set the pattern for what followed: extreme danger, a narrow escape, and a certain amount of farce. The *Seraph* was fired on by an RAF plane, but escaped serious damage. Then, in the waters off Norway, Jewell spotted a U-boat, and blew it to pieces with a single torpedo. The *Seraph*'s first kill turned out to be a whale.

In October 1942, during the run-up to Operation Torch, the invasion of North Africa, Bill Jewell was given his first secret mission: transporting the American General Mark Clark, Eisenhower's deputy, to the Algerian coast, for secret negotiations with the French commanders there. The invasion, led by General Patton, was already underway, and the neutrality of the Vichy forces in French Algeria was considered critical if it was to succeed. Many Vichy officers were deeply hostile to the British following the sinking of much of the French fleet at Mers-el-Kebir. Clark faced an extremely delicate situation. Jewell had the equally tricky task of getting him ashore without being spotted. On 19 October, the *Seraph* and her American passengers arrived at the designated spot, a remote coastal villa some fifty miles west of Algiers. Soon after midnight, Jewell brought the submarine to within 500 yards of the shore, and the American negotiating party disembarked in four collapsible canoes, accompanied by a protection squad of three British Marines of the Special Boat Service, led by Roger 'Jumbo' Courtney, a former big-game hunter with a 'bashed-in sort of face and a blunt no-nonsense manner'.

The all-night negotiations went well, but at one point the visitors were forced to hide in a dusty cellar to avoid an impromptu visit from the gendarmes. Courtney suffered a coughing fit, which threatened to give them away. General Clark passed the choking commando some chewing gum.

'Your American gum has so little taste,' whispered Courtney, once the spasm subsided.

'Yes,' said Clark. 'I've already used it.'

When the time came to pick up the party, Jewell brought the *Seraph* perilously close to shore, until she was almost aground. Clark appears to have been betrayed, and moments ahead of a French raiding party, the general and his party dashed for the boats, paddled through the surf, and scrambled aboard the *Seraph*. Jewell gave the order to turn tail, and then dive. Sir Andrew Cunningham, the addressee of one of the Mincemeat letters and Royal Navy commander-in-chief in the Mediterranean, described the joint Anglo-American adventure as 'a happy augury for the future'.

Jewell's unflappability had marked him out for secret work, and his next assignment was even stranger: to pick up, from the south coast of France, General Henri Honoré Giraud. A charismatic, self-important, and popular veteran of the Great War, the sixty-three-year-old French general was seen as the only officer able to deliver French North African forces to the Allies. Giraud was hiding out with the French resistance after escaping from the Germans. Allied command decided that Giraud could be an important figurehead to galvanise Vichy opposition to the Germans, if he could be safely collected. The mission was codenamed 'Operation Kingpin'. The only problem was that the crusty general, like De Gaulle, was said to entertain a hearty loathing for the British, and had insisted that if he were to be rescued, the Americans must do it. The *Seraph*, therefore, would briefly have to adopt a new nationality. An American captain, Jerauld Wright, was placed in nominal command.

Flying the Stars and Stripes, the *Seraph* duly waited off Le Lavandou, until Jewell spotted the light signals from the shore, and sent a boat to pick up Giraud. The French general managed to miss his footing while transferring to the submarine, and was hauled aboard dripping wet. To maintain the charade, the crew of the *Seraph* had attempted to adopt American accents, and spent the rest of the voyage imitating Clark Gable and Jimmy Stewart. General Giraud, it turned out, spoke English, and was not remotely fooled. But he was far too proud to acknowledge the trick.

In the wake of the North African invasion, the *Seraph* roamed the Mediterranean, conducting more traditional submarine operations, and attacking any and every enemy vessel. In the space of a few weeks, she sank four cargo ships destined to supply Rommel's army, and disabled an Italian destroyer. Back in Algiers harbour, the piratical Jewell raised the Jolly Roger. Late in December 1942, the *Seraph* was assigned to another secret mission: the reconnaissance of the Mediterranean island of Galita, eighty miles north of the African coast. The island was occupied by German and Italian troops and was used as a lookout post to monitor the movements of Allied ships. Jewell's mission – codenamed 'Operation Peashooter' – was to reconnoitre the island in secret, and establish whether it could be successfully attacked by a commando force led by an American, Colonel William Orlando Darby of the US Rangers. On 17 December, Jewell had set off for Galita, with Bill Darby as his passenger.

The two Bills struck up an immediate friendship, which was hardly surprising, since Darby was, in Jewell's words, 'a two-fisted fighting man', with a taste for danger that matched Jewell's own. The 1st Ranger Battalion, an elite and highly trained assault force (the counterpart to the Royal Marine Commandos) had been formed under Darby's leadership in 1942. They had already distinguished themselves in North Africa by their courage and devotion to their leader: 'We'll fight an army on a dare, we'll follow Darby anywhere . . .' At thirty-one-years old, 'El Darbo', as his troops called him, gave the impression of having been hewn out of Arkansas granite: three times in his career, he spurned promotion in order to stay at the head of his troops, a varied crew that included a jazz trumpeter, a hotel detective, a gambler and several toughened coalminers. At Arzew in North Africa, Darby had led the 1st Ranger Battalion into battle, hurling hand grenades in the face of heavy machine-gun fire, 'always conspicuously at the head of his troops'.

On the way to Galita, Darby regaled Jewell and his crew with ribald stories. For two days, the *Seraph* prowled around the island charting possible landing spots, while the American took photographs. 'I think we can do it,' declared Darby. Eventually, it was ruled that no troops could be spared for the assault on Galita, and Operation Peashooter was called off, but not before Darby got a taste of Jewell's methods. All friendly forces had been cleared from the operational area, and Jewell's orders invited him to 'sink on sight any vessel'. On the way back to Algiers, Jewell rammed one U-boat underwater, and attacked another with three torpedoes, one of which failed to detonate on impact while the other two veered off target owing to the damage sustained in the earlier collision. Even the unshakable Darby found the experience of underwater combat alarming, telling Jewell: 'Put me ashore, give me a gun and there isn't anyone or anything I won't face. But, gee, Bill, I haven't been so scared in my life as in the last two days.'

The *Seraph* had sustained serious damage to her bows, and her crew was suffering from the 'constant strain', as became apparent when two former friends fell out and 'one grabbed a large, evil-looking carving knife from the galley and tried to stab the other in the back'. The *Seraph* was ordered to return home for rest, recuperation and repairs. On the return journey, the submarine was attacked, once again, by a flight of Allied bombers.

The repairs at Blyth dockyard had reset the submarine's 'broken nose', giving the *Seraph* 'a lithe, graceful look'. A cartoon of Ferdinand the Bull had been painted on her conning tower – a reference to the children's story about the bull who shunned the bullring, and a nickname reflecting the fact that *Seraph* spent more time on special missions than operational patrols.

As the *Seraph* made towards Huelva, Jewell was itching for another scrap, but knew he must avoid contact with the enemy if possible. 'We were told that we were not going to be required to attack anything, as this was more important.' The RAF had issued strict instructions to aircraft not to attack any submarines on the route, and naval intelligence confirmed that there were no known enemy vessels in the Gulf of Cadiz. But then, west of Brest, about midway through the voyage, the submariners heard a noise they all knew, and dreaded: 'The unmistakable sounds of a submarine being depth-charged.' Somewhere, very close at hand, a duel was underway. 'We knew that at least one of our boats was in the vicinity,' wrote Lieutenant Scott, 'and as each series of explosions hit our pressure hull like a hammer, despite the distance, we feared for the safety of our friends.' Jewell had his orders, and the *Seraph* continued south. Scott returned to *War and Peace*.

At the precise moment Bill Jewell was uncharacteristically turning his back on a fight, Ewen Montagu and Jean Leslie were in London preparing to go out to the theatre and dinner, for the last time, as Bill Martin and his fiancée Pam.

14

Bill's Farewell

Ewen Montagu had been planning 'Bill Martin's Farewell Party' for some time, but did not tell Jean Leslie until the afternoon of 22 April. He sent a note from 'Bill' inviting 'Pam' to see the variety star Sid Field in *Strike A New Note* at the Prince of Wales Theatre, to be followed by dinner at the Gargoyle Club. The MI5 secretary was thrilled by the invitation from her office admirer: 'I rushed home, changed out of office clothes, and threw on some makeup.' Cholmondeley had bought four tickets for the evening performance – that way they could demonstrate that the tickets had been bought in a block, even though the counterfoils of the two in the middle were missing, and already en route to Spain in the dead man's pocket. Wasting the tickets, Montagu later wrote, would have been 'absurd'. Besides, it was an ideal opportunity to continue the courtship of his imaginary fiancée. Charles Cholmondeley's date for the evening was Avril Gordon, another young secretary in the office who had helped Hester Leggett compose 'Pam's' letters. Both women were 'in the loop' on Operation Mincemeat, although ignorant of its details.

Montagu remained firmly in character. The death of Bill Martin, presumed drowned at sea following an air crash, would shortly be announced, but in the meantime Montagu composed a personal tribute to him, to be published in *The Times* in due course. The ruse would have to be maintained and reinforced long after Mincemeat had landed.

The notice described the life of a deskbound literary genius who had insisted on fulfilling his patriotic duty, only to die tragically.

> Bill Martin's death 'on active service' came as a complete surprise to many of his friends when it was announced in your columns. Few of them knew that he had for some time been serving with the Commandos where hitherto unsuspected qualities had been revealed.
>
> Martin was a unique personality and his loss is tragic. An ever-growing number of his more discerning contemporaries were convinced that he had genius. He made little mark at school where he was more interested in his own reading and music than in the normal work and athletics of his friends. After a university career during which he impressed with his literary talents and qualities of leadership a small circle of dons and college friends, he retired into the country to farm, fish and write.
>
> On the outbreak of war, Martin, who had already been profoundly stirred by the growing menace to all that he loved most deeply, hastened to offer his services to his country. He found himself placed in an office job, and although it was an important one and well suited to his talents, the determined, if unorthodox, efforts which he made to escape and prepare himself for more active and dangerous work, were ultimately successful.
>
> As to others of an imaginative and artistic temperament, Martin's experiences with the Commandos had brought a new meaning into life, an immense stimulus to creative activity. He had refused, until the war was over, to publish any of his work. We will therefore have to wait some time before a wider public can appreciate his rare talent.

The fake obituary was never published, but it gives a fascinating insight into the spymaster's level of emotional involvement.

The two couples made an attractive sight as they entered the Prince of Wales Theatre, the men in full uniform, the women in their best dresses and heels. Montagu handed the tickets to an usherette. 'We were terribly agitated when she tore the tickets,' said Jean. 'Would she notice that two were missing?' She did, and summoned the manager, who accepted that the middle counterfoils had been torn off 'as a joke'.

The lights dimmed, and the four settled into the plush seats of the circle to watch Sid Field open his new show. A veteran performer, Field had toured the provincial music halls for thirty years, singing, dancing and performing comic skits. He had recently broken into the big time, playing the part of 'Slasher Green', a cockney spiv. *Strike A New Note* was his first West End appearance, and he was supported by a group of young theatrical hopefuls 'gathered from every part of the country', performing together as 'George Black and the Rising Generation'. Black, a theatrical impresario, is today as obscure in public memory as Sid Field, but some of the rising generation rose very high indeed. Among the cast were two unknowns, Eric Morecambe and Ernie Wise, aged sixteen and seventeen respectively.

Strike A New Note had opened to rave reviews a month earlier: *The Times* hailed Field as 'definitely "a find"'; the *Daily Mail* noted 'the loudest laughter we have heard in years'; the *Daily Telegraph* was gratified that 'all his jokes are clean'. By April the show was playing to packed houses. Sid danced, told jokes, performed sketches and sang:

I'm going to get pickled when they light up Piccadilly,
I'm going to get pickled like I've never been before.

In fact, Sid was already well pickled, since he never went on stage without 'an adequate ration of gin'. *Strike A New Note* was tailor-made escapism for wartime theatregoers. Many in the audience were American GIs, and the satires on Anglo-

American relations raised the loudest cheers. The war seemed impossibly distant, even irrelevant. A note on the back of the programme read: 'If an Air Raid Warning should be received during the performance the audience will be informed. Those desiring to leave the theatre may do so, but the performance will continue.' The show ended with Sid's fan song:

When you feel unhappy
And if you're looking blue
We recommend
Sid Field to you.

Even the cast seemed a little bemused by the rapturous audience reception. Jerry Desmonde, Sid Field's straight-man sidekick, wrote: 'The laughs came like the waves of a rough sea, breaking on a shingle beach, and when they came they lasted. They lasted a long, long time.'

Eight hundred miles away, far out at sea, Lieutenant Scott stood on the deck of the *Seraph*, listening to the waves breaking, and peered through the darkness towards the coast of Portugal. 'The weather was warm at last, and it was a delight to keep a watch on the bridge at night beneath a cloudless sky.'

Submarine crews develop a sixth sense for the peculiar. Long periods spent underwater, in close proximity with little to do, when the faintest noise or smallest mistake can mean death, render submariners acutely sensitive to anything out of the ordinary. Bill Jewell firmly believed he was the only person aboard with an inkling of the additional passenger, but at least some members of the crew suspected that the strange tubular canister in the forward torpedo room did not contain optical or meteorological instruments. It was a telltale length, and oddly heavy. When the submarine lurched, a faint sloshing noise could be heard inside. Crewmen began joking about 'John Brown's Body' mouldering in the torpedo rack, and 'our pal Charlie the weatherman coming for a ride'. Jewell himself had no idea of the identity of the body, real or fictional. In his mind he, too, had begun to refer to his passenger as 'Charlie'.

Jean Leslie left the theatre on Montagu's arm, high with excitement, her ears ringing with the applause. Bill Martin's farewell party continued at the Gargoyle, the raffish rooftop club above Meard Street in Soho. Founded in 1925, the Gargoyle was the haunt of artists, writers and actors, the epitome of decadent glamour. It could only be reached by a tiny, rickety lift, the dimensions of which 'were such that strangers entering it left as intimate friends at the top'. The interior was decorated in Moorish style, the walls adorned with mirrored shards of eighteenth-century glass inspired by Henri Matisse, who was a member, as were Noël Coward, Augustus John and Tallulah Bankhead. Spies, including Guy Burgess and Donald Maclean, were drawn to its dark corners and air of secret assignation. The Gargoyle was half-lit, avant-garde, and slightly louche. The film-maker Michael Luke described the atmosphere inside this den as 'mystery suffused with a tender eroticism'. Jean Leslie had never been anywhere like this before. Her mother would have been scandalised.

It was a 'very cheerful evening', Montagu recalled. It was also distinctly flirtatious. The foursome was shown to a corner table, with a banquette and two chairs. Montagu suggested that the women sit together on the banquette. Getting into the dramatic spirit, Avril Gordon remarked playfully: 'Considering Bill and Pam are engaged, they are the least affectionate couple I know. They don't even want to sit together at his farewell party before he goes abroad.' An American couple eavesdropping at the next table looked round sharply. Warming to his own role, and sensing they were being overheard, Montagu replied that he had only known Pam for a few days before getting engaged to her. 'It would be different if Pam and I knew one another better,' he said loudly. 'My boss has said in a letter that although I am quiet and shy at first, I really do know my stuff' – a reference to Mountbatten's fake letter to Admiral Cunningham, in which he used these words to describe Major Martin. It was also a deliberate double entendre.

The couple looked daggers at this naval officer, engaged to a young woman on such brief acquaintance, and now joking about his own romantic prowess. The man was clearly a cad. Registering strong disapproval, they got up to dance. Still, if they did not like that sort of suggestive conversation, they should not have come to the Gargoyle Club. The foursome spent the evening drinking and dancing. Cholmondeley proposed a toast 'to Bill', and they clinked glasses. The men were relaxed and plainly enjoying themselves, but Jean sensed an undercurrent of tension. 'They kept looking at their watches and saying things like: "I wonder if he's afloat now."' She noticed that Ewen Montagu seemed anxious, as if his life was about to change.

The next morning, Montagu wrote to Iris as usual, in a tone of forced indifference: 'I had to go and take someone officially to the theatre. We went to see a new comedian who has been a lot in the North but hadn't been in London before. He was called Sid Field and is frightfully funny. A thoroughly good evening.'

In a few days, the engagement of Pam and Bill would come to its predestined end, and so would the strange parallel bond between a naval officer and his secretary. Montagu, who had been so 'smitten' in the early days of the fantasy, was never quite as flirtatious after the farewell dinner. Lady Swaythling's report to Montagu's wife about the suspicious signed photograph on his dressing table had had its intended effect. The letter from Iris demanding an explanation has not survived, but it is not hard to imagine what was in it. Montagu asked a colleague, who happened to be passing through New York, to visit his wife and clarify matters on his behalf. Iris seems to have accepted his explanation. 'I am glad that Verel told you about my doings,' he wrote. 'I was more nervous of what you might think about the photo and its compromising inscription than what Mother might think!!!' 'Pam' and 'The Girl from the Elms' disappeared from Montagu's life. But nearly half a century later, he was still writing to Jean as 'Pam', and signing himself 'Bill'.

As the *Seraph* neared the drop point, the anxiety levels in Room 13 rose steadily. 'We were all very excited, but also worried, and we couldn't tell anyone outside the room what was happening,' Pat Trehearne recalled. Any number of things might go wrong, and the stakes could hardly have been higher.

Operation Barclay was to be, in Clarke's words, 'the peak of the deception effort in the Mediterranean'. Although never formally integrated into Operation Barclay, the Mincemeat plan was a key element in the expanding operation to deceive the Germans into believing that the next blow would fall simultaneously in Sardinia and Greece, as a prelude to a major campaign in the Balkans. To keep as many German troops as possible away from Sicily and the Central Mediterranean, the plans devised by Johnnie Bevan in London and Dudley Clarke of 'A' Force now encompassed double agents, Greek partisans, false rumours and the imaginary British 12th Army, poised to invade the Balkans.

The host assembled at Cyrenaica in Libya, within range of German reconnaissance planes, consisted of dummy landing craft, dummy gliders and dummy tanks, as well as real anti-aircraft batteries and fighters to be scrambled at the first sign of enemy aircraft, reinforcing the lie. A genuine sabotage operation was planned to concentrate German attention on Greece. Hints of an impending Greek invasion were dropped at diplomatic dinner parties in neutral countries, in the hope that these would filter back to Germany. Greek troops underwent amphibious training in Egypt, calls for Greek speakers were sent out, and Greek drachmas were bought on the Cairo foreign exchange. 'One patriotic Greek managed to remain with a British unit and was no doubt amazed to find himself landing in Sicily instead of his homeland.' Leaflets were distributed on 'hygiene in the Balkans'. Similar, though less intensive, efforts were made to indicate an impending assault on Sardinia at the other end of the Mediterranean: fishermen in Algeria were quizzed on their knowledge of Sardinian waters.

At the same time, preparations for the real invasion of Sicily were progressing swiftly, with troops assembling at North African ports. If Mincemeat and Barclay worked, then the Germans would see those preparations as elements of Brimstone, the fake plan for attacking Sardinia, and the supposed attacks on Greece. The airfields in Sicily would have to be bombed, since, in Montagu's words, 'no major operation could be launched, maintained, or supplied until the enemy airfields and other bases in Sicily had been neutralised'. If the plan succeeded, the bombing would be seen as supporting action for the invasions in the eastern and western Mediterranean, and not as a prelude to what they were: a full-scale assault on Sicily itself. Various false dates for an imminent invasion were spread through numerous channels, and then 'postponed'. The false dates were selected to coincide with the darkest lunar periods. That way, it was hoped, the enemy might assume a dark night was the only time to fear an attack, and relax its guard when the moon was high.

Operation Mincemeat was just one cog in the deception machine, but it was a pivotal one. If it failed, then all the other elements of the deception might be revealed as part of an enormous fraud, allowing the Germans to reinforce Sicily and see the preparations for invading Greece as the sham they were. As Montagu had warned at the outset, 'if they should suspect that the papers are a "plant" it might have far-reaching consequences of great magnitude'. The responsibility weighed heavily on Montagu's shoulders. 'I had to carry the can (and have it on my conscience) if anything happened to *Seraph*.'

There would be no second chance. John Godfrey, the former boss of Naval Intelligence, had always insisted that deception was a dish best served piping hot: 'Intelligence, like food, soon gets stale, smelly, cold, soggy and indigestible, and when it has gone bad does more harm than good. If it ever gets into one of these revolting conditions, do not try to warm it up. Withdraw the offending morsel, and start again.' Once Mincemeat went bad, it would have to be discarded. Jewell was under no illusions: the smallest hitch, and the operation would be aborted, the body taken to Gibraltar, and the documents handed to the Staff Officer (Intelligence) 'with instructions to burn the contents unopened'. Contingency plans were also laid in case matters went awry after the body was launched.

On 22 April, a coded message was sent to the senior intelligence officer in Gibraltar: 'Operation known as Mincemeat repeat Mincemeat has been mounted . . . If body is sent to Gibraltar with documents in despatch case please advise Robertson MI5 immediately and give opinion whether such documents have or have not been tampered with. If such documents come into your hands they are to be sent complete with seals intact by direct weighted air bag addressed Colonel Robertson MI5.'

On the evening of 28 April, the *Seraph* rounded Cape St Vincent, and headed for Huelva. Jewell summoned his officers to the wardroom. Seated around the table, in addition to Jewell and his second-in-command, David Scott, were Lieutenants Dickie Sutton, John Davis and Ralph Norris. Taking a large envelope from the safe, Jewell proceeded to describe the gist of Operation Mincemeat. As Scott remarked, the contents of the canister came as 'something of a shock'. What seemed to upset him most was the thought that 'sailors had been sleeping alongside it, possibly using part of it as a pillow'. The officers nodded and asked no questions. After dropping off a genial American general in one part of the Mediterranean, picking up a grumpy French one in another, blowing up a whale and becoming, briefly, an American submarine, their new mission was just about par for the course. Jewell stressed 'the vital need for absolute secrecy'. Submariners are notoriously superstitious. When Jewell was out of earshot, one of the officers remarked: 'Isn't it pretty unlucky carting dead bodies around?'

At dawn the next day, just off Punta Umbria, Jewell gave the order to dive. For the next few hours, he and Scott carried out 'a close-range reconnaissance of the beach, making sure we knew every landmark'. The place seemed all but deserted, with just a handful of fishing huts and a few boats drawn up on the sand. This mission, Scott reflected, wrongly, was going to be 'easy, even enjoyable'. The only impediment was a strong offshore wind. Their orders were clear: 'The operation had to be carried out as near as we could manage to the time of low water' with 'an onshore wind, or no wind at all'. Jewell decided to wait.

'The next day turned out to be ideal,' Scott wrote. 'The wind was light and Southerly and the sky overcast.' The *Seraph* withdrew twelve miles off the coast, to recharge her batteries, and waited for low tide and complete darkness. In London, the Admiralty requested the Air Ministry to 'arrange total bombing restrictions' in the area. Naval Intelligence reported: 'No known defensive dangers' near Huelva.

At 0100 hours on 30 April, the submerged submarine stealthily approached the shore once more. Two hours later, the *Seraph* reached the prearranged spot, 148 degrees off Portil Pilar, and some eight cables, a little under one mile, from the beach. 'We were just about to surface,' Jewell described, 'when the fishing fleet went over the top of us, going out to collect sardines.' Waiting until the boats were well clear, the *Seraph* surfaced and Jewell surveyed the area with his binoculars. 'A large number of small fishing boats were working in the bay. The closest about a mile off' – too far, he calculated, to be able to spot the dark submarine. The sky was overcast with low clouds and patchy visibility, and the wind was picking up.

The crew had been told that the officers were 'landing some pseudo-secret instruments on the beach in order to try to trap a German agent known to be operating in the vicinity of Huelva, and that we hoped enough evidence against him could be gathered to result in his expulsion from neutral Spain'. Three of the ratings hauled the canister through the torpedo hatch, which would usually only be opened in harbour. The metal tube was laid on the forecasing, and the crewmen ordered to return below. Scott manned the bridge, while Lieutenant Norris acted as lookout. Lieutenants Sutton and Davis set to work, unscrewing the bolts in the canister lid. Scott ran the echo sounder, which showed almost two fathoms of water beneath the keel. 'We crept in a little closer to the beach.'

Major Martin was lifted out of the steel tube at 0415 hours. There was, as Jewell put it with his usual understatement, 'some little stink'.

Perhaps through oxygen trapped in the dead man's uniform and blanket, decomposition had accelerated during the passage from Scotland. Several of the officers recoiled. They had seen the worst of wartime underwater combat, but as Jewell observed, 'I doubt if any of them had seen a dead body at that time.' Jewell himself was sublimely unconcerned. 'I had seen bodies before. My father was a doctor, a surgeon. My brothers were doctors. I wasn't that worried by it.' Jewell's official report described the extent of the decay: 'The blanket was opened up and the body examined. The briefcase was found to be securely attached. The face was heavily tanned and the whole of the lower half from the eyes down covered with mould. The skin had started to break away on the nose and cheek bones. The body was very high.'

Working quickly, Jewell inflated the Mae West, transferred the documents from envelope to briefcase, locked it, and placed the keys in the pocket of the corpse. He then selected the identity card picturing Ronnie Reed, and added that to the pocket. Up on the bridge, Lieutenant Scott was becoming steadily more anxious. It was now 0430, and a glimmer of dawn light was spreading over the water. More worryingly, the wind was strengthening and the submarine was drifting closer to the shore. 'We seemed to be practically on the beach.' The *Seraph*'s draft was 6.4 metres. The depth at low water in her current position was just 4.5 metres. The tide was almost out, and the submarine was very nearly aground.

Bill Jewell straightened, took off his officer's cap and, bending his head, briefly recited 'what I could remember of the funeral service' – a fragment of the 39th Psalm. The choice was oddly appropriate, given the extreme secrecy of their mission: 'I will keep my mouth as if it were with a bridle: while the ungodly is in my sight. Held my tongue, and spake nothing: I kept silence, yea, even from good words; but it was pain and grief to me.'

The three officers then picked up the body, and gently slipped it into the sea. Jewell turned to Scott on the bridge and gave the thumbs-up sign. 'With some relief', Scott jammed the submarine full speed astern. 'The wash of the screws helped Major Martin on his way.' As the submarine headed seawards, Scott could just make out the grey shape, drifting towards the shore. In the official report on the operation, Jewell was praised for steering so close to the beach, even though the submarine had almost grounded: 'He virtually assured success by approaching as close inshore as he did.'

A half-mile south, the partially inflated rubber dinghy and oar were thrown overboard, while the officers stuffed the blankets, tapes, and dinghy packaging inside the canister. Still on the surface, powered by the quieter electric motor, Scott steered the submarine into deep, open water. Twelve miles out, the *Seraph* stopped for the last time, and the canister was thrown overboard. The seafloor here was 200 fathoms down. The canister would never be found. If, that is, it could be made to sink. Charles Fraser-Smith had made Major Martin's capsule too well. 'Because it had been designed to keep the ice from melting, it had pockets of air all the way around it.' The double skin acted as an inbuilt buoyancy tank.

A Vickers gun was brought up from below, and the canister was 'riddled by fire'. Still it would not go down and, worse, it was drifting towards the shore. Jewell then handed Scott a .455 service revolver, and instructed him to stand on the foreplanes, while he manoeuvred the submarine until the canister was directly below him. 'He did this with his usual skill, and I fired all six shots into the top of the canister.' Still the steel tube bobbed defiantly on the surface. It was, Jewell reflected, 'a hell of a time', and time was now running out. 'Daylight was fast approaching, and we could see some fishing boats not far off.' Jewell opted for radical measures. The steel tube, now resembling a large colander with some 200 bullet holes in it, was hauled back on to the casing, and packed with plastic explosive, inside and out. The fuse was lit, the canister lowered overboard, and the submarine hastened to get out of the way. The resulting explosion was exceptionally loud. In Jewell's laconic epitaph: 'It then disappeared, finally.' Jewell was relieved, but he knew he had taken a risk. His orders were to sink the canister in one piece, not to blow it to smithereens. Fragments of the casing, or even bits of blanket and tape, might now wash ashore. Perhaps these would be assumed to be debris from the downed aircraft, but not necessarily. Moreover, even if the Spanish fishermen in the bay had not spotted the submarine setting off the explosion, they would surely have seen the flash and heard the sound echoing through the still dawn. In his final report, Jewell made no mention of having to explode the canister, merely observing that after being shot full of holes, 'it was seen to sink'. Indeed, he did not tell anyone how the canister had been blown to shreds until 1991, when he was seventy-seven years old.

'We dived and set course for Gibraltar,' wrote Scott. 'Breakfast tasted wonderful, and so was the deep sleep into which I fell immediately afterwards.'

At 0715 hours, Lieutenant Bill Jewell of HMS *Seraph* sent a wireless message to the Admiralty in London: 'Mincemeat Completed.' Back on land in Gibraltar, Jewell scribbled a postcard, which he posted to Montagu: 'Parcel delivered safely.'

15

Dulce et Decorum

All morning the body lay in the dunes, beneath the pines, where the fisherman José Antonio Rey María had carried it. As the sun rose, the sand grew hotter, and the smell grew worse. A series of important visitors came to look at the dead man.

The officer in command of the 1st Company of the 2nd Battalion of the 72nd Infantry Regiment (in charge of coastal defence around Huelva), who had been drilling his men on the beach before the body was brought ashore, sent word to the police at Punta Umbria. The police duly informed the port authority at Huelva that a drowned soldier had washed up on the beach at La Bota. The case therefore came under the military jurisdiction of the port. In late morning, the rotund figure of navy lieutenant Mariano Pascual del Pobil Bensusan, second in command of the port and acting military judge, appeared at the beach in a canoe, paddled by two Spanish seamen. Lieutenant Pascual del Pobil was sweating profusely, very hot, and he wanted his lunch. With some distaste, he made a cursory examination of the body, noting the military uniform, and the briefcase with the crest 'G VI R and the royal crown' attached to the dead man by a chain 'which had penetrated the muscles of the neck as a result of the swelling'. He also extracted the wallet, and noted down Major Martin's name from his identity card. Pascual del Pobil then unclipped the locked case from its chain, ordered that the body be taken to Huelva, and climbed back into his boat, taking the case with him. He did not think to look in the dead man's pocket for a key. The next to arrive, on foot, was a local doctor, José Pablo Vázquez Pérez, who came to certify that the body was really dead. The stench wafting from under the pines suggested this was not strictly necessary.

There was no road to the dock at Punta Umbria, merely a sandy track winding five miles through the dunes. The body was loaded on to a donkey, which set off, led by a child, through the sweet afternoon scent of wild rosemary and jacaranda. The two infantrymen followed behind. In the late afternoon, the grim little procession arrived at the infantry headquarters by the dock, too late to arrange transport of the body across the estuary mouth. The corpse was placed in an outhouse, ready to be taken over to Huelva in the morning.

Lieutenant Pascual del Pobil had by now sent word to the British consulate that a dead British soldier, found on La Bota beach, would be arriving by motor launch at Huelva dock the next morning. Francis Haselden was profoundly relieved. For the last forty-eight hours the British vice consul had been waiting anxiously, unaware that the delivery of the body had been delayed by the weather.

Gómez-Beare had left Haselden with very specific instructions: as soon as he received word that the body had come ashore, the vice consul 'should telephone him at Madrid and inform him of the finding of the body, its particulars, etc.'. Gómez-Beare would then verbally instruct Haselden to arrange the burial while he notified London. A few days later, 'when a signal from London might be expected to have reached him', Gómez-Beare would call again to ask if anything had washed ashore with the body. The assistant naval attaché 'would say that he could not talk on the 'phone but would come down to Huelva. He would then do so and make discreet inquiries whether any bag or paper had been washed ashore.' Gómez-Beare knew that the telephones at the Madrid embassy were bugged. It was likely that Adolf Clauss also had spies inside the consulate, and that anything said on the telephone there would be reported back to the Germans. At the same time, Alan Hillgarth in Madrid would send cables to Huelva backing up the story, again in the knowledge that these would be intercepted at source, and relayed to Karl-Erich Kuhlenthal and his colleagues at Abwehr headquarters in Madrid. The entire performance was for German benefit: London, and the embassy in Madrid, should appear to be increasingly agitated about the loss of top-secret documents. Parallel to these 'breakable' messages, Hillgarth would despatch 'a separate series in his personal cipher, keeping London in the picture of what was going on'.

Haselden must play the part of a harassed official under mounting pressure from his bosses to trace a missing briefcase. The role required nuance. Haselden would have to make inquiries, with increasing urgency, for the missing papers, but he must not do so too 'energetically', as this might lead to the documents actually being returned before they reached the Germans. In that case, Operation Mincemeat would have failed.

Here lay an additional, but crucial, consideration. The British *did* want to get the documents back, intact, once the Germans had had a good look at them. Under international law, as a neutral country, Spain was obliged to return any property belonging to a British national who had died in Spain. The precedent of Lieutenant Turner suggested that the briefcase would, eventually, be returned by the Spaniards. But in reality if top-secret plans really had fallen into enemy hands, and the breach of security was detected, then those plans might well be abandoned, or at least substantially altered. The Germans must be made to believe that they had gained access to the documents undetected; they should be made to assume that the British believed the Spaniards had returned the documents unopened, and unread. Operation Mincemeat would only work if the Germans could be fooled into believing that the British had been fooled. All of this would require the most careful stage management.

Francis Haselden was not an actor. Nor was he a spy, novelist or fly fisherman. He did not even particularly want to be a vice consul, but had inherited the post after the sudden death of his predecessor in 1940. He was a gentle, civilised, sixty-two-year-old mining engineer and businessman, who had settled in Huelva two decades earlier, and might reasonably have expected to spend the rest of his life playing golf and running his mine supplies company, a pillar of the community in a small and sunny British outpost. War had made a new man of Haselden: he now ran an underground network helping escaped prisoners of war, harboured downed Allied pilots, monitored the nefarious doings of Adolf Clauss and his agents, and did everything he could to help the Allied secret services respond in kind. In most parts of Spain, Franco was content simply to monitor the espionage battle between the Germans and the British, and leave the two sides to get on with it. But in Huelva the civilian governor, Joaquín Miranda González, was a keen member of the fascist Falange, strongly pro-German, and keen to help his friend Clauss root out British spies. To Haselden's annoyance, three members of Huelva's British community had already been expelled on suspicion of spying, including Montagu Brown, the head of a local railway company. Here, then, was Haselden's opportunity to strike back at Clauss and his Spanish allies, by playing – but not overplaying – the part of a worthy functionary looking after the interests of a dead British officer. He rose to the occasion magnificently.

Emilio Morales Candela, Huelva's undertaker, was waiting at the jetty when the ferry from Punta Umbria pulled in the following morning, carrying a handful of passengers and one dead body. Beside him stood Francis Haselden, who had asked Candela to transport the body to the cemetery. The vice consul had also, as instructed, made the first telephone call to Gómez-Beare in Madrid informing him that a dead British soldier had washed ashore. The body was lifted into a wooden coffin, and loaded on to the horse-drawn cart provided by 'La Magdalena' funeral services of Huelva (it would be another decade before the town had its own motorised hearse). Pulled by an ancient horse and steered by Candela, the square wooden funeral carriage, locally known as the 'Soup Bowl' (La Sopera), set off up the hill towards the cemetery, with Haselden following in his car. The route to Nuestra Señora de la Soledad cemetery led through the area of Huelva known as Concepción, little more than a cluster of fishing huts surrounding the ancient Torre de Vigilancia, one of the circular brick watch towers built in the sixteenth century to spot pirates.

News spreads fast in a small town, and word that a dead British soldier had been found at La Bota travelled well ahead of the slow-moving cortège. A small knot of people gathered outside the Church of Nuestra Señora de Lourdes to watch it pass. Several made the sign of the cross. The priest, Father José Manuel Romero Bernal, muttered a prayer. The carriage continued through the centre of the town, and past the Teatro Mora, which was showing *Pygmalion* starring Leslie Howard. The sun was already baking.

The cemetery of Nuestra Señora de la Soledad sits on a small hill just outside Huelva, a high-walled compound surrounded by fields of sunflowers. Alongside it is the much smaller British cemetery, in which members of the Protestant German community, in a strange alliance of religion in defiance of politics, were also interred. The horse was sweating by the time the lumbering funeral carriage reached the cemetery. Waiting at the gates were Lieutenant Pascual del Pobil, the naval judge, with the briefcase under one arm. Alongside him stood Dr Eduardo Fernández del Torno, and his son, Dr Eduardo Fernández Contioso, who would together carry out an autopsy. The final member of the reception committee was a young American pilot called Willie Watkins.

Three days before the body was brought ashore, an American P-39 Airacobra plane crash-landed in a field in Punta Umbria. The pilot was Watkins, a twenty-six-year-old from Corpus Christi, Texas, who had been flying from North Africa to Portugal when his plane ran out of fuel. Unable to open the cockpit cover, Watkins had come down with his plane, escaping with only minor injuries. He had been taken into custody by the infantry detachment guarding the coast, briefly lodged at the Hotel La Granadina in Huelva, and then transferred to the home of Francis Haselden, the refuge of all Allied soldiers since there was no American consulate in Huelva. Lieutenant Pascual del Pobil had requested that the American pilot be brought to the cemetery in case the dead body and the downed plane were connected in some way, and Watkins might be able to identify the body.

The coffin was carried to the small building on the edge of the cemetery that served as a morgue. Glyndwr Michael's body was lifted out, and placed on the raised marble slab. Methodically, the mortuary attendant went through the pockets, extracted the contents, and laid them out on the table: cash, sodden cigarettes, matches, keys, receipts, identity card, wallet, stamps, and theatre ticket counterfoils. Pascual del Pobil barely glanced at these. Lunch was already beckoning. Haselden did his best to seem uninterested. The Spanish officer now turned his attention to the briefcase, which he unlocked with one of the dead man's keys. The contents were soaked, but the writing on the envelopes was still clearly legible. Pascual del Pobil carefully 'examined the names on the envelopes', and motioned Haselden over to look. Haselden had been told only the outline of Operation Mincemeat. But from the red seals and embossed envelopes, these were clearly confidential military letters. Pascual del Pobil also seems to have registered their importance, for he now did exactly what Montagu and Cholmondeley had hoped would not happen. He gestured towards the case, and asked Haselden if he would like to take it. Since these items would have to be returned to the British eventually, would the vice consul like to take custody now? Pascual del Pobil liked the English vice consul;

he believed he was doing Haselden a favour; and he wanted his lunch and siesta.

Haselden knew he had to 'react swiftly'. Indeed, he had mentally prepared himself for the possibility that Pascual del Pobil would cut corners, and simply hand over the briefcase. With as much nonchalance as he could muster, he said: 'Well, your superior might not like that, so perhaps you should deliver it to him, and then bring it back to me, following the official route.' Pascual del Pobil shrugged, and closed the briefcase.

Willie Watkins had observed this exchange. Although he spoke little Spanish, it was clear what was going on. Haselden's 'attitude, in refusing the briefcase, struck him as odd'. The American pilot was now beckoned over by Pascual del Pobil, and asked if he could identify the dead man. Needless to say, he could not, and said so. The dead man's lifebelt, he pointed out, was 'of an English pattern, whereas he himself had flown an American plane, which carried a completely different type of lifebelt'. Pascual del Pobil stated the obvious: 'There are clearly two completely unconnected accidents.'

Packing up the briefcase, wallet, and other possessions, the naval judge explained that these would be formally handed over to his commanding officer, the naval commander of the port of Huelva. The tubby Spanish officer departed, taking the case and other items with him. Haselden casually announced that he would stay to watch the autopsy. If it seemed odd to Watkins that the British vice consul should decline the offer of the briefcase, it was surely even odder that he should choose to remain in a broiling hut with a tin roof while two Spanish doctors cut up a half-rotted corpse. The American pilot was only too happy to escape the foetid room with its stench of death, and smoke a cigarette in the shade of the willow tree outside.

The autopsy would usually have been carried out by a military pathologist, but since he was away, the task fell to Dr Fernández, the civilian forensic pathologist, and his son Eduardo, a recent medical graduate. Contrary to Spilsbury's dismissive remark about the poor state of Spanish forensic expertise, Fernández was a good and experienced pathologist. A native of Seville, he had studied medicine at Seville University, and then spent many years working as the company doctor for a large mining concern. Since 1921 he had been senior pathologist for the Huelva area. Fernández may not have been in Spilsbury's forensic league, but he had a wide practical knowledge of dead bodies in general and, given his coastal location, of drowning victims in particular.

Haselden later described the autopsy. 'On the first incision being made, there was a minor explosion, for while the body externally was in good preservation, the inside had deteriorated badly.' The lungs were filled with fluid, but given the state of decomposition and without further tests, Dr Fernández would have been unable to say whether this was sea water. He examined the ears and hair of the corpse, and its strangely discoloured skin. Haselden knew nothing of the real circumstances surrounding the body, but he knew enough of the plot to realise that the more detailed the autopsy, the more likely it was that the pathologist would find some clue to the real cause of death. The British vice consul was friendly with the Spanish doctor. The stench of putrefaction in the room was now almost overwhelming. With what was later described as 'remarkable presence of mind', he decided to intervene. 'Since it was obvious the heat had done its worst,' he said, there was no need for a detailed autopsy. 'On receiving this assurance from the VC that he was quite satisfied, the doctor, not without relief perhaps, agreed to call it a day and issued the necessary certificate.'

The postmortem verdict was straightforward: 'The young British officer fell in the water while still alive, showed no evidence of bruising, and drowned through asphyxia caused by submersion. The body had been in the water between eight and ten days.'

The body was returned to its plain wooden coffin, and formally transferred into the care of the British vice consul.

Fernández had missed the telltale discolouration of the skin, indicating phosphorus poisoning. He made only a cursory examination of the lungs, and took no samples from the lungs, liver or kidneys for testing. Yet there were other aspects of the case that troubled him. The doctor had examined hundreds of drowned fishermen over the years. In every case, there was evidence of 'nibbling and bites by fish and crabs on the earlobes and other fleshy parts'. The ears of the British officer were untouched. On bodies that have been in sea water for more than a week, the hair on the head becomes dull and brittle. 'The shininess of the hair did not correspond to the time which he had supposedly spent in the water', and there was also, in Fernández's mind, some 'doubt over the nature of the liquid in the man's lungs'. Privately, Fernández also noted something peculiar about the clothing. The man's uniform was waterlogged, but it had not attained the shapeless, soggy form of clothing that has been in sea water for a week. 'He seemed very well dressed to be in the water for so many days,' the doctor reflected. The two doctors had also compared the photograph on the identity card with the dead man, but concluded that these were 'identical'. Yet even here, there was room for doubt, for the father and son medical team noted 'that a bald patch on the temples was more pronounced than in the photograph'. The William Martin in the photograph had a thick head of hair, but the one on the mortuary slab was thinning on top. Fernández concluded that 'either the photograph was taken some two or three years ago or the baldness on the temples was due to the action of sea water'. This was an odd conclusion: sea water has many effects on the human body, but male-pattern baldness is not one of them.

It is impossible to know how many of Fernández's doubts found their way into his final report: the autopsy was passed to the port authority, filed in the archives by Pascual del Pobil, and then destroyed in a fire in 1976.

There was one additional, far more glaring inconsistency, which Fernández did spot, although he did not realise its significance. The degree of decomposition, according to Fernández, indicated that the body had been at sea for a minimum of eight days, or possibly longer. According to the evidence in Major Martin's pocket, he flew from London late on 24 April; and the body was retrieved in the early hours of 30 April. The decayed state of the body was simply inconsistent with a body submerged in cold sea water for only a little over five days. Fernández, of course, was unaware of the supposed timing of Major Martin's death. That evidence was contained in his wallet, which was now in the possession of Captain Francisco Elvira Alvárez, commander of the port of Huelva and, as it happened, the best friend of Ludwig Clauss, Huelva's elderly German consul.

At 8.30 that evening, Francis Haselden sent a cable to assistant naval attaché Don Gómez-Beare in Madrid: 'With reference to my phone message today, body is identified as Major W. Martin R. M. identity card 148228 dated 2nd Feb. 1943 Cardiff. Naval judge has taken possession of all papers. Death due to drowning probably 8 to 10 days at sea. I am having funeral Sunday noon.'

Normally, in such circumstances, the naval attaché would have sent a message to the Admiralty in London, with the name and rank of the dead man. In this case, no such Royal Marines officer existed, and if the cable was distributed through normal channels someone in London might well spot the anomaly. Hillgarth had arranged that just before he was ready to send the telegram reporting the death of Major Martin, he would send a separate message, in code, to 'C' at MI6, 'so that the action for suppressing it could be taken'. The plan went wrong. The message to 'C' duly arrived, but by the time MI6 got around to acting on it, the signal from Hillgarth had already begun to be distributed to various Admiralty departments: one of these might well be conversant with the names of Royal Marines officers, and start making embarrassing enquiries. A flurry of telephone calls to the heads of the departments that had received the message ordered 'the suppression of the signal on the excuse that the individual in question was not a naval officer, but had, with the authority of the First Sea Lord, been given the cover of rank in the Royal Marines when he was setting out on a secret and very special mission abroad . . . the secrecy of his task rendered it necessary that the signal should be suppressed and no action taken on it'. In a way, the excuse was true.

Haselden's message was addressed to 'Sadok', Gómez-Beare's cable name, but its intended recipient was Adolf Clauss, the senior Abwehr officer in Huelva and the man identified by Montagu as the 'super-super-efficient agent' most likely to intercept the documents. Clauss was living up to his billing, for he was already fully aware that the body of a British officer carrying letters had washed up in his bailiwick. It may have been Lieutenant Pascual del Pobil himself who told the German agent about the body and its accompanying briefcase, or the harbour master, or the mortuary attendant, or even Dr Fernández, who had conducted the autopsy. Whoever it was, by the time the British vice consul informed Madrid that the papers had arrived, Clauss had already mobilised his extensive spy network to intercept them.

This was proving rather difficult, for the briefcase and its contents had fallen, from the point of view of both the British and the Germans, into the wrong hands. Had the case simply been handed over to the Huelva police, as the British intended, then Clauss would have obtained it within hours. The same thing would have happened had the documents ended up in the possession of Huelva's civilian governor, the harbour master, or the army authorities, for these, too, were in the pay of Clauss. Instead, the Spanish navy had them, and this was an altogether trickier nut for German espionage to crack. Montagu himself later admitted that the fact that the documents had been 'taken into naval custody' very nearly derailed the entire operation. Many Spanish naval officers were pro-British, and there was a tradition of mutual respect between the British and Spanish navies. The Navy Minister, Admiral Moreno, was a personal friend of Alan Hillgarth, who had made a point of cultivating naval officers: 'The Spanish navy is not in German hands,' he wrote.

Clauss's first approach was the most direct one: he instructed his father, the consul, Ludwig Clauss, to ask his friend and golfing partner, Captain Francisco Elvira Alvárez, to hand over the documents. Captain Elvira refused. Politely, he explained that these documents were now locked away in his safe at the Navy Office at 17 Avenida de Italia, where they would remain until he received orders from Cadiz about what should be done with them. Elvira was a cheerful, garrulous and sociable man. He liked Clauss, was happy to eat the dinners laid on by the German consul, and the hospitality he provided at Huelva Golf Club. But there is no evidence he was on Clauss's payroll. Elvira was also a stickler for the rules, 'a rigid disciplinarian', and a firm believer in hierarchy. He would await instructions from above.

At midday on 2 May 1943, a group of mourners, official and unofficial, public and secret, gathered for the funeral and burial of Major William Martin. It was a day of 'suffocating heat', according to the local newspaper, yet the turnout was impressive. Representing Britain were Francis Haselden, the vice consul, and Lancelot Shutte, a British mining company executive who had been expelled from Spain once already by Governor Miranda on suspicion of espionage. Here, too, was the Frenchman Pierre Desbrest, a Gaullist and close friend of Haselden. Officially, Desbrest was the representative in Spain of a French-owned pyrites company. Less officially, he organised an underground route for Free French forces from occupied France through Spain to North Africa, and conspired with Haselden against the Germans. The port commander, Elvira, and the naval judge, Pascual del Pobil, attended in full naval uniform. The military governor of Huelva was in Seville, meeting General Franco, but sent an army lieutenant to represent the Spanish armed forces.

Glyndwr Michael had died without a single mourner. His funeral, as someone completely different, was carried out with full military honours, and all the ceremony and solemnity Huelva could muster. In addition to the officials and military brass, a small crowd of civilians also gathered at Nuestra Señora de la Soledad cemetery: the curious, the pious, and the clandestine. Haselden does not seem to have spotted the tall, cadaverous figure of Adolf Clauss among the crowd. Clauss would later claim that he had only come to the funeral in his capacity as German vice consul, 'as a mark of respect to the fallen soldier'. In truth, of course, he was there to observe, to see if he might pick up any useful information about the dead man, and his intriguing briefcase.

The death certificate, filled out by funeral director Candela, formally marked the passing of 'W. Martin, aged between thirty-five and forty, native of Cardiff (England) [sic], officer of the British marines, found on the beach known as "La Bota" at half past nine on 30 April 1943. Death by drowning.' After a brief funeral service in the cemetery chapel, the coffin was carried along a cobbled path, down a neat avenue of cypresses, to the section of the cemetery known as San Marco. Swallows dipped and dived among the palm trees, and the strong scent of jasmine trees rose in the midday heat. The funeral procession passed the large and imposing mausoleums of Huelva's wealthiest Spanish families, marble tombs surrounded by iron railings. Here was the grave of Huelva's most famous son, Miguel Biez, 'El Litri', a bullfighter famously gored to death in 1929. Litri's huge and ostentatious tomb depicted the matador wearing the 'suit of lights'.

As the procession neared the northwest corner of the cemetery, the graves grew smaller and humbler. The San Marco section was where the poor and ordinary folk of Huelva were buried. Haselden had ordered a 'Class Five' burial, the cheapest available: total cost, including coffin, being just 250 pesetas. The British consulate contracted to pay the cost of renting and maintaining the grave in perpetuity. Major Martin was not the first tenant of grave number 46, in the fourteenth avenue of the

San Marco section, backing up to the cemetery wall. In 1938, a ten-year-old girl named Rosario Vilches had been buried there, but her parents had been unable to keep up payments on the plot, and two months earlier the body had been removed and reburied elsewhere.

At half past twelve, the coffin was lowered into the grave. Of the official mourners, only Francis Haselden knew that the man inside had not died at sea, and even he was ignorant of the full scale of the imposture taking place: a Welsh Baptist in a Spanish Catholic grave, a derelict who had never worn uniform accorded rank and honour, a man with no relatives (at least none who seemed to care) invested with a parent to mourn him, and buried with full military pomp by a grateful nation. Glyndwr Michael had probably killed himself on the spur of the moment, or through insanity, or by accident. The fatal dose of poison had carried him 500 miles, into another country, and another personality. The inscription on his tomb would eventually read: *Dulce et decorum est pro patria mori*, the line from Horace's *Odes*: 'It is sweet and fitting to die for your country.' There was nothing remotely decorous or patriotic about the way Glyndwr Michael died. Yet in a way, the epitaph was apt: Michael had, indeed, given his death, if not his life, to his country, even if he was given no choice about it.

The officials climbed into their hot cars, the gravediggers began to fill in the hole, and the mourners trailed away down the hill towards the town. Adolf Clauss watched them leave, and then headed back to the German consulate on foot. He did not sign the mourners' book, and he spoke to no one, but his presence did not go unremarked. Among the other mourners was an innocuous-looking middle-aged man in a nondescript suit. The Spaniards had assumed he must be part of the official delegation. The officials assumed he was a local Spaniard. From the shade of a Cyprus tree, Don Gómez-Beare watched Adolf Clauss leave the cemetery, and then quietly slipped out, and followed him down the hill.

16

Spanish Trails

Clauss had much to occupy his mind. His attempts to obtain the briefcase had so far failed. The Spanish naval authorities were proving vigorously uncooperative. Perhaps they would be more amenable to an approach from a fellow Spaniard. Frustrated, the German spy resolved to try a more indirect approach. Lieutenant Colonel Santiago Garrigos was commander of the Guardia Civil, the Spanish paramilitary police, for the Huelva district, and an enthusiastic recipient of German largesse. Clauss instructed Garrigos to 'do everything necessary to obtain copies of the documents which were found in the briefcase'. Garrigos may have been a keen collaborator, but he was also a coward, and knew that if he asked Elvira or Pascual del Pobil to show him the documents, they would conclude that he was on the German payroll, and send him packing. 'Notwithstanding his great desire to serve the Germans, this Lt Colonel apparently did not have the courage to approach the naval judge' and simply demand that he open the letters.

Garrigos did, however, persuade someone in the naval office to tell him what was in the briefcase. He sent the list to Clauss:

a) Three British Operation bulletins
b) Two plans
c) 33 photographs
d) Three envelopes addressed to Cunningham, General Eisenhower and General Alexander.

Helpfully, but unnecessarily, Garrigos added: 'These three persons are in command of the Allied troops in North Africa.'

Clauss knew that whatever was in that briefcase must be extremely interesting. Heavier guns were mobilised. The German consul, Ludwig Clauss, was once again wheeled out, and asked by his son to approach his 'intimate friend' Joaquín Miranda González, the civilian governor of Huelva and head of the provincial Falange. A keen fascist, Miranda 'nursed a profound antipathy towards the British, in common with the sentiment among most officials, and maintained excellent relations with the German consulate . . . he treated the Germans with favouritism and the British with a heavy hand'. Miranda was anxious to help, and made discreet enquiries at the naval office, but he too stopped short of demanding that the letters be opened. 'This gentleman,' reported one of Hillgarth's agents, 'did not dare to ask the naval judge for copies of the documents.' Clauss received this fresh rebuff with mounting frustration and growing curiosity. He had spent a small fortune bribing the local officials. 'In Huelva, Don Adolfo can open every door,' it was said. Yet the door to Captain Elvira's safe remained firmly shut. A bag full of secret British documents had been sitting in Huelva for three days, and, so far, these had been 'neither copied nor photographed [and] were only seen and read in the naval judge's office'. The three envelopes, which Clauss knew must contain the most important information, were still sealed.

Back in London, Cholmondeley and Montagu were equally frustrated that the information appeared to have reached its target, only to become lodged in the annoyingly honest hands of the Spanish navy. They decided to give the pot a stir.

Alan Hillgarth sent a cable to London, unencrypted, reporting that Major Martin of the Royal Marines had been laid to rest with due decorum: 'I am glad to say the naval and military authorities were well represented and extremely sympathetic.' Two days after the funeral – enough time, it was estimated, for news of Major Martin's death to filter through the British military bureaucracy – the Naval Intelligence Department in London sent a much less casual-sounding cable to Hillgarth in Madrid, numbered '04132'. It was marked 'Top Secret' but intended for German eyes, and carefully flavoured with rising anxiety. 'Some papers Major Martin had in his possession are of great importance and secrecy. Make formal demand for all papers and notify me by personal signal immediately of addressees of any official letters recovered. Such letters should be returned addressed to Commodore Rushbrooke, Personal, by fastest safe route and should not repetition not be opened or tampered with in any way. If no official letters are recovered make searching but discreet inquiries at Huelva and Madrid to find whether they were washed ashore and if so what has happened to them.'

At the same time, Montagu sent a separate message to Hillgarth, using the secret personal cipher that was the only safe method of communication with the spy-riddled embassy in Madrid. 'Carry out instructions in my Naval Signal as this is necessary cover but lack of success is desirable.' The message merely confirmed what Hillgarth already knew. The novelist-naval attaché would be creating a fiction especially for Kuhlenthal and his informants but, once again, this would need to be done with extreme subtlety. The Germans knew British diplomatic methods by now: if a bag full of secrets really had been lost, the British would still not rush in and demand its return, as this would tip off the Spanish to its importance. Hillgarth must start with an apparently routine enquiry, and then gradually give the impression of greater and greater urgency. It was a tricky balancing act, since enquiries must be 'kept on such a plane as (theoretically) not to arouse Spanish suspicions that we were really frightened that someone might get those documents, but in fact making it plain to them that we were so frightened'.

Hillgarth passed on London's message to Haselden in Huelva, instructing him to make a 'searching but discreet' investigation into the whereabouts of these important and secret papers. At the same time, he set the first cog of Madrid's mighty rumour mill grinding into action. In wartime Spain, practically the only commodity freely available everywhere was gossip: spies traded in it, the government was saturated with it and just about everyone, from Franco down, indulged in it. Gossip was currency. Gossip was power. 'Rumours are extremely easy to spread in Spain,' wrote Hillgarth. 'The country lives on word-of-mouth stories. A casual word in a club or café is often enough.' To get a rumour flying, he told London, all he need do was 'select from among his acquaintance the most inveterate gossips and, taking into account their connections, use them accordingly'. Hillgarth quietly began to spread word that the British were searching for an important set of documents in Huelva: he knew that, like any game of Chinese whispers, the story would be mangled and inflated as it passed from one gossip to the next, and with any luck, it would soon reach the Germans, who would react accordingly.

The British naval attaché also made an unobtrusive approach to Rear Admiral Moreno, the Navy Minister. Hillgarth liked Moreno, believing him to be 'sincerely anti-war'. The two men were friends, although perfectly happy to use their friendship for mutual manipulation. On an earlier occasion, Hillgarth recalled, 'I managed to make the Minister of Marine so sorry for me because he could not do what I wanted that in the end he did it, at considerable hazard to himself, just because he felt he was letting a friend down if he didn't.' Through a contact in the Spanish navy, Hillgarth sent word to the admiral, asking for assistance in securing the return of the briefcase. Hillgarth was careful to make the request a verbal one, and commit nothing to paper. Moreno was a reliable and well-informed source, and almost certainly one of the prime recipients of British gold. But Hillgarth also knew that the Spanish Minister of Marine, while professing his attachment to Britain, and Hillgarth personally, was in close contact with the German Embassy, and spoke frequently to the German ambassador, Hans-Heinrich Dieckhoff. Moreno was the ideal conduit: he was the government minister in command of the navy, and thus likely to see the documents sooner rather than later; he would make strenuous efforts to retrieve them and return them to Britain; but he could also be relied upon to pass on the information to the Germans, or at least enable access to the documents, thus ensuring the continued goodwill of both sides.

Four days after the funeral of Major Martin, Hillgarth secretly reported to London 'that the Minister of Marine, who knew nothing of the papers or effects, was expecting an early report' from naval authorities in the south, and had pledged to keep him abreast of developments. Hillgarth gave Moreno no indication of what might be in the briefcase, and was careful to avoid any impression of undue anxiety.

Finally, Hillgarth mobilised his most trusted informant, the senior Spanish naval officer codenamed 'Agent Andros', and asked him to keep track of what happened to the briefcase and its contents. To judge from results, Andros was perfectly placed to do this, reinforcing suspicion that he may have been the chief of Spanish naval intelligence. The report he subsequently sent to Hillgarth and MI6 was astonishingly detailed, an almost daily account of the fate of Major Martin's briefcase.

Hillgarth's rumour-mongering paid swift dividends. On 5 May, Captain Elvira, the senior navy officer in Huelva, informed Vice Consul Haselden that he had been ordered to pass the dead man's effects, under guard, to his superior officer in San Fernando, Cadiz, who would arrange for their onward transfer to the Ministry of Marine in Madrid. He also shared this information with the German vice consul, Adolf Clauss. Haselden passed the information on to Hillgarth, who sent a telegram to London through the normal, permeable channels:

> Vice Consul Huelva saw body. Postmortem performed. Verdict drowning several days previously. Funeral attended by representative military and naval officers.

> 1. Pocket book containing private letters
> 2. Identity disc
> 3. Identity papers
> 4. Medal and crucifix
> 5. Black leather documents case, locked and attached to strap. By lifting flap envelope could be seen inside. Presumably this is what is referred to in your [telegram] 041321
>
> Vice Consul was informed all effects must be sent C in C, Cadiz (who is unfortunately pro-German). In due course they will reach Ministry of Marine and be handed to me. Vice Consul had no (repeat no) chance of obtaining possession of the case. Am trying everything possible, but fear too much display of interest will only increase official curiosity, which is already aroused.

Montagu and Cholmondeley sent back a message in kind, subtly infused with the flutter of rising panic: 'Secret papers probably in black briefcase. Earliest possible information required whether this came ashore. If so, it should be recovered at once. Care should be taken it does not get into undesirable hands if it comes ashore later.'

At the same time, they sent a separate message, by 'Most Secret Special Route', urging Hillgarth to maintain the guise of a harassed official being asked to perform the impossible. 'Normally you would be getting frantic messages asking you to get the secret documents at once, and to hurry the Spaniards. You must adjust your actions to achieve desired results and maintain normal appearance.' Hillgarth needed no stage directions: 'Understood and acted on throughout,' he replied.

While Hillgarth played the part of a spy under pressure, there was nothing remotely fake about the strain Adolf Clauss was now under. The German spy had sent word to Abwehr headquarters in Madrid as soon as the body was discovered. When he learned that a briefcase containing British documents had also come ashore, he confidently told Madrid that he would be able to copy the contents within days. The messages flying between London and Madrid had been picked up by the Germans' eavesdroppers, as predicted, and the Abwehr spy chiefs in Madrid were now thoroughly alerted to the existence of a cache of secret documents that the British were desperate to retrieve. What had seemed, at first, to be a golden intelligence opportunity was turning into a nightmare for the Abwehr's man in Huelva. Clauss had 'promised to obtain copies of the documents, but was unable to keep his promise'. Gómez-Beare was also in Huelva, making 'discreet inquiries whether any bag or paper had been washed ashore'. The presence of the Gibraltarian was undoubtedly communicated to Clauss, ratcheting up the strain another notch.

Agent Andros reported: 'As the local Germans were not able to obtain copies of these documents, to which they attached the utmost importance, the matter was taken up in Madrid by either Leissner personally, or by Kuhlenthal.' The ambitious Karl-Erich Kuhlenthal saw an opportunity to add another feather to his espionage cap.

Clauss's reputation was at stake, and to make matters worse, his colleagues and bosses were muscling in. Through its own informants, the Abwehr in Portugal had got wind of what was happening, and offered to help. Clauss was 'summoned to Villarreal de San Antonio [in nearby Ayamonte] for a conference' on what to do about the situation. The full might of the German secret services on the Iberian peninsula was now unleashed in an effort to obtain the British documents that the British, with equal determination, were trying to put into their hands.

Clauss insisted he could still get the documents through his Spanish contacts. He instructed the willing Colonel Santiago Garrigós to go immediately to Seville and make contact with a fellow member of the Guardia Civil, Major Luis Canis, a man described by Agent Andros as 'very pro-German and in German pay'. Canis was probably Clauss's most important contact. 'This individual,' Hillgarth's spy reported, 'who is under complete German control, is in charge of the contra-espionage services in the Seville Captain General's headquarters and therefore of all Andalucia.' In theory, Canis was responsible for tracking espionage activities aimed at Spain; in reality, he was an employee of the German Abwehr. Garrigós explained the situation to Canis, and instructed him, on behalf of Clauss, 'to do everything possible to obtain copies of the documents, availing himself of his official position'. The head of counterespionage for the region might reasonably claim an interest in anything of intelligence value washing up on the coast. Canis selected one of his junior officers from the counterespionage unit, and told him to go to San Fernando, where Major Martin's effects were now lodged with the Cadiz naval authorities. 'Urging him to use the utmost discretion', Canis told this officer to sniff around the naval headquarters, talk to the naval commander there, and obtain, by whatever means necessary, 'accurate information regarding the contents of the documents'.

He very nearly succeeded. Someone in the naval office in Cadiz agreed to photograph the contents of the briefcase: the letters, photographs, and the proofs of Hilary Saunders's book about the commandos. This person, however, flatly refused to open the letters, 'either because they were afraid to break the seals lest the Minister of Marine should disapprove, or more probably because they had no experience in opening them without leaving a trace'. Admiral Moreno was known to be sympathetic to the British; if he found out that someone had opened official letters without the highest authorisation, the minister would hit the roof. The naval commander in Cadiz, it transpired, was not quite as pro-German as the British thought. He refused to hand over the letters, and Canis's officer trailed home with a flea in his ear, and a handful of photographs of no intelligence value whatever. 'Either because of the junior rank of his envoy, or because this person acted with excessive discretion or perhaps because this is the usual procedure in the navy, he had to return to Seville and confess that he had not been able to obtain any information whatever and stated that he had been told by the naval authorities that if the Captain General of Seville wanted any information about the documents he should address himself to the Ministry of War in Madrid.' Furious and embarrassed, Canis prepared to head to Cadiz and confront the naval authorities in person. But it was already too late.

Admiral Moreno, the Minister of Marine, had sent explicit orders that the briefcase and its contents must be 'forwarded, unopened, to the Admiralty, Madrid' and they were now en route, in the custody of an official from the Marine Commandant's Office in Cadiz. Adolf Clauss had failed to intercept the documents in Huelva; his agent Luis Canis has failed to obtain them in Cadiz; it was now up to Karl-Erich Kuhlenthal to try to snare them in Madrid, and quickly. The items belonging to Major Martin had been in Spanish custody for more than a week. The British were apparently agitating to get them back, and sooner or later the Spanish authorities would have to comply in order to avoid a major diplomatic row, even though this was the very last thing the British wanted.

Back in London, Johnnie Bevan sent a progress report to the Chiefs of Staff. There was, he warned, 'only scanty information' so far. 'Mincemeat was found by the Spaniards washed ashore at Huelva on 1 May . . . It seems that certain documents were taken from him by Spaniards and that these have been passed back to the Spanish authorities in Madrid.'

For Montagu and Cholmondeley, the slow progress was worrying, and the uncertainty agonising. Agent Andros's report describing German efforts to obtain the papers would not reach London for many weeks. All they knew for certain was that Major Martin's effects had been passed to the navy, the least pro-German of the Spanish services. Hillgarth had laid an obvious trail for the Germans to follow, but had they picked up the scent? The codebreakers at Bletchley Park combed the messages passing between the Abwehr stations in Huelva, Madrid and Berlin, but found nothing to indicate that the Germans were aware of the documents' existence, much less of their contents. Mincemeat, it seemed, might simply work its way through Spanish military bureaucracy and back to Britain without ever reaching the Germans.

The operation organisers reacted to the tension in different ways. Cholmondeley went for long walks around St James's, a tall, gangling figure, plunged in thought. He spent hours in his garage at Queen's Gate Mews, tinkering with the Bentley he was restoring. Montagu's primary reaction to tension was irritation. Reality's stubborn refusal to conform to his expectations made him peevish. With the fraud apparently in stasis, he complained bitterly, largely about little things. 'We sweat away, eleven of us, in far too small and low a room, with often foul potted air and five typewriters often all going at once, jaded and headachy from the conditions. By giving up many of my days off, by coming in after dinner, I have managed to keep up with essential work although I am usually too tired in the evening to do anything but go to bed straight after dinner. No one has any idea, or will even consider, how hard pressed we are.'

With the departure of Bill Martin, his alter ego, and stuck once more behind a desk, Montagu appears to have turned in on himself, wondering if the complex ruse he had created would prove an abject and potentially calamitous failure. The strain brought out his sarcasm. Bitterly, he reflected that the Abwehr chiefs were more appreciative of his work than his own bosses, since the Germans, at least, sent money and praise to the double agents, real and invented, that he was helping to run. He wrote a half-joking letter of resignation: 'It is requested that I may be given permission to relinquish my commission in the RNVR in order to be free to join the German navy. The reason for this request is that my services are appreciated more highly by Admiral Canaris than they appear to be by their Lordships.

The former has just awarded me a special bonus and has agreed to my pay being increased. Signed, E. S. Montagu Failed-Commander RNVR.' He never sent the letter. Montagu knew he sounded petty – 'I always was a selfish shit' – but could not help himself. Cholmondeley was the ideas man, content to see his inspirations float away, in this case literally, to whatever outcome fate intended. But Montagu was a perfectionist, and a workaholic: 'I have never been able to half-do a job,' he wrote, 'even if it means working to a standstill.'

At the forefront of Montagu's mind was the knowledge that thousands of Allied soldiers were massing on the coast of North Africa, whose future depended on a ruse that had once seemed like a jolly game, but was now a matter of life and death on a massive scale. 'If I had made a slip in the preparation and devising of Mincemeat,' Montagu reflected, 'I could have ballsed-up Husky.'

That anxiety would have been at least partially relieved, had he been able to witness the frantic scenes taking place at Abwehr headquarters in Madrid, where Leissner, Kuhlenthal and the other German spies were now focused on a single task: getting inside Major Martin's briefcase. A week after the funeral, the documents had arrived at the Admiralty in Madrid, and passed immediately into the hands of Admiral Moreno himself. Then they seemed to vanish into the labyrinth of Spanish military officialdom. The Germans were desperate to get them; the British were equally determined that they should do so; the only obstacle was Spanish bureaucracy, inefficient, self-important and leisurely in the extreme. 'Official procedure is always slow,' Hillgarth had warned. In this case, it appeared to have ground to a halt.

Major Kuhlenthal was tying himself in knots trying to find out where the papers might be, and whom he needed to bribe in order to get them. Admiral Moreno, it seemed, had taken receipt of the briefcase personally, and then handed over everything to the Alto Estado Mayor, the Supreme General

Staff. Kuhlenthal had several high-level contacts within the General Staff, but when enquiries were made there, the Abwehr was 'informed that they had not received the documents or copies of them and in fact that they knew nothing at all about the matter'. Next stop was the Spanish Ministry of War, but the response was the same. The Abwehr now turned to the Gestapo, which maintained a permanent office in Spain. The Gestapo chief in Spain was asked to get in touch with his informants in the Dirección General de Seguridad, or DGS, the state security apparatus, and get them working on the case. 'Again they failed, as nothing was known about the matter.' The last person known to have had the package was Admiral Moreno, who received it from 'an official of the [Cadiz] Marine Commandant's Office'; but no one seemed to know whom he had passed it to, and the Germans 'did not dare approach the Ministry of Marine' to ask him, as Moreno would almost certainly tip off the British to the hunt.

For help, the Germans turned to one of their most trusted spies, a Spanish air force officer named Captain Groizar, 'an assiduous worker for the Germans', in the words of Agent Andros, with wide-ranging military contacts. Groizar reported 'that he had heard about the body and documents being washed ashore and promised to get into touch with the Army General Staff'. Groizar appears to have worked, in some undefined capacity, for Spanish intelligence, enjoying 'many privileges and facilities to investigate anything in which he may be interested'. The Spanish captain went first to the General Staff, without success; he then applied to the DGS, but was 'unable to obtain any fresh information'; then he made contact with 'certain high officials in the police', with the same negative result. Groizar's enquiries produced nothing, but by poking sticks into every corner of the Spanish military hierarchy, the Germans stirred up a swarm of speculation surrounding the missing briefcase. 'Great interest was aroused in these documents,' Andros later reported. 'Groizar fostered this interest to such an extent that eventually Lt Colonel Barrón, Secretary General of the Directorate General of Security, took a personal interest in the matter.'

This was the turning point. Colonel José López Barrón Cerruti was Spain's most senior secret policeman, a keen fascist and an exceptionally tough cookie. He had fought in the Blue Division, the Spanish volunteer unit sent to the Russian front to fight alongside Hitler's troops, and he now ran Franco's security service with ruthlessness and guile. The Blue Division, formed in 1941 and so called for the colour of its Falangist shirt, represented the high-water mark of Spanish military collaboration with Nazi Germany. If the Condor Legion, in which both Adolf Clauss and Kuhlenthal had served, was Germany's gift to Franco, then the Blue Division was Spain's gift to Hitler. No other non-belligerent country raised an entire division to fight in the war. Some 45,000 Spaniards volunteered to fight for fascism, and Barrón was among the first. Like all members of the division, he had sworn a personal military oath to Hitler. The Blue Division had fought fiercely on the Eastern Front in appalling conditions for over two years, leaving 5,000 dead. 'One can't imagine more fearless fellows,' declared SS General Sepp Dietrich. Hitler had been so impressed by the division that he ordered a special medal for its members.

The unit was formally disbanded in 1943. By then, José Barrón had become Franco's head of security. Hillgarth had his own spies within the state security apparatus, but the prevailing attitude in the DGS was vigorously pro-German. Under Barrón, the unit actively worked to gather information for the Germans, and ordered provincial governors to compile files on every Jew in Spain. Colonel Barrón, then, was a battle-hardened fascist veteran, an avowed Germanophile presiding over a secret police force riddled with spies and German sympathisers. Once Colonel Barrón was on the scent, it was only a matter of time before the documents were located, and made available to the Germans.

Karl-Erich Kuhlenthal, ambitious and paranoid, was becoming frantic. He was now in the same uncomfortable position in which he had placed Adolf Clauss, under growing pressure from above to produce documents he had promised but could not deliver. Word of the elusive British briefcase had by now reached the upper echelons in Berlin, most notably Wilhelm Canaris, the head of the Abwehr. Canaris had close links with the Spanish government, dating back to the First World War, when he had worked as a secret agent in Spain under civilian cover, gathering naval intelligence. In 1925 Canaris had established a German intelligence network in Spain. He spoke fluent Spanish, and cultivated close relations with the nationalists, including General Franco himself and Martínez Campos, his intelligence chief. It was almost certainly Kuhlenthal, the Abwehr chief's protégé, who informed Canaris of the so-far fruitless hunt for the documents, 'in the hope that he will come to Spain where they think he will be able to obtain copies because of his great friendship with many high military officers, especially General Vigon, Minister for Air, and General Asensio, Minister for War'.

Juan Vigón, former head of the Supreme General Staff, had personally negotiated with Hitler, on behalf of Franco, in the early days of the war. Carlos Asensio was keenly pro-German, and had long argued that Spain should enter the war in support of Hitler. According to a British intelligence report, 'approaches were made by the Germans' to both men, but in the end, the aid of these two powerful generals, and the intercession of Canaris, proved unnecessary.

Nine days after arriving in Spain, the faked letters landed in the Germans' lap.

17

Kuhlenthal's Coup

British intelligence would not discover the name of the man who had handed over the Mincemeat papers to the Germans for another two years. In April 1945, as the Nazis retreated, a group of British naval intelligence commandos, a unit set up by none other than Ian Fleming, captured the entire German admiralty archives at Tambach Castle near Coburg. Fleming himself travelled to Germany to supervise the unit he referred to as his 'Red Indians', and ensure the safe return of the German files to Britain.

Among the documents were several relating to Operation Mincemeat, including one revealing the identity of the officer on the Spanish General Staff who had presented the documents to the Abwehr: this was a Lieutenant Colonel Ramón Pardo Suárez, described by the Germans as 'a Spanish Staff Officer with well-established connections' and an informant 'with whom we have been in contact for many years'. Years later, Wilhelm Leissner was still covering up Pardo's identity, describing him merely as 'my Spanish agent in the General Staff'. Pardo's brother, José, was Civil Governor of Zaragoza and Madrid, and a senior figure in the Franco regime. Ramón Pardo would go on to become a general, Governor of the Spanish Sahara and, finally, General Director of the Spanish Department of Public Health.

Ramón Pardo was not acting alone, and German documents clearly indicate he was under instructions from a higher authority, and may even have been assigned as 'case officer' to liaise between the General Staff and the Germans. Agent Andros indicates, though he does not state explicitly, that pressure from the security chief Colonel Barrón brought about the decision to pass over the documents. It may well have been agents of Barrón's security service who successfully extracted the letters from their envelopes, and then replaced them, leaving barely a trace.

The British later worked out exactly how the Spanish had performed this delicate and difficult task. The letters had been stuck down with gum, and then secured with oval wax seals. 'Those seals held the envelopes closed as all the gum had washed off.' By pressing on the top and bottom of the envelope, the lower flap of the envelope, which was larger than the top one, could be bent open. Inserting a thin metal double prong with a blunt metal hook into the gap, the Spanish spies snagged the bottom edge of the letter, wound the still-damp paper tightly around the probe into a cylindrical shape, and then pulled it out through the hole in the bottom half. Even the British, normally so dismissive of the espionage efforts of others, were impressed by the Spaniards' ingenuity: 'It was possible to extract all the letters through the envelopes by twisting them out [leaving] the seals intact and untampered with.'

The letters were then carefully dried with a heat lamp. No one, needless to say, noticed a microscopic eyelash falling out of the unfolded sheet of notepaper. The letters were then almost certainly copied by the Spanish officials, although no copies have ever come to light. 'The Spaniards had, very intelligently, not bothered to supply photographs of the letter to Eisenhower, which only dealt with the pamphlet on Combined Operations, and was mere padding.' The two other letters, however, were clearly very significant indeed.

These letters were taken by Colonel Pardo of the General Staff to the German Embassy and handed, in person, to Leissner, the Abwehr chief in Spain, who was told he had one hour to do whatever he wanted with them. Leissner understood English, while Kuhlenthal spoke and read the language fluently. The Germans immediately realised that they had stumbled on something explosive, an impression doubtless compounded by the difficulties they had encountered in obtaining the documents. 'They seemed to me to be of the highest importance,' Leissner later recalled. The letters not only indicated an imminent Allied landing in Greece, and possibly Sardinia too, but specifically identified Sicily as a decoy target.

'A short white-haired man with a birdlike brightness of eye', Leissner 'gave more the impression of a diplomat than an intelligence officer'. By 1943 he had been all but supplanted by the energetic Kuhlenthal, but he was no fool. Even on this first, swift reading, something about the documents struck him as odd: 'These letters mentioned the operational name "Husky". That stuck in my memory, because it seemed to me a dangerous thing to name the codeword in the same document as discussed the possible destinations.' He was also cautious about drawing firm conclusions from a single letter, and considered 'the strategic considerations not definite enough to suggest an already fixed target on the North Mediterranean coast . . . the final choice seemed to be left to General Alexander'. Kuhlenthal, by contrast, with the mixture of eagerness and gullibility that defined him, seems to have entertained no such doubts. Just as he had run the Garbo network for years without once questioning its veracity, so he believed the Mincemeat letters, instantly and unquestioningly.

The German spies moved quickly, knowing that the documents must be returned within the hour. 'I took them to the basement of the German Embassy,' Leissner later recalled, 'and had my photographer photocopy them there. I even stood over him while he worked, so that he could not read the documents.' Leissner informed Dieckhoff, the German ambassador to Spain, of the discovery, and described the contents of the letters to him.

The original documents were now returned to Colonel Pardo, who took them back to the offices of the General Staff, accompanied by Kuhlenthal. The German spy observed as the Spanish technicians reinserted the letters into the envelopes, reversing the method used to extract them. It is hard enough to remove a damp letter from an envelope this way, but harder still to get one back in without creasing the paper, leaving telltale marks or breaking the seals. The Spanish spy responsible must have been astonishingly dextrous, for, to the naked eye, 'there was no trace whatever' to show that the letters had left their envelopes. The letters were then placed in salt water, and soaked for twenty-four hours, to return them to their damp condition. Finally, the envelopes and book proofs were replaced in the briefcase, which was relocked, and then passed back to the Spanish Ministry of Marine, along with Major Martin's wallet and other personal property. The entire process – opening the letters, transferring them to the Germans, the copying, resealing and restitution – was completed in less than two days. But even before the documents were back in Spanish hands, the copies were winging their way to Berlin.

The letters had been handed over to Leissner, as head of the Abwehr in Spain, but it was Karl-Erich Kuhlenthal who bore them back in triumph to Germany. The copied documents were far too secret and significant to be sent by wireless or telegram. As Leissner later observed, the decision to send Kuhlenthal in person was a measure of 'the importance attached to them'. It appears that Berlin may already have been informed that the documents had been intercepted, and summoned the wunderkind of the Madrid station to bring them by hand. He, and only he, should present this new intelligence coup to the high command and, since it came from Kuhlenthal, it was far more likely to be believed. From the British point of view, this was ideal. The credibility of intelligence often depends less on its intrinsic value than on who finds it, and who passes it on. Presentation is critical and, from the British point of view, Major Martin's documents were now in the hands of the ideal courier.

Colonel Pardo of the Spanish General Staff was interviewed once more, in order to obtain more details about how and when the body and its hoard of secrets had been found. This information, written up some time later, would go into a long report entitled 'Drowned English Courier picked up at Huelva':

> On the 10th May, 1943, a further conversation with the case officer clarified the following questions:
>
> 1. The courier carried, clutched in his hand, an ordinary briefcase which contained the following documents:
>
> a) An ordinary white paper as a cover for the letters addressed to General Alexander and Admiral Cunningham. This white paper carried no address.
>
> The letters were contained each in its own envelope with the usual superscription and addressed personally to the recipients, and apparently sealed with the private seal of the sender (signet ring). The seals were intact. The letters themselves, which I have already had replaced in their original envelopes, are in good condition. For the purposes of reproduction they were dried by artificial heat by the Spaniards, and thereafter were again placed for some 24 hours in salt water, without which their condition would undoubtedly have been altered.
>
> b) In the portfolio there were also the proofs of the pamphlet on the functions of Combined Operations Command referred to by Mountbatten in his letter of the 22nd April, 1943, as also the photographs mentioned in the letter. The proofs are in excellent condition, but the photographs are completely ruined.

> 2. In addition the courier carried in his breast pocket a letter case containing personal papers, among them his military papers with photographs. (These papers connect up with Mountbatten's reference to Major Martin in his letter of 22nd April.) There were, too, a letter to Major Martin from his fiancée and another from his Father, also a London night-club bill dated 27th April.
> Therefore Major Martin left London on the forenoon of the 28th April and during the afternoon of the same day the aircraft met with an accident in the neighbourhood of Huelva.
>
> 3. The British Consul was present at the discovery and knows all about it. On the pretext that anything found on the corpse, including all documents, must be made available to competent Spanish authorities, we anticipated representations which the British Consul would probably have made for the immediate delivery of the documents. All the documents were, after reproduction, replaced in their original condition in such a way that even I would have been convinced, and definitely give the impression that they have not been opened. In the course of the next few days they will be handed back to the British by the Spanish Foreign Office.
>
> Enquiries regarding the remains of the pilot of the aircraft, presumably wounded in the crash, and interrogation of the same concerning other passengers, are already being put in hand by the Spanish General Staff.

The report was unsigned, but the phrase 'even I would have been convinced' was typical of Kuhlenthal's braggadocio. Equally characteristic were the mistakes and exaggerations, the over-egging that was his Achilles heel. He implied that a pilot had been found and was being interrogated; he claimed to have overseen the reinsertion of the letters, a process at which he was merely an observer; he described the seals as personal signet-ring seals, when they were standard military seals; he made no mention of the chain attaching the briefcase to the body, but instead added the melodramatic (and inaccurate) detail that the corpse had been found clutching the briefcase. Describing the theatre tickets as nightclub receipts was an easy mistake to make, but getting the date wrong was not. The date on these was 22 April, not 27 April. The body was discovered on 30 April. According to Kuhlenthal's report, the body had been immersed for less than three days when it was picked up, a timescale flatly contradicted by the state of decomposition and the autopsy, which estimated that death had occurred at least eight days earlier.

Bletchley Park intercepted a message indicating that Kuhlenthal 'left Madrid hurriedly for Berlin in order to consult at the latter's request with Oblt von Dewitz, the evaluator of KO [Abwehr] Spain's reports at the Luftwaffenführungsstab'. Kuhlenthal was booked into the Adlon Hotel in Berlin, but apparently travelled directly to Abwehr headquarters, south of the city. On 9 May he presented his delighted bosses with the greatest intelligence feat of his career.

Oddly, the significance of Kuhlenthal rushing to Berlin does not seem to have been picked up at the time. The intercept may have been accidentally backdated, or decoded too late to be of use, and the dates in Kuhlenthal's MI5 files are contradictory. Montagu and Cholmondeley remained unaware that Kuhlenthal had flown to Germany in a hurry: as far as they knew, the documents were still marooned somewhere in the byzantine Spanish bureaucracy.

On 11 May, Admiral Alfonso Arriago Adam, the Spanish Chief of Naval Staff, arrived at the British Embassy carrying a black briefcase and a buff envelope, and asked to see the naval attaché, Alan Hillgarth. The Spanish officer explained that the Spanish Naval Minister, Rear Admiral Moreno was currently away in Valencia, but had given him instructions to hand over to Hillgarth in person 'all the effects and papers' found on the body of the British officer. 'They are all there,' said Admiral Arriago, with a knowing look. The key, removed from Major Martin's keyring, was in the briefcase lock, and the case was unlocked. 'From his manner it was obvious the Chief of Naval Staff knew something [of the] contents,' wrote Hillgarth. 'While expressing gratitude I showed both relief and concern. Neither [the] secretary nor I showed any wish to discuss [the] matter further.' Having handed over the envelope containing the wallet and other items, the Spanish admiral saluted crisply, and departed.

Locking his office door, Hillgarth gingerly opened the case and peered inside. This was his first glimpse of the hard evidence he had worked so strenuously to pass to the Germans. He was under strict instructions not to open the letters or rearrange the contents in any way, since these would need to be microscopically studied back in London. The Spaniards did not disguise that the case had been opened. 'It is obvious [that the] contents of bag have been examined though some of the documents appear to be stuck together by sea water,' Hillgarth reported to London. He wrapped the case and other effects in paper, addressed the parcel to Ewen Montagu, Naval Intelligence Department, Whitehall, and sent a telegram explaining that the package would be included in the sealed diplomatic bag on the first flight to London, leaving Madrid on 14 May. Hillgarth was convinced that the Spanish Chief of Naval Staff knew what was in the case, but added: 'While I do not believe he will divulge his knowledge to the enemy it is clear [a] number of other people are in [on the] secret. It is to say the least extremely probable that it has been communicated to [the] enemy. In any case notes or copies have certainly been made.' Hillgarth also requested permission to ask the SIS head of station to try to find out through whose hands the documents had passed. 'If you concur I will ask 23000 to discover through his channels whether Germans have got them as he can do if they get to

Combined General Staff (which they almost certainly will).' In fact, of course, the letters had come back to the naval authorities *from* the General Staff.

Hillgarth's telegram was the first solidly good news since the body had come ashore, yet it did not amount to hard evidence that the Germans had obtained the documents, and still less that they believed the contents.

Unbeknown to anyone on the British side, by the time the letters were back in British hands, the Germans had been poring over them for at least forty-eight hours. On 9 May, the Abwehr forwarded the letters to the German high command, with an accompanying message stating that 'the genuineness of the report is held as possible', though that note of caution would swiftly evaporate. The task of authenticating the letters would fall to the intelligence branch of the German army's high command, Fremde Heere West (Foreign Armies West) or FHW, the linchpin of German military intelligence.

At its headquarters in a two-storey bunker in Zossen, south of Berlin, FHW received and evaluated all intelligence connected to the Allied war effort. The unit was run by professional officers from the General Staff, but also staffed by reserve personnel, journalists, businessmen and bankers with the ability to think beyond structured military ideas. At FHW, every scrap of intelligence was subjected to scrutiny and analysis: Abwehr reports, communications intercepts, prisoner interrogations, reconnaissance data, and captured documents. FHW issued long-range assessments of enemy planning and, every two weeks, a detailed survey of the Allied armies and their dispositions, the order of battle. These top-secret documents were distributed not only to Hitler and the Supreme Command of the Armed Forces, the Oberkommando der Wehrmacht (OKW) under Field Marshal Wilhelm Keitel, but also to German commanders in the field. Daily situation reports assessing Allied strength and intentions were sent directly to the Führer himself, together with information on troop movements, enemy activity, and any newly discovered intelligence. The FHW reports represented the cream of German intelligence, and the most direct access route into Hitler's mind.

The Führer was in need of some good news. In four months, Hitler had lost one-eighth of his fighting men on the battlefields of North Africa and the Eastern Front. Fleets of bombers were tearing German cities and industries to shreds. Germany was now losing the underwater war: forty-seven U-boats had been sunk in May, and triple that number in March, thanks to the codebreakers pinpointing the 'wolfpacks'. Hitler blamed his military leaders. 'He is absolutely sick of the generals,' Joseph Goebbels noted in his diary. 'All generals lie. All generals are disloyal.' Hitler needed to be told something he could believe in, to counter the lies of his generals, to bolster the mad myth of his own invincibility. The German intelligence service would now oblige.

Presiding over FHW was Lieutenant Colonel Alexis Baron von Roenne, a small, bespectacled aristocrat whose family had once ruled swaths of Baltic Germany. Von Roenne was a former banker, and still looked like one: he was meticulous, pedantic, snobbish, intensely Christian and glintingly intelligent. 'Behind his rimless spectacles and compressed lips there worked a brain as clear as glass.' Von Roenne had volunteered to fight on the Eastern Front, suffered a serious wound, and been transferred back to military intelligence, where he ascended rapidly, developing his own intelligence technique which involved piecing together a picture of the enemy, a *Feinbild*, from tiny fragments of information. As a result he enjoyed an almost mystical reputation for divining and predicting Allied intentions. The myth of Von Roenne's infallibility was largely undeserved but, critically, it was believed by Hitler, who held Von Roenne in the highest regard: when the command of FHW fell vacant in the spring of 1943, the Führer personally ordered the appointment of the small, clever Latvian-born aristocrat. Von Roenne had been in control of the western intelligence arm of the German army for just two months when the Mincemeat letters landed on his desk at Zossen.

Montagu had rightly predicted that the Germans would examine such a trove of information with profound suspicion and extreme caution. The Spaniards had handed over the two crucial letters, but the Germans had also obtained a full inventory and description of every item in the briefcase, wallet and pockets of the dead man: 'The Germans studied each phrase of the material letters with great care and also were fully informed about the documentary build-up of Major Martin's personality.'

The first full German intelligence assessment of the documents was written on 11 May, and signed by Baron von Roenne himself. It was addressed to the OKW Operations Staff, or Wehrmachtführungsstab, headed by General Alfred Jodl, and entitled, portentously, 'Discovery of the English Courier'. It began: 'On the corpse of an English courier which was found on the Spanish coast, were three letters from senior British officers to high Allied officers in North Africa . . . They give information concerning the decisions taken on the 23 April 1943, regarding Anglo-American strategy for the conduct of the war in the Mediterranean after the conclusion of the Tunisian campaign.' Major Martin is described as 'an experienced specialist in amphibious operations'.

Von Roenne went on to lay out, point by point, the misinformation prepared by Cholmondeley and Montagu. 'Large-scale amphibious operations in both the western and eastern Mediterranean are intended. The proposed operation in the eastern Mediterranean, under the command of General Wilson, is to be made on the coast round Kalamata, and the section of the coast south of Cape Araxos. The codename for the landings on the Peloponnesus is "Husky" . . . The operation to be conducted in the Western Mediterranean by General Alexander was mentioned, but without naming any objective.' Von Roenne, however, had picked up on the reference to sardines. 'A jocular remark in this letter refers to Sardinia,' he wrote. 'The codename for this operation is "Brimstone".' The attack on Sardinia, he surmised, must be 'a minor "commando type"' since Mountbatten had requested the return of Major Martin after the operation. 'This indication points to the invasion of an island rather than of a major undertaking . . . This is another point in favour of Sardinia.'

Just as importantly, Von Roenne relayed the news that Sicily was not a real target for the Allies, but a decoy: 'The proposed cover operation for "Brimstone" is Sicily.' That lie would sit, immovably, at the centre of German strategic thinking over the coming months: the attacks would come in the East, in Greece, and the West, most probably Sardinia; evidence of any planned assault on Sicily could safely be dismissed as a hoax. The only uncertainty, Von Roenne warned, was that of timing. If the two divisions identified in Nye's letter – the 56th Infantry attacking Kalamata and the 5th Infantry Division aimed at Cape Araxos – were deployed at less than full strength, then the 'operation could be mounted immediately', and the offensive might start at any time. However, the 56th Division, Von Roenne noted, had two brigades 'still in action' at Enfidaville. If the entire division was to be used in the assault, these troops 'must first be rested and then embarked. This possibility, which necessitates a certain time lag before the launching of the operation, is, judging by the form of the letters, the most likely.' In Von Roenne's mature estimation, Germany still had 'at least two or three weeks' to reinforce the Greek coast before the attack.

That was also enough time for the British to change their plans, which they might well do if they knew the information had reached the Germans. Von Roenne now turned to this important consideration. 'It is known to the British Staff that the courier's despatches to [sic] Major Martin fell into Spanish hands,' he wrote, '[but] it is not perhaps known to the British General Staff that these letters came to our notice, since an English Consul was present at the examination of the letters by Spanish officials.' The letters had been reinserted in the envelopes and returned to the British, and a senior officer of the Madrid Abwehr station had personally inspected the resealed envelopes before they were returned to Alan Hillgarth. The British might suspect, but would have no proof, that the letters had been read, let alone passed to the Germans and copied. 'It is, therefore, to be hoped that the British General Staff will continue with these projected operations and thereby make possible a resounding Abwehr success.' In order to convince the British that their secrets were still safe, Von Roenne suggested that the Germans mount their own deception: they should give no indication that they feared simultaneous attacks in the East and West Mediterranean, and instead 'initiate a misleading plan of action which will deceive the enemy by painting a picture of growing Axis concern regarding Sicily'. The Germans should pretend to reinforce Sicily, while doing nothing of the sort.

Von Roenne ended with a security warning. 'News of this discovery will be treated with the greatest secrecy, and knowledge of it confined to as few as possible.' The Baron's assessment was remarkable in many ways: it hauled on board every single aspect of the deception, and even launched a corresponding deception plan to reinforce it. But perhaps most astonishing of all was the ringing endorsement that accompanied the appraisal: 'The circumstances of the discovery, together with the form and contents of the despatches, are absolutely convincing proof of the reliability of the letters.' The army's chief intelligence analyst, from the outset, utterly dismissed the possibility of a plant.

This was, to say the least, strange. The analysts of FHW usually distrusted uncorroborated information emanating directly from the Abwehr, knowing the inefficiency and corruption of that organisation, and tended to be sceptical of Abwehr revelations 'unless these were clearly corroborated by more tangible evidence'. Von Roenne's natural scepticism seemed to have deserted him. He knew only what the Madrid Abwehr station had told him about the discovery of the body, which was second-hand information derived through Adolf Clauss. The report detailing the results of the second meeting with Pardo on

10 May had not yet reached Berlin. No additional checks had been made, the body had not been examined, and the original documents had remained in German hands for only one hour, far too short a time for forensic testing. And yet he chose to describe the documents as incontrovertibly genuine.

Deception is a sort of seduction. In love and war, adultery and espionage, deceit can only succeed if the deceived party is willing, in some way, to be deceived. The betrayed lover sees only the signs of love, and blocks out the evidence of faithlessness, however glaring. This unconscious willingness to see the lie as truth – 'wishfulness' was Admiral Godfrey's word for it – comes in many forms: Adolf Clauss in Huelva wanted to believe the false documents because his reputation depended on believing them; for Karl-Erich Kuhlenthal, any intelligence breakthrough to his credit, no matter how fantastic, made him safer, a Jew among anti-semitic killers. Von Roenne, however, may have chosen to believe in the fake documents for an entirely different reason: because he loathed Hitler, wanted to undermine the Nazi war effort and was intent on passing false information to the high command in the certain knowledge that it was wholly false, and extremely damaging.

It is quite possible that Lieutenant Colonel Alexis Baron von Roenne did not believe the Mincemeat deception for an instant.

18

Mincemeat Digested

Alexis Baron von Roenne appeared, on the outside, to be the consummate Nazi intelligence officer: a veteran of the First World War, a wounded war hero, holder of the Iron Cross, loyal to his oath, and the Führer's favourite intelligence analyst. 'Hitler had implicit faith in Von Roenne and in his reasoning ability, and seems to have liked him personally.' The aristocratic former banker had fought in the celebrated Potsdam Regiment, attended the War Academy, and demonstrated his intellectual mettle from the outset of the war. In 1939 he had been entrusted with the task of assessing whether Britain and France would come to Poland's aid if Germany attacked that country, and had sent a special report to Hitler, predicting that 'the Western allies would protest a German attack, but would take no military action'. Von Roenne's prediction was 'exactly what Hitler wanted to hear'; he was exceptionally attuned to what the Führer wanted to hear. 'Hitler was greatly impressed by Von Roenne's intuition, as well as by the accuracy of his evaluation'.

Again, in 1940, Von Roenne predicted that the Maginot Line, supposedly protecting France's eastern border, could be circumvented, enabling a successful German assault. Again, he was correct. By May 1943, Von Roenne had become Hitler's most trusted reader of the intelligence runes – a fearsome responsibility. 'It was his mission to produce for the high command the definitive intelligence they needed . . . It was at his desk that the buck-passing ended.'

Colleagues described Von Roenne as cold and distant, 'an intellectual but aloof person, impossible to make friends with'. Von Roenne's unapproachable manner was, perhaps, unsurprising, for there was another side to him, the obverse of the prim fascist functionary, of which his Nazi colleagues – and, most importantly, Hitler – knew nothing whatsoever. Von Roenne was a secret but committed opponent of Nazism, living a double life. He detested Hitler and the uncouth thugs surrounding him. His was an old-fashioned, monarchist, military cast of mind, steeped in feudal tradition and the belief that certain people (like himself) 'because of their origins, have title to be a higher class among the people'. His Christian conscience had been outraged by the appalling SS terror unleashed in Poland. Quietly, but with absolute conviction, he had turned against the Nazi regime.

From 1943 onwards, he deliberately and consistently inflated the Allied order of battle, overstating the strength of the British and American armies in a successful effort to mislead Hitler and his generals. His precise motive is still uncertain. Von Roenne may simply have been compensating for the tendency of his superiors to deflate military numbers. He may have been trying to impress his bosses. He was a fanatical opponent of Bolshevism, which threatened to destroy the class system to which he was heir, and he may have calculated, in common with other German anti-communists, that 'if Germany should give in to superior force in the West the Allies would help hold back the Soviets: and inflating Allied strength was a means to that end'. Perhaps, like other German anti-Nazi conspirators, he just wanted Germany to lose the war as swiftly as possible, to avoid further bloodletting and remove Hitler and his repellent circle from power. Whatever his reasons, and despite his reputation as an intelligence guru, by 1943 Von Roenne was deliberately passing information he knew to be false, directly to Hitler's desk.

Von Roenne's finest hour would come with the invasion of Normandy in 1944. In the build-up to D-Day, he faithfully passed on every deception ruse fed to him, accepted the existence of every bogus unit regardless of evidence, and inflated forty-four divisions in Britain to an astonishing eighty-nine. Without Von Roenne's willing connivance, the entire elaborate net of deception woven for D-Day might have unravelled. In the words of one historian, 'his way of fighting the Nazi war machine was to inflate estimates of Allied troop strength in England and convince Hitler and OKW that the main attack would be at Calais', when he may well have known that the real attack was aimed at Normandy. His determination to be deceived played a crucial part in the last chapter of the war.

Von Roenne was not directly involved in the failed plot, led by Claus von Stauffenberg, to assassinate Hitler in July 1944. But he was close friends with Stauffenberg and the other conspirators of the Schwarze Kapelle, the Black Orchestra, and his links with the planned rebellion were sufficient to ensure a grim fate in the ferocious Gestapo reprisals that followed. Hitler's revenge was breathtakingly brutal. A month after the July plot, Von Roenne was arrested, tried, and sentenced to death after a show trial by the 'People's Court'. In his own defence, Von Roenne simply declared that Nazi race policies were inconsistent with Christian values. On 11 October 1944, with other alleged conspirators, he was bound hand and foot in Berlin-Plötzensee prison, hanged on a meat hook by his throat, and left to die slowly. In an additional exercise in barbarity, Hitler ordered some of the executions to be filmed for his viewing pleasure. On the eve of his death, Von Roenne wrote a martyr's epitaph to his wife: 'In a moment now I shall be going home to our Lord in complete calm and in the certainty of salvation.' Von Roenne undoubtedly helped the Allies to win the war, but his precise reasons for doing so are an enduring mystery. If Kuhlenthal was losing the intelligence war by accident, then Von Roenne seemed to be losing it by design.

In May 1943, the allegation that Colonel von Roenne was

an anti-Nazi conspirator, working to undermine Hitler, would have been unthinkable, even treasonable. The diminutive baron was still Hitler's favourite intelligence analyst, and if he declared that there was 'absolutely convincing proof of the reliability' of this 'resounding Abwehr success', then that is what Hitler was most likely to believe.

For two weeks, during the wait for news from Spain, the atmosphere in Room 13 had been 'frousty, peevish and petulant'. Montagu's grumbling had intensified; he complained that 'he had to duck each time he had to go under the air duct, and approach Room 13 in a stooping position'. Given the pressure, he muttered, it was 'surprising that we only have five breakdowns among the female staff'.

On 14 May, the very day that Hillgarth reported the safe return of the briefcase, Juliette Ponsonby, the secretary of Section 17M, went to collect the latest Bletchley Park despatches from the teleprinter room in the Admiralty. Montagu began leafing through the printouts, and then suddenly uttered a loud whoop, and banged the table so hard his coffee cup flew off the desk. That morning, the interceptors had picked up a wireless message sent by General Alfred Jodl, the OKW Chief of the Operations Staff responsible for all strategic, executive, and war-operations planning, stating that 'an enemy landing on a large scale is projected in the near future in both the East and West Mediterranean'. The information, sent to the senior German commanders Southeast and South, with copies to the Naval Staff Operations Division and Air Force Operations Staff, was described by Jodl as coming from 'a source which may be regarded as being absolutely reliable'. The message then furnished full details of the planned attack on Greece, precisely as described in Nye's letter. Jodl himself gave his seal of approval to the documents: 'It is very unusual for an intelligence report to be passed on in operational traffic or by someone of [such] seniority with so high a recommendation of reliability,' wrote Montagu, who had studied thousands of such signals. 'So far as I can recollect it is almost unknown that such a thing should happen.'

The mood in the Admiralty basement changed instantly with the arrival of Most Secret Source message 2571. 'Everyone jumped up and down. We were so thrilled,' recalled Pat Trehearne. The ladies hugged one another. The gentlemen shook hands. The fly had been taken, and the tension seemed to vanish.

No corresponding message relating to the fake assault in the west on Sardinia was picked up, but the British concluded it was 'almost certain' that German commanders in the western theatre had received by teleprinter 'similar details from the letter which concerned that area'. Jodl's message was only the hors d'oeuvre. From this moment on, evidence steadily accumulated showing that 'the Germans were reinforcing our imaginary invasion areas in Greece . . . and at the same time spreading their available forces into Sardinia'. These were, in Montagu's words, 'wonderful days'.

Winston Churchill was in Washington for the war conference codenamed 'Trident', working on plans with Roosevelt for the invasion of Italy, the bombing of Germany and the Pacific War. A telegram was immediately despatched to the Prime Minister, stating cryptically that 'Mincemeat' had reached 'the right people and from best information they look like acting on it'.

Cholmondeley was quietly jubilant. Montagu scribbled a celebratory note on a postcard and sent it to Bill Jewell of HMS *Seraph*: 'You will be pleased to learn that the Major is now very comfortable.' He also wrote to Iris in New York: 'Friday was almost too good to be true. I had marvellous news of the success of a job that I was doing (it was so good that I feel a snag must arise).' Montagu was deeply relieved, yet he remained cautious, knowing that the deception was still at an early stage. The Abwehr in Madrid had fallen for the hoax, and so, it seemed, had the intelligence analysts in Berlin. The initial messages, wrote Montagu, 'proved that we had convinced them. Now would they convince the general staff?'

He had no cause to fret, for back in Germany the Mincemeat

lie was building up steam. On the day Jodl's cable was sent to Germany's Mediterranean commanders, Hans-Heinrich Dieckhoff, the German ambassador in Madrid, sent a telegram to the Foreign Office in Berlin: 'According to information just received from a wholly reliable source, the English and Americans will launch their big attack on southern Europe in the next fortnight. The plan, as our informant was able to establish from English secret documents, is to launch two sham attacks on Sicily and the Dodecanese, while the real offensive is directed in two main thrusts against Crete and the Peloponnese.'

Dieckhoff was clearly writing without the benefit of Von Roenne's analysis, for he missed the reference to Sardinia. An hour later, Dieckhoff sent another message, reporting that Francisco Gómez-Jordana y Souza, the Spanish Foreign Minister, had told him 'in strict confidence' that Allied attacks should be expected in Greece and the western Mediterranean. The secret was now streaming through the upper echelons of the Spanish government, and being fed back to the Germans. 'Jordana begged me not to mention his name,' reported Dieckhoff, 'especially as he wanted to exchange further information with me in the future. He considered the information wholly trustworthy, and felt it his duty to pass it on.'

The Mincemeat letters were now, finally, homing in on the ultimate target. Three weeks, and 3,000 miles, after their journey began, the forgeries finally landed on the desk of the man for whose eyes they had always been intended, the only person whose opinion really mattered.

Hitler's initial response was sceptical. Turning to General Eckhardt Christian of the Luftwaffe, he remarked: 'Christian, couldn't this be a corpse they have deliberately planted on our hands?' General Christian's response is not recorded, but by 12 May, the day after Von Roenne's enthusiastic report, any doubts in Hitler's mind had evaporated. That day, the Führer issued a general military directive: 'It is to be expected that the Anglo-Americans will try to continue the operations in the Mediterranean in quick succession. The following are most endangered: in the Western Med, Sardinia, Corsica and Sicily; in the Eastern Med, the Peloponnese and the Dodecanese . . . Measures regarding Sardinia and the Peloponnese take precedence over everything else.' The orders reflected a dramatic shift in priorities since, as Montagu observed, 'the original German appreciation had been that Sicily was more likely to be invaded than Sardinia'. Sicily now appeared to be, in German thinking, the least vulnerable of the Mediterranean islands, with the focus firmly trained on Greece and Sardinia. Hitler ordered 'all German commands in the Mediterranean to utilise all forces and equipment to strengthen as much as possible the defences of these particularly endangered areas during the short time which is probably left to us'.

In Washington DC, Roosevelt and Churchill were hammering out the next stage of the war, looking beyond Operation Husky. 'Where do we go from Sicily?' the President asked. The Americans favoured assembling a mighty army in Britain to attack across the Channel, as soon as possible. Churchill and his advisers preferred an invasion of the Italian mainland itself, disembowelling the soft underbelly. 'The main task which lies before us,' the British argued, 'is the elimination of Italy' – this would force Hitler to divert troops from elsewhere and undermine German strength on both the Eastern and Western Fronts. After three days in the presidential retreat in the mountains of Maryland, later named Camp David, Churchill addressed a joint session of Congress: 'War is full of mysteries and surprises,' he said. 'By singleness of purpose, by steadfastness of conduct, by tenacity and endurance – such as we have so far displayed – by this and only this can we discharge our duty to the future of the world and to the destiny of man.' The Anglo-American conference broke up with the agreement that Eisenhower would continue the fight in the south of Europe, while a great cross-Channel offensive would be prepared for the following May. But first, Sicily.

At the press conference ending the Trident meeting, Churchill was asked: 'What [do] you think is going on in

Hitler's mind?' There was laughter, and Churchill replied: 'Appetite unbridled. Ambition unmeasured – all the world!' But secretly, Churchill now knew that in one corner of Hitler's mind another conviction had settled: that the Allied armies in North Africa were aiming at Greece in the east and Sardinia in the west, while Sicily would be left alone.

With the effects of Operation Mincemeat appearing in intercepted German messages, a security issue arose. If someone outside the secret saw reports referring 'to a document that had been captured from a dead body' there would be a serious 'security flap', and questions would be asked about why top-secret documents had been carried abroad in this way, in defiance of wartime regulations. Bletchley Park had been instructed to ensure that any messages referring to the intercepted Mincemeat documents were initially sent only to 'C', the head of MI6, and to Montagu himself. 'Arrangements could then be made to warn recipients or to limit the distribution.'

Von Roenne had chosen to accept the documents at face value, and his analysis was now hurtling up the German power structure. Not everyone was entirely convinced. Major Percy Ernst Schramm, who kept the OKW war diary, recalled the intense discussion among senior officers over whether the letters might be forged: 'We earnestly debated the question "Genuine or not? Perhaps genuine? Corsica, Sardinia, Sicily, the Peloponnese?"' On 13 May, a sceptical officer at FHW in Zossen, identified by the codename 'Erizo', sent a message to the Abwehr in Madrid demanding more details about the discovery of the documents. 'The evaluation office attach special importance to a more detailed statement of the circumstances under which the material was found. Particular points of interest are: when the body was washed ashore, when and where the crash is presumed to have taken place. Whether aircraft and further bodies were observed, and other details. Urgent Reply by W/T if necessary.'

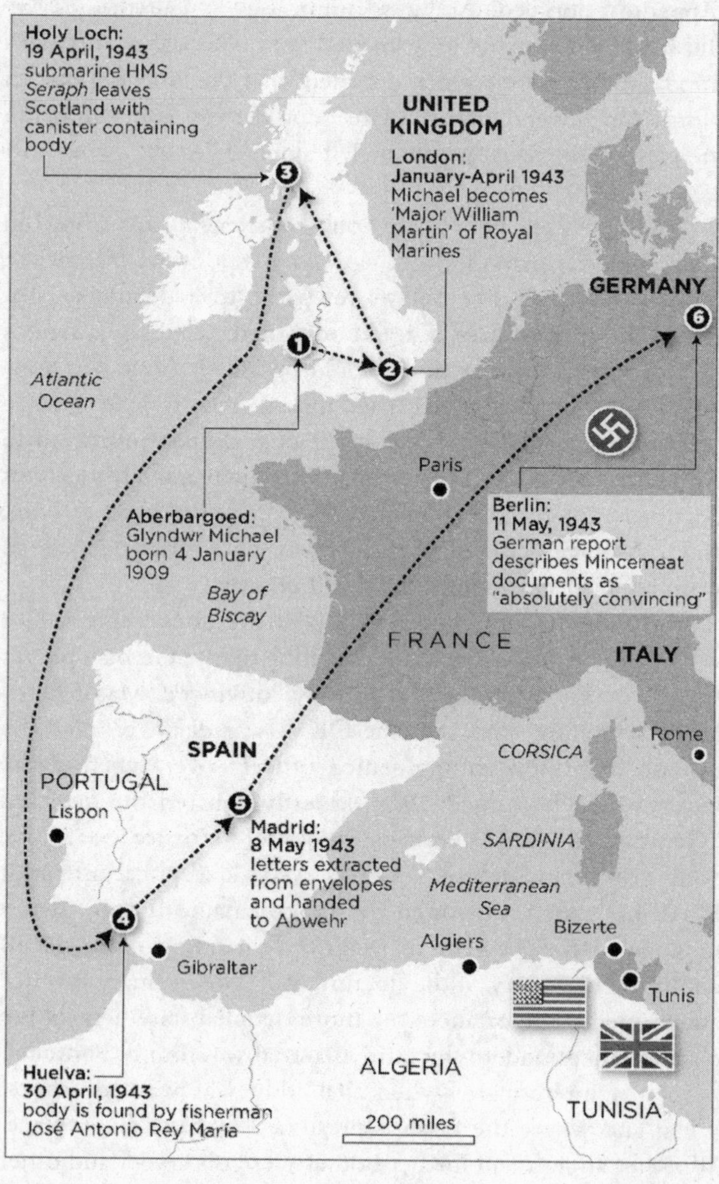
Holy Loch:
19 April, 1943
submarine HMS
Seraph leaves
Scotland with
canister containing
body
UNITED
KINGDOM
London:
January-April 1943
Michael becomes
'Major William
Martin' of Royal
Marines
GERMANY
Atlantic
Ocean
Paris
Aberbargoed:
Glyndwr Michael
born 4 January
1909
Berlin:
11 May, 1943
German report
describes Mincemeat
documents as
"absolutely convincing"
Bay of
Biscay
FRANCE
ITALY
SPAIN
CORSICA
Rome
PORTUGAL
Lisbon
Madrid:
8 May 1943
letters extracted
from envelopes
and handed
to Abwehr
SARDINIA
Mediterranean
Sea
Bizerte
Algiers
Gibraltar
Tunis
Huelva:
30 April, 1943
body is found by fisherman
José Antonio Rey María
ALGERIA
TUNISIA
200 miles

German analysts had now spent several days studying the letters, and the accompanying reports. The demand for greater detail on the discovery suggests that the inconsistency between the postmortem, indicating at least eight days of decomposition, and Kuhlenthal's timing of just three days between crash and discovery, had not gone unnoticed. The FHW also appears to have questioned how a decomposing corpse, at sea for more than a week, could still be holding a full briefcase when it reached the shore. And if a plane had crashed in the Mediterranean, where was the wreckage? The cable was followed by a telephone call from FHW, again pressing for more details.

The Madrid Abwehr office replied, somewhat huffily, that it had already requested, four days earlier, a detailed report on the discovery from the Spanish General Staff: 'The latter immediately despatched an officer to the spot. The results of the officer's findings partly differ in detail from the facts of the case as first represented by the general staff. Detailed report will arrive at Tempelhof [airport in Berlin] on evening of 15/5. Have it collected.'

Kuhlenthal had clearly picked up the new note of scepticism in Berlin, and, as he always did when under pressure, he simultaneously covered his back and passed the buck: 'Oberst Lt Pardo on the 10 May was emphatic that the answers he gave us were a complete story of the whole affair without reservations, but it seems, however, that this was not so.' The Spanish officer sent by the General Staff to Huelva to find out more about the discovery of the body, and the papers, had now returned to Madrid. 'The result of his investigations was communicated to us this morning in the presence of Oberst Lt Pardo's commanding officer.'

The Spanish staff officer had done his job well, interviewing most of the protagonists in the story, including the fishermen, the naval authorities and the pathologist: his verbal report added numerous corroborating details, and corrected others. 'In contrast to the first statement of Oberst Lt Pardo, that the corpse carried the briefcase clutched in his hand, it appears that the above mentioned briefcase was secured to the corpse by a strap around the waist. The briefcase was fastened to this strap by a hook.'

The new report, sent from the Abwehr office in Spain to Colonel Von Roenne at FHW as well as the Abwehr chiefs, accurately described how the papers and briefcase had travelled up the Spanish chain of command, from Huelva to Cadiz to Madrid, before being presented to Admiral Moreno himself. 'He [the Minister for Marine] handed the whole collection – the courier's briefcase, together with all papers found in his breast pocket – to AEM [Alto Estado Mayor, the Spanish General Staff] who undertook the opening, reproduction and resealing, and then returned them to him. He then gave the whole collection to the British naval attaché in Madrid.' The British plane carrying the courier seemed to have vanished into the sea without a trace, at least none that Adolf Clauss and his agents in Huelva could find. 'A search for the remains of Major Martin's aircraft and also for the corpses of any other passengers in this plane was unsuccessful.' But, as ever, Kuhlenthal had an excuse: 'The fishermen state that in the area where the corpse was found there are strong currents and other corpses together with parts of the aircraft might later on be found in other places.'

Far harder to explain away was how the body had so thoroughly decomposed in such a short time. But Kuhlenthal was up to the task:

> A medical examination of the corpse showed that there were no apparent wounds or marks which could have resulted from a blow or stab. According to medical evidence, death was due to drowning (lit: the swallowing of sea water). The corpse carried an English pattern lifebelt and was in an advanced state of decomposition. According to medical opinion, it had been in the water from five to eight days. This contradicts the evidence provided by the discovery of a nightclub bill on the corpse dated 27th April, and the

> discovery of the corpse at 9.30 in the morning of the 30th April. It is, however, considered possible that the effect of the sun's rays on the floating corpse accelerated the rate of decomposition. The doctors also stated that the corpse was identical with the photographs in its military papers with the sole exception that a bald patch on the temples was more pronounced than in the photographs. Either the photograph of Major Martin had been taken some two or three years ago or the baldness on the temples was due to the action of sea water.

Here was a classic example of willingness to believe, blended with self-deception and outright falsification. The earlier report had got the date of the theatre tickets wrong, but rather than correct the error, this report fudged the time gap. The Spanish pathologists had concluded that death took place at least eight days before 30 April, but in order to fit in with his own (erroneous) timing, Kuhlenthal changed this to between five and eight days. Two spurious but plausible-sounding scientific explanations were adduced to explain why the corpse was rotting, and why Major Martin looked substantially older than his photograph. The Abwehr had decided, from the outset, that the discovery was genuine, and moulded the evidence, despite obvious flaws, towards that belief. Kuhlenthal stood by his intelligence coup. With the information now swirling around the upper reaches of the Nazi war machine, he had no choice.

In the foetid basement of the Admiralty, Montagu and Cholmondeley were sweating over an entirely unforeseen development that would have been funny, had it not been so deeply alarming: Major Martin's briefcase had disappeared, again. Hillgarth had taken receipt of the case and other personal effects on 11 May, and promised to send them in the diplomatic bag to London on 14 May. By 18 May, the package had still not arrived at Room 13, and the Mincemeat team was starting to panic. That evening, Hillgarth received a telegram in secret cipher: 'Bag not yet arrived. Urgent that letters should be received earliest possible. Was bag sent by air or sea?' Hillgarth immediately replied that the items, packed in 'a small, sealed bag', had left Madrid for Lisbon, as planned, and should have arrived by air, addressed personally to Ewen Montagu. For months, they had been working to get the bag into the wrong hands, as if by accident. Now it might very well have fallen into the wrong hands, by accident.

In the same telegram, Montagu asked whether the rubber dinghy set adrift by the *Seraph* had ever washed up. He also passed on the news that initial signs seemed to show that Mincemeat was working: 'Evidence that operation successful but vital that no suspicion should be aroused.' Hillgarth replied that there was no trace of the dinghy, which had almost certainly been appropriated by the fishermen of Punta Umbria.

From his own discreet investigations, Hillgarth already knew that the deception was taking satisfactory shape. Agent Andros had 'reported that there was great excitement over some official documents found on the body of a British officer at Huelva'. The rumour mill was grinding away: 'I naturally asked him to find out what he could.' A few days later, Hillgarth ran into Admiral Moreno at a cocktail party for foreign diplomats. The Minister of Marine brought up the subject of the documents without prompting, and 'said that immediately he heard they had reached Madrid (he was in Valencia) he gave Chief [of] Naval Staff orders to hand over to me at once'. This was a bald lie. German documents show that Moreno took personal custody of the papers, and then handed them, unopened, to the General Staff.

There then followed a most revealing conversation between Hillgarth and his Spanish friend:

'Why did you go to so much trouble?' Hillgarth asked nonchalantly.

'I was anxious no one should have an unauthorised look at them,' Moreno replied. 'Which might be a serious matter.'

Moreno had tripped himself up. Hillgarth had requested the return of the case through a third party, but had never indicated that this was anything other than a routine matter, let alone that the contents were secret and should be kept from 'unauthorised' eyes. 'He obviously did not know the exact terms of my request which was verbal and could never alone have led him to say what he did,' Hillgarth reported to London. 'It can be taken as a certainty that Spanish government know contents of documents. I am not so certain they have [reached] enemy. Yet they were more than a week in Huelva and Cadiz.'

The Spanish admiral was playing a dangerous double game. On 19 May, the German ambassador, Dieckhoff, sent another message to Berlin, describing a meeting with Moreno: 'He told me that all his information indicated that strong forces would be concentrated in preparation for an attack on Greece and Italy . . . The Navy Minister regards an attack on Greece as especially likely.' While reassuring the British that their secrets were safe, Moreno was simultaneously passing those secrets to the Germans. The duplicitous Spanish admiral would make a very useful tool for reinforcing the deception. 'The operation has given conclusive proof of the extent to which the Spaniards will go in assistance to the Axis.'

On 21 May, to the intense relief of the Mincemeat team, the package containing Major Martin's briefcase and other effects finally arrived in London. No satisfactory explanation was offered for its week-long, heart-stopping disappearance. Spanish bureaucracy was not alone in moving in mysterious ways. The letters were immediately sent to the Special Examiners ('Censorship') for microscopic analysis. First they inspected the wax seals, and found that despite all that had happened over the preceding weeks, these were still perfectly intact. 'The seals were photographed and marked by us before they were despatched, and they have been photographed also after their return. They have not been altered in any way.'

Imperial War Museum

FIGURE 1.

Left-hand seal
before despatch

FIGURE 2.

Left-hand seal
after return.

But that was only part of the story. 'Although we can say that there has been no tampering with the seals [it is] quite possible that the letters have been rolled out, from under the bottom flaps . . . as the bottom flap was very much deeper than the upper, there was plenty of room for the contents to be taken out.' The eyelash was missing from each envelope, but the examiners had laid another, rather more scientific trap. Before being placed in the briefcase, back in April, each letter was folded into three, symmetrically, just once. A letter when folded dry creates a crease that is noticeably 'sharper than one made in it when it was well soaked and soft, more like that which would be made in a piece of cloth'. Under the microscope, it was revealed that at least one of the letters had been folded twice, 'once symmetrically and secondly irregularly . . . while the letter was wet'. Thus the examiners deduced that when the Spaniards closed up the key letter, 'it was not done on exactly the same folds and there were damaged fibres in the paper minutely separate from the new folds'.

There was one other test. To extract the letters, the paper must have been tightly wound around a metal prong. The letters had been soaked again before being replaced inside the envelopes, and despite the delayed journey from Spain, they were still slightly damp. A piece of paper rolled up when wet will tend to curl up when dried out. The censors extracted the letters and then carefully watched to see whether or not the paper would lie flat. Sure enough, 'as the letter began to dry naturally, outside the envelope, the edges began to curve upward, that is to say as they would if the letter had been rolled out of the back of the envelope'. Moreover, the rolling up must have happened when the letter was folded in three, since the examiners noted that 'when the letter is folded up, it all curves the same way'. Here was solid physical proof that the letters had been opened, corroborating the evidence now appearing in the intercepted wireless messages.

The Germans would be expecting the British to examine the returned letters carefully to see if they had been tampered with. The deception would be reinforced if the Germans could be made to believe that such an examination had been carried out and that the British scientists were satisfied the letters had never been opened. The best person to pass on that message would be the fickle Admiral Moreno.

A message was drafted to Captain Hillgarth, referring to his earlier conversation with the admiral. 'Inform Minister of Marine as soon as possible that sealed envelopes have been tested by experts and there was no trace of opening or tampering before they reached care of Spanish navy and that you are instructed to express our deep appreciation for the efficiency and promptitude with which Spanish navy took charge of all documents before any evilly disposed person could get at them. You should say that you may tell him in confidence that one of the letters was of the greatest importance and secrecy and the appreciation expressed at this token of friendship is most sincere.' This message was not sent in cipher, but by naval cable. A second, secret cable informed Hillgarth that the 'letters [were] in fact opened', but he should spread the word to anyone 'likely to pass it on' that the British were confident the letters were never read in Spain. 'Important there should be no repetition no suspicion that we believe letters were read so that present success may not be endangered.'

Despite the misgivings of some at FHW, and Kuhlenthal's blustering excuses for the gaps and contradictions in the story, the lie had by now firmly embedded itself in German strategic thinking, and was beginning to metastasise, spreading out through the veins of Axis intelligence. Important and exciting information, whether true or false, develops its own momentum. So far from being questioned, the expected attacks in Greece and Sardinia were fast becoming accepted wisdom.

19

Hitler Loses Sleep

Four days after Von Roenne's initial analysis, one Captain Ullrich, an officer on the German General Staff, offered a fresh assessment of the intelligence. This report, dated 14 May, 'consisted of comments for the perusal of Admiral Doenitz'. Ullrich was, if anything, even more wildly enthusiastic about the Mincemeat information than Von Roenne.

'No further doubts remain regarding the reliability of the captured documents. Examination as to whether they were intentionally put into our hands shows that this is most unlikely.' It is not clear what examination, if any, had been made in order to clear up 'remaining doubts'. No new evidence had been found, and no formal investigation had been undertaken. Yet the impetus of wishful thinking was unstoppable.

Captain Ullrich next addressed the question of 'whether the enemy is aware of the interception by us of these documents or whether he is only aware of the loss of a plane over the sea'. The analyst was confident that Germany now had the upper hand. 'It is possible that the enemy knows nothing of the capture of these documents but it is certain that he will know they have not reached their destination. Whether the enemy intend to alter the operations they have planned or accelerate the timing is not known but remains improbable.' The letter from Nye to Alexander was 'urgent'; Alexander had been asked to 'reply immediately "since we cannot postpone the matter any longer"'.

On the other hand, there had been sufficient time to send the letter by air courier, rather than by wireless, and to await a response. 'It is the opinion of the German General Staff that sufficient time remains for alteration in the planning of both the eastern and western Mediterranean operations.'

With Germanic precision, Ullrich laid out his conclusions: the attacks in the east and west would be simultaneous 'since only in this case would Sicily be unsuitable as cover for both'; the troops attacking Greece would probably leave from Tobruk, in northeastern Libya; Alexandria would not be used as an embarkation point, since it would be 'absurd' to pretend that such forces could reach Sicily, in conformity with the cover plan. ('This shows how wrong a staff can be, as Sicily was invaded from Alexandria,' Montagu remarked, when Captain Ullrich's report was eventually recovered.) It was possible, thought Ullrich, that the 5th and 56th Divisions would 'comprise the whole of the assault forces' in the Peloponnese. As for the decoy attack on Sicily, this might be a brief commando-style assault followed by an immediate retreat, but it could also 'be continued after the launching of the actual operation'. The report concluded by stressing that the German defensive focus should shift, emphatically, to Greece. 'It must be especially emphasised that this document indicated extensive preparations in the eastern Mediterranean. This is especially important because from that area, on account of the geographical situation, there has, up to this time, been considerably less news about preparations than from the area of Algiers.' There was, of course, another very good reason why the Germans had less evidence of an attack in the east: the Allies, in reality, had no plans to launch one. Once again, when the truth did not fit, the Germans willingly manoeuvred the facts in favour of the deception.

Grand Admiral Karl Doenitz, who had been made commander-in-chief of the German navy three months earlier, undoubtedly read Captain Ullrich's analysis, since he wrote on it. Among the documents seized at Tambach in 1945 was Ullrich's original report: in the margin, Doenitz's 'personal squiggle' is clearly visible, the initials indicating that he had read it, and absorbed its contents. Doenitz was one of Hitler's most trusted decision makers, and would become his heir: his influence was critical.

Benito Mussolini had long believed that the next Allied attack would be aimed at Sicily, the key strategic point for a full-scale assault on Italy. His German allies now set about convincing him otherwise. Doenitz returned from Rome and sent a report of his meeting with Mussolini to Hitler. In his official war diary for 14 May, the German admiral noted: 'The Führer does not agree with the Duce that the most likely invasion point is Sicily. Furthermore, he agrees that the discovered Anglo-Saxon order confirms the assumption that the planned attack will be directed mainly against Sardinia and the Peloponnesus.' A few days later, Hitler wrote to Mussolini: 'It is also clear from documents which have been found that they intend to invade the Peloponnese and will in fact do so . . . if the British attempts are to be prevented, as they must be at all costs, this can only be done by a German division.' Hitler's faith in his Italian ally was fading fast, and Italian troops could not be relied on to do the job. 'Within the next few days or weeks, a large number of German divisions must be sent immediately to the Peloponnese.' With regard to the Balkan threat, the Nye letter had not changed Hitler's mind; it had merely bolstered what he already, wrongly, believed. As one intelligence historian wrote in his assessment of Operation Mincemeat: 'It is very unusual and very difficult for deception to create new concepts for an enemy. It is much easier and more effective to reinforce those which already exist.'

Corroborative titbits flooded in from all sides, as Mincemeat's false information spread through German sources, official and unofficial. Ernst Kaltenbrunner, chief of the RSHA – the Reichssicherheitshauptamt, Reich Security Main Office – the organisation formed by Himmler combining the Security Service and Gestapo, told the Foreign Minister, Joachim von Ribbentrop, that his spies in the British and American embassies in Madrid confirmed that 'targets of enemy operation [are] Italy and her islands as well as Greece'. The Turkish embassies in London and Washington picked up the news, and reported to Germany that 'the Allies wanted to advance into the Balkans via Greece'. General Jodl was overheard on the telephone telling German commanders in Rome: 'You can forget Sicily, we know it's Greece.'

Additional Ultra intercepts showed that the German Abwehr station in Rhodes, citing the Italian high command as its source, reported 'that the Allied attack would be directed against Cape Araxos and Kalamata', and added a little embroidery of its own: 'Allied submarines had received orders to assemble at an unknown assembly point for massed operations.' The warning was passed from Athens to German commanders in the Aegean and Crete, the army commander in southern Greece, and the Abwehr in Salonika, which 'forwarded it to Belgrade and Sofia'. The deception was reinforcing itself, to London's delight: 'The reports coming from opposite quarters seemed to confirm each other and have evidently, for the time being at least, been accepted as true.'

The information had all originated in the same place, but having trickled out in the form of gossip, rumour and information passed from source to source, it now filtered back to Germany, confirming itself like an echo growing ever louder.

On 19 May, Hitler held a military conference in which he referred to the expected assault on Greece and the thrust up through the Balkans. The Führer's 'congenital obsession about the Balkans', stoked by the Mincemeat letters, was keeping him awake. 'In the last few days, and particularly last night, I have again been giving much thought to the consequences which would follow if we lost the Balkans, and there is no doubt that the results must be very serious.' The ravenous German war machine could not survive without raw materials from the Balkans and Romania, the source of half its oil, all its chrome, and three-fifths of its bauxite. German commanders had emphasised the threat of an Allied offensive in Greece since the previous winter, and discussions between the Axis allies in February had concluded that Greece was vulnerable. The documents had crystallised Hitler's pre-existing anxieties: 'the danger is that they will establish themselves in the Peloponnese'; he now proposed 'as a precaution to take a further preventive measure against an eventual attack on the Peloponnese'. Partisan activity was increasing in the German-held Balkans, and from Hitler's perspective the area seemed, in his own words, the 'natural' target. Greece was the thin end of an exceedingly sharp wedge: 'If a landing takes place in the Balkans, let us say the Peloponnese, then in a foreseeable time Crete will go,' he told his generals at the conference on 19 May. 'I have therefore decided whatever happens to transfer one armoured division to the Peloponnese.'

While the fake letter from General Nye concentrated Hitler's mind on Greece, Montagu's joke about sardines focused German attention on Sardinia. 'Sardinia is particularly threatened,' observed General Walter Warlimont, Deputy Chief of the Operations Staff. 'In the event of the loss of Sardinia, the threat to Northern Italy is extremely acute. This is the key point for the whole of Italy.' German fears for the vulnerability of Greece and the Balkans were mirrored by Hitler's anxiety over Sardinia: 'He foresaw that from Sardinia the enemy could threaten Rome and the main ports of Genoa and Leghorn, strike simultaneously through upper Italy and at southern France, and strike at the heart of the European fortress.'

A British spy within Italian government circles, meanwhile, reported that the Mincemeat information had reached Rome, 'through the Spaniards and not directly through the Germans' – confirmation that the Spanish General Staff had made its own copies of the documents, and passed these on to the Italians. 'The Italian high command have the details of the letter and have accepted it as genuine.' The Italian ambassador in Madrid told the Germans that he had obtained 'information from an absolutely unimpeachable source that the enemy intend landing operations in Greece in the very near future'. The German ambassador in Rome passed on the news, now no longer new, to Berlin. It is an intriguing comment on the state of the Axis alliance that the Italians delivered this high-grade information to the Germans, but the Germans, who had known it for considerably longer, felt no such obligation to share intelligence with its Italian ally.

Fragments of corroborative information were swirling around the diplomatic world. British intelligence discovered that the German ambassador in Ankara had informed the Turkish minister in Budapest that the German army would soon be reinforcing its military stance in Greece, but that it had no hostile intention towards neutral Turkey: 'There would be troop and transport movements towards the south which will affect Greece but that the Turkish government should not be worried in any way as these were not aimed against Turkey.' As always with Chinese whispers of gossip, the information tended to get mangled in transition. From Madrid, Hillgarth reported wryly: 'German circles here have a story that they have obtained warning of our plans through papers found on a British officer in Tunis.'

Soon after, Hillgarth received a report from Agent Andros describing, in minute detail, how the documents had reached German hands. 'The degree of Spanish complicity' was laid bare: 'This exchange of information with the Germans in fact took place at the highest levels in Madrid.' Andros confirmed that Leissner and Kuhlenthal, the two most senior Abwehr officers, had been directly involved in obtaining the documents from the Spaniards, and the entire episode, as Montagu wrote to 'C', was 'adding to our knowledge of German intrigues in Spain'.

Months later, shards of the false intelligence continued to ricochet from one source to another, breaking up in the process. A spy in Stockholm reported that the local Germans had information from a British aircraft shot down in the

Mediterranean, with battle orders showing 'simultaneous landings in Sardinia and the Peloponnese', and a secondary attack on Sicily. Almost every other detail in the report was inaccurate, but it was plain that it had come, as the report put it, from 'our refrigerated friend'.

One by one, Hitler's key advisers were being drawn into the deception, either by access to the documents themselves, or through independent 'confirmation', as the same intelligence arrived by other routes: Canaris, Jodl, Kaltenbrunner, Warlimont, Von Roenne. By 20 May, Mussolini 'had come round to the same view'. A collective willingness to believe seems to have gripped the upper reaches of the Nazi war apparatus, driven by Hitler's own belief. It takes a brave man to stand up to the boss in such circumstances. The men surrounding Hitler were not made of such stuff.

Nazi confidence was in dire need of reinforcement: with the Axis powers defeated in North Africa, bogged down in blood on the Eastern Front, facing an increasingly confident Allied enemy, before the arrival of the Mincemeat letters, the entire southern coast of Europe had appeared vulnerable. Now, instead of waiting for the Allied armies to attack, somewhere, anywhere, the Germans and their Italian allies could lie in wait at Kalamata, Cape Araxos and Sardinia, and then hurl the British and Americans back into the sea. The papers washed up in Spain represented more than just an intelligence coup: here was a real chance to strike back. The tide of war was turning, but here, floating in on the waves, was an opportunity to reverse the current. Fate was smiling on Germany. No wonder they chose to believe.

There was one man in Hitler's circle who remained sceptical. Joseph Goebbels was alone among the Nazi elite in wondering whether the letters that had so conveniently arrived in German hands at this opportune moment were nothing more than 'camouflage', an elaborate effort by the British to put Germany off the scent. The Nazi propaganda minister knew better than most that reality, in war, is a malleable and fickle substance. 'The truth is whatever helps bring victory,' he wrote. Goebbels had no faith in the Abwehr, which made such extravagant claims for its spy networks but produced so little of real use. 'Despite all the assertions, our political and military intelligence just stinks,' he complained. Having bungled and blustered its way through four years of war, the Abwehr was now trumpeting a 'resounding' success, with a set of letters that revealed Allied planning down to a comma. Goebbels thought he knew the British mind. He had *The Times* translated for him daily, and complained about the newspaper exactly as if he was a retired general living in the Home Counties, rather than the master of Nazi propaganda. '*The Times* has once again sunk so low as to publish an almost pro-Bolshevik article,' he harrumphed. 'It praised the Bolshevik revolution and used words that make one blush with shame.' Doctor Goebbels may have been one of the most repulsive creatures in the bestiary of Nazism, but he had a sensitive nose for a lie, and the British letters smelled wrong. To use the favourite expression of Admiral Cunningham, one of the notional recipients, something about the letters was just too 'velvety-arsed and Rolls-Royce'.

'I had a long discussion with Admiral Canaris about the data available for forecasting English intentions,' Goebbels wrote in his diary for 25 May 1943. 'Canaris has gained possession of a letter written by the English general staff to General Alexander. This letter is extremely informative and reveals English plans almost to the dotting of an "i". I don't know whether the letter is merely camouflage – Canaris denies this energetically – or whether it actually corresponds to the facts.' Unlike most of Hitler's advisers, and Hitler himself, Goebbels tried to test the reality presented in the letters against what he knew of British strategic thinking. 'The general outline of English plans for this summer revealed here seems on the whole to tally. According to it, the English and Americans are planning several sham attacks during the coming months: one in the west, on Sicily, and one on the Dodecanese islands. These attacks are to immobilise our troops stationed there, thus enabling English forces to undertake other and more serious operations. These operations are to involve Sardinia and the Peloponnesus. On the whole, this line of reasoning seems to be right. Hence, if the letter to General Alexander is the real thing, we shall have to prepare to repel a number of attacks which are partly serious and partly sham.' No other senior Nazi wondered if the letter was the real thing. Goebbels kept his doubts to himself, and his diary.

The trickiest aspect to lying is maintaining the lie. Telling an untruth is easy, but continuing and reinforcing a lie is far harder. The natural human tendency is to deploy another lie to bolster the initial mendacity. Deceptions – in the war room, boardroom, and bedroom – usually unravel because the deceiver lets down his guard, and makes the simple mistake of telling, or revealing, the truth.

The invasion of Sicily was planned for 10 July. That left a gap of two months in which the elaborate fabrication had to be protected, buttressed and fortified. For weeks, Allied deception planners had built up the fictional '12th Army' in Cairo, the dummy force apparently poised to strike at the Peloponnese, by spreading modern Greek myths: recruiting Greek fishermen familiar with the coast, distributing Greek maps to Allied troops, employing Greek interpreters.

On 7 June, Karl-Erich Kuhlenthal sent a message to Juan Pujol, asking his star spy to find out whether the British were recruiting Greek soldiers in preparation for the assault. The First Canadian Division was already training in Scotland, and preparing to embark for Sicily. Kuhlenthal assumed they were heading for Greece. 'Try to find out if Greek troops are stationed close to the First Canadian Army or elsewhere in the South of England, and if so, which Greek troops are these?' wrote Kuhlenthal. 'It is of greatest importance to discover the next operation.' Garbo told his handler that Agent No. 5, a wealthy Venezuelan student, would immediately head to Scotland 'to investigate the presence of Greek troops'. The Greek troops did not exist, of course; but then, neither did Agent No. 5.

The Germans had clearly taken the bait, but they would also be watching closely for any evidence confirming or disproving what they now believed. Dudley Clarke sent a message suggesting that 'the only serious danger' of the deception being rumbled would be a 'legal or illegal exhumation with a view to more thorough autopsy' on the body in Huelva cemetery. Montagu arranged another meeting with the St Pancras coroner Bentley Purchase, who reassured him that an autopsy at this late stage would probably be inconclusive. 'By the time that he had been buried for a short period his internal organs must have been, according to the coroner, in a very mixed up condition [and] the lungs would probably have been liquefied', making it even harder to establish death by drowning. Montagu sent a message to Bevan: 'Although no one in this world can be certain of anything it does not seem that the fear that the Germans may learn anything from a disinterment and subsequent autopsy is well founded.'

Still, a large slab of engraved marble might help to discourage any grave-robbing, while giving William Martin the sort of dignified gravestone he deserved. On 21 May, Alan Hillgarth received an encoded message from London: 'Suggest unless unusual that a medium-priced tombstone should be erected on grave with inscription such as quote William Martin, born 29 March 1907 died 24 repetition 24 April 1943 beloved son of John Glyndwyr repetition Glyndwyr Martin and the late Antonia Martin of Cardiff, Wales. *Dulce et Decorum Est Pro Patria Mori*. RIP. end quote.'

Montagu spelled Glyndwr Michael's first name wrong in his cable: the error was duly transferred to the stone. For a moment, the spies had second thoughts. Would a large marble gravestone look suspicious? 'This to be done unless restrictions on making payment from England to Spain or other wartime difficulties would have made it too difficult for a father to get this done in normal circumstances.' Hillgarth replied immediately: 'Please send me ordinary cipher signal saying that relations would like this stone put up telling me to get on with it I will then get exchange in normal way and proceed immediately.'

Germany's spies within the British Embassy could be relied on to pick up the message, and relay it to the Abwehr in the usual way. In a final element of stage design, the Mincemeat team wrote: 'Suggest Consul place wreath now with card marked quote From Father and Pam end quote.' Mario Toscana, the Huelva gravestone carver, was instructed to make the stone 'as fast as possible'. Francis Haselden sent the wreath, as well as several bouquets picked from the garden of the Casa Colón, the headquarters of the Rio Tinto Company. 'The purpose of this was not only to carry out what would probably have occurred in real life, but also to enable the grave to be visited often enough to discourage any chance of a secret and illicit disinterment for further autopsy.' Lancelot Shutte, Haselden's sidekick, would make a daily pilgrimage to the graveside, ostensibly as an official mourner, in reality to see if the flowers had been moved and the grave disturbed.

Hillgarth composed and dictated a letter, addressed to 'John G. Martin ESQ' but for the attention of Kuhlenthal and his spies:

Sir,

In accordance with instructions from the Admiralty, I have now arranged for a gravestone for your son's grave. It will be a simple white marble slab with the inscription which you sent to me through the Admiralty, and the cost will be 900 pesetas.

The grave itself cost 500 pesetas, and, as I think you know, it is in the Roman Catholic cemetery.

A wreath with a card on it with the message you asked for has been laid on the grave. The flowers came from the garden of an English mining company in Huelva.

I have taken the liberty of thanking the Vice Consul, Huelva, on your behalf for all he has done.

May I express my deep sympathy with you and your son's fiancée in your great sorrow?

I am, Sir, Your obedient servant,

Alan Hillgarth

At the same time, Montagu sent a message to Hillgarth, with the same audience in mind: 'I have been asked by Major Martin's father, fiancée and friends, to thank you for the trouble you and the vice consul have taken in connection with his funeral and to say how much they appreciate the promptitude with which you returned his personal effects. Few though they were, as Major Martin was an only son and just engaged to be married, they will be greatly treasured.' Here was confirmation for the Germans that all Martin's accoutrements were safely back in Britain. 'Could you possibly procure for him a photograph of the grave after the tombstone has been erected?' Hillgarth duly obliged.

As far as the Germans knew, the British authorities were deeply relieved to get their valuable documents back intact. Another small outlay by Hillgarth would bolster that impression, by way of local gossip: 'A reasonable reward of not more than £25 should be given to the person who handed the papers to the safe custody of naval authorities. It is left to your judgement whether this should be done by you through naval authorities or by Consul Huelva direct.' The sum of £25 was a small fortune in wartime Huelva: José Rey's fishing trip would turn out to be the most lucrative of his life.

While 'Pam' and 'Father' grieved in private, the news of Major William Martin's death now needed relaying to a wider, public audience. The Germans had access to the British casualty lists, and if Martin's name failed to appear on them, suspicions might be aroused. At least equal suspicion might be provoked among Royal Marines officers if one of their number was suddenly declared dead without warning. A letter, marked 'Most Secret and Personal', was sent to the commanders of the three Royal Marines Divisions, as well as the colonel who edited the *Globe and Laurel*, the Marines' official newsletter: 'No action is to be taken in respect of the notification of the death of Major William Martin. This officer was detached on special service and no mention will be made in General Orders.' The casualty section received a curt order: 'Insert the following entry in the next suitable casualty list "Tempy Captain, (Acting Major) William Martin, R.M." This should appear at the earliest possible moment.' But it was not so easy to slip a false death past the authorities. The department of the Medical Director-General later demanded to know whether Major Martin had died in action, and if so, how. The Navy's legal department wanted to know if the gallant major had left a will, 'and, if so, where was it?' Both departments were politely, but firmly, told to mind their own business.

The announcement of Major William Martin's death on active service duly appeared in *The Times* on Friday, 4 June 1943. By pure chance, the names of two other real naval officers, whose death in an aircraft accident had previously been reported in the newspaper, appeared on the same list. The Germans, Montagu speculated, might link the reported death of Martin with that accident. The death of Leslie Howard, 'distinguished film and stage actor', was reported in a news story alongside the Roll of Honour featuring W. Martin. The civilian plane carrying the actor had been shot down by a German fighter over the Bay of Biscay. Somewhat eerily, an Abwehr informant may have mistaken Howard for Winston Churchill, who had recently visited Algiers and Tunis. It is safe to assume that more public attention was paid to this 'severe loss to the British theatre and to British films' than to the obscure death of an officer whom no one, bar a few spies, had ever heard of.

The Times was the place all important people wanted to be seen dead in, and it is not possible to be deader than in the death columns of Britain's most venerable newspaper. That said, several people have been pronounced dead in the press while being very much alive, including Robert Graves, Ernest Hemingway, Mark Twain (twice) and Samuel Taylor Coleridge. In July 1900, George Morrison, the Peking correspondent of *The Times*, read of his own death in his own newspaper after he was believed to have perished during the Boxer Rebellion. (The obituary described him as devoted and fearless. A friend remarked: 'The only decent thing they can do now is double your salary.' They didn't.) This, however, was the first time in the newspaper's history that a person was formally pronounced dead without ever having been alive.

At the end of May, the Director of Naval Intelligence noted in his secret diary that 'the first German Panzer Division (strength about 18,000 men) is being transferred from France to the Salonika region'. The information was graded 'A1'. This was the first indication of a major troop movement in response to the Mincemeat papers. An intercepted message added further details of the 'arrangements for the passage through Greece to Tripolis, in the Peloponnese, of the 1 German Panzer Division'. The movement seemed directly linked to the information in Nye's letter, since Tripolis, Montagu noted, was a 'strategic position well suited to resist our invasion of Kalamata and Cape Araxos'. The 1st Panzer Division, with eighty-three tanks, had seen fierce action in Russia, but was now 'completely reequipped'. Last located by British intelligence in Brittany, the Panzer division was a formidable, hardened force, and it was now being rolled from one end of Europe to the other, to counter an illusion.

On 8 June, Montagu wrote an interim report on the progress of Operation Mincemeat. 'It is now about half way between the time when the documents in MINCEMEAT reached the Germans and the present D-Day for Operation HUSKY, and I have therefore considered the state of the Germans' mind in so far as we have evidence.' Montagu summarised the intercepted messages, known troop movements, diplomatic gossip, and the double agent feedback, all of which suggested the most 'gratifying' progress. 'The present situation is summed up in the [7 June] message to Garbo which to my mind indicates the Germans are still accepting the probability of an attack in Greece, and are still anxiously searching for the target we foreshadowed in the Western Mediterranean.' Whatever suspicions there may have been on the German side now seemed to be allayed: 'They raised (but did not pursue) the question [of] whether it was a plot.'

'Mincemeat has already resulted in some dispersal of the enemy's effort and forces. It is to be hoped that, as visible signs in the eastern Mediterranean increase, the story we have put over may be "confirmed" and lead the enemy to take their eye off Sicily still more, although they obviously cannot entirely neglect the re-inforcement [sic] of so vulnerable and imminently threatened a point. It already appears to be having the desired effect on the enemy and (as the preparations for Husky grow) its effect may become cumulative.'

There was still time for Mincemeat to go horribly wrong, but so far, Major Martin's secret mission was going swimmingly. Montagu's interim report declared: 'I think that at this halfway stage Mincemeat can still be regarded as achieving the objective for which we hoped.'

20

Seraph and Husky

Bill Jewell steered the *Seraph* towards the jagged silhouette of the coastline, as the wind whipped and wailed around the conning tower. It was past ten o'clock, and curtains of thick fog draped an irritable sea, the rearguard of a nasty summer storm. Jewell shivered inside his sou'wester. The weather, he reflected, was 'moderately vile', but the reduced visibility would work to his advantage.

Once again, the *Seraph* was creeping towards the southern coast of Europe in the darkness, to drop off an important item. Once again, she had been entrusted with a mission of profound secrecy and extreme danger, and the lives of thousands depended on her success. The difference between this mission, and the one successfully executed three months earlier, was that the canister in the hold really did contain scientific instruments, a homing beacon to guide the largest invasion force ever assembled to the shores of Sicily. Having played her part in the secret build-up to 'Husky', the *Seraph* had been selected to lead in the invasion itself.

A week earlier, Jewell had been summoned to Submarine HQ, Algiers, where he was briefed by his commanding officer, Captain Barney Fawkes: 'You are to act as a guide and beacon submarine for the Army's invasion of Sicily.' The *Seraph*'s mission would be to drop a new type of buoy containing a radar beacon 1,000 yards off the beach at Gela on the island's south coast, just a few hours before D-Day: 10 July, 0400 hours. Destroyers leading flotillas of landing craft carrying the troops of America's 45th Infantry Division would lock on to the homing beacon, and the assault troops would then storm ashore in the early hours of the Sicilian morning. The *Seraph* should remain in position as a visible beacon 'for the first waves of the invasion force', and retire once the attack was underway. The submarine would act as the spearhead for a mighty host, an armada of Homeric proportions comprising more than 3,000 freighters, frigates, tankers, transports, minesweepers and landing craft carrying 1,800 heavy guns, 400 tanks, and an invasion force of 160,000 Allied soldiers made up from the United States's 7th Army under General George Patton and Montgomery's British 8th Army.

Sicily may be the most thoroughly invaded place on earth. From the eighth century BC, the island had been attacked, occupied, plundered and fought over by successive waves of invaders: Greeks, Romans, Vandals, Phoenicians, Carthaginians, Ostrogoths, Byzantines, Saracens, Normans, Spaniards and British. But never had Sicily witnessed an invasion on this scale. If Operation Mincemeat had succeeded, then the Allied troops would face only limited resistance. Jewell had no idea whether his strange cargo had ever reached the coast of Huelva, but as he absorbed his new orders, he found himself wondering whether the dead body 'had delivered his false information to the Germans and whether, as a result, the thousands of troops preparing to assault the island would meet less resistance'. If the ruse had failed, and tipped off the Axis powers to the real target of Operation Husky, then the *Seraph* might be leading the vast floating host into catastrophe.

After receiving his orders, Jewell had reported to the 7th Army headquarters for a briefing from General Patton himself. Swaggering, foul-mouthed and inspirational, Patton was a born leader of men, and a deeply divisive figure. Jewell detested him on sight. With a pearl-handled revolver on each hip, the general strode around the briefing room, barking orders at Jewell and the two other British submarine commanders who would help to guide in the American ground troops. 'His force was to land in three parts, each on its own beach; he wanted reconnaissance checked and the submarines allocated to the beaches to stay in their position over the beacon buoys to ensure that the right forces landed on the right beaches.' The briefing lasted all of ten minutes. 'He was really very short with us, somewhat conceited and very rudely outspoken,' Jewell recalled.

Outside the conference room, Jewell heard a loud American voice call his name, and turned to find Colonel Bill Darby of the US Rangers, his friend from the earlier Galita reconnaissance. Darby explained that he would be leading his troops ashore in the *Seraph*'s wake, at the head of Force X, made up of two crack Ranger battalions. 'Do as good a job for us as you did at Galita,' said Darby, 'and we'll be mighty grateful.' Jewell promised to do his best. Yet the submarine commander was privately apprehensive. If the enemy spotted the *Seraph* laying the beacon buoy, they would certainly realise that an invasion was imminent, and rush reinforcements to that section of the coast. 'Discovery,' Jewell reflected, 'would throw the whole Husky plan into jeopardy.' Eisenhower himself had warned that if the Germans were tipped off, the attack on Sicily would fail. The American general told Churchill: 'If substantial German ground troops should be placed in the region prior to the attack, the chances for success become practically nil and the project should be abandoned.' Even a few hours' warning would be paid for in greatly increased bloodshed. Surprise was essential; lack of it was potentially suicidal. Patton's closing remark also stuck in Jewell's mind, both irritating and alarming him: 'The submarines would be less than a mile from the enemy, but come what may they must stay there until the Task Force with the army arrived, no matter how late.' The *Seraph,* codenamed 'Cent', would be left on the surface as the sun rose, isolated and defenceless, a sitting duck for the Italian guns ranged along the

From The Unknown Courier, Ian Colvin

Wilhelm Leissner, alias Gustav Lenz, codename 'Heidelberg', head of German military intelligence in Spain.

Galerie Huesken

Lieutenant Colonel Alexis Baron von Roenne, chief German intelligence analyst and anti-Nazi conspirator.

Courtesy of Federico Clauss

Adolf Clauss, butterfly collector and the senior Abwehr officer in Huelva.

Courtesy of Tristan Hillgarth

Courtesy of Tristan Hillgarth

Alan Hillgarth: spy-master in Madrid (*above*), gold-hunter in South America (*top right*), novelist in his spare time and, in the words of Ian Fleming, a 'war-winner'.

Courtesy of Jesus Copeiro del Vilar

Francis Haselden, Britain's vice consul in Huelva.

Churchill Archives

Churchill Archives

Two photographs taken by the Spanish police of Lieutenant Colonel Dudley Wrangel Clarke, the officer in command of deception for Operation Husky. Clarke was arrested in women's clothes in Madrid. He was then allowed to change into more conventional attire before being photographed again.

The National Archives

Juan Pujol García, Agent Garbo, the most celebrated double agent of the Second World War.

EFE Agency

Colonel José López Barrón Cerruti, the Spanish security chief who played a key role in obtaining the documents.

Courtesy of Jesus Copeiro del Vilar

Lieutenant Mariano Pascual del Pobil Bensusan, the Spanish naval officer and acting judge in Huelva.

Courtesy of Jesus Copeiro del Vilar

Dr Eduardo Fernández del Torno, the Spanish pathologist who carried out the autopsy.

Courtesy of Nicholas Jewell

Lieutenant Bill Jewell, commander of the *Seraph*

Courtesy of Nicholas Jewell

Rosemary Galloway, fiancée of Bill Jewell

Hulton / Getty Images

Churchill and his senior officers plan the invasion of Sicily at the George Hotel in Algiers. Admiral Andrew Cunningham and General Sir Harold Alexander, the two intended 'recipients' of the Mincemeat letters, are standing behind Churchill, centre and right; the addressee of the third letter, General Dwight Eisenhower, is seated right. General Bernard Montgomery is standing far right.

Samuel Goldstein / Keystone / Getty Images

General Sir Harold Alexander, the commander of Allied ground forces, who usually looked 'as if he had just had a steam bath, a massage, a good breakfast and a letter from home'.

Topfoto

Admiral Wilhelm Canaris, the formidable chief of the Abwehr, German military intelligence.

Courtesy of Leverton & Sons

Derrick Leverton, undertaker, gunnery officer and unsung hero of the Sicilian invasion.

H A Mason / Imperial War Museum

The invasion flotilla steaming towards Sicily.

Crown copyright

The tanks roll ashore on the south coast of Sicily.

The Times

British soldiers pass shells ashore.

IMW/Camera Press

Sicilians greet the Allied invaders as liberators.

Galerie Huesken

Alexis von Roenne on trial before the Nazi People's Court, accused of plotting against Hitler. He was found guilty, inevitably, and hanged in Berlin-Plötzensee prison on 11 October 1944.

Courtesy of Tom Cholmondeley

Charles Cholmondeley hunting locusts in the Middle East in Bedouin costume.

Twentieth Century Fox / Kobal Collection

A still from the 1956 film *The Man Who Never Was*: Ewen Montagu, right, plays an air vice marshal; the American actor Clifton Webb, left, plays Montagu.

coast. This was undoubtedly Jewell's most dangerous mission, with every probability that it might also be his last.

Jewell was sublimely indifferent to his own safety. He had faced danger and discomfort on an extravagant scale in a gruesome war. Time after time he had demonstrated his willingness to die. But now he had something new to live for. Bill Jewell had fallen in love.

After performing his part in Operation Mincemeat, Jewell had returned to Algiers for some well-earned shore leave. Among the new arrivals at Allied Headquarters in the city was Rosemary Galloway, a young officer in the Wrens, the Women's Royal Naval Service. Rosemary was a cipher clerk, coding and decoding the messages passing in and out of Allied Headquarters, and thus was privy to secret and sensitive information. She was vivacious, intelligent and exceedingly attractive. Jewell and Rosemary had met once before, in Britain, and in the sultry heat of wartime Algiers that acquaintance rapidly bloomed into romance. Once Bill Jewell had spotted Rosemary on his emotional periscope, he pursued her with unswerving determination. She proved a most cooperative quarry. There were limited opportunities for courtship in wartime Algiers, and Jewell seized all of them.

At Sidi Barouk, just outside the city, the American forces had created a rest camp that was the nearest thing in Algeria to an American country club, with bar, restaurant, tennis court and swimming pool. Jewell recalled: 'The American High Command had taken possession of a strip of beach and olive grove and converted it into an Arabian Night's dream – barring the houris, of course!' (Actually, these were available too.) An evening at Sidi Barouk was, in Jewell's words, 'a really de luxe experience'. Jewell's friendly relations with senior American officers earned him access to this 'most exclusive spot', and even the use of an American driver, one Private Bocciccio, a Brooklyn native, who drove with one leg permanently hanging out of his jeep. When Bocciccio was unavailable, Jewell squired

Rosemary around town in an ancient Hillman acquired by the 8th Flotilla and known as 'The Wren Trap', less for its romantic allure, which was zero, than its captive potential: 'None of the doors opened from the inside and, no matter how urgent the need for fresh air, Wrens who accepted the risk had to rely on the chivalry of their companions to release them.' Bocciccio, who had picked up some fruity British slang, was scathing about the Wren Trap, and what went on in it: 'Bloody heap ain't got no springs left.'

The Hotel St George was the best hotel in Algiers, and Eisenhower's headquarters. Built on the site of an ancient Moorish palace, it was surrounded by botanical gardens with hibiscus, roses and flowering cacti; in both war and peace, visitors sipped cocktails in the shade of vast umbrellas beneath the palms and banana trees, served by Algerian waiters in starched uniforms with epaulettes. The hotel chef, in Jewell's estimation, 'could turn out a meal, even in the depleted Algiers of that day, in keeping with the finest traditions of French cuisine'. Rudyard Kipling, André Gide, Simone de Beauvoir, and King George V had all stayed at the St George. On 7 June 1943, the hotel hosted the crucial conference at which Churchill and Eisenhower finalised plans for the Allied invasion of Sicily. That same month, it was the setting for the culmination of Jewell's campaign to win Rosemary Galloway. For two joyful weeks, he had wooed her with every weapon at his disposal: French food, an American swimming pool and a British car with doors that wouldn't open. Rosemary was in no mind to resist, and at the end of this sustained bombardment she had sunk, unresistingly, into Lieutenant Jewell's arms.

It was therefore with even more than his usual alertness that Jewell scanned the foggy seas off the Sicilian coast at midnight on 9 July: he had captured Rosemary Galloway's heart and he did not intend to lose his prize by getting killed. If Mincemeat had failed – or worse, had backfired – then Jewell, his crew, and the thousands of British and American troops steaming into battle behind him might not live through the next few hours. If the plan had worked, and he survived, then perhaps he would see Rosemary again. Jewell, who had never paid much attention to his own mortality, was surprised at how much this mattered to him.

The crew of the *Seraph* had already laid out a trail of small marker buoys, each primed with a fuse that would set off simultaneous blinker lights in exactly four hours, to lead the flotilla to shore. The heavier beacon buoy was brought up on deck, and the submarine slowly edged towards the drop point. Jewell was about to give the order to lower the buoy, when the lookout's hushed voice cut through the darkness. 'E-boat on port quarter, Sir.'

The German *Schnellboot*, known to the Allies as the E-boat, was a motor torpedo launch with three 2,000-horsepower Daimler-Benz engines, carrying four torpedoes, two 20mm-cannon, and six machine guns. It was better armed, and three times faster, than the *Seraph*. And it was about 400 yards away, motionless, 'a clearly visible silhouette standing out blackly against the dark blueness of the night'. The E-boat had also spotted the British submarine, and was attempting to determine whether it was friend or foe. 'It was a ticklish moment,' wrote Jewell. 'That Nazi, I knew, was faster than we and much better armed. I knew her gunners were at battle stations, manning their weapons and waiting for the word to fire.' For seconds that passed like minutes, Jewell 'waited tensely for the E-boat to make its move'. At a whispered order, the submarine's gun crews and torpedo men moved to action stations. If the German attacked, the *Seraph* would have to try to fight it out. Even if he won that duel, the coastal defenders would be alerted to what was coming over the dark horizon.

The British submarine lay low in the water; the swirling fog made identification doubly difficult. The German captain was plainly 'undecided about her identity, expecting only friendly submarines so near his coast'. Suddenly, he flashed his navigation lights. 'I knew that would be a recognition signal of some sort that I'd be expected to answer immediately.' The German captain's challenge gave Jewell the vital few seconds he needed. The decks were cleared, the buoy manhandled below, the hatch slammed shut, and Jewell barked the order to dive. 'Down she went in a few seconds. To the enemy she must have seemed literally to vanish.' With luck, reflected Jewell, the encounter would not tip off the defenders to the impending invasion: 'The captain of the E-boat would still be victim to his own indecision [and] so long as he couldn't be sure whether we were friend or enemy it was not likely the Germans would take alarm.' But time was short. The buoy would have to be laid within the next hour, for the mighty Allied army of invasion was now only a few hours away, strung out in a vast flotilla just over the horizon to the south.

The broad plan for the invasion of Sicily had been agreed at Casablanca back in January, but the process of working out the specifics of Operation Husky had turned into a dogfight, with intense disagreements among commanders, and rising tensions between the British and American allies. Patton found Montgomery 'wonderfully conceited' and noted that Alexander, the commander of Allied ground forces, had 'an exceptionally small head'. This from a man whose big-headedness was legendary. Montgomery said of Eisenhower: 'His knowledge of how to make war, or to fight battles, is definitely nil.' The British general flatly refused to accept Eisenhower's initial battle plans, which called for an American invasion in the west of Sicily aimed at Palermo, while the British took Augusta and Syracuse on the southeast coast. Monty insisted that he knew better, which he did, and predicted a 'military disaster' if the plan was not scrapped. Montgomery was adept at tactical manoeuvres: he finally got his way after cornering Major General Walter Bedell Smith, Eisenhower's Chief of Staff, in the toilets at Allied Forces HQ in Algiers. First at the urinal, then by drawing a map of Sicily on the steamy mirror above the hand basin, Montgomery laid out his alternative plan: a consolidated assault on the southeast coast by both armies.

Agreement was reached. Before dawn on 10 July, Patton's 7th Army would assault the coast at the Gulf of Gela, while Montgomery's 8th Army would storm ashore farther east at the Gulf of Noto and Cassibile. In all, some twenty-six beaches would be attacked along a hundred miles of Sicily's southern coast, by troops assembled in the ports of Algeria, Tunisia, Libya and Egypt. The invasion would be preceded by intensive bombing of Sicilian airfields. Immediately before the assault, paratroopers would drop behind enemy lines to sever communications, forestall counterattacks, secure vital road junctions and confuse the enemy. The Combined Chiefs approved the plan for Husky on 12 May, the very day that London intercepted the first message indicating that Hitler had seen, and believed, the documents in Major Martin's briefcase.

The logistics of the operation would have boggled most minds: the American contingent alone called for 6.6 million sets of rations, 5,000 crated aeroplanes, 5,000 carrier pigeons and accompanying pigeoneers, and a somewhat unambitious 144,000 condoms, fewer than two each. The task of assembling this plethora of kit was rendered yet more complex by the need for absolute secrecy. Amphibious landings are notoriously hard, as Gallipoli and Dieppe attested. They are all but impossible if the defenders are ready and waiting. Eisenhower was insistent on the paramount importance of surprise, predicting that the operation would fail if more than two divisions were waiting, and the defenders put up strong resistance. The Germans could hardly fail to spot the 160,000 soldiers and 3,000 boats assembling on the north coast of Africa: the key would be to keep them guessing as to where, exactly, the attack might come.

Once the offensive was underway, a secondary deception plan, Operation Derrick, would try to convince the enemy that the assault on the south was diversionary, and the real attack would still come in the west of Sicily, keeping more troops out of the battle zone. Maps of Sicily were kept under lock and key. The soldiers of the invasion force would not be told where they were going until the task force was at sea. Letters home were strictly censored to ensure that the intended target remained secret, with officers only half-joking when they instructed their men that when writing home: 'You cannot, you must not, be interesting.'

Yet word, inevitably, had leaked out, on to the docks of North Africa. *The Soldier's Guide to Sicily* was accidentally distributed too early. A British officer in Cairo sent his uniform to be cleaned with the Husky battle plans in the pocket. The papers were retrieved, but not before several pages had been used to write out customer invoices: somewhere in Cairo was a person with clean clothes, and the Allies' most secret plans. Still more alarmingly, an officer of the British 1st Airborne Division accidentally left a top-secret cable on the terrace of Shepheard's Hotel in Cairo. The document not only gave the date and time of the Sicily invasion, but also the timing for dropping paratroops and even 'the availability of aircraft and gliders for such operations'. The paper was missing for at least two days before the hotel manager returned it to the military authorities. Dudley Clarke was confident, however, that if it had fallen into enemy hands through such an obvious and 'gross breach of security' then it would probably be dismissed as a plant, pointing to Sicily as the cover target in accordance with Mincemeat. He concluded that 'the accident may well have assisted rather than hindered us'.

Operation Barclay, the overall deception plan to disguise Allied intentions and keep as many Axis forces as possible away from Sicily, reached a climax in the days leading up to 10 July. Submarines had dropped men on the coasts of Sardinia and the Greek island of Zante, to leave behind unmistakable signs of reconnaissance for the Germans to find, as if in preparation for major assaults. 'Operation Waterfall', simulating the gathering of an army in the eastern Mediterranean as if to invade the

Balkans, assembled huge numbers of dummy tanks and planes. SOE organised a genuine sabotage operation by Greek resistance fighters, codenamed 'Animals', to suggest increased partisan activity in the Greek target area.

Double agents were used to bolster the deception, most notably André Latham, a dodgy, high-living French aristocrat and career army officer with a rabid loathing for communism, who had been recruited by the Abwehr in Paris in 1942. Latham was introduced to the rest of his spy team in the Elizabeth Arden Beauty Parlour on Faubourg St Honoré: a playboy called Dutey-Marisse (or possibly Duthey Harispe), a former French naval officer named Blondeau, and a pimp and saboteur called Duteil who, unbeknown to Latham, had orders from the Germans to kill him if he showed any sign of betrayal. The team had headed to Tunis, with orders to gather information for the Abwehr. On 8 May, as the preparations for Sicily were gathering pace, Latham – 'athletic, middle-aged, of medium height, with grey hair and military moustache' – presented himself to the head of French intelligence in North Africa, and declared his intention to spy against the Germans. He was given the codename 'Gilbert' and put to work sending false information to his German spymasters, who considered him 'an agent of very high class'. Gilbert reported that a large invasion force was assembling at the Tunisian port of Bizerte, which was in fact composed of dummy landing craft, to divert attention from the genuine preparations.

The Garbo network was deployed to muddy the waters still further: Agent 6 in Garbo's stable was Dick, an anti-communist South African recruited in 1942 by Pujol, 'who had promised him an important post in the New World Order after the war' if he would spy for Germany. Dick had been taken on by the War Office 'on account of his linguistic abilities', and sent to Allied Headquarters in Algiers. Pujol supplied him with secret ink, and the South African was soon reporting back via Garbo to Kuhlenthal in Spain on preparations for the coming assault.

The Germans were 'delighted with their new agent'. To draw attention away from Sicily, and further disperse the available German forces, Agent 6 'speculated that on account of certain documents which had come to his notice whilst working in the Intelligence Section at Headquarters the landing would probably be made in Nice and Corsica'. Soon after, Dick managed to 'steal some documents relating to the impending invasion' and promised to forward these to Pujol hidden in a packet of fruit.

On 5 July, however, Garbo relayed sad news to Kuhlenthal: Dick's 'unmarried wife', Dorothy, had informed him that Agent 6 had been killed in an air crash in North Africa. The Germans had lost a key spy just as he was getting into his stride. This small tragedy was, of course, entirely fictitious. Dick and Dorothy did not exist. The invented spy had been terminated because of a real death: the 'officer who had been acting as scribe for Agent No. 6 met with a fatal air accident whilst returning from leave in Scotland'. Dick had had distinctive handwriting. MI5 debated whether to 'pretend that the agent had damaged his right hand and was therefore obliged to write with his left, or to attempt to forge his handwriting'. Neither option seemed safe, so Dick, the South African spy who never was, was summarily put to death.

Despite the tight security surrounding the Sicilian campaign, and the vast clouds of disinformation thrown up by Operation Barclay and the double agents, German and Italian intelligence could hardly fail to spot the signs of an imminent invasion: the hospital ships assembled at Gibraltar; the 8 million leaflets dropped over Sicily warning that Hitler was a fickle ally: 'Germany will fight to the last Italian.' Even more significantly, the fortified island of Pantelleria, sixty miles southwest of Sicily, surrendered on 11 June after a three-week bombardment in which 6,400 bombs were dropped. The assault on Pantelleria, 'Operation Corkscrew', was the obvious prelude to a full-scale invasion of Sicily itself, since its capture would furnish the Allies with an airbase within range of the larger island. In London it was feared that the successful capture of the island 'would give the game away altogether'. Double agent Gilbert told his controllers 'not to be alarmed as the attack on Pantelleria was merely a feint', and the real attack would come elsewhere.

Even so, some on the German side correctly anticipated what was to come, and German messages deciphered at Bletchley Park suggested that the Germans were increasingly concerned about Sicily. Even Karl-Erich Kuhlenthal, watching from Spain, began to wonder whether the plans detailed in the intercepted letters had changed. After the capture of Pantelleria, Kuhlenthal 'received increasing reports that Sicily would be the next invasion goal. Numerous reports to that effect were sent to Berlin, but Berlin discounted the validity of such information.' Field Marshal Albert Kesselring, the canny German commander in the Mediterranean, had believed for six weeks before D-Day that the most likely point of attack would be Sicily. Yet for the most part, the German high command appeared wedded to the belief that the main assaults would come in the eastern and western Mediterranean, while the assault on Sicily might still be a feint.

The false picture of Allied strength painted by Mincemeat and the other deception operations had left Germany attempting to mount defences across an impossibly wide front. 'Operation Cascade' successfully convinced the Germans that the Allies had some forty divisions available to participate in the offensive – almost twice the real figure – and could therefore easily mount two or more attacks simultaneously. In truth, the Allies never had enough landing craft for more than one operation. In the same way, the Allies' strategic thinking rejected the launching of an amphibious assault without adequate air cover: realistically, this ruled out Sardinia and Greece as objectives for major landings. The two targets identified by Mincemeat were simply not on the genuine Allied agenda. The Germans never realised this.

German intelligence was quite unable to tell the high command where or when the main attack would come. Confusion and hesitation reigned, as the Germans struggled to see through the murk of deception, and their own flawed and limited sources of intelligence. The agenda of possible landing sites included not only Sardinia and Greece, but also Corsica, southern France, and even Spain, while Hitler's fear for the Balkans coloured his every strategic move. In Sardinia, which the Japanese chargé d'affaires in Rome reported 'was still regarded as the favourite target', troop strength was doubled to more than 10,000 men by the end of June, and bolstered with additional fighter aircraft. At the critical moment in the Kursk tank battle on the Eastern Front in July, two more German armoured divisions were placed on alert to go to the Balkans. German torpedo boats were ordered from Sicily to the Aegean; shore batteries were installed in Greece, and three new minefields were laid off its coasts. Between March and July 1943, the number of German divisions in the Balkans was increased from eight to eighteen, while the forces defending Greece increased from one division to eight.

Despite Italian intelligence warnings that an attack on Sicily was coming, and urgent Italian calls for German reinforcements, 'no measures were taken to reinforce the island'. As the official assessment of Operation Mincemeat later noted, 'it was never possible for the Germans to cease reinforcements and fortifications of Sicily altogether, as we might have changed our plans and it was always too vulnerable a target'. Yet the Germans clearly continued to believe that Sicily, if it were attacked at all, would not face a full Allied onslaught. At the end of May, an Ultra intercept from Kesselring's quartermaster revealed how chronically underprepared the Germany forces were: rations for just three months, and less than 9,000 tons of fuel. Confidence that Mincemeat was doing its job rose higher still. 'Compared with the forces employed in Tunisia, this was a tiny garrison.' Four days before the invasion, Kesselring reported that his troops in Sicily had 'only half the supplies they needed'. Eisenhower's fears of meeting 'well-armed and fully organised German forces' on the shores of Sicily were unfounded. Germany simply did not know what was coming, or where, and by the time it became clear that Sicily was the real target after all, it was too late.

The Allies, by contrast, had a clear-cut idea of Sicily's defences, and the Axis failure to reinforce them. The British and American invaders would face some 300,000 enemy troops defending 600 miles of coastline. More than two-thirds of the defenders were Italian, poorly equipped and ill-trained. Many were Sicilian conscripts, men with little stomach for this fight, old, unfit, unenthusiastic and, in some cases, armed with ancient weapons dating back to the previous war. The Italian coastal defence troops, according to one Allied intelligence report, suffered from 'an almost unbelievably low standard of morale, training and discipline'. The German forces, some 40,000 men in two divisions, were made of more motivated material. The newly rebuilt Hermann Goering Armoured Division, three battalions of infantry, had seen hard fighting in Tunisia, and had been transferred to Sicily by Kesselring after the seizure of Pantelleria. The 15th Panzer Grenadier Division was a battle-scarred, war-toughened unit with 160 tanks and 140 field artillery guns. The Italian defenders would probably put up little resistance, it was predicted, but the Germans would be 'hot mustard'.

'It will be a hard and very bloody fight,' Montgomery gloomily predicted. 'We must expect heavy losses.' Bill Darby was also expecting the worst, and rather looking forward to it: 'If casualties are high, it will not be a reflection of your leadership,' the Ranger commander told his officers. 'May God be with you.'

21

A Nice Cup of Tea

The weather forecast was grim, and the weather deteriorating, as the great invasion force set sail. In Malta, Admiral Sir Andrew Cunningham, naval commander in the Mediterranean and the recipient of the second Mincemeat letter, received the news that the flotilla had set off with more resignation than hope. The admiral had recorded a message for the troops, to be broadcast on loudspeakers once the task force was underway: 'We are about to embark on the most momentous enterprise of the war, striking for the first time at the enemy in his own land.' The upbeat tone contrasted with Cunningham's gloomy feelings, as the flotilla set off into 'all the winds of heaven', with every possiblility that the entire force might perish at sea. 'The die was cast. We were committed to the assault. There was nothing more we could do for the time being.' Over dinner in the Malta headquarters, Admiral Lord Louis Mountbatten, the signatory of two Mincemeat letters, was even gloomier: 'It doesn't look too good.'

The weather steadily deteriorated, and the wind began to bellow, creeping up to gale force 7. The troop ships lurched and bucked through the 'breakers and boiling surf, whipped into needle spray'. Landing craft tore free of their davits and smashed into the decks. Cables snapped. The gale – some called it 'Mussolini's wind' – screamed louder. Some soldiers prayed or cursed, but most 'lay in their hammocks, green and groaning', surrounded by the stench of vomit and fear.

While all around him retched, Major Derrick Leverton of the 12th Light Anti-Aircraft Regiment of the Royal Artillery, jovial heir to a long line of British undertakers, played another hand of bridge with himself in the officers' mess and happily munched the latest rations: 'We are now getting Cadbury's-filled blocks,' he told his mother. 'I had a Peppermint Crème and a Caramello – very nice.' Derrick, known to all as 'Drick', was thoroughly enjoying 'the show', as he referred to the invasion. He would have been happier still had he known of the small but important part played by his brother Ivor in paving the way for the invasion, by ferrying a dead body to Hackney mortuary in the middle of the night. Like Ivor, Drick had an irrepressible talent for looking on the bright side of everything, the consequence of being brought up in a family dedicated to dealing with death. 'It was a most excellent cruise,' he wrote, describing the hellish trip to Sicily. 'Once we were clear of land, everyone was told the whole plan: date, time and everything. We had maps, plans, models, a copy of *A Soldier's Guide to Sicily* and a copy of Monty's message each.' Drick was particularly impressed by the naval officer who briefed the troops on the strategic importance of Sicily. 'He was excellent. He looked like a masculine edition of Noël Coward.' Major Leverton's task would be to set up his field battery on the beach and shoot down any enemy planes attacking the invasion forces.

Leverton could not sleep. 'I went up on deck just before the sun set and could see the Sicilian mountains quite clearly in the distance.' The wind was now dropping. 'The sea had been wickedly rough all afternoon, but it had now calmed down. I definitely believe it was a miracle.' The soldiers had already set to work with chalk on the landing craft, on which were scrawled a variety of joking messages: 'Day Trips to the Continent' and 'See Naples and Die'. Shortly before midnight, Leverton watched the heavy bombers passing overhead, followed by towed gliders, packed with troops for the assault.

'I was standing up on deck by myself then. I had previously often wondered what my feelings would be when the party started. I was disappointed to find that I had absolutely none. Although I was perfectly conscious that quite a lot of people I knew were about to be killed and that I might be just about to kick the bucket myself, I wasn't really interested. I didn't feel excited or heroic or anything like that. I seemed to be watching a play.'

Drick trotted below for a final hand of bridge ('rather a nice small slam') and another Cadbury's Caramello.

At the same moment, just a few miles ahead, in the darkness, Bill Jewell was setting the stage for the next act of the play. Submerged, the crew had heard the noise of the E-boat propellers fade as the torpedo attack vessel moved off. After twenty more minutes of listening, the *Seraph* cautiously resurfaced. The German boat was nowhere to be seen. Perhaps she was lying in wait for an ambush. If so, the two vessels would have to fight it out. The deadline was now less than an hour away. 'There could be no more diving – this time the buoy had to be laid.' The wind had dropped, but the sea was still choppy, making the task of dropping the homing buoy 'three times as difficult as it should have been'. Just after midnight, the buoy was hauled back on deck for a second time, and dropped at the precise spot indicated, 1,000 yards offshore. Jewell now heard, for the first time, the low, thickening drone in the skies above, hitherto masked by the wind. 'Unseen planes, hundreds of them, were roaring through the dark skies overhead. The vanguard of the invasion! "Invasion!" That electrifying word.'

For the first time, Jewell wondered if victory might finally be in sight: 'The invasion of Sicily would be a long stride in the direction of Europe, and at least a short step on the road to Berlin,' he reflected. If it succeeded. The same thoughts were echoed among the assault troops. An American journalist sailing with the 5th Division wrote: 'Many of the men on this ship believe that the operation will determine whether this war will end in stalemate or whether it will be fought to a clear-cut decision.'

Jewell heard a series of loud explosions and, looking back towards the land, he could see 'great fires springing up in every direction'. Those paratroopers who had survived the flight and the drop were now at work. At the same time, above the echo of detonations and the drone of aircraft, Jewell picked up another noise. The wind had now dropped completely, as it often does in the Mediterranean, and he could now hear 'the faint throb of approaching engines'. Italian coastal radar had also picked up the shape of the advancing fleet. Seconds later, a battery of searchlights from the shore turned night to day, and the British submarine found herself in the limelight. 'Their blindingly brilliant beams cut across the water and blended into a dazzling ball of light concentrated on *Seraph*.' In normal circumstances, this would have been the cue to dive, but Jewell's orders were to stay put until the flotilla arrived. The shore guns opened fire, and for the next ten minutes – 'a nerve-tightening, shell-packed eternity' – the *Seraph* sat immobile, as hell exploded all around her. The cook, crouched behind a machine gun, cursed eloquently. Each shell sent up a plume of water, and the lookouts huddled into the sides of the conning tower, 'as much to avoid the cascading water as to find protection from flying shrapnel'. Between explosions, the 'throbbing beat' grew louder.

Then, out of the gloom, came 'a flicker of light from the leading destroyer of the mighty invasion fleet'. Moments later the ships took on form, as 'dark shapes emerged slowly from the shadows'. Forgetting the shells dropping around him, Jewell thought he had never seen anything so lovely. 'The English language needs a new descriptive noun to replace the hackneyed word *armada*,' he wrote. 'As far as my night glasses would carry, I saw hundreds of ships following in orderly fashion.' The destroyer searchlights now picked out the gun emplacements on shore, 'like footlights on a stage', and opened fire. 'Shells whistled high overhead.' Enemy planes screamed over, dropping flares to aid the onshore gunners.

Out at sea, Derrick Leverton admired the flak pouring into the sky 'with different coloured tracer', and the shimmering light in the sky as the dry wheat fields above the beaches ignited. It was horribly beautiful. 'With flares, searchlights and blazing fires, plus the vivid chromatic effects of bomb bursts and shell explosions, all of Sicily so far as the eye could reach was like nothing in the world so much as a huge pyrotechnical show.' The first destroyer passed the *Seraph*, her American crew 'cheering the stubborn little submarine'. Moments later, a small landing craft approached, with an American naval captain standing in the stern. Above the noise, he shouted: 'Ahoy *Seraph*! The Admiral has sent me over to thank you for a great job of work.' Jewell gave what he later admitted was 'a slightly astonished salute'. But the captain had not finished his peroration. 'You know, those boys who landed are going to remember for a long time how you guided 'em in . . .'

This was the moment for the *Seraph* to 'slide warily back into the protective darkness'. Jewell took a last look back at the shore, where 'tiny, darting flashes marked the progress of the assault force as the tommy guns blazed a path through the defenders'. Bill Darby's US Rangers had hit the beach at Gela. Jewell 'hoped the friendly, ever-joking colonel would do nothing foolhardy'.

Leading from the front, since he knew no other place to lead from, Bill Darby stormed up the beach like a man possessed, which he was; through the defences, and straight on to the town of Gela, much of which had already been demolished by the naval guns. Italian troops of the Livorno Division attempted to make a stand at the town's cathedral, and were swiftly overwhelmed by the Rangers. Darby personally held off an Italian counterattack by light Renault tanks, armed only with a .30-calibre machine gun mounted on his jeep. Realising that something more substantial was needed, he ran back to the beach, obtained a 37mm anti-tank gun, opened its ammunition box with an axe, and then, with the help of a captain, used it to blow up another Italian tank as it bore down on his command post. For good measure, he popped a grenade on the tank hatch. Its terrified Italian crew immediately surrendered.

Some twelve hours into the invasion, Darby took a rolled-up American flag from his backpack and nailed it to the door of the Fascist Party headquarters in Gela's main square. After the battle of Gela, Patton awarded Darby the Distinguished Service Cross, and a promotion to full colonel. He accepted the medal, and turned down the promotion, again. 'Darby is really a great soldier,' marvelled Patton.

To the east, Major Derrick Leverton was taking the invasion at a more leisurely pace. Having 'wished my chaps good luck. All perfectly normal and matter-of-fact', the undertaker waited on deck to be called to the landing craft. 'As there was still a bit of time in hand, I went to sleep.' Leverton holds the distinction of being the only man to doze off in the middle of the biggest seaborne invasion man had yet staged. There was, he recalled, 'quite a bit of banging about going on in the background', but Derrick had no problem dropping off. As acts of heroism go, this very nearly compares to the exploits of Colonel Darby.

'It was getting close to dawn, and the hills could just be seen in silhouette' when Leverton clambered into the landing craft. In a few minutes he was ashore, after wading through the wreckage of gliders that had made 'slightly premature landings'. Two dead paratroopers lay on the beach. Leverton was the last man to be upset by the sight of dead bodies ('The first thing I was conscious of was the delicious smell of crushed thyme'). He and his men headed to the spot chosen for the gun emplacement, straight through a minefield. 'Occasional mines went off, making a hell of a row and a lot of black smoke.' While his guns were unloaded, Leverton decided it was time for a cup of tea. His rations, he was delighted to find, contained 'tea-sugar-and-milk powder', which could be brewed simply by adding hot water. 'Most nourishing, appetising and intelligent,' thought Drick. Then he was dive-bombed.

This, he told his mother in a letter, 'added zest to the party'. 'As the bombs came down, I hopped down beside a stone wall. A lot of dust and stuff flew about, and when I got up I found a bit of stone as big as a football had been blown out of the wall a few feet from my head.' Only an incurable optimist like Leverton could see the bright side of being bombed. 'Another bomb fell in the sea and splashed us with nice cool water.' In case of further attacks, the undertaker instructed his men to dig 'little graves about three feet deep which were most comfortable'. The guns had still not been unloaded, so Leverton tucked himself up in his foxhole, and went back to sleep. Unlike his nourishing kip on the boat, this sleep was less restful. 'I had rather an awful sort of dream of dive bombing and so forth and I woke up with a glorious sort of feeling that it was only a dream, when I realised it wasn't a dream and the blighters were just above me in their dive.' The bombs caused only minor damage, although, as he wrote to his parents, 'the concussion in my grave jarred a bit'.

By nightfall, the guns were assembled, and in action. To Leverton's satisfaction, one dive-bomber was shot down on the first day. Over the next six weeks, eleven more kills would follow, 'plus quite a lot of "possibles" and "damaged"'. Leverton was happy. 'Our chaps are very bucked at knowing we were the first battery to go into action in Europe since Dunkirk.'

It was hot on the beach, and organising the guns in long drill slacks and gaiters was sweaty work. 'I didn't feel I was suitably dressed for the job,' wrote Major Leverton. 'I therefore designed myself a utility invasion suit, consisting of a thin shirt, my blue Jantzen swimming shorts, a pair of blue gym shoes and a tin hat. An excellent and highly recommended costume.'

And so, as the bombs fell around him, this heroic British undertaker sat in his own grave, wearing his swimming trunks and a helmet, drinking a nice cup of tea.

He looked ridiculous and, at the same time, bloody magnificent.

Mussolini was woken by an army colonel at six in the morning, to be told that the invasion of Sicily was underway. Il Duce was bullish: 'Throw them back into the sea, or at least nail them to the shore.' He had been right all along: Sicily was the obvious target. 'I'm convinced our men will resist, and besides, the Germans are sending reinforcements,' he said. 'We must be confident.'

Never was confidence more misplaced. By the end of the day, more than 100,000 Allied troops were ashore, with 10,000 vehicles. The Italian defenders surrendered in large numbers, often simply stripping off their uniforms and walking away, or running. Sicilian cheers, not bullets, greeted the invaders in many places. The British 8th Army had expected some 10,000 casualties in the first week of the invasion; just one-seventh of that number were killed or wounded. The Navy had anticipated the loss of up to 300 ships in the first two days; barely a dozen were sunk.

At 11.00 the previous evening, André Latham, Agent Gilbert, had sent a wireless message to his German handlers: 'Most important. Have learned from reliable source that large force now on its way to Sicily. Invasion may be expected hourly.' He was only telling the defenders what they already knew, for the first major alert had reached Italian coastal units several hours before Jewell dropped his homing buoy. By then, it was far too late for the defenders to make adequate preparations, and the bombing of the Sicilian telephone network ensured that many units remained unaware of the attack until it was well underway. Some went to bed, assuming the enemy would not be so rash as to attack in the middle of a storm. The Italian commander in Sicily was fully expecting an attack – indeed, the Italian intelligence services were never as taken in by the deception as their German counterparts – yet owing in part to Operation Derrick, the secondary deception, the assault was expected in the west, not the south.

As predicted, the response of the German divisions, stationed inland, was more vigorous. But by the time the Germans counterattacked on Sunday, 11 July, crucial time had been lost, and the Allied beachhead was firmly in place. Spitfires attacked the Luftwaffe's Sicilian headquarters, disorientating what remained of German air defences at the crucial moment. Field Marshal Kesselring had sent the 15th Panzer Division to intercept the expected invasion in the west of the island, leaving the Hermann Goering Panzers to absorb the brunt of the assault. The Germans did nothing to hide their disgust as the Italian troops melted away, and the coastal defences collapsed like sandcastles in a hurricane. A message to Berlin, sent on the day after the landings, reported the 'complete failure of coastal defence' and noted sourly that 'on enemy penetration many of the local police and civil authorities fled. In Syracuse, the enemy landings gave rise to plundering and rioting by the population, who accepted the landings with indifference.' So many Italians surrendered in the first two days that the long lines of prisoners impeded the advancing troops. Kesselring complained that 'half-clothed Italian soldiers were careering around the countryside in stolen lorries'.

At 5.15 on the afternoon of D-Day, Kesselring ordered the Hermann Goering Division: 'at once and with all forces attack and destroy whatever opposes the division. The Führer has ordered all forces to be brought into operation immediately in order to prevent the enemy from establishing itself.' The German tanks could not break through. Some forty-three were destroyed, in bitter and bloody combat. The commander of the Goering Division conceded: 'The counterattack against hostile landings has failed.' The German tanks rumbled north, to continue the fight inland. General Patton, screeching around the battlefield in his jeep, called it 'the shortest Blitzkrieg in history'. Montgomery agreed with him on this, if nothing else. 'The German in Sicily is doomed. Absolutely doomed. He won't get away.'

The conquest of the island was just beginning, more ferocious fighting was to come, but the Sicilian D-Day was over, and won.

22

Hook, Line and Sinker

A loud cheer erupted from Room 13 as the news of success in Sicily broke. Cholmondeley performed a shuffling dance, and a strange ululation. 'Auntie' Joan Saunders wiped her eyes.

The strain of waiting had been almost unbearable. As the success of Operation Mincemeat became clear, Montagu privately feared his part in the war might be coming to an end. 'Even if I have once brought off something really important and worthwhile . . . I'm never going to be allowed to do anything of the kind again.' The pressure had left the planners hollow-eyed and, in Montagu's words, 'too keyed-up to read a book or to get to sleep'.

Looking back, Montagu recalled the flooding relief as the Allies surged through Sicily. 'It is really impossible to describe the feeling of joy and satisfaction at knowing that the team must have saved the lives of hundreds of Allied soldiers during the invasion – a feeling mixed with the delight that we had managed to do what we said we could do and what so many of our seniors had said was impossible – and what I have always thought even Churchill really thought was only worth trying as a desperate measure.' For Montagu, a special pleasure lay in the subsequent discovery that Hitler himself had fallen for the phoney documents: 'Joy of joys to anyone, and particularly a Jew, the satisfaction of knowing that they had directly and specifically fooled that monster.'

The deception had succeeded beyond every expectation, and Montagu was jubilant: 'We fooled those of the Spaniards who assisted the Germans, we fooled the German intelligence service both in Spain and in Berlin, we fooled the German operational staff and supreme command, we fooled Keitel, and, finally, we fooled Hitler himself, and kept him fooled right up to the end of July.' The operation was also gratifyingly economical: 'One specially made canister, one battledress uniform, some dry ice, the time of a few officers, a van drive to Scotland and back, about sixty miles added to HMS *Seraph*'s passage and a few sundries: about £200 at most.'

There was no grand celebration over the success of Operation Mincemeat, no return to the Gargoyle Club with Montagu and Jean Leslie playing the parts of Bill Martin and his beloved Pam. Montagu's wife, Iris, perhaps prompted by the dark hints from her mother-in-law, had announced that she was returning from America with the children. Montagu knew that Hitler was still planning to unleash pilotless flying bombs on London, and that the capital remained deeply unsafe. Since this information came from Ultra, however, he could not tell Iris. 'The most I could do was make vague references to Hitler's last fling. But this made no impression on her.' It was probably not Hitler's fling that worried her. Iris and the children returned to London while the invasion of Sicily was underway. The reunion was a joyful one. The photograph of Pam in her bathing suit, lovingly signed, was swiftly removed from Montagu's dressing table. Montagu could not yet explain what that was all about. Perhaps this was just as well.

Secret messages of congratulation flooded in from those who had touched, or been touched by, Operation Mincemeat. Dudley Clarke, the cross-dressing maverick behind 'A' Force, wrote: 'I do congratulate you most warmly on the success of your "M" operation. It was very remarkable and a fine piece of organisation and whatever the developments may be you have achieved 100 per cent success.' General Nye also applauded the planners: 'It is a most interesting story, and it seems it was swallowed [whole].' Frank Foley, the celebrated MI6 officer who had helped thousands of Jews to escape from Germany before the war, told Montagu that the operation had been 'the greatest achievement in the [deception] line ever brought off'. In his diary, Guy Liddell celebrated: 'Mincemeat has been an outstanding success.'

There was already talk of medals for the framers of Operation Mincemeat. Johnnie Bevan and Ewen Montagu had spent months at loggerheads, but to Bevan's great credit he insisted that both Montagu and Cholmondeley deserved formal recognition, albeit secretly. 'From evidence at present available it appears that a certain deception operation proved a considerable success and influenced German dispositions with all-important strategical and operational results. The fact that it achieved such very successful results must be attributed in large measure to the ingenuity and tireless energy on the part of these two officers.' Montagu had pushed the operation through by force of personality, while Cholmondeley 'was the originator of this ingenious scheme and was responsible, in conjunction with a certain naval officer, for the detailed execution of the operation'. Both men, Bevan recommended, 'should receive a similar decoration, since each seems to have played equally vital parts on the plot'.

Montagu was so delighted by the success of Mincemeat that he proposed a sequel. A plane carrying the Polish Prime Minister in exile, Władysław Sikorski, had crashed on take-off from Gibraltar on 4 July. Six days later, on Sicilian D-Day, Montagu sent a note to Bevan pointing out that 'papers from Sikorski's aircraft are still washing up and likely to reach the Spanish shore', and suggesting that this might be an opportunity to plant some false documents among the debris. The object would be 'to show that Mincemeat was genuine and that we are going to attack Greece, etc., and that we only delayed it and switched from Brimstone [Sardinia] to Sicily because we suspected that the Spaniards might have shown the papers in

Mincemeat to the Germans'. Mincemeat Mark II was vetoed by Commodore Rushbrooke, the Director of Naval Intelligence, because the Germans could not be expected to fall for the same ruse twice. 'Not worth trying. The Spaniards will know that everything of importance has been recovered, and a valuable secret "wash up" could have no verisimilitude.'

The success of the Sicily invasion could not, of course, be attributed to Operation Mincemeat alone. To an important degree, the deception plan reinforced what the Germans already believed. Every element of Operation Barclay – of which Mincemeat was but one strand – tended to back up that misperception. Moreover, the comparative weakness of German forces in Sicily reflected Hitler's mounting doubts about Italy's commitment to the war. Sicily was a strategic jewel, but it was also an island, physically separated from the rest of the Axis forces. If large numbers of German troops were committed to defend it, but Italy dropped out of the war, they would be isolated, and Sicily would become, in Kesselring's words, a 'mousetrap for all German and Italian forces fighting down there'.

Yet up to, and even after, the invasion of Sicily, the effects of Mincemeat lingered on in German tactical planning, slewing attention to east and west. The night before the attack, Keitel had distributed a 'Most Immediate' analysis of Allied intentions, predicting a major Allied landing in Greece, and a joint attack on Sardinia and Sicily: 'Western assault forces appear to be ready for an immediate attack while the eastern forces appear to be still forming up,' he wrote. 'A subsequent landing on the Italian mainland is less probable than one on the Greek mainland.' Half the Allied troops available in North Africa, Keitel predicted, would be used 'to reinforce the bridgehead which . . . would be established in Greece'.

Ultra intercepts showed that four hours after the landings, twenty-one ground-attack aircraft took off from Sicily, which was now under attack, heading for Sardinia, which was not. The same day, the Abwehr in Berlin sent a message to its

Spanish office 'stating that the High Command in Berlin were particularly anxious that a sharp lookout should be kept for convoys passing through the straits of Gibraltar which might be going to attack Sardinia. It gave as a reason for these orders that the high command appreciated that the attack on Sicily was possibly only a feint and that the main attack was going to be elsewhere.' That assessment, Naval Intelligence noted with satisfaction, was 'entirely consistent with the Mincemeat story'.

The same effects were visible at the other end of the Mediterranean, where the fictional attack on Greece was directly undermining Germany's ability to repel the genuine attack on Sicily. The 'R-boats', or *Räumboote*, were 150-ton minesweepers and a key component of German naval strength, used to pick up mines but also for convoy escort, coastal patrol, mine-laying and rescuing downed air crews. On 12 July, Sicilian D-Day +2, the commander of German naval forces in Italy sent a cable to headquarters 'complaining that the departure of the 1st R-boat Group, sent to the Aegean for the defence of Greece, had prejudiced the defence of Sicily, as the Gela barrages were no longer effective, the shortage of escort vessels was "chronic", and the departure of any more boats, as ordered, would have a serious effect.' Yet the belief in an impending Greek attack remained rooted: in late July, Rommel was despatched by Hitler to Salonika to take command of the defence of Greece if and when the Allies attacked. The Abwehr laid intricate plans in anticipation of the expected assault on Greece, including teams of secret agents and saboteurs to be left behind if the Germans were forced to withdraw.

The recriminations on the Axis side started almost immediately after the invasion. When he heard that the Italian coastal defenders had failed to repulse the attack, Goebbels muttered darkly about 'macaroni-eaters', but refrained from pointing out that he had never quite believed in the Abwehr's great intelligence coup. Hitler never admitted he had been fooled, but his military response to the invasion was proof enough that he knew he had made a major strategic error in failing to reinforce Sicily. 'Hitler's own reaction was immediate. He ordered two more German formations, 1st Parachute and 29th Panzer Grenadier Division to be hurried to Sicily to throw the invaders into the sea.' Again, it was too late.

Others within the German hierarchy realised they had been sold a fantastic and extremely damaging lie, and responded with fury. Joachim von Ribbentrop, the Nazi Foreign Minister, demanded a full explanation of why Major Martin's documents indicating that the attack on Sicily was a decoy had been so blithely accepted as genuine: 'This report has been proved to be false, since the operation directed by the English and Americans against Sicily, far from being a sham attack, was of course one of their planned major offensives in the Mediterranean . . . The report from "a wholly reliable source" was deliberately allowed by the enemy to fall into Spanish hands in order to mislead us.' Von Ribbentrop suspected that the Spaniards were in on the ruse all along, and ordered his ambassador in Madrid, Dieckhoff, to conduct a full-scale witch-hunt: 'Undertake a most careful reappraisal of the whole matter and consider in so doing whether the persons from whom the information emanated are directly in the pay of the enemy, or whether they are hostile to us for other reasons.' Dieckhoff blustered, and tried to swerve out of the way: 'The documents had been found on the body of a shot-down English officer, and handed over in the original to our counterintelligence here by the Spanish general staff. The documents were investigated by the Abwehr and I have not heard their investigations cast any doubt on their authenticity.' Rather weakly, Dieckhoff argued that the enemy must have altered their plans after losing the documents. 'The English and Americans had every intention of acting in the way laid down in the documents. Only later did they change their minds, possibly regarding the plans as compromised by the shooting down of the English bearer.'

Von Ribbentrop was having none of it. 'The British Secret Service is quite capable of causing forged documents to reach the Spaniards,' he insisted. The deception had been intended to persuade Germany 'that we should not adopt any defensive measures . . . or that we should adopt only inadequate ones'. With the Allies storming through Sicily, he wanted names, and he wanted heads to roll. 'It is practically certain that the English purposely fabricated these misleading documents and allowed them to fall into Spanish hands so that they might reach us by this indirect route. The only question is whether the Spaniards saw through this game, or whether they were themselves taken in.' The finger of suspicion pointed at Admiral Moreno, the double-dealing Minister of Marine, and at Adolf Clauss and his Spanish spies. Further up the chain of command, it cast a shadow over the Abwehr in Spain, and the intelligence analysts in Berlin who had verified the fakes. 'Who originally circulated the information?' demanded Von Ribbentrop. 'Are they directly in the pay of our enemies?'

Karl-Erich Kuhlenthal was also in the firing line. 'After the invasion of Italy had actually taken place, Berlin reprimanded [the Abwehr office in] Spain for having failed to submit adequate data.' Kuhlenthal, as adept at escaping blame as he was skilled at gathering credit, kept his head down until the storm passed. He must have known that the documents passed to Berlin back in May had been proven entirely misleading, but he said nothing. Kuhlenthal watched the invasion of Sicily with mounting consternation, but at least one of his fellow intelligence experts, who had played an equal role in facilitating the fraud, may have witnessed the unfolding of events with secret satisfaction. Not until 26 July, more than a fortnight after the landings in Sicily, did Alexis von Roenne, the head of Foreign Armies West (FHW) and secret anti-Nazi conspirator, issue a report stating, 'at present at any rate, the attack planned against the Peloponnese had been given up'. Von Roenne was too canny to acknowledge that the letters were fakes; he merely asserted, like Dieckhoff, that the plans had changed. In Hitler's world there was no room for an honest mistake.

The most significant victim in the fallout, on the Axis side, was Mussolini himself. From the first Allied footfall in Sicily,

Il Duce was doomed, though he refused to acknowledge it. Goebbels noted: 'The only thing certain in this war is that Italy will lose it.' The Pact of Steel was cracking up. By 18 July, the Allied front line had moved halfway up Sicily. That day, Mussolini sent an almost defiant cable to Hitler: 'The sacrifice of my country cannot have as its principal purpose that of delaying a direct attack on Germany.' The Führer summoned him to an urgent meeting. Il Duce did not care to be summoned anywhere, but went meekly.

The two fascist leaders met in Feltre, fifty miles from Venice, where Hitler launched into a long harangue, lambasting the 'inept and cowardly' Italian troops in Sicily and insisting: 'What has happened now in Sicily must not be allowed to happen again.' In the midst of the tirade, an aide interrupted to inform Mussolini that Rome was under massive air attack, the first time the capital had been targeted. Mussolini sat impassively through the two-hour monologue. The great Italian bull seemed to be fatally gored, diminished and distant. At the end of the excruciating meeting, he said simply: 'We are fighting for a common cause, Führer.' It sounded more like an epitaph than a statement of solidarity.

On 22 July, Palermo fell to Patton's American troops. Three days later, Mussolini was outvoted by the Fascist Grand Council, summoned by King Victor Emmanuel III to a private audience, and toppled. 'It can't go on any longer,' said the King: Mussolini must resign at once, to be replaced by Marshal Pietro Badoglio, the former chief of the armed forces. Italy's deposed dictator left the royal Villa Savoia hidden in an ambulance, and the new government in Rome began the secret task of extracting Italy from the war, and Hitler's poisonous embrace. In Badoglio's words: 'Fascism fell, as was fitting, like a rotten pear.' The next day, Rommel was recalled from Greece to defend northern Italy.

Would it have fallen so fast, or rotted so quickly, without Operation Mincemeat? The invasion of Sicily was a far from perfect military operation, bedevilled by poor planning and personal rivalries between selfish and powerful men. The airborne landings were horrifically costly: only 12 out of 147 British gliders landed on target, and 67 crashed into the sea. A relatively small contingent of German troops successfully held up the advance of an Allied host seven times larger, and then evacuated the island to continue the battle up mainland Italy. The fight for Sicily was grim and bitter. But how much worse would it have been had the Nazi high command been prepared for it? What if, say, the full-strength, battle-tempered First Panzer Division, instead of being despatched to Greece to await an imaginary invasion, had been deployed along the coast at Gela?

It is impossible to calculate how many lives, on both sides of the conflict, were saved by Operation Mincemeat, nor exactly how much it contributed to hastening the end of the war and the defeat of Hitler. The Allies had expected it would take ninety days to conquer Sicily. The occupation was completed on 17 August, thirty-eight days after the invasion began. Looking back after the war, Professor Percy Ernst Schramm, keeper of the OKW war diary, left no doubt that the fake documents had played a critical role: 'It is well known that under the influence of the letters, Hitler moved troops to Sardinia and southern Greece, thereby preventing them from taking part in the defence against [Husky].' In September, Italy formally surrendered, although the war in Italy would not end until May 1945.

The impact of the Sicilian invasion was felt 1,500 miles away on the blood-soaked Eastern Front, and most importantly around the Russian city of Kursk. On 4 July, Hitler had launched Operation Citadel, his massive, long-awaited offensive against the Red Army following the German defeat at Stalingrad. The Battle of Kursk would be history's largest tank battle, the most costly day of aerial warfare yet fought, and Germany's last major strategic offensive in the east. With 900,000 troops and 3,000 tanks, Field Marshal Erich von Manstein planned to eliminate the bulge in the lines known as the Kursk salient, encircle the Soviets, and then head south to reconquer more lost territory.

Repeated delays, and excellent Soviet intelligence, ensured that the Red Army had a good idea of what was coming. Like Sicily, Kursk was an obvious target; unlike Sicily, by the time the attack came, it was massively fortified, with layered, in-depth lines of defence, a million mines, 3,000 miles of trenches, and an army of 1.3 million men, with reserves strategically placed to strike back when German troops were exhausted. After five days of furious combat, the battle still hung in the balance. The German blitzkrieg in the north of the battlefront had stalled, with terrible losses on both sides, but in the south the German forces, although heavily depleted, pushed on. By 12 July, the German forces had broken through the first two Soviet lines of defence, and believed that the final breakthrough was at hand.

But by now, events in the Mediterranean had changed the strategic picture, and the cast of Hitler's mind. Three days after the invasion of Sicily, the Führer summoned Von Manstein to the Wolf's Lair, his headquarters in East Prussia, and announced that he was suspending Operation Citadel. The Field Marshal insisted that the Red Army was tottering, and the German offensive was at a critical stage: 'On no account should we let go of the enemy until the mobile reserves which he had committed were decisively beaten.' But Hitler had made up his mind. 'Inescapably faced with the dilemma of deciding where to make his main effort, he gave the Mediterranean preference over Russia.' One week after Allied troops landed on the shores of Sicily, Hitler cancelled the Eastern Front offensive, and ordered the transfer of the SS Panzer Korps to Italy. Hitler's decision to call off the attack, partly in order to divert forces to threatened Italy and the still-feared threat to the Balkans, marked the turning of the tide. For the first time, a blitzkrieg attack had failed before breaking through enemy lines. The Red Army launched a devastating counterattack, taking first Belgorod and Orel and then, on 11 August, the city of Kharkov. By November, Kiev itself would be liberated. The Third Reich never recovered from the failure of Operation Citadel, and from now until the end of the war, the German armies in the east were on the defensive as the Red Army rolled, inexorably, towards Berlin. 'With the failure of *Zitadelle* we have suffered a decisive defeat,' wrote General Heinz Guderian, the foremost German theorist of tank combat. 'From now on, the enemy was in undisputed possession of the initiative.'

Unsurprisingly, those involved in the planning and execution of Mincemeat were unanimous in their self-congratulation. A 'top secret' assessment of the operation, written shortly before the end of the war, described it as 'a small classic of deception, brilliantly elaborate in detail, completely successful in operation . . . The Germans took many actions, to their own prejudice, as a result of Mincemeat.' At the very least, the deception had encouraged Hitler to do what he already wanted to do, which was exactly what the Allies wanted him to do. The German defences in southern Europe had been spread 'as widely and thinly as possible', by stoking fears of multiple assaults, instead of the one, massive attack on southern Sicily. 'There can be no doubt that Mincemeat succeeded in the desired effect [and] caused the dispersal of the German effort at a crucial time . . . it was largely responsible for the fact that the east end of Sicily, where we landed, was much less defended both by troops and fortifications.' Even more gratifying, the progress of the lie had been tracked at every stage: 'Special intelligence enabled us to know that the enemy was deceived by it.' In one of his last private messages to Churchill from Madrid, Alan Hillgarth described how the success of the Sicilian campaign had transformed public and official opinion in Spain: 'Sicily has impressed everyone and delighted most. Mussolini's resignation and what it presages has stunned opponents.' The fear that Franco might side with the Axis was now over, and so was Hillgarth's role in Spain.

Bill Jewell often wondered, in later years, how much Operation Mincemeat 'really affected the outcome in Sicily'. He was told that this was 'impossible to estimate'. Deception may not be measured in battlefield yards won, or soldiers lost, but it can be gauged in other ways, large and small: in the toppling of Mussolini and the buttressing of Hitler's fixation with the Balkans; in the thin defences on Sicily's coast that allowed the Allied army ashore with so little bloodshed; in the Axis troops tied up in Sardinia and the Peloponnese, and the great retreat at Kursk; in the Panzers, waiting on the shores of Greece for an attack that never came; in Derrick Leverton, sitting unscathed in his foxhole, as the German counterattack petered out.

Later historians have been equally convinced that the deception not only worked, but succeeded dramatically, and with a profound impact. Hugh Trevor-Roper called Operation Mincemeat 'the most spectacular single episode in the history of deception'. The official history of Second World War deception described it as 'perhaps the most successful single deception of the entire war'. It was also the luckiest. The deception depended on skill, timing and judgement, but it would never have succeeded without an astonishing run of good fortune.

Wars are won by men like Bill Darby, storming up the beach with all guns blazing, and by men like Leverton, sipping his tea as the bombs fall. They are won by planners, correctly calculating how many rations and contraceptives an invading force will need; by tacticians, laying out grand strategy; by generals, inspiring the men they command; by politicians, galvanising the will to fight; and by writers, putting war into words. They are won by acts of strength, bravery and guile. But they are also won by feats of imagination. Amateur, unpublished novelists, the framers of Operation Mincemeat, dreamed up the most unlikely concatenation of events, rendered them believable, and sent them off to war, changing reality through lateral thinking, and proving that it is possible to win a battle fought in the mind, from behind a desk, and from beyond the grave. Operation Mincemeat was pure make-believe; and it made Hitler believe something that changed the course of history.

This strange story was conceived in the mind of a writer, and put into action by a fisherman, who cast his fly on the water with no certainty of success but an angler's innate optimism and guile. The most fitting, and aptly fishy, tribute to the operation was contained in a telegram, sent to Winston Churchill on the day the Germans took the bait: 'Mincemeat swallowed rod, line and sinker.'

23

Mincemeat Revealed

Ewen Montagu began lobbying the British government for permission to reveal Operation Mincemeat before the war had even ended. In 1945 he was offered the 'considerable sum' of £750 to reveal the story, although who made the offer, and how they learned of Operation Mincemeat, is unclear. Montagu wrote to the War Cabinet Office asking to be allowed to publish his account of what had happened. 'I am a prejudiced party, but I feel strongly that no harm could result and good might well be obtained,' he wrote, adding that the story had already 'leaked fairly widely'. Anticipating the objection that the operation would reveal how Britain had partly lied its way to victory, he argued: 'It would pay to release Mincemeat as a specialised ad hoc operation to draw attention away from the fact that deception was a normal operation.'

Montagu's request was turned down flat. Guy Liddell of MI5 told him 'the Foreign Office would never allow publication in any form in view of the inevitable effect on our relationship with Spain'. Yet it was true that the story was starting to leak. Indeed, a copy of the report on Operation Mincemeat, one of only three made, had gone missing in March 1945. Another remained in Montagu's possession, apparently with Guy Liddell's blessing, 'in case the embargo should eventually be lifted'.

Two months after the Normandy landings, a British radio journalist named Sydney Moseley picked up the scent from a contact in British intelligence. Moseley had worked for the *Daily Express* and the *New York Times*; he was also John Logie Baird's business manager and a tireless promoter of the new technology of television. And he knew a good story when he heard one. In August 1944, Moseley broadcast an item on the Mutual Broadcasting System radio network in America: 'Our intelligence obtained over in England the body of a patient that had died, and dressed it up in the uniform of a senior officer. In due course this body . . . floated across the Channel to the enemy-occupied coast where, as was hoped, it was picked up. As a result of a set of faked documents, orders, and plans, the Nazis actually did concentrate their forces elsewhere, and when we made the big move into Normandy, they still regarded it as a feint.' Moseley concluded his report: 'I believe this story is the greatest of the war.' Moseley had the wrong location, and the wrong D-Day, but his story was close enough to the truth to put a gale-force wind up the Secret Service.

'Tar' Robertson wrote to Bevan, pointing out that while the Official Secrets Act could silence the inquisitive in Britain, it had no power in the US: 'Unless some action is taken fairly soon, this, being such an attractive subject, will produce sooner or later, a flood of stories in America, some of which will be true, others invented.' On the other hand, if the journalist was approached and urged to keep quiet, that would show that 'there was in fact some truth behind what Moseley says'. It would be better to ignore the story, and 'leave the American authorities and Moseley in ignorance on this whole question'. Even so, it was only a matter of time before others came hunting. Britain's spymasters were adamant: 'We should do our utmost to stop the true story getting out.'

The story, when it finally emerged, came not from an inquisitive journalist, but from Winston Churchill himself. In October 1949, Alfred Duff Cooper, later Viscount Norwich, the wartime Minister for Information, began work on a novel based on the story of Operation Mincemeat. *Operation Heartbreak* tells the story of 'William Maryngton', a man unable to serve his country in life, but deployed in death in a way that was equally unmistakable. The last chapter reads:

> Dawn had not broken, but was about to do so, when the submarine came to the surface. The crew were thankful to breathe the cool, fresh air, and they were still more thankful to be rid of their cargo. The wrappings were removed, and the Lieutenant stood to attention and saluted as they laid the body of the officer in uniform as gently as possible on the face of the waters. A light breeze was blowing shoreward, and the tide was running in the same direction. So Willie went to war at last, the insignia of field rank on his shoulders, and a letter from his beloved lying close to his quiet heart.

Operation Heartbreak is a charming fiction, quite obviously based on fact.

Duff Cooper had learned of the case in March 1943, while head of the Security Executive, but he must also have obtained access to the Mincemeat file itself after the war was over. Montagu believed 'Duff Cooper learned of Mincemeat from Churchill in one of his expansive "after-dinner" moods and then was (I'm pretty sure, but my evidence doesn't amount to proof) shown a copy of the report by someone I won't name.' It is just possible that Montagu himself showed Duff Cooper the file, as a way of bringing pressure on the Government to allow him to tell the non-fiction version. Churchill may well have wanted the story to be told. When the other Operation Mincemeat – a simple minefield-laying operation – was revealed in the 1950s, Alan Brooke, former Chief of the Imperial General Staff, apparently got his Mincemeats confused and wrote: 'Sir W always wanted to hear this story told.'

The authorities in 1950, however, most emphatically did not want the story told, and when Whitehall got word of the contents of *Operation Heartbreak*, Duff Cooper came under intense pressure – possibly from the Prime Minister, Clement Attlee, himself – not to publish. The story, it was pointed out, might damage Anglo-Spanish relations, and British intelligence might want to use the same ruse in the future. Duff Cooper 'considered the objections to be ridiculous'. According to Charles Cholmondeley, Cooper threatened to say that he had learned the story 'direct from Churchill if prosecuted'. *Operation Heartbreak* was published on 10 November 1950, prompting a ripple of critical acclaim and 'consternation in security quarters'. It sold 40,000 copies.

The cat was now out of the bag, at least in fictional form, and Montagu renewed his demand to be allowed to publish, since 'there could not be one law for a Cabinet minister and a different one for the blokes who do the work'. He wrote to Emanuel 'Manny' Shinwell, the Defence Secretary, demanding to know whether Cooper would be prosecuted for breaching the Official Secrets Act and, if not, whether there was any reason why he should not now publish his own, non-fiction account. Again, the authorities resisted. Publication of the facts would be 'wholly contrary to the public interest', wrote Sir Harold Parker, Permanent Secretary to the Minister of Defence. 'Any true account would have to show how the law was manipulated to secure possession of a corpse, the forgery of documents from well-known firms (whether with their consent or not) and the use made of beliefs of Catholics' as part of the plot. Sir Harold also ordered Montagu to return the Mincemeat files, since 'there is no longer any reason for you to retain a copy of the record of the operation'.

Montagu immediately fired back: 'One would not think even the most ardent Catholic would be offended that a man of unknown religious belief was buried as a Catholic to save thousands of lives and render the invasion of Sicily more certain of success.' The Mincemeat files would remain firmly in his possession until the minister saw sense: 'I see no reason why I should hand over my copy.'

After months of wrangling, the authorities partly relented. In a later letter to John Godfrey, Montagu wrote: 'I forced Shinwell to agree that, if they did not prosecute Duff Cooper, they must give me permission to publish . . . Shinwell gave me a clear consent.'

The deal came with strings attached: Montagu must write an outline of what he planned to write, submit the finished manuscript for vetting, and 'sympathetically consider advice as to modification'. He began writing immediately. Initially he envisaged an extended magazine article, and contacted the editor of *Life* magazine, who was wildly enthusiastic. By April 1951, a first draft outline was completed. Now he hesitated, wondering whether 'it would be wrong to publish'.

Meanwhile an enterprising journalist named Ian Colvin, who had worked in Berlin before the war and would go on to become deputy editor of the *Daily Telegraph*, had picked up rumours that there was more to *Operation Heartbreak* than fiction, and went digging. In 1952, the diaries of Erwin Rommel were published, in which the Field Marshal described being sent to Greece soon after the invasion of Sicily to resist an expected attack. A footnote, written by Basil Liddell Hart, hinted at the connection to the story told in *Operation Heartbreak*. Ian Colvin, in Montagu's words, 'shot off to Spain' and began asking questions. When Britain's ambassador to Spain learned what the journalist was up to, he 'cabled back in a frenzy', fearful of a major breach in Anglo-Spanish relations. 'The Foreign Office's chief worry was that Colvin had been told by our ex vice-consul in Huelva that he had been in the know and had taken part in deceiving the Spanish government.' The Foreign Office took a dim view of 'using diplomats to lie and deceive their host government'.

The Foreign Office was not the only branch of the British government fearful of what Colvin might find, and urged the Joint Intelligence Committee to intervene. 'Further pressure was applied by the Home Office who were very worried lest it became known that a coroner had handed over a corpse with no one's permission.'

The Joint Intelligence Committee decided on a pre-emptive strike. Colvin had already been commissioned by the *Sunday Express*, and was getting close to the truth in Spain. A spoiling operation was launched. Montagu was told he should now write his account as long as he did not reveal any information on 'the true means by which the corpse was obtained and any details from which the man's real identity could be inferred'. He would have to do so very fast. He was 'rushed round to the *Sunday Express* who had first claim on Colvin's work and they said they would consider it if they got the story written by Monday so that they could decide before they got Colvin's'. This was an underhand trick. Colvin had worked hard on the story for two years: the Government, and the newspaper that had commissioned him, were now conniving to scoop him.

Montagu later wrote, disingenuously, that government permission to write his account had been 'wholly unexpected' and that permission to do so had been unsolicited. 'The request not to publish, which I had accepted, was altered to a request that I should write the true story and publish it as soon as possible so as to kill these dangerous untruths.' The reason given for the volte-face was that Colvin's account was likely to be 'so wildly inaccurate as to be dangerous'. The reverse was true: the danger of Colvin's account was its probable accuracy, in particular the fear that it would reveal the way British diplomats had deceived the Spanish government, and how Bentley Purchase had simply conjured up a corpse to order. The guardians of official secrecy knew they could edit and mould what Montagu might write. This would be a 'controlled version, in which delicate points could be modified', whereas Colvin, in Montagu's own words, was 'someone not under any control or influence'. If the story of Operation Mincemeat must be told, it would be told in a way that would not upset the Spanish, and conceal how the body was obtained.

Writing to John Godfrey, Montagu was quite explicit about the terms of his deal with the intelligence censors: he would not reveal secret information, most importantly the Ultra intercepts, and he would write nothing that could embarrass the Foreign or Home Offices. 'The return that the country got was therefore not only the protection of "our sources", but also the other two quite important points' – concealing the roles of Haselden and Hillgarth in Spain, and Purchase in London. The newspaper could edit the serialisation, but the final version would need to be approved by the Secret Service before publication: 'The *Express* will submit and get passed anything that they may add or any alterations that they may make.' The story of Operation Mincemeat would be an official publication in all but name.

Montagu claimed to have written his authorised account in the space of forty-eight hours 'with much black coffee and no sleep' in order to get it to the newspaper's offices by Monday, 24 January. In fact, a draft was complete, and had already been approved by the authorities and sent to the *Sunday Express*, at least three weeks before the newspaper's deadline. On 8 January, Montagu wrote to Jean Gerard Leigh ('or should it be "Pam"?'), warning her that his book was about to be published: 'The powers that be have decided that an accurate story by me "under control" would be less dangerous than an inaccurate one which might lead anywhere.' Montagu asked Jean for permission to use her photograph as 'Pam': 'We don't want to alter anything of that kind as we want to be able to say "this is true".' Montagu assured her that she would be identified only as 'a girl working in my section'. Montagu sent a simultaneous letter to Bill Jewell, informing him that 'Mincemeat is soon going to be published', and that his draft had been approved by Whitehall. 'My account has been vetted and passed,' he wrote. 'I felt that you ought not to be taken by surprise.'

Jewell raised no objection, but Jean was concerned: 'I was most interested to hear that parts of your and Bill's doubtful past are to be revealed to the unsuspecting public,' she wrote.

'But what should my answer be if someone sees through the ravages of time and identifies me with Pam!? . . . Perhaps you would come and have a drink one evening and put me "in the picture" if it is not too late.' Montagu suggested that if anyone made the connection and asked what she had done during the war, she should 'merely say that you were working in a branch of the War Office'.

Charles Cholmondeley wanted nothing to do with the project. As an MI5 officer, he refused to be named, but his natural reticence would have prevented his participation in any case. Montagu had first raised the idea of writing a book together two years earlier, after the appearance of *Operation Heartbreak*. He now offered to cut his former partner in on the deal, with a 25 per cent share of the profits from 'book, film rights, or other uses to which the story might be put'. Cholmondeley's response was typically polite, but firm. 'As you will recall, when you originally broached the subject in 1951, I felt, due to my position, that I could not take part in it.' In the interim, Cholmondeley had left MI5. 'Whilst the general situation has changed considerably,' he wrote, 'I do not feel that my own rather peculiar position has done so and therefore I must reaffirm my decision to take no part and accept no benefit from this publication. I am sure you will appreciate this difference in our positions, but reaching this decision has not been easy and believe me I am not less appreciative of your very generous offer.'

The first instalment of the story, proclaiming 'The war's most fantastic secret disclosed for the first time', appeared in the *Sunday Express* on 1 February, under the headline 'The Man Who Never Was' – the title was the inspiration of the news editor, Jack Garbutt. This was followed by two more instalments. Ian Colvin was understandably furious at being elbowed out of the story, but as a sop he was allowed to write an introduction and analysis to the pieces. His own book of the story – necessarily incomplete, but nonetheless a remarkable piece of investigation – appeared later that year under the title *The Unknown Courier*.

Montagu's book, *The Man Who Never Was*, was published a few months later by Evans Brothers, with the image of a faceless Marine on the cover (wrongly wearing service dress). It was an instant bestseller, and went on to sell more than 3 million copies. It has never been out of print.

Opinion among Montagu's former colleagues in the intelligence world was sharply divided over the decision to reveal Operation Mincemeat. Charles Cholmondeley made no comment on the contents, but was generous, as ever: 'I shall look forward to a gripping and soul-searing saga on the silver screen at some future date.' Mountbatten gave qualified support: 'Although I heartily disapproved of *Operation Heartbreak*, and told the author so when I saw him, once the beans had been spilt in that way I think it was probably a good thing that the true story should be told.' However, Archie Nye, the author of the plot's centrepiece, was sharply critical, telling Montagu that he would need 'a good deal of persuasion that the merits of publication exceeded the drawbacks'. John Masterman was also opposed. 'You and I don't agree on the wisdom of publishing Mincemeat in this form,' he wrote. 'I always thought that a good deal could be published with advantage but I also thought that such publication should be anonymous and with official sanction.' (Such scruples did not endure. In 1972, Masterman would publish his own account of the Double Cross System, under his own name, and in the teeth of strong official opposition.) The most trenchant criticism came from Admiral John Godfrey. 'Uncle John blitzed me on the phone in quite the old way,' Montagu told another former denizen of Room 13. The old admiral testily pointed out that the book claimed to be non-fiction, while withholding key truths: 'Your admirable *Man Who Never Was* covers up the real final secret – how did we know that the Germans had access to the despatches?'

The Man Who Never Was remains a classic of postwar literature. With a lawyer's precision, Montagu laid out the plot in careful steps, to reveal 'an exploit more astonishing than any story in war fiction'. More than half a century later it is still gripping, a tour de force of reconstruction.

Yet the book is – and was always intended to be – partial, in both senses. In some ways, it fulfilled the demands of postwar propaganda. In Montagu's telling, the British planners made no mistakes, and the Germans were duped without the slightest hint that anything might go wrong. Montagu can be forgiven for presenting himself as the hero of his own drama – many of those involved could or would not be identified – but in so doing, he made Operation Mincemeat appear to be a one-man show. Cholmondeley appears fleetingly in the book, under the pseudonym 'George'. The others who played roles, large or small – Alan Hillgarth, Gómez-Beare, Johnnie Bevan, Charles Fraser-Smith, Juan Pujol, Jean Leslie and many others – were not only unnamed, but in some cases simply excised from the story. The Ultra secret would not be revealed until the 1970s, so Montagu was unable to describe how the success of the operation had been tracked. The book was carefully vetted, and contained nothing that might embarrass the government: the extent to which British diplomatic officials had cooperated in deceiving the Spanish was glossed over, as was the level of Spanish collaboration with the Germans; the way the body had been obtained was made to seem entirely official and above board. Partly for dramatic effect, partly in obedience to the guardians of official secrecy, and partly because that is the way he was, Montagu 'managed to give the impression', wrote one detractor, 'that he was single-handedly responsible for the entire deception scheme'.

As for Glyndwr Michael, he was removed from the story, permanently, or so Montagu believed. In a first draft of *The Man Who Never Was*, he concocted a story in which the 'real' identity of the dead man was hinted at, misleadingly, as 'an only son, an officer of one of the services, from an old service family'. He wrote: 'His parents were then alive and we decided to take a chance on their agreeing to our plan. We could not tell them the whole story but we felt we could not in decency keep them completely in the dark. They did not like the idea – who would? – but they agreed on the strict condition that neither the real name nor any identifying particulars of their son would ever come out.'

In the final version of the book, however, he opted for an even vaguer explanation, claiming that relatives of the dead man had been asked for permission to use the body 'without saying what we proposed to do with it and why', and that 'permission, for which our indebtedness was great, was obtained on condition that I should never let it be known whose corpse it was'. Montagu couched his refusal to divulge the name as a matter of honour, since he had given his word to the relatives of the dead man. In 1977 he claimed that all those relatives had since died: 'I gave a solemn promise never to reveal whose body it was and, as there is no one alive from whom I can get a release, I can say no more.' The truth, of course, was that none of Michael's few relatives had ever been contacted, let alone asked for permission to use his body. This was a cover-up, to spare the blushes of the British government, and to avoid the admission that the body had been obtained by falsifying a legal certificate indicating burial outside the country, and used entirely without permission.

While not exactly a white lie, this untruth was surely an excusable shade of grey. In the midst of a ferocious war, Montagu and Cholmondeley had persuaded a coroner to bend the law in the national interest. Bentley Purchase had done so on the understanding that he would not be later called to account. The Joint Intelligence Committee would never have allowed Montagu to publish a book revealing that the body of Glyndwr Michael had, in effect, been seized illegally by government intelligence officers: that would have provoked a scandal, as well as undermining the moral high ground upon which *The Man Who Never Was* rested. If the identity had been revealed, then Glyndwr Michael's relatives might, with some reason, have kicked up an almighty stink. So Montagu hid the truth with another deception, and continued to hide it for the rest of his life.

During the war, Montagu had complained: 'My work is such that I will never be able to mention its importance and people will merely say "Oh, he didn't do much good in the war". I will therefore go down as someone who was a failure when tested in the war.' The publication of *The Man Who Never Was* turned him, almost overnight, into a celebrity. He toured the US, gave lectures, and appeared on American television alongside a chimpanzee named J. Fred Muggs. Hollywood swiftly came calling, as Cholmondeley had predicted, and a vigorous auction ensued. The film rights were finally purchased by 20th Century Fox.

The film of *The Man Who Never Was*, an Anglo-American Technicolor Cinemascope production directed by Ronald Neame, opened with a royal premiere attended by the Duchess of Kent, on 14 March 1956. Shot in Britain and Huelva, it starred the American actor Clifton Webb playing Montagu, and Gloria Grahame as 'Lucy', his secretary's fictional flatmate. André Morell played Sir Bernard Spilsbury. The screenplay, by Nigel Balchin, used the truth where convenient, and made up the rest, including an Irishman spying for the Nazis, played by Stephen Boyd, tasked with verifying the body's identity. Montagu declared himself entirely happy with the 'thrilling incidents which, although they did not happen, might have happened'. Mountbatten got an early look at the script, and complained that it made him 'appear to be grudging and rather "Old Blimpish"'. 'I would like to make it clear that I was the most enthusiastic supporter of this idea from the beginning.' He even tried to insert a line to make his character more appealing: 'I would have no objection to the addition of a phrase like "Nice of Mountbatten to take a dead man on his Staff."'

Among those on set during filming was a tall, ungainly man with an extravagant Air Force moustache, who was described as a 'technical adviser' and known only as 'George'. He did not appear in the credits. Even Ronald Neame never knew that George was Charles Cholmondeley, content, as ever, to organise matters anonymously, from the wings.

In the film, Montagu makes a cameo appearance as an air vice marshal with doubts about the plan's feasibility. At one point, Montagu leans over to Webb, looks him in the eye, and declares: 'I suppose you realise, Montagu, that, if the Germans see through this, it will pinpoint Sicily.' This was a wonderfully surreal moment: the real Montagu addressing his fictional persona, in a work of filmic fiction, based on reality, which had originated in fiction.

The film was a box-office and critical success, winning a Bafta for best British screenplay. Perhaps the ultimate accolade, the sign that Operation Mincemeat had truly and permanently entered British culture, came in 1956, when *The Goon Show* devoted an entire episode to the story. Monty saw the film in Holland and, rather missing the point, complained that Archie Nye had looked quite different. Adolf Clauss went to see *The Man Who Never Was* in Huelva's Teatro Mora. He told his son: 'There's nothing true in it. It was nothing like that.' Someone tipped off the press to the identity of 'Pam'. Jean Gerard Leigh was besieged by journalists, and denied everything.

Montagu had hoped that by framing his refusal to identify the body as a promise he could never break, he would end all attempts to attach a name to it. The very title of his book seemed to imply that the corpse had no previous existence worthy of mention. But there *was* a man, and the runaway success of the book and film ensured that the speculation over whom he might have been started immediately. The body was variously identified as 'a derelict alcoholic found beneath the arches of Charing Cross Bridge', a professional soldier, and 'the wastrel brother of an MP'. Numerous candidates were put forward, with evidence ranging from possible to wishful to fanciful. The conspiracy theories continue to this day.

24

Aftermath

Three weeks after the invasion of Sicily, Lieutenant Bill Jewell was reunited with Rosemary Galloway in Algiers: they immediately became engaged. While Rosemary went on to serve at Allied Headquarters in Italy, Jewell continued to attack enemy shipping in the Mediterranean, eastern Atlantic and Norwegian Sea. At the Normandy landings in June 1944, the *Seraph* once again guided the invading forces ashore. The same month, Bill Jewell and Rosemary were wed in a ceremony in Pinner. They remained married, and 'absolutely devoted to one another', for the next fifty-three years. Jewell was awarded the DSC and the American Legion of Merit, and appointed MBE, for his part in Operation Husky, along with the French Croix de Guerre. He rose to the rank of captain in command of a submarine flotilla, and died in 2004 at the age of ninety.

HMS *Seraph* also remained on active service. In recognition of her role in the run-up to the invasion of North Africa, a brass plaque was nailed to the door of the submarine toilet: 'General Mark Wayne Clark, Deputy Supreme Commander in North Africa, sat here.' She served as a training ship at Holy Loch on the Clyde, the port from which she had set off for Huelva in 1943. The submarine was decommissioned in 1963, twenty-one years to the day after her launch, and finally scrapped at Briton Ferry in South Wales, close to the birthplace of Glyndwr Michael. The *Seraph*'s conning tower, forward torpedo hatch and periscope were all preserved and erected as a memorial to Anglo-American cooperation during the Second World War at the Citadel, the American military training college in South Carolina. US and British flags fly jointly over the memorial, the only place in America permitted to fly the white ensign.

Lieutenant David Scott of the *Seraph* finished reading *War and Peace* shortly before the end of the war. He served on ten submarines, in war and peace, commanding five of them, and was promoted to Rear Admiral in 1971.

Derrick Leverton fought through the Italian campaign, was mentioned in despatches, took over command of his artillery regiment, and then returned to Britain to resume his rightful place, alongside his brother Ivor, in the family funeral business. Ivor Leverton would boast that he had 'played a tiny part in ending the war'; he liked to tease Drick that he had saved his life on the beach at Sicily by taking a dead body to Hackney in the middle of the night. In a quiet way, he felt 'redeemed' by the part he had played. Ivor's sons took over the business, and have since passed it on to an eighth generation of undertakers.

Colonel Bill Darby of the US Rangers was killed in northern Italy, two days before the final German surrender in Italy. As Darby was giving orders to cut off the German retreat, an 88mm shell burst outside his command post, killing him instantly. He was thirty-four. Darby was unable to turn down the promotion to brigadier general which was awarded to him posthumously. James Garner played Darby in the 1958 film *Darby's Rangers*.

With the success of Operation Mincemeat, and the Mediterranean under Allied control, Alan Hillgarth looked to new pastures. At the end of 1943 he was transferred to Ceylon as chief of intelligence for the Eastern Fleet, going on to become head of Naval Intelligence for the entire eastern theatre. There he 'developed an intelligence organisation [that] materially aided the Allied war effort at sea against Japan', and once more his intelligence advice was sent directly to Churchill.

The war won, he retired from the Navy, and purchased an estate in Ireland, where he planted a forest. 'He walked several miles a day, inspecting his trees.' But he also continued to cultivate exotic human flora, most notably Juan March, the dubious financier who had helped to bribe the Spanish generals, and Winston Churchill. Through a series of questionable financial manoeuvres, March's fortune and notoriety expanded in tandem: by 1952 he was the seventh richest man in the world. Hillgarth had once described Juan March as 'the most unscrupulous man in Spain', but his own scruples did not prevent him from becoming director of the Helvetia Finance Company, March's nominee business in London. It has been suggested that Hillgarth and MI6 may have helped smooth over March's business dealings as payback for his help in paying off the Cavalry of St George. March was killed in a car accident outside Madrid in 1962.

While looking after March's business interests, Hillgarth continued to act as Churchill's unofficial adviser on intelligence. Between the end of the war and Churchill's return to Downing Street in 1951, Hillgarth met regularly with the once and future Prime Minister, at Chartwell, at his Hyde Park Gate apartment, and in Switzerland. Mining his intelligence and diplomatic contacts, Hillgarth briefed Churchill on Spanish affairs, American plans for atomic warfare and, above all, the threat of Soviet espionage in Britain, which he described as a 'quiet, cold-blooded war of brains in the background'. The Soviet codes would be far harder to crack than the German Enigma, Hillgarth warned: 'The Russians are cleverer than the Germans.' Hillgarth's secret correspondence with Churchill in opposition, disguised under the codename 'Sturdee', lasted six years and played a crucial part in framing Churchill's attitude in the early years of the Cold War.

A few years after the war, Hillgarth received a letter from Edgar Sanders, his partner in the disastrous Sacambaya expedition, adding a postscript to that fiasco: according to Sanders, the American engineer, Julius Nolte, had spotted an entrance to the treasure cavern while everyone else was digging the huge hole, but did not share his discovery with the others. Nolte had returned to Sacambaya in 1938 with an American team of explorers and heavy digging equipment, extracted $8 million worth of gold, and then retired to California, where he built himself a castle. 'Thus ends the story of the Sacambaya treasure,' wrote Sanders, who had visited Nolte and tried, unsuccessfully, to extract some money from him. 'Crazy Nolte is rich, while you and I are poor, at least I am, certainly. Hell! Let's have another drink.'

Hillgarth had no idea whether to credit a word Sanders wrote. He had long ago learned not to believe what one reads in letters.

Alan Hillgarth remained a close friend of Churchill, converted to Catholicism, never breathed a word about his wartime and postwar intelligence activities, and died in 1978 at Illannanagh in County Tipperary, surrounded by mystery, and trees.

Don Gómez-Beare was appointed OBE, although quite what for was never fully explained. He spent his retirement in Seville and Madrid, playing bridge and golf. When a British journalist asked him what he had done during the war, he responded with exquisite politeness: 'I am sorry, but I am not free to discuss some subjects.'

On 16 December 1947, Sir Bernard Spilsbury, the great forensic scientist, dined alone at the Junior Carlton Club, then went to his rooms in University College London, locked the door, turned on the Bunsen burner tap, and gassed himself to death. Spilsbury had become increasingly conscious that his mental faculties were deserting him; he was making mistakes, and Sir Bernard did not tolerate mistakes. The scientist, who had studied, investigated and catalogued so many thousands of deaths, left no note to explain his own. His friend Bentley Purchase, the coroner, examined Spilsbury's body and pronounced a verdict of suicide: 'His mind was not as it used to be.'

The cheerful coroner was appointed CBE in 1949 and knighted in 1958. Purchase retired the following year, to look after his pigs and listen to Gilbert and Sullivan. He resisted writing his memoirs: 'Every time I tell a story I am likely to rattle a skeleton in someone's cupboard.' This applied particularly to his role in Operation Mincemeat. Sir Bentley Purchase died in 1961, after falling off his roof while fixing a television aerial. Having performed some 20,000 inquests himself, Sir Bentley, typically, left behind a small postmortem mystery: the coroner in his case could not tell whether he had suffered a fatal heart attack before or after falling off the roof.

Adolf Clauss, the Huelva spy, also declined to discuss his wartime work, although for rather different reasons. At the end of the war, retribution against Germans who had been active in espionage was unevenly applied. Luis Clauss was accused of spying because his fishing fleet had been used to track Allied shipping, and spent two dreary years under house arrest in the little village of Caldes de Malavella in northeast Spain. Don Adolfo, although far more senior in the Abwehr, was never punished. 'His wife was the daughter of a powerful Spanish general, and so he was protected.' Clauss went back to collecting butterflies, and building chairs that still broke if you sat on them. Years later, when the truth about Operation Mincemeat began to emerge, like the super-spy he was, Clauss invented a new version of reality. His son still insists: 'He was always suspicious because the papers came into his hands too easily. He immediately realised it was a trick, and warned his superiors in Berlin and Madrid, but they refused to believe him. He thought the people in Berlin were useless for failing to realise they were being duped.' Gustav Leissner, alias Lenz, the Abwehr chief in Madrid, was more honest in defeat. He was arrested and interrogated by the Americans in 1946, but then permitted to return to Spain. When presented with the evidence of what British intelligence had done, ten years later, he 'admitted the possibility with a long-drawn "*Schön!* Ach, if that is so, I really must congratulate them . . . I take off my hat".'

Karl-Erich Kuhlenthal, the linchpin of the Abwehr in Spain, was far too busy trying to save his own skin to worry about keeping up appearances, or admitting his own errors.

As the Nazi power structure crumbled, Juan Pujol,

Kuhlenthal's Agent Arabel and Britain's Agent Garbo, kept up a steady stream of Nazi jingoism in messages to his German spymaster. In response to a letter from Kuhlenthal bemoaning 'the heroic death of our beloved Führer', Garbo wrote with typical bombast: 'News of the death of our dear chief shook our profound faith in the destiny which awaits our poor Europe, but his deeds and the story of his sacrifice will save the world . . . the noble struggle will be revived which was started by him to save us from chaotic barbarism.'

Kuhlenthal told his star spy that he intended to go into hiding. Their roles had reversed. 'If you find yourself in any danger let me know,' Pujol wrote. 'Do not hesitate in confiding your difficulties fully in me. I only regret not being at your side to give you real help. Our struggle will not terminate with the present phase. We are entering a world civil war which will result in the disintegration of our enemies.' This was all part of an elaborate ruse to find out if remnants of the German intelligence service might be planning to re-establish some sort of underground Nazi network after the war. In the wake of the German defeat, Kuhlenthal fled Madrid, having systematically destroyed the Abwehr's records, and took refuge under an assumed name in Ávila, west of the capital. Britain's MI5 despatched Pujol to track him down and find out what the former golden boy of the Abwehr was planning to do next. Pujol traced Kuhlenthal to Ávila, and knocked on his door. 'Kuhlenthal was overcome with emotion when he welcomed Garbo into his sitting room.' The two men talked for three hours, with Pujol studiously maintaining his guise as a Nazi fanatic. 'Kuhlenthal made it abundantly clear, not only that he still believed in the genuineness of Garbo but that he looked upon him as a superman.'

Kuhlenthal explained that Pujol had been awarded the Iron Cross in recognition of his work for the Third Reich, and that Hitler had 'personally ordered that the medal should be granted. Unfortunately the certificate in evidence of this had not reached

Madrid prior to the German collapse.' Still, it is the thought that counts. As for himself, Kuhlenthal explained that he was desperate to escape Spain, and would not consider returning to Germany, where he was sure to be arrested. Pujol told Kuhlenthal to 'remain patiently in his hideout until Garbo could evolve a plan to facilitate his escape'. Pujol was stern, telling his former spymaster 'he should obey instructions to the letter if he wished to save himself . . . This Kuhlenthal promised to do.' The Spanish spy explained that he planned to get to South America, via Portugal, and solemnly pledged to work for Germany again, should the Abwehr ever be restored. When Kuhlenthal asked him how he intended to get out of the country, Pujol replied, truthfully, with one word: 'Clandestinely'.

MI5 concluded that Karl-Erich Kuhlenthal was no threat to the postwar world. The former Abwehr chief waited, paranoid but patient, for word from his former protégé, but no message came. Like Clauss, he later put a rather different gloss on the past. He had stayed in Spain, he explained, because the country was 'a melting pot of many races, conveying an atmosphere of tolerance and understanding of human nature'. In truth, he was too terrified to budge, waiting for a message from the spy who had double-crossed him so spectacularly. Kuhlenthal's wife, Ellen, was heiress to the Dienz clothing company in Germany, and before 1939 Karl-Erich had worked in his wife's family business. The company premises were bombed at the end of the war, but the business was slowly rebuilt. In 1950, the couple slipped back to Germany, moved into a house in Koblenz, and took over running the clothing company. Kuhlenthal turned out to be much better at buying and selling clothes than buying and selling secrets. The House of Dienz prospered. In 1971, the former spy was elected president of the Federal Association of German Textile Retailers, representing about 95 per cent of German textile retailers, with a purchasing power of about 390 billion deutschmarks. He inaugurated the first pedestrian shopping zone in Koblenz. He gave long, dull speeches on the subject of tax reform, business promotion, and parking in his hometown. No one ever enquired about his past. A more solid member of the German establishment it would be impossible to imagine, worthy, dependable and predictable. The German spy and textile magnate died in 1975 still wondering, perhaps, whether his star agent would reappear from the past. The most interesting thing his obituary could find to say was that 'he always tried to dress correctly as an example to his colleagues'.

Kuhlenthal's life perfectly exemplified what Juan Pujol, Alexis von Roenne and Glyndwr Michael had already proven: it is possible to fit at least two people into one life.

Agent Garbo went to ground. With a gratuity of £15,000 from MI5 and an MBE, he moved to Venezuela, and vanished. After he was tracked down by the spy writer Rupert Allason (Nigel West), he re-emerged, briefly, to accept formal recognition at Buckingham Palace of the debt owed to him. He then disappeared into obscurity again. Garbo wanted to be alone. He died in Carácas in 1988.

With victory, the denizens of Room 13 emerged, blinking, into the light. An anonymous poet in Section 17M marked the occasion with a verse entitled 'De Profundibus'.

In the depths of the fusty dungeons,
In the bowels of NID
Where wild surmise or blatant lies
Are digested for those at sea,
The in-trays are all empty,
The dreary toil is done,
And with mental daze and bleary gaze
The Troglodytes see the sun.

The year after the war ended, Jean Leslie married a soldier, an officer in the Life Guards named William Gerard Leigh, a dashing and handsome polo player with a reputation as a 'bold man to hounds'. He, too, had gone ashore at Sicily, and then 'fought through Italy', the unknowing beneficiary of a plot in which his future wife had played a crucial part. Gerard Leigh, known as 'G', was brave, upright, and utterly correct, not entirely unlike the gallant and doomed William Martin.

Jock Horsfall, the chauffeur on the night drive to Scotland, returned to motor racing after the war. He won the Belgian Grand Prix, and then took second place in the British Empire Trophy Race in the Isle of Man. In 1947 he joined Aston Martin as a test driver, and in 1949 he entered the Spa 24-Hour Race, and finished fourth out of a field of thirty-eight, covering 1,821 miles at an average speed of over 73 mph. On 20 August 1949, he entered the *Daily Express* International Trophy Race at Silverstone: on the thirteenth lap, at the notorious Stowe Corner, the car left the track, hit a line of straw bales intended as a buffer, and flipped over. Horsfall's neck was broken and he died at once. The St John Horsfall Memorial Trophy, a race open only to Aston Martins, is awarded at Silverstone every year, in his memory.

Ivor Montagu listed his activities in *Who's Who* as 'washing up, pottering about, sleeping through television'. This was not quite accurate, for 'pottering' was never Ivor's style: frenetic activity in multiple causes, both public and secret, was closer to the mark. In 1948 he co-wrote the film *Scott of the Antarctic* with Walter Meade; he translated plays, novels and films by a new generation of Soviet writers and film-makers; he travelled extensively in Europe, China and Mongolia; he wrote polemical pamphlets attacking capitalism, and a book about Eisenstein; he championed cricket, Southampton United, and the Zoological Society, but his two greatest passions remained communism and table tennis, a dual obsession that earned him the lifelong suspicion of MI5. He was awarded the Lenin Peace Prize by the Soviet Union in 1959.

Ivor Montagu was never publicly exposed as Agent Intelligentsia. The Venona transcripts cease abruptly in 1942. Whether Montagu learned of Operation Mincemeat, and whether he passed on what he knew to Moscow, will never be known for sure unless the files of the Soviet secret services are finally opened to scrutiny.

What is certain is that Moscow knew all about Operation Mincemeat and, very probably, obtained its information before the operation took place. A secret report by the NKVD, Stalin's intelligence service, dated May 1944 and entitled *Deception during the Current War*, provided an astonishingly detailed account of the operation, its codename, planning, execution and success. The Soviet report described the precise contents of the letters, the exact location of the dummy attacks in Greece, and noted that the operation had been 'somewhat complicated by the fact that the papers ended up with the [Spanish] general staff'. The author of the report also provided a description of the role of Ewen Montagu within British intelligence, and his position on the Twenty Committee: 'Captain [sic] Montagu is in charge of the dissemination of misinformation through intelligence channels. He is also engaged in researching special intelligence sources.' Moscow's spymasters were in no doubt that Operation Mincemeat had worked: 'The German general staff apparently were convinced that the documents themselves were genuine,' the report concluded. 'When the [invasion] was launched, it was clear that the German and Italian commands were somewhat taken by surprise and ill-prepared to repel the attack.'

Much of the information on Operation Mincemeat was supplied to the Soviets by Anthony Blunt, the MI5 officer tasked with overseeing the illegal XXX (Triplex) Operation to extract material from the diplomatic bags of neutral missions in London. Blunt was recruited by the NKVD in 1934, and between 1940 and 1945 he passed huge volumes of secret material to his Soviet handlers. Two other members of the 'Cambridge Five' spy ring probably supplied additional intelligence on the Sicily deception: John Cairncross, who had access to the Ultra decrypts at Bletchley Park, and Kim Philby, the most notorious Soviet mole of all, who headed the Iberian subsection of MI6's counterintelligence branch. Some of the material in Soviet intelligence files on Operation Mincemeat may have come from Ivor Montagu.

MI5 and MI6 continued to watch him and Hell closely. Kim Philby was partly responsible for coordinating reports on the shambolic figure of Ivor Montagu, as he trailed through Vienna, Bucharest and Budapest in 1946. In one report, Philby described Montagu as 'intelligent and agreeable, and an expert at ping-pong'. Philby almost certainly knew more about Montagu than he let on. Montagu's handler, the Soviet air attaché in London, Colonel Sklyarov, alias 'Brion', left London that year. Did Ivor Montagu continue to supply intelligence to the Soviet Union? If so, MI5 could find no hard evidence, although in 1948 it was reported that 'information from secret sources shows that Montagu has recently been in touch with the Soviet embassy'.

By the time the Venona transcripts were decoded in the mid-1960s, and agent 'Intelligentsia' was identified as Ivor Montagu, it was impossible to do anything about him. Venona was simply too secret and too valuable to be revealed in court, and the spies it had unmasked could not be prosecuted. In spite of the many fruitless years spent trying to establish a link between table tennis and Soviet espionage, MI5 had been right all along. Montagu never knew he had been rumbled, and took his role as Agent Intelligentsia to the grave, another double life concealed. Ivor Montagu died in Watford in 1984, leaving behind a clutch of Soviet decorations, his correspondence with Trotsky and the unpublished second volume of his autobiography misleadingly entitled *Like It Was*, which avoided any mention of his activities as a secret agent.

The second half of Charles Cholmondeley's life was, perhaps, the most mysterious of all. The last reference made to him by Guy Liddell of MI5 noted that he was 'somewhere in the Middle East, chasing locusts'. This was an accurate, although partial, description of what Cholmondeley was up to. In October 1945, he joined the 'Middle East Anti-Locust Unit' as 'First Locust

Officer', a job that involved chasing swarms of locusts all over the Arab states, and feeding them bran laced with insecticide.

Another English locust hunter, named George Walford, met Cholmondeley in the desert in 1948, and described a man obsessed: 'His objective was the destruction, at almost any price, of all living locusts in Arabia. It was an impossible task. Only a person with a rare combination of patience, tact and strength of purpose could have achieved any success at all.' The qualities that had served Cholmondeley so well as a wartime intelligence officer were now put to work waging war on the locust. For months on end, he would simply vanish into the desert, disguised as a Bedouin. In the Yemen, he visited villages so remote that when he arrived, women came out with hay offering to feed his jeep. From Arabia, he moved on, in 1949, to the International Council for the Control of the Red Locust in Rhodesia. Cholmondeley was certainly keen on killing locusts ('they are loathsome insects'). Equally certainly, he was still working for the British Secret Service, using his cover as a locust officer for more clandestine work, although quite what this might have been has never been revealed.

Cholmondeley was appointed MBE in 1948, and two years later he signed up with the RAF for a five-year commission on 'intelligence duties'. By December of that year he was in Malaya, using his 'wide experience of deception work' to coordinate with MI5 and Special Branch on bamboozling a rather different enemy – the guerrillas of the Malayan National Liberation Army.

Charles Cholmondeley left MI5 in 1952. He moved to the West Country, married, and set up a business selling horticultural machinery. He regarded the vow of secrecy he had made on joining MI5 as a blood oath, and he never broke it. In the words of his wife, Alison, 'He would not give information to anyone who did not "need to know". Infuriatingly I found this included me.' He still enjoyed shooting with a handgun, although his deteriorating eyesight made this extremely hazardous, except for the birds. 'He would take a revolver when we walked up partridges,' recalled his friend John Otter. 'I never saw him hit one.' No one in the Somerset town of Wells had a clue that the tall, short-sighted, courtly gentleman who sold lawnmowers had once been an officer with the Secret Service, and the inspiration behind the most audacious deception of the war. When the story of Operation Mincemeat finally emerged, he refused to be identified or accept any public credit. Cholmondeley died in June 1982. He never wanted to be recognised, let alone celebrated. Even his headstone is discreet and understated, simply bearing the initials 'CCC'. An obituary letter written to *The Times* by Ewen Montagu drew attention to his 'invaluable work during the war . . . work which, through circumstances and his innate modesty is not adequately known'. As Montagu observed: 'Many who landed in Sicily owe their lives to Charles Cholmondeley.'

Ewen Montagu was appointed OBE for his part in Operation Mincemeat. He returned to the law, as he had always intended, and in 1945 he was appointed Judge Advocate of the Fleet, responsible for administering the court-martial system in the Royal Navy. He would hold that post for the next eighteen years, while also serving as a judge in Hampshire and Middlesex, and Recorder, successively, of Devizes and Southampton. Montagu lived a double life: alongside the feared judge and pillar of Anglo-Jewish society was another Ewen Montagu: the dashing wartime intelligence officer with an extraordinary story to tell.

As a judge, Montagu proved scrupulously fair, wonderfully rude and almost always embroiled in one controversy or another. The press nicknamed him 'The Turbulent Judge'. In 1957, he remarked in court, while trying a merchant seaman: 'Half the scum of England are going into the Merchant Navy to escape military service.' He apologised. Four years later, he told an audience of Rotarians: 'A boy crook should have his trousers taken down and should be spanked by a policewoman with a hairbrush.' He apologised again. When deliberations in court displeased or bored him, he would groan, sigh, roll his eyes and crack inappropriate jokes. Barristers complained often about his offensive behaviour. He apologised, and carried on. His corrosive humour was usually misunderstood; his wit was so sharp and sarcastic it could humble the most arrogant barrister, and did so, frequently. In 1967, a pimp appealed against his conviction, arguing that Montagu had been so rude to his lawyer that he deserved a retrial. The appeal was rejected on the grounds that 'discourtesy, even gross discourtesy, to counsel, however regrettable, could not be a ground for quashing a conviction'.

Often he would impose a lenient sentence on an offender, acting on a hunch that the man or woman genuinely planned to go straight. His hunches were seldom wrong. 'If a man can't have a stroke of luck once in his life, it's not much of a life.' But to those who should know better, or seemed incorrigible, he was merciless. Sentencing the actor Trevor Howard for drinking at least eight double whiskies and then driving into a lamppost, he said: 'The public needs protecting from you, you are a man who drinks vast quantities, every night, yet you have so little care for your fellow citizens that you are willing to drive.'

Summing up Montagu's career, one contemporary wrote: 'Few judges have trodden so hard on the corns of so many people's dignity as this tall, witty, testy, wartime naval commander with the sensitive face and the turbulent tongue. But few judges have been so quick to apologise with the air of a boxer shaking hands after a fight.' Montagu was aware of his own shortcomings. 'Perhaps I should have been more patient,' he once said. 'It is fair, I think, to say that I don't suffer fools gladly.' In truth, he did become more patient and tolerant with age. He also became more devout, plunged into numerous charitable works, and became President of the United Synagogue.

Montagu had lived an extraordinary life, as a lawyer, intelligence officer, and writer: a judge of deep seriousness, he had also retained a boyish side, and a talent for self-mockery. Without his combination of 'extreme caution and extreme daring', Operation Mincemeat could never have happened. The entire plan was, in a way, a reflection of his sense of the ridiculous, and his love of the macabre, of playing a part. In 1980, a photograph of Jean Gerard Leigh appeared in *The Times* after her husband was made CBE. 'Dear "Pam",' wrote Montagu, now seventy-nine years old. 'It was a voice from the past to see you in today's papers and I can't resist being another such voice and sending you congratulations. Ever yours, Ewen (alias Major William Martin).'

Shortly before his death, Montagu received a letter from the father of two young Canadian girls, who had read of his wartime exploits, requesting a memento. He immediately replied, enclosing 'one of the buttons I wore when carrying out Operation Mincemeat', along with some advice: 'Keep a real sense of humour. By real I don't mean just to be able to see a joke, but to be able to really and truly laugh at oneself.'

Ewen Montagu died in 1985, at the age of eighty-four, believing he had successfully hidden, for all time, the identity of the body used in Operation Mincemeat.

Roger Morgan, a council planning officer in London and an indefatigable amateur historian, began researching the story of Operation Mincemeat in 1980. He wrote to Montagu, and later met him, and like every other would-be sleuth, received a response that was as courteous as it was unhelpful. Like most others, Morgan concluded that the secret of Major Martin's identity had died with Montagu: the man who never was would never be. But then, in 1996, Morgan was leafing through a newly declassified batch of government files, when he came across a three-volume report on Ewen Montagu's wartime activities, including a copy of the official account of Operation Mincemeat, written just before the end of the war. 'There, at the end of the last volume, staring out at him was the answer to many sleepless nights.' The official censor, perhaps unaware of the extraordinary efforts of concealment made over the preceding half-century, had failed to redact a name. 'On 28

January there had died a labourer of no fixed abode. His name was Glyndwr Michael and he was thirty-four years old.'

Nuestra Señora de la Soledad cemetery is a ghostly but tranquil place at dusk. Swallows swoop over the cobbled paths, and the cypresses stand sentry. Far out in the bay, you can see the fishing boats, bringing in the sardines. As the sun sinks and the dusk settles, the graves seem to merge into one long field of engraved marble, stories of lives long and short, full and empty. One of the gravestones is different. It tells of a double life, one brief, sad and real, the other a little longer, entirely invented, and oddly heroic. The body in this grave washed ashore wearing a fake uniform and the underwear of a dead Oxford don, with a love letter from a girl he had never known pressed to his long-dead heart. No one in this story was quite who they seemed to be. The Montagu brothers, Charles Cholmondeley, Jean Leslie, Alan Hillgarth, Karl-Erich Kuhlenthal and Juan Pujol – each was born into one existence, and imagined themselves into a life quite different.

Grave number 1886 in Huelva's cemetery was taken over by the Commonwealth War Graves Commission in 1977. In a small local armistice, it is now maintained, on behalf of Britain, by the German consulate in Huelva. Every year, in April, an Englishwoman from the town lays flowers on the gravestone.

In 1997, half a century after Operation Mincemeat, the British government added a carved postscript to the marble slab:

Glyndwr Michael
served as
Major William Martin, RN

WILLIAM MARTIN
BORN 29TH MARCH 1907
DIED 24TH APRIL 1943
BELOVED SON OF JOHN
GLYNDWYR MARTIN
AND THE LATE ANTONIA MARTIN OF
CARDIFF, WALES.
DULCE ET DECORUM EST PRO PATRIA MORI
R. I. P.

Appendix

COPY

7

OPERATION MINCEMEAT

1. Object

To cause a brief-case containing documents to drift ashore as near as possible to HUELVA in Spain in such circumstances that it will be thought to have been washed ashore from an aircraft which crashed at sea when the case was being taken by an officer from the U.K. to Allied Force H.Q. in North Africa.

2. Method

A dead body dressed in the battle-dress uniform of a Major, Royal Marines, and wearing a "Mae West" will be taken out in a submarine, together with the brief case and a rubber dinghy.

The body will be packed fully clothed and ready (and wrapped in a blanket to prevent friction) in a tubular air-tight container (which will be labelled as "Optical Instruments").

The container is just under 6' 6" long and just under 2' in diameter and has no excresences of any kind on the sides. The end which opens has a flush fitting lid which is held tightly in position by a number of nuts and has fitted on its exterior in clips a box-spanner with a permanent tommy-bar which is chained to the lid.

Both ends are fitted with handles which fold down flat. It will be possible to lift the container by using both handles or even by using the handle in the lid alone, but it would be better not to take the whole weight on the handle at the other end as the steel of which the container is made is of light gauge to keep the weight as low as possible. The approximate total weight when the container is full will be 400 lbs.

When the container is closed the body will be packed round with a certain amount of "dry-ice". The container should therefore be opened on deck as the "dry-ice" will give off carbon dioxide.

3. Position

The body should be put into the water as close inshore as prudently possible and as near to HUELVA as possible, preferably to the North West of the river mouth.

According to the Hydrographic Department the tides in that area run mainly up and down the coast, and every effort should therefore be made to choose a period with an on-shore wind. South Westerly winds are in fact the prevailing winds in that area at this time of year.

The latest information about the tidal streams in that area, as obtained from the Superintendant of Tides is attached.

4. Delivery of the Package.

The package will be brought up to the port of departure by road on whatever day is desired, preferably as close to the sailing day as possible. The brief case will handed over at the same time to the Captain of the submarine. The rubber dinghy will also be a separate parcel.

/5.

9A

5. Disposal of the body

When the body is removed from the container all that will be necessary will be to fasten the chain attached to the brief case through the belt of the trench-coat which will be the outer garment on the body. The chain is of the type worn under the coat, round the chest and out through the sleeve. At the end is a "dog-lead" type of clip for attaching to the handle of the brief case and a similar clip for forming the loop round the chest. It is this loop that should be made through the belt of the trench coat as if the officer has slipped the chain off for comfort in the aircraft, but has nevertheless kept it attached to him so that the bag should not either be forgotten or slide away from him in the aircraft.

The body should then be deposited in the water, as should also be the rubber dinghy. As this should drift at a different speed from the body the exact position at which it is released is unimportant, but it should be near the body but not too near if that is possible.

6. Those in the know at Gibraltar

Steps have been taken to inform F.O.I.C. Gibraltar and his S.O.(I). No one else there will be in the picture

7. Signals

If the operation is successfully carried out a signal should be made "MINCEMEAT completed". If that is made from Gibraltar the S.O.(I) should be asked to send it addressed to D.N.I. (PERSONAL). If it can be made earlier it should be made in accordance with orders from F.O.S.

8. Cancellation

If the operation has to be cancelled a signal will be made "Cancel MINCEMEAT". In that case the body and container should be sunk in deep water; as the container may have positive buoyancy it may either have to be weighted or water may have to be allowed to enter. In the latter case care must be taken that the body does not escape. The brief case should be handed to the S.O.(I). at Gibraltar, with instructions to burn the contents unopened, if there is no possibility of taking that course earlier. The rubber dinghy should be handed to the S.O.(I) for disposal.

9. Abandonment

If the operation has to be abandoned a signal should be made "MINCEMEAT abandoned" as soon as possible (See para 7 above).

10. Cover

This is a matter for consideration. Until the operation actually takes place it is thought that the labelling of the container "Optical Instruments" will provide sufficient cover. It is suggested that the cover after the operation has been completed should be that it is hoped to trap a very active German agent in this neighbourhood and it is hoped that sufficient evidence can be obtained by this means to get the Spaniards to eject him.

/The

The importance of dealing with this man should be impressed on the crew together with the fact that any leakage that may **ever** take place about this will compromise our power to get the Spaniards to act in such cases; also that they will never learn whether we were successful in this objective as the whole matter will have to be conducted in secrecy with the Spaniards or we won't be able to get them to act.

It is in fact most important that the Germans and Spaniards should accept these papers in accordance with para 1. If they should suspect that the papers are a "plant" it might have far-reaching consequences of great magnitude.

(Sgd) E.E.S. Montagu,
Lt.Cdr. R.N.V.R.

31.3.43.

Appendix

I am afraid there is nothing to add to the remarks in S.D.'s "West Coasts of Spain &Portugal Pilot" page 13, lines 31-39. There would be a probability that an object freed near Cape St. Vincent would drift towards the Straits of Gibraltar, while winds between S and W might set it towards the head of the bight near P. Huelva. If it was drifting off the port at L.W. Lisbon it would probably be carried inwards by the flood stream, but if it did not strand it would be carried out again on the ebb.

The Spaniards and Portuguese publish practically nothing about tides, tidal streams and currents off their coasts.

(Initialled)

22.3.43.

PERSONAL DOCUMENTS AND ARTICLES IN POCKETS

Identity discs (2) "Major W. MARTIN, R.M., R/C" attached to braces.

Silver cross on Silver chain round neck.

Watch, wrist.

Wallet, containing:-

Photograph of Fiancee
Book of stamps (2 used)
2 letters from Fiancee
St. Christopher plaque
Invitation to Cabaret Club
C.C.O. Pass } In cellophane container
Admiralty Identity Card }
Torn off top of letter.
1 £5 note - March 5th 1942 C/227 45827

3 £1 notes X 34 D 527008
W 21 D 029293
X 66 D 443119

1 Half crown

2 Shillings

2 six pences

4 pennies

Letter from "Father"

Letter from "Father" to McKenna & Co., Solicitors

Letter from Lloyds Bank

Bill (receipted) from Naval & Military Club

Bill (cash) from Gieves Ltd.

Bill for engagement ring

2 bus tickets

2 counterfoil stubs of tickets for Prince of Wales' Theatre 22.4.43

Box of matches

Packet of Cigarettes

Bunch of keys

Pencil Stub

Letter from McKenna & Co. Solicitors.

TEL. NO. 88.

BLACK LION HOTEL.
MOLD.
N. WALES.

13th April 1943.

My dear William,

I cannot say that this Hotel is any longer as comfortable as I remember it to have been in pre war days. I am, however, staying here as the only alternative to imposing myself once more upon your aunt whose depleted staff & strict regard for fuel economy (which I agree to be necessary in war time) has made the house almost uninhabitable to a guest, at least one of my age. I propose to be in Town for the nights of the 20th & 21st of April when no doubt we shall have an opportunity to meet. I enclose the copy of a letter which I have written to Gwatkin of McKenna's about your affairs. You will see that I have asked him to lunch with me at the Carlton Grill (which I understand still to be open) at a quarter to one on Wednesday the 21st. I should be glad if you would make it possible to join us. We shall not however wait luncheon for you, so I trust that, if you are able to come, you will make a point of being punctual.

Your cousin Priscilla has asked to be remembered to you. She has grown into a sensible girl though I cannot say that her work for the Land Army has done much to improve her looks. In that respect I am afraid that she will take after her father's side of the family.

Your affectionate
Father.

In reply, quote SR.1924/43.

COMBINED OPERATIONS HEADQUARTERS,
1A, RICHMOND TERRACE,
WHITEHALL, S.W.1.

21st April,
1943.

Dear Admiral of the Fleet,

I promised V.C.I.G.S. that Major Martin would arrange with you for the onward transmission of a letter he has with him for General Alexander. It is very urgent and very "hot" and as there are some remarks in it that could not be seen by others in the War Office, it could not go by signal. I feel sure that you will see that it goes on safely and without delay.

I think you will find Martin the man you want. He is quiet and shy at first, but he really knows his stuff. He was more accurate than some of us about the probable run of events at Dieppe and he has been well in on the experiments with the latest barges and equipment which took place up in Scotland.

Let me have him back, please, as soon as the assault is over. He might bring some sardines with him - they are "on points" here!

Yours sincerely

Louis Mountbatten

Admiral of the Fleet Sir A.B. Cunningham, G.C.B., D.S.O.,
Commander in Chief Mediterranean,
Allied Force H.Q.,
Algiers.

THE MANOR HOUSE
OGBOURNE ST. GEORGE
MARLBOROUGH
WILTSHIRE
TELEPHONE OGBOURNE ST. GEORGE 242

Sunday 18th

I do think dearest that seeing people like you off at railway stations is one of the poorer forms of sport. A train going out can leave a howling great gap in one's life & one has to try madly – & quite in vain – to fill it with all the things one used to enjoy a whole five weeks ago. That lovely golden day we spent together – oh! I know it's been said before, but if only time could sometimes stand still just for a minute – But that line of thought is too pointless. Pull your socks up Pam & don't be a silly little fool.

Your letter made me feel slightly better – but I shall get horribly conceited if you go on saying things like that about me – they're utterly unlike ME, as I'm afraid you'll soon find out. Here I am for the week-end in this divine place with Mummy & Jane being too sweet & understanding the whole time, bored beyond words & panting for Monday so that I can get back to the old grindstone again. What an idiotic waste!

Bill darling, do let me know as soon as you get fixed & can make some more plans, & don't please let them send you off into the blue the horrible way they do nowadays – now that we've found each other out of the whole world, I don't think I could bear it –

All my love,

Pam

PLAYER'S
CIGARETTES
"MEDIUM"
MASTERS
SAFETY
MATCHES

31

MOST SECRET

From The Commanding Officer, H.M. Submarine "SERAPH".

Date: 30th April, 1943.

To Director of Naval Intelligence.

Copy to F.O.S.

(for Lt. Cdr. The Hon. E.E.S. Montagu,R.N.V.R.) personal.

OPERATION MINCEMEAT

Weather: The wind was variable altering between SW and SE, force 2. It was expected that the sea breeze would spring up in the morning, close inshore, as it had on the previous morning in similar conditions.
Sea and swell - 2.0. - Sky overcast with very low clouds - visibility was patchy, 1 to 2 miles - Barometer 1016.

2. **Fishing boats:** A large number of small fishing boats were working in the bay. The closest was left, about a mile off, and it is not thought that the submarine was observed by them.

3. **Operation:** The time of 0430 was chosen as being the nearest to Low Water Lisbon, (0731) which would allow the submarine to be well clear by dawn. The Cannister was opened at 0415 and the body extracted. The blanket was opened up and the body examined. The brief case was found to be securely attached. The face was heavily tanned and the whole of the lower half from the eyes down covered with mould. The skin had started to break away on the nose and cheek bones. The body was very high. The Mae West was blown up very hard and no further air was needed. The body was placed in the water at 0430 in a position 148° Portil Pillar 1.3 miles approximately eight cables from the beach and started to drift inshore. This was aided by the wash of the screws going full speed astern. The rubber dinghy was placed in the water blown up and upside down about half a mile further south of this position. The submarine then withdrew to seaward and the cannister, filled with water, and containing the blanket, tapes and also the rubber dinghy's container was pushed over the side in position 36°37'30 North 07°18'00 West in 310 fathoms of water by sounding machine. The container would not at first submerge but after being riddled by fire from Vickers gun and also .455 revolver at very short range was seen to sink.
Signal reporting operation complete was passed at 0715.
A sample of the water close inshore is attached.

N. L. A. JEWELL.

Lieutenant-in-Command.

Postscript

The story of Operation Mincemeat is far from over. The events themselves took place sixty-six years ago, and all but a handful of those involved in the planning and execution of the operation are now gone. Yet the story continues to grow, as new information, new memories, and new documents come to light.

The Black Lion

A week after publication, I received the sort of telephone call writers of non-fiction routinely receive, and usually dread. 'I believe you have got something wrong…' said a polite voice. My heart sank a little. The voice continued: 'In Chapter Seven you wrote, "The plot would never have stood up to scrutiny if German spies in Britain had made even the most cursory checks on it … A glance at the hotel register for the Black Lion Hotel would have showed that no J. G. Martin had stayed there on the night of 13 April."' I braced myself. I had indeed written that the letter supposedly written by Bill Martin's 'Father' at a specific hotel on a specific date was a dangerous hostage to fortune. 'Well, I happen to have the old register for the Black Lion open in front of me. And if you look at the page for April, 1943, you will clearly see the name J. G. Martin.'

I was flabbergasted, and my respect for the planners of Operation Mincemeat rose another notch. They had thought of everything: they had even despatched someone to Mold, in North Wales, to stay at the hotel and pose as the fictional father of a fictional officer, simply to ensure that the hotel register would look correct if anyone came snooping afterwards. That was true spycraft.

When the caller sent me a photograph of the page from the register, I studied it carefully. The handwriting appeared to be that of Charles Cholmondeley, the originator and co-creator of Operation Mincemeat. The false address given for 'J. G. Martin' was Scotts House, Eynsham, in Oxfordshire (now a day care centre).

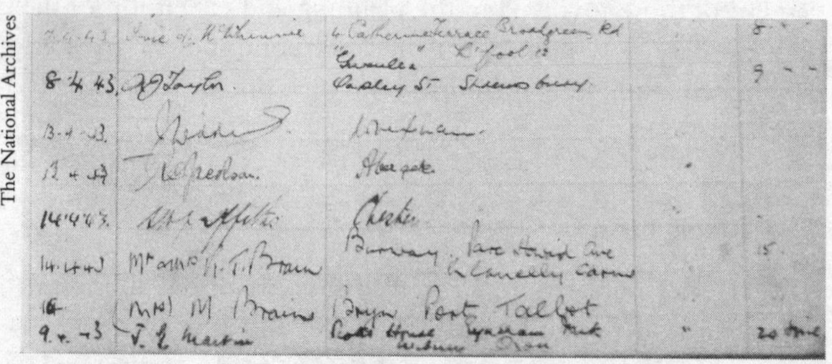

The National Archives

The faked letter in Major Martin's pocket clearly indicated that 'Father' had been staying at the hotel for some time ('the only alternative to imposing myself once more on your aunt'). According to the register, he had arrived at the hotel on 9 April, and checked out on 20 April, in time for the fake meeting with his son in London. So far, so convincing.

But closer examination revealed something very odd. The name and signature of J. G. Martin did not appear in the correct date sequence, but was added in the space at the bottom of the page. It was clearly an afterthought, written in at a later date; and possibly much later. To even the most casual investigator this would have set off loud alarm bells: far from covering up the mistake, Cholmondeley had compounded it, by drawing attention to the fact that there was something distinctly out of the ordinary about John Martin and his sojourn at the Black Lion.

One can speculate about what must have happened. As Operation Mincemeat got underway, the planners began to realise that it was working far more effectively than they had dared to hope. They began to wonder and worry about possible loose ends. The coroner, Bentley Purchase, was contacted again and quizzed over whether, if the Germans exhumed the body and carried out another post mortem, they would be able discover that he had died of poisoning, rather than drowning. (The cheery coroner, ever optimistic, was confident they would not.) They also, I suspect, took another look at the letters, and despatched Cholmondeley to Mold to doctor the record. The result was not a cover-up, but a giveaway. A register without the name J. G. Martin would merely have presented a mystery; a register with the name so obviously added in was patently a botched attempt to deceive.

In the end, it did not matter. There is no evidence that the Germans ever carried out any checks in Britain on the Bill Martin backstory. Had they attempted to do so, this would almost certainly have been picked up by British intelligence since the entire German espionage system in the UK was effectively controlled by MI5. Once the lie was embedded in German strategic thinking, no effort was made to disprove it.

Still, it is a sobering thought, that if a single German agent had travelled to Mold to examine the register of the Black Lion, he would surely have spotted the obvious subsequent addition of 'J. G. Martin', realised there was something fishy going on, and warned the Germans before the invasion of Sicily, with incalculable consequences. That single register entry could have changed the course of the Second World War.

The planners deliberately placed John Martin in a hotel to ensure there was no home address for the Martins that a German spy might be able to investigate. To his credit, Montagu felt rather guilty for casting aspersions on the hotel in the fake letter: 'I cannot say that this hotel is any longer as comfortable as I remember it to have been in pre-war days'. Even so, 'Father' may have had a point. The Black Lion went out of business after the war. It is now the Halifax bank.

The help of the Post Office

A letter from another reader drew my attention to a different anomaly. The letter from the bank manager to Bill Martin was addressed to him at the Army and Navy Club, yet all the other documents, including a bill from the club itself, clearly showed that he had been staying at the Naval and Military Club, an entirely different establishment. This looked like a glaring error. Whoever typed up the letter from the bank had, it seemed, mixed up the two armed forces clubs. Why had Cholmondeley and Montagu, usually so meticulous and entirely absorbed in the fictional character and habits of their creation, failed to spot the mistake? Why, for that matter, had the Germans missed this clear proof that these were not genuine documents, but fabrications?

But when I went back to the archives, I discovered that so far from being a mistake, the wrongly addressed letter was part of the plan. The envelope containing the bank manager's dunning letter was indeed addressed to Martin at the Army and Navy Club, but the club name had been crossed out – scrawled below were the words 'Not known at this address. Try Naval and Military Club, 94 Piccadilly'. The envelope had even been postmarked twice: the first time 14 April, and the second, when it was forwarded to the correct address, 18 April – the very day that Bill Martin supposedly checked in.

The National Archives

Far from being a mistake, the wrongly addressed letter was yet another way to bolster the apparent genuineness of the documents, a tiny, subtle twist to the story. If the Germans spotted it, it would only serve to show that Bill Martin was a real person, with a real bank manager, who made a real (though unimportant) mistake when demanding that he pay off his overdraft. And if Bill Martin was real, then his official documents would also seem the more believable.

I can't help thinking that the wrongly addressed envelope was also a sly joke, of the sort that serving officers might appreciate, at the expense of Ernest Whitley Jones, the pompous Joint General Manager of Lloyds Bank. Bank managers may be most efficient, even peremptory, in demanding that we pay off an overdraft, but they don't know the difference between one services club and the other.

Out of date

There is one other oddity in Bill Martin's 'wallet litter' that was brought to my attention after publication. The Major's pass for Combined Operations Headquarters was out of date, since it clearly states 'Not Valid after March 31st, 1943'. Here was yet another reinforcement of the character – disorganised, dreamy and inclined to overlook details. His photographic identity card also underlined this aspect of his personality, since it was 'issued in lieu of No. 09650 lost'. This would also allay the suspicions of any German intelligence officer who wondered why the identity card seemed so new (despite Montagu's attempts to give it the patina of wear). Major Martin was simply the sort of person who spent £53 on a diamond ring despite a thumping overdraft, lost his identity card, and forgot to renew his official pass. But the expired pass poses a small mystery: if the fictional Major Martin could not get into Combined Operations Headquarters, how did he manage to pick up the letters from Lord Mountbatten? We will never know because, of course, no such thing ever happened.

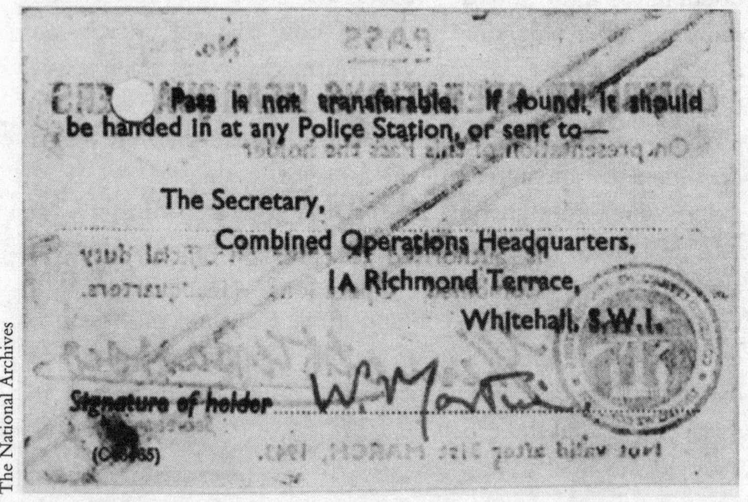
Pass is not transferable. If found, it should be handed in at any Police Station, or sent to—

The Secretary,
Combined Operations Headquarters,
1A Richmond Terrace,
Whitehall, S.W.1.

Signature of holder W Martin

The National Archives

The name Martin was chosen partly because there were several Martins in the Royal Marines, and also because the real William Martin was the right age, rank and far enough away not to make trouble. William Hynd Norrie Martin's son, Peter Martin, wrote to me explaining that in 1943 his father was 'the

Assistant Superintendent of British Air Training at Quonset Point, Rhode Island, in charge of training and converting British aircrews to Avenger and Vought Corsair aircraft'. But the name was also chosen because it began with 'M'. Montagu knew – through the Ultra intercepts passed on by Bletchley Park – that the Germans only had the first volume of the Navy List, covering letters A to L. If they tried to check up on the identity, they would have to obtain the second volume, or use intermediaries who had access to it, and any such attempt at verification would probably appear in the intercepts.

Dudley Clarke

After the war, Colonel Clarke, the chief of deception in the Mediterranean, was unstinting in his praise for Operation Mincemeat. 'Preparation of the body had called for infinite pains and untold ingenuity: not the smallest detail had been overlooked and every conceivable contingency had been provided for. It was a masterpiece of planning and stage-management'.

Yet the mystery of Clarke's own transvestite brush with the Spanish police was one detail of the story that many readers seemed to find particularly intriguing. Several went to the trouble of digging up more details on this episode.

Clarke was arrested on 18 October 1943, on a street in Madrid. He was apparently in Spain to recruit agents to help with his deception work, although the specifics of his mission remain tantalisingly vague. Whether he was arrested on suspicion of espionage, or because he looked like a man in women's clothes, is not revealed. He first told the Spanish police that he was a novelist and 'wanted to study the reactions of men to women in the streets'. He then changed his story, insisting he was 'taking the feminine garments to a lady in Gibraltar' and thought that he would 'try them on for a prank'.

The British embassy was sceptical, pointing out, in a telegram that could hardly contain its mirth, that the shoes fitted him perfectly, and he had 'unusually big feet'. The police decided that Clarke must be a 'homosexualist'; the Gestapo in Spain concluded he must be a spy. His colleagues could not work out *what* he was.

Once liberated from jail by Alan Hillgarth, Clarke played down the whole incident with magnificent nerve. Indeed, he brazenly asserted that the affair had been intentional, and had helped to reinforce his cover as a correspondent for *The Times* – although as a former foreign correspondent of *The Times* myself, I am not sure how flattered I am by this line of argument.

The incident even merited a small footnote in the most famous spy scandal of all. On 31 October 1941, Kim Philby, in a message that can only have reinforced the KGB's belief in Western decadence, reported to his Moscow handlers: 'So far, no reason has reached London as to why he was found in women's clothes.'

Franco's hand in the matter

I had always suspected that General Franco must have known about the Mincemeat documents, but with the publication of *Deathly Deception* by Denis Smyth (Oxford University Press, 2010), came proof. According to Smyth, an authority on Spanish history, the documents were translated into Spanish and forwarded to the *Caudillo*. Franco himself must therefore have approved the appointment of Colonel Pardo as a go-between, and then personally authorised the passing on of the secret documents in direct contravention of Spain's supposed neutrality.

Professor Smyth also sheds additional light on the route the information took to Berlin. On 8 May, soon after the documents had been extracted from their envelopes but before handing them over to the Germans, a Spanish officer (almost certainly Pardo) briefed an Abwehr officer (either Leissner or

Kuhlenthal) on the gist of the Nye letter. This information was written up in a 'Most Secret Letter', and taken by hand to Berlin by Kurt von Rohrscheidt of the Madrid Abwehr counter-espionage section, who had no idea of its contents. According to this timetable, Alexis Von Roenne, the head of FHW, gave his initial seal of approval to the intelligence contained in this letter before he had even seen the photographs of the original documents – yet more evidence of his determination to believe them, without question or investigation. A few days later, with Berlin's appetite thoroughly wetted, Kuhlenthal arrived bearing copies of the letters themselves.

Fisher's knickers

The use of H. A. L. Fisher's underwear to clothe the dead man prompted a remarkable correspondence in *The Times*. Unlike other types of clothing, underwear was available only with ration coupons, and could not simply be bought in a shop. None of the officers, understandably, was willing to surrender his own.

On 14 January 2010 *The Times* published a letter from Harry Judge, fellow of Brasenose College, Oxford, and an authority on the life of Fisher, under the headline 'Upper-class unmentionables – No upper-class corpse would be convincing without appropriate underwear.' Garments that had previously belonged to Fisher were given by his widow to her nephew, Courtenay. He handed them over to intelligence officers (in circumstances that are not clear), who wisely removed the Cash's name tapes. I was first told of this unlikely detail by [the historian] Hugh Trevor-Roper in 1978 and, doubting it, secured confirmation from Fisher's late daughter, at that time the Principal of St Hilda's College.'

Courtenay Young, an intelligence colleague of John Masterman, appears to have obtained the underwear from his aunt Lettice, Fisher's widow, in response to a request from

Masterman himself. Lettice does not seem to have found the request remotely odd. As her nephew, Robin Ilbert, wrote: 'She was indeed a remarkable combination of keen intellect and common sense, needing to spend a portion of each day either gardening and being a keen hen wife, or playing her violin. Household economics, and household economy, were in her bones. Add that to "Make Do and Mend" and clothes rationing during the war, and you will find it entirely credible that Lettice should, after Herbert's death, post Herbert's clothes to Courtenay. And then the presence of mind to remove the then ubiquitous Cash's name tapes!' In fact, the planners of Operation Mincemeat carefully had the underwear laundered again, to make sure the laundry marks were the same as those on the rest of Bill Martin's clothing.

Mr Judge's letter triggered the sort of exchange that could only take place in the letters page of *The Times*. Stanley Martin, author of *The Order of Merit*, an account of Fisher's life, wrote to report that in the 1980s the story of the underwear was part of New College folklore. Alistair Cooke wrote from London: 'Sir, H. A. L. Fisher, Warden of New College, Oxford, from 1925 to 1940, was not the kind of man who would have wanted his underwear to end up on a dead young tramp to help to deceive the Germans. He followed his godfather, the Prince Consort, in reserving his approval for "anything that he found exalted". He had no time for life's failures. As Lloyd George's Minister for Education, his one objective was to help "young ambition starving for knowledge and stinted in opportunities". Nor would the destruction of Germany have appealed to him. His last published article, which appeared in February 1940, expressed the hope that "a *modus vivendi* with the Germans" would be found. A contribution to Operation Mincemeat should have been sought from the clothes closet of Oxford's most zealous supporter of the war, A. L. Rowse, of All Souls.'

Here, then, was the sort of debate that John Masterman, don

and spy, would have relished: which Oxford academic would most willingly have surrendered his underwear to confound Hitler?

'Animals'

The SOE operation in Greece to bolster the deception was codenamed 'Animals' (p. 281), and it played a crucial role in maintaining German focus on the Eastern Mediterranean, long after it became obvious that Sicily would be attacked by the Allies. After parachuting into Northern Greece, Lieutenant Colonel Eddie Myers and Captain Monty Woodhouse were ordered to launch a coordinated campaign of sabotage, starting in late June 1943 and continuing throughout the invasion period. The intention was quite specific, according to a memo written by Woodhouse now in the National Archives: 'To create the utmost havoc in the enemy's communications throughout the length and breadth of Greece, in order to deceive the enemy into thinking that this was the preliminary to the invasion of Greece'.

On 21 June 1943, a six-man sabotage team destroyed the railway viaduct at Asopos, after scaling down a cliff and through a waterfall. Across the country, roads were blown up, railways ruptured and telephone lines cut. With the viaduct down, the 1st German Panzer division was effectively trapped. The guerrilla campaign made it practically impossible to reinforce Sicily with troops from Greece, but more importantly it redoubled the German conviction, sown by the Mincemeat deception and Operation Barclay, that Greece was facing imminent Allied attack.

Cholmondely's romance

The most touching letter I received in the wake of publication came from a former girlfriend of Charles Cholmondely, who also worked in intelligence during the war.

Courtesy of Tom Cholmondely

'I am so glad that Charles Cholmondeley has at last been given the credit due for his idea. I knew him when he was in MI5 and I worked in MI6. I inadvertently sent him some wrong papers in the diplomatic bag. He met me to return the papers and took me to the Piccadilly Hotel to dinner. He was a charming and modest companion, almost ashamed of being "chairborne" instead of "airborne". And if he was eccentric – well, so were a lot of others in MI6. He had a little car which he drove with the sunroof open and his head almost poking through and he unflatteringly described himself as "like toothpaste squeezed out of a tube", but I was used to tall men as my father was 6 ft 4 in. He gave me an opal ring which he had made himself, saying "It is not an engagement ring". He didn't want to settle down, as his life was too full of adventure. He loved the film *The Third Man* and we often danced to the signature tune. It might have been the start of a beautiful romance … thank you for reminding me of him and of London during the war.'

The flirtatious aspect of Ewen Montagu's character is clear from his letters to 'Pam'. Here was the correspondingly romantic side of his partner, the self-effacing, self-mocking, and chairborne Charles Cholmondeley.

Something in the words of his girlfriend – recalling him so fondly, so many years later – reminded me of the fictional relationship between 'Pam' and 'Bill', the doomed wartime love affair that never was.

Ben Macintyre, June 2010

Courtesy of Judith Kuhlenthal

Karl Erich Kuhlenthal is standing second from left in a family photograph. Blurred as it is, this is the only surviving image of the German intelligence officer from the time he was working in Spain as head of the Abwehr's espionage section.

Courtesy of Patricia Davies

Patricia Trehearne, working in Room 13. Miss Trehearne addressed the envelopes of the official letters: the only other person to handle the documents was Ewen Montagu. Too many sets of fingerprints might have alerted the Germans that these were no routine letters.

Courtesy of Lawrence and Wisam

Ivor Montagu, table tennis aficionado, film maker and vole-expert. In this photograph Ivor looks indisputably (and somewhat self-consciously) like the Soviet spy he was.

Courtesy of Jeremy Montagu

Ewen Montagu smoking his pipe. In the cramped confinement of Room 13, which housed fourteen people without windows or ventilation, no one ever forgot the smell of Montagu's pipe.

Notes

Epigraph

'Who in war will not have . . .' Winston Churchill, *The Second World War*, Vol. V *Closing the Ring* (London, 1951), p. 91.

Preface

'some memoranda which . . .' Ewen Montagu, *Beyond Top Secret Ultra* (London, 1977), p. 14.

Chapter 1: The Sardine Spotter

'lump' Cited in Jesús Ramírez Copeiro del Villar, *Huelva en la II Guerra Mundial* (Huelva 1996), p. 408.
'no-one wanted . . .' Ibid., p. 409.

Chapter 2: Corkscrew Minds

'The Trout Fisher' TNA ADM 223/478.
'marked flair' Cited in Ben Macintyre, *For Your Eyes Only: Ian Fleming and James Bond* (London, 2008), p. 42.
'romantic Red Indian daydreams' Ibid., p. 43.
'deception, ruses de guerre' TNA ADM 223/478.
'At first sight' Ibid.
'The business of deception' John Godfrey, 'Afterthoughts', TNA ADM 223/619, p. 51.
'pushing quicksilver' Ibid.
'treasure ship' TNA ADM 223/478.
'an unimpeachable and immaculate' Ibid.
'with instructions on the' Ibid.

'A Suggestion (not a very nice one)' Ibid.
'research' *Time* magazine, 'The Thomson Case', 18 Jan 1926.
'I know the stuff' Basil Thomson, *The Milliner's Hat Mystery* (London, 1937), p. 64.
'offers us far more' Godfrey, 'Afterthoughts', TNA ADM 223/619 p. 26.
'the target date' David Kahn, *Hitler's Spies: German Military Intelligence in World War II* (New York, 2000), p. 471.
'extremely worried' *After the Battle*, 54, 1986.
'not been tampered with' Kahn, *Hitler's Spies*, p. 471.
'quite legible' Ibid.
'It was highly unlikely' Ibid.
'All the documents' TNA CAB 163/1.
'no greater importance' Kahn, *Hitler's Spies*, p. 471.
'documents had likely' Frank J. Stech, 'Outguessed and One-Behind: The Real Story of The Man Who Never Was,' paper presented to conference, University of Wolverhampton, Jul 2004.
'This suggested that' TNA ADM 223/794.
'lifting his toes as he walked' Interview with Jean Gerard Leigh (JGL), 5 Mar 2008
'This was a terrible' Interview with Tom Cholmondeley, 1 Oct 2007.
'ideas man' Thaddeus Holt, *The Deceivers: Allied Military Deception in the Second World War* (London, 2004), p. 370.
'extraordinary and delightful' Ibid.
'one of those subtle' Ewen Montagu, *The Man Who Never Was* (Oxford, 1996), p. 116.
'a plan for introducing documents' IWM 97/45/1, folder #2.
'A body is obtained from one' Ibid.
'the drop' Ibid.
'double for an actual officer' Ibid.
'and injuries inflicted after death' Montagu, *Man*, p. 116.
'a full and capable postmortem' Memo to XX Committee, 4 Feb 1943, IWM 97/45/1 folder #2.
'Of these, Spain was clearly' Ibid.
'Meinertzhagen knew no half measures' T. E. Lawrence, *Seven Pillars of Wisdom* (London, 1991), p. 452.
'Good-bye, my darling!' John Lord, *Duty, Honour, Empire* (London, 1971) p. 332.
'easy, reliable and inexpensive' Meinertzhagen, *Army Diary*, cited in ibid., p. 336.
'fair going' Holt, *The Deceivers*, p. 95.
'there was never any evidence' Ibid., p. 297.

Chapter 3: Room 13

'The Germans, having cause to regret' Jimmy Burns, *Papa Spy: Love, Faith and Betrayal in Wartime Spain* (London, 2009), p. 233.
'strongly supported' Draft of report on Operation Mincemeat, 29 May 1943, IWM 97/45/1 folder #2.
'go into the question' Ibid.
'fertile brain' Montagu, *Man*, p. 108.
'My memory is of' Ewen Montagu, Untitled, unpublished autobiography in manuscript, in Montagu Papers, courtesy of Jeremy Montagu. Henceforth Ewen Montagu, *Autobiography*.
'*Montagu, first Baron Swaythling he*' Ivor Montagu, *The Youngest Son: Autobiographical Chapters* (London, 1970), p. 18.

'exquisite chandelier' Ewen Montagu, *Autobiography*.
'Statesmen (British and world)' Ibid.
'like a very animated piece' Ibid.
'It was a *servants'* lift' Montagu, *Younger Son*, p. 14.
'Born as I was' Ewen Montagu, *Autobiography*.
'idiotic' Ibid.
'the sort of American social life' Ibid.
'I felt a great debt' Ibid.
'The 'spread' among us three' Ibid.
'already had a banker's attitude' Ibid.
'He and I were much' Ibid.
'we had nothing to do' Ibid.
'I advised him to choose' Ibid.
'Our great ambition was' Ibid.
'to study something' Ibid.
'I put it in my pocket' Ibid.
'one of the best fly-fisherman' Anthony Cave Brown, *Bodyguard of Lies*, Vol. I (London, 1975), p. 278.
'never better than a mediocre' Ewen Montagu, *Autobiography*.
'the thrill of the strike' Ibid.
'an exceedingly primitive vole' Montagu, *Younger Son*, p. 283.
'Baron's Son Weds Secretary' *Evening News*, 23 Mar 1927.
'Dear Gladys, I feel for you' Obituary of Lord Swaythling, *Daily Telegraph*, 4 Jul 1998.
'remarkably obscene curse' Ivor Montagu, *Like it Was*, unpublished, undated autobiography, manuscript in Montagu Collection, Labour History Archive and Study Centre (People's History Museum), Manchester. Henceforth Ivor Montagu, *Autobiography*.
'a certain sympathy with rogue characters' Montagu, *Ultra*, p. 9.
'see the point of view' Ibid.
'gentle manners' M. R. D. Foot, entry in *Oxford Dictionary of National Biography*
'If he could see a really artistic lie' Ewen Montagu, *Autobiography*.
'looking out to sea' Ibid.
'It is quite useless' TNA ADM 223/478.
'two stockbrokers, a schoolmaster' Godfrey, 'Afterthoughts', TNA ADM 223/619 p. 26.
'The permanent inhabitants' Ibid.
'worked like ants' Ibid.
'learning a new language' Ewen Montagu, 'History of Section 17M (now section 12Z)', 26 Oct 1942, courtesy of Jeremy Montagu. Henceforth Montagu Papers.
'the cream of all intelligence' TNA ADM 223/792.
'The Germans have a passion' Ewen Montagu, 'History of Section 17M', Montagu Papers.
'to do the detailed work' Ibid.
'Auntie' Interview with Pat Davies (née Trehearne), 4 Oct 2009.
'She is extraordinarily good' EM to Iris Montagu (IM), 31 Jan 1941, courtesy of Rachel Montagu. Henceforth Montagu Letters.
'watchkeepers' TNA ADM 223/792.
'far too small' Montagu, *Ultra*, p. 51.
'which made everyone' Interview with Pat Davies (née Trehearne), 5 Oct 2009.
'were not supposed to listen to' TNA ADM 223/792.

'a brilliant band of . . .' John Godfrey (JG) to EM, 13 Sep 1964, Montagu Papers.
'began to regard some almost as friends' 'History of Section 17M', Montagu Papers.
'They were so kind to us unconsciously' Montagu, *Ultra*, p. 52.
'in the racket too' EM to Vera Ruth Filby, 3 Feb 1979, Montagu Papers.
'The most fascinating job' Montagu, *Ultra*, p. 50.
'If I am killed there are' EM to IM, 17 Aug 1941, Montagu Letters.
'very entertaining but useless' 'History of Section 17M', Montagu Papers.
'A great number who' Montagu, *Ultra*, p. 36.
'it might be an indication' Naval Intelligence Department memo, 12/13 Sep 1945 TNA ADM 223/794.
'Though I have kept' Victor Rothschild to EM, 13 Nov 1941, TNA ADM 223/794.
'had heard and believed the propaganda' TNA ADM 223/794.
'I thought you had realised' Montagu, *Ultra*, p. 59.
'an out and out traitor' TNA ADM 223/794.
'a four-letter man' EM to IM, 13 Nov 1942, Montagu Letters.
'Fleming is charming' Ibid.
'The bare idea of the dead airman' JG to EM, 13 Sep 1964, Montagu Papers.
'I quite honestly don't remember' EM to JG, 19 Sep 1964, Montagu Papers.

Chapter 4: Target Sicily

'underbelly of the Axis' Churchill speech, 11 Nov 1942.
'no major operation could be' Ewen Montagu, unpublished critique of Constantine Fitzgibbon, *Secret Intelligence in the Twentieth Century* (London, 1976), Montagu Papers.
'and might be the beginning' Cited in Rick Atkinson, *The Day of Battle: The War in Sicily and Italy 1943–1945* (London, 2007), p. 7.
'Everyone but a bloody fool' Montagu, *Ultra*, p. 143.
'prepare deception plans' Christopher Andrew, *The Defence of the Realm: The Authorized History of MI5* (London 2009), p. 284.
'When things were looking pretty' Holt, *The Deceivers*, p. 184.
'an ingenious imagination' Nicholas Rankin, *Churchill's Wizards: The British Genius for Deception 1914–1945* (London, 2008), p. 178.
'fourteen of the biggest Nigerians' Ibid., p. 181.
'special section of intelligence' Ibid., p. 253.
'The idea of knocking' 'Future Anglo Saxon Operative Possibilities', FHW of OKW 8/2/43, cited in Ralph Bennett, *Ultra and Mediterranean Strategy 1941–1945* (London, 1989), p. 227.
'wishfulness' and 'yesmanship' Godfrey, 'Afterthoughts', TNA ADM 223/619, p. 10.
'If the authorities were clamouring' Ibid.
'inclined to believe the one' Ibid., p. 12.
'He could achieve single-handed' Colin Evans, *The Father of Forensics: How Sir Bernard Spilsbury Invented Modern CSI* (London, 2009), p. 122.
'He formed his opinion' Ibid., p. 27.
'just carried on' Ewen Montagu, *Autobiography*.
'England's modern Sherlock Holmes' *Washington Post*, 30 Mar 1938, p. 3.
'haughty, aristocratic bearing' Evans, *The Father of Forensics*, p. 5.
'unlucky sixteen' *After the Battle*, 11, Nov 2006.
'that extraordinary man' Montagu, *Man*, p. 122.
'wanted the Germans and Spaniards' Ibid.
'never once did he ask why' Ibid.
'clear, resonant, without any trace' Evans, *The Father of Forensics*, p. 27.

'Many die from exposure' Montagu, *Man*, p. 122.
'doing a Burke and Hare' Ibid.
'A depressing job?' Robert Jackson, *Coroner: The Biography of Sir Bentley Purchase* (London, 1963), p. 5.
'They were found in Auntie's bag' Ibid., p. 260.
'rugged in appearance and character' Ibid., p. 15.
'an impish sense of humour' Ibid.
'an old friend from my barrister days' EM to Roger Morgan, 19 Apr 1982, Montagu Papers.
'An alternative means of getting' Bentley Purchase to EM , 25 Aug 1953, Montagu Papers.
'conspicuous gallantry and devotion to duty' Jackson, *Coroner*, p. 28.
'aching to get into the war' Ibid., p. 104.
'distort the truth in the service of security' Roger Morgan in *After the Battle*, 54, 1986.
'cursory in the extreme' Ibid.
'a warlike operation' Jackson, *Coroner*, p. 148.
'did not wish to disclose why a body' Ibid.
'You can't get bodies just' Ibid.
'of national importance' Ibid.
'public confidence in coroners' Ibid.
'At what level has this scheme . . .' Ibid.
'The Prime Minister's' Ibid.
'well-developed sense of comedy' Ibid., p. 313.
'absolute discretion' EM to JG, 19 Sep 1964, Montagu Papers.
'A coroner' Ibid.
'remained unidentified' Jackson, *Coroner*, p. 196.
'After one or two possible corpses' Ibid., p. 148.
'the inevitable misery of separation' Montagu, *Ultra*, p. 65.
'I miss you most frightfully' EM to IM, 11 Aug 1941, Montagu Letters.
'In a way it was like a mixture' Montagu, *Ultra*, p. 61.
'It was lovely . . .' EM to IM, 11 Jun 1941, Montagu Letters.
'super-secret papers' Montagu, *Ultra*, p. 68.
'as long as I always wore' Ibid.
'one of the best cooks in London' Ibid., p. 28.
'Mother is too awful' EM, 11 Aug 1941, Montagu Letters.
'crossword puzzles' Montagu, *Ultra*, p. 61.
'who had been in the family' Ewen Montagu, *Autobiography*.

Chapter 5: The Man Who Was

'senile decay' Medical records of Angelton Mental Hospital, Bridgend, 11 Dec 1924, Glamorgan Record Office.
'melancholic' Ibid., 12 Dec 1924.
'confused and very depressed' Ibid.
'deep mental depression' Ibid.
'Hair is grey and thin' Ibid.
'a hectic temperature' Ibid., 28 Mar 1925.
'on condition that the scale' House of Commons Debate, 6 Jul 1926, Hansard, Vol. 197.
'led men and women to London' Jackson, *Coroner*, p. 196.

'It still surprised him' Ibid.

'a common lodging house' Draft of report on Operation Mincemeat, 29 May 1943, IWM 97/45/1 folder #2.

'kept in suitable cold storage' Montagu, *Man,* p. 123.

'lunatic' Glyndwr Michael, death certificate.

'labourer, no fixed abode' Ibid.

'phosphorus poisoning' Ibid.

'removed out of England' Draft of report on Operation Mincemeat, 29 May 1943, IWM 97/45/1 folder #2.

'a minimal dose' EM to J. H. Bevan (JHB), 28 May 1943, TNA CAB 154/67.

'This dose was not sufficient' Ibid.

'phosphorus is not one of' Ibid.

'except possibly faint' Draft of report on Operation Mincemeat, 29 May 1943, IWM 97/45/1 folder #2.

'a highly skilled medico-criminal' EM to JHB, 28 May 1943, TNA CAB 154/67.

'bet heavily against anyone' Ibid.

'You have nothing to fear' Montagu, *Man,* p. 123.

'I am a martyr to Spilsburyism' Andrew Rose, *Lethal Witness: Sir Bernard Spilsbury, the Honorary Pathologist* (London, 2008), p. 139.

'died from pneumonia after exposure' Montagu, *Man,* p. 123.

'really worthwhile purpose' Ibid.

'on condition that I should never' Ibid.

'feverish enquiries into his past' Ibid.

'The most careful possible' Draft MS of *Man*, IWM 97/45/2.

'a ne'er do well, and his relatives' EM to Billy Bob Crim, 26 Dec 1981, Montagu Papers

'extra-cold refrigerator' TNA ADM 223/794, p. 450.

'would have to be used within' Minutes of XX Committee, 4 Feb 1943, IWM 97/45/1 folder #2.

'They ought not to be given names' Winston Churchill to General 'Pug' Ismay, minute, 8 Aug 1943.

'stupidity' Montagu, *Ultra*, p. 52.

'no deductions could be' Ibid.

'sense of humour' Montagu, *Man*, p. 125.

'good omen' Ibid.

'This Operation is proposed' Memo to XX Committee, 4 Feb 1943, IWM 97/45/1 folder #2.

'a courier carrying important' Ibid.

'the real target is omitted from' Ibid.

'the Germans will be looking' Ibid.

'The body must be dropped' Ibid.

'find out a suitable position' Minutes of XX Committee, 4 Feb 1943, IWM 97/45/1 folder #2.

'into the question of providing' Ibid.

'so he will be able to cope' Ibid.

'continue with preparations' Ibid.

Chapter 6: A Novel Approach

'active and well-distributed team' J. C. Masterman, *The Double Cross System in the War 1939–1945* (London, 1972), p. 119.

'The one-man band of Lisbon' Ibid., p. 146.

'for deception, "notional"' Ibid., p. 33.
'The Germans could seldom resist' Ibid., p. 21.
'How difficult it was' Montagu, *Ultra*, p. 43.
'must *never* step out of character' Ibid.
'The more real he appeared' Montagu, *Man,* p. 149.
'Would the ink of the manuscript' Manuscript of 'Post Script' to Montagu, *Man*, p. 4, Montagu Papers.
'give the game away' Ibid.
'Many inks on a freshly written' Ibid., p. 6.
'We talked about him until' Montagu, *Man*, p. 149.
'He does not have to look like' Ibid. p. 123.
'complete failure' Ibid., p. 140.
'appearance that would have' Ibid., p. 141.
'rudely staring at anyone' Ibid.
'almost the same build' Ibid., p. 146.
'The difficulty of obtaining' Masterman, *Double Cross*, p. 137.
'one enormous mausoleum' Michael Ignatieff, *Isaiah Berlin*, p. 60.
'brilliant' 'Obituary' of William Martin, TNA CAB 154/67.
'Keen for more active and dangerous' Ibid.
'a thoroughly good chap' Undated note in CAB 154/67.
'could sometimes come from head' EM to Miss Winton, Lloyds Bank, 29 Feb 1978, Montagu Papers.
'a father of the old school' Montagu, *Man,* p. 154.
'a brilliant tour de force' Ibid.
'. . . at the last moment' TNA, WO 106-5921-15.
'effort to find a flaw in' Montagu, *Man,* p. 149.
'We decided that a' Ibid., p. 150.

Chapter 7: Pam

'What on earth are we going to do' Interview with JGL, 5 Mar 2008.
'glaring inconsistencies' Ibid.
'I was frightfully willing' Ibid.
'Don't run, Miss Leslie!' Ibid.
'In fact, he was trailing me' Ibid.
'charming' Montagu, *Man,* p. 152.
'very attractive' Draft of Operation Mincemeat report EM and CC, 27 April 1943, IWM 97/45/1 folder #2.
'The more attractive girls in' Montagu, *Man*, p. 152.
'I think he had every intention' Interview with JGL, 5 Mar 2008.
'The swimming there was horrible' Ibid.
'quite a collection' Montagu, *Man,* p. 152.
'Uncle John gave specific orders' Interview with Pat Davies (née Trehearne), 4 Oct 2009.
'We were all rather jealous' Ibid.
'I knew it was going to be planted' Interview with JGL, 5 Mar 2008.
'Has anybody else got that' Ibid.
'I never realised how lonely' EM to IM, 17 Aug 1941, Montagu Letters.
'How ultra-happy our life was' EM to IM, 30 Dec 1940, Montagu Letters.
'Bugger Hitler' Ibid.
'You must have gone off' EM to IM, 2 Dec 1940, Montagu Letters.

'I am always the gooseberry' EM to IM, 28 Sep 1941, Montagu Letters.
'It was a question of whether' EM to IM, 22 Dec 1940, Montagu Letters.
'I took a girl from the office' EM to IM, 19 Apr 1942, Montagu Letters.
'no German could resist the "Englishness"' Montagu, *Man,* p. 152.
'achieved the thrill and pathos' Ibid.
'P.L. from W.M. 14.4.43' TNA, WO 106-5921-19.
'We will insert the legacy of £50' Montagu, *Man,* p. 156.
'since the wife's family will not' Ibid.
'The nearer the approach' John Godfrey, 'Afterthoughts' TNA ADM 223/619.
'He is very old' EM to IM, 13 Nov 1942, Montagu Letters.
'He was the world's prize shit' EM to Captain A. N. Grey, 12 Dec 1980, IWM 97/45/1 folder #5.
'the unhoped-for benefit' EM to 'Ginger', 6 Jul 1943, Montagu Papers.
'preparation and devising' Ibid.
'was entirely unsupervised' Ibid.
'How will that argument' Montagu, *Ultra*, p. 90.
'There was almost complete' TNA ADM 223/794.
'Masterman raised the question' Ibid.
'execution subcommittee' Ibid.
'the only deceptioneer' Ibid.
'enthusiasm for all things Russian' TNA KV2/598.
'attracted by Marxism' Ivor Montagu, *Autobiography*.
'We have had a request' Ibid.
'the keenest players' Ibid.
'Dear Comrade Trotsky' Ivor Montagu to Leon Trotsky, 1 Jul 1929, in Montagu Collection, Labour History Archive and Study Centre (People's History Museum).
'able, even brilliant' Ivor Montagu, *Autobiography*.
'allowed this quality to divorce' Ibid.
'like Edinburgh at its worst' Ibid.
'Two Turkish policemen' Ibid.
'to put under my pillow' Ibid.
'I did not know what precautions' Ibid.
'The memory I shall always . . .' Ibid.
'fascinating and commanding' Ibid.
'repelled by his self-admiration' Ibid.
'I felt I understood' Ibid.
'Ivor Montagu has' Leon Trotsky to Reg Groves, 13 Jul 1932, KV2/598.
'Montagu has for some time' Memo, 10 May 1926, KV2/598.
'Montagu has dark curly hair' Ibid.
'What is the use of living' Ivor Montagu, *Autobiography*.
'Last night Ivor came dinner' EM to IM, 30 Jun 1942, Montagu Letters.
'Hell is digging for victory' EM to IM, 4 Aug 1940, Montagu Letters.
'Ivor is really bad' EM to IM, 2 Dec 1940, Montagu Letters.
'He is busy working for the Russian' EM to IM, 30 Jun 1942, Montagu Letters.
'knew in advance practically' Montagu, *Ultra*, p. 30.
'that particularly unpleasant' RHH to DP, MI5 report, 3 Mar 1942, TNA KV2/599.
'I have met representatives' TNA HW 15/43.
'Intelligentsia considers there is' Ibid.
'removed from the leadership' Ibid.
'secret parliamentary session' Ibid.
'influential relatives' TNA HW 15/43.
'Intelligentsia has not yet found' Ibid.

'Although one is somewhat deaf' J. B. S. Haldane, *What is Life* (London, 1949), p. 32.
'I think that Marxism' J. B. S. Haldane, *The Marxist Philosophy and the Sciences*, (New York, 1939) p. 4.
'Intelligentsia has handed over' TNA HW 15/43.
'three military sources' Ibid.
'that this was a matter' Ibid.
'I promised to bring' Ibid.
'reported that a girl' Ibid.
'an officer of the air ministry' Ibid.
'the organisational structure' Ibid.
'The coastal defence is' Ibid.
'30 Sausage Dealer bombers' Ibid.
'he still seems to be going on with . . .' EM to IM, 11 Jun 1941, Montagu Letters
'Intelligentsia has reported' TNA HW 15/43.

Chapter 8: The Butterfly Collector

'We felt that we knew' Montagu, *Man,* p. 160.
'joined up to go to sea' Montagu, *Ultra,* p. 20.
'an incurable romantic' Andrew, *Defence of the Realm*, p. 285.
'Ewen *lived* the part' Interview with JGL, 5 Mar 2008.
'He wrote me endless letters' Ibid.
'Till death us do part' Montagu, *Man,* p. 168.
'Pam dearest' EM to Jean Leslie, undated letter, courtesy of Jean Gerard Leigh.
'The girl from the Elms' EM to IM, 9 Jan 1943, Montagu Letters.
'One of her appealing virtues' EM to IM, 29 Jun 1943, Montagu Letters.
'She has been much connected' EM to IM, 15 Apr 1943, Montagu Letters.
'I took the girl from the Elms' Ibid.
'I feel definitely that you ought' Ibid.
'If Mother did touch my things' EM to IM, 29 Jun 1943, Montagu Letters.
'I told her truthfully that it was' Ibid.
'writing in her letters' Montagu, *Man,* p. 168.
'would not carry enough weight' TNA ADM 223/794 p. 442.
'to fake documents of a sufficiently' EM to Thomas Thibeault, 18 Mar 1980, Montagu Papers.
'a crooked lawyer's dream of heaven' Montagu, *Ultra,* p. 150.
'bone from the neck up' Atkinson, *Day of Battle*, p. 130.
'as if he had just had a steam bath' Ibid., pp. 130-31.
'Will Eisenhower go ahead' EM, first draft, 16 Feb 1943, TNA CAB 154/67.
'So and so [naming a general]' Ibid.
'personal and "off the record"' Ibid.
'the contents of such a letter' JHB report to T. A. Robertson (TAR), TNA CO/43/66, 12 Feb 1943.
'almost completely ignorant' EM memo, 5 Mar 1943, TNA ADM 223/794.
'is almost completely inexperienced' Ibid.
'From reports coming out' German high command to command in Tunisia, 26 Feb 1943, MSS 2180/T.28 IWM 97/4/1 folder #1.
'Sicily has now been allowed' EM memo, 5 Mar 1943, TNA ADM 223/794.
'It is much easier' Ibid.
'He still has no deception' Ibid.

'now in a highly dangerous situation' Ibid.
'It would be a very great pity' EM to TAR, 16 Feb 1943.
'Spanish police records' Tomas Harris, *Garbo: The Spy Who Saved D-Day* (London, 2004), p. 38.
'worked in military intelligence' Burns, *Papa Spy*, p. 232.
'a Spaniard to Spaniards' Ian Colvin, *The Unknown Courier* (London, 1953), pp. 98–9.
'because of his enormous' Hector Licudi, *Gibraltar Chronicle*, Aug 1989.
'no more than a smattering of' TNA ADM 223/490.
'padding about Madrid' Colvin, *Unknown Courier*, p. 98.
'exceptionally favoured by character' TNA ADM 223/490.
'He was invaluable' TNA ADM 223/490.
'privileges and facilities' Ibid.
'Spain contained a large' Ibid.
'Madrid was full of spies' Ibid.
'danger of the body' TNA ADM 223/794, p. 444.
'German influence in Huelva' Ibid.
'a reliable and helpful man' Ibid.
'very pro-German chief of police' Cyril Mills to EM, 8 Nov 1983, Montagu Papers.
'active and influential' TNA ADM 223/794, p. 444.
'The Shadow' Copeiro, *Huelva*, p. 306
'the viceroys' Interview with Jesús Ramírez Copeiro del Vilar, 3 Jun 2009.
'First the Romans' Ibid.
'the black sheep' Interview with Isabel Naylor, 3 Jun 2009.
'the only clever one in the family' Ibid.
'He didn't dispute' Interview with Federico Clauss, 2 Jun 2009.
'cold, distant and silent' Interview with Jesús Ramírez Copeiro del Vilar, 3 Jun 2009.
'He was an active and intelligent' Copeiro, *Huelva*, p. 306.
'very efficient German agent' EM to Lynne Gladstone-Miller, 1 Nov 1983, Montagu papers.
'a super-super efficient agent' 'History of section 17M', Montagu Papers.
'first rate' EM to Lynne Gladstone-Miller, 1 Nov 1983, Montagu Papers.
'No ship can move without being' 'History of section 17M', Montagu Papers.
'one of the most difficult' J. C. Masterman, cited in David Stafford, *Roosevelt and Churchill: Men of Secrets* (London 1999), p. 94.
'the tiniest jewel in the imperial' TNA KV4/260.
'increased and spread' 'History of section 17M', Montagu Papers.
'in all Spanish and Spanish owned ports' Ibid.
'one of the most important' Copeiro, *Huelva*, p. 306.
'sufficient evidence can be obtained' Draft of Operation Mincemeat Report, EM and CC, 27 April 1943, IWM 97/45/1 folder #2.
'They would have to' Ibid.
'the washing ashore of any' Ibid.
'was to be told the outline of the plan' Ibid.

Chapter 9: My Dear Alex

'owing to the need for placing' Charles Cholmondeley (CC), memo, 6a, TNA W0 106/5921.
'if the body were dropped in this way' Ibid.
'come in from out at sea' Ibid.

'After the body has been' Ibid.
'technical difficulties in keeping' Ibid.
'Of these methods' Ibid.
'unswerving logic of the German' Macintyre, *For Your Eyes Only*, p. 108.
'if most of the oxygen had previously' TNA ADM 223/794, p. 446.
'keep perfectly satisfactorily' EM to JHB, 26 Mar 1943, TNA ADM 223/464.
'an enormous Thermos flask' Montagu, *Man*, p. 126.
'HANDLE WITH CARE' TNA ADM 223/794, p. 445.
'the Spaniards and Portuguese' N. L. A. Jewell (NLAJ) operational orders, 31 Mar 1943, TNA ADM 223/464.
'the tides in that area' Ibid.
'wind between S and W' Hydrographer's Report, 22 Mar 1943, TNA W0 106/5921
'if it did not strand' Ibid.
'The currents on the coast' EM to JHB, 26 Mar 1943, TNA CAB 154/67.
'I am not quite clear as to who' JHB to EM, 1 Mar 1943, TNA CAB 154/67.
'thinking it couldn't come off' EM to 'Ginger', 6 Jul 1943, Montagu Papers.
'Mincemeat will be taken out' EM to JHB, 26 Mar 1943, TNA ADM 223/464.
'All the details are now 'buttoned up''' Ibid.
'alteration and improvement' Ibid.
'more personal' JHB to A. Nye (AN), 8 Apr 1943, TNA CAB 154/67.
'a letter in answer to one from' EM draft, 6 Apr 1943, TNA CAB 154/67.
'should not be undertaken' Admiralty amendment to official report, 3 Jun 1945, TNA CAB 154/67.
'rather too official' JHB to AN, 10 Apr 1943, TNA CAB 154/67.
'we must get Dudley Clarke's' JHB memo TNA CAB 154/67.
'danger of overloading' Dudley Clarke to JHB, 2 Apr 1943, TNA CAB 154/67.
'a mistake to play for high' Admiralty amendment to official report, 3 Jun 1945, TNA CAB 154/67.
'If anything miscarries' JHB, memo 12 Apr 1943, TNA CAB 154/67.
'merely a lowish grade innuendo' Excised paragraph 13 in 'Draft history of Operation Mincemeat', 29 May 1943, IWM 97/45/1 folder #2.
'Mincemeat should be capable' Admiralty amendment to official report, 3 Jun 1945, TNA CAB 154/67.
'of a type which could have' Excised paragraph 14 in 'Draft history of Operation Mincemeat', 29 May 1943, IWM 97/45/1 folder #2.
'If it isn't too much trouble' EM, undated draft letter, TNA CAB 154/67.
'How are you getting on' Ibid.
'Do you still take the same size' Ibid.
'What is wrong with Monty?' Ibid.
'the best way of giving it' EM, draft letter, 6 Apr 1943, TNA CAB 154/67.
'ideally suited to the purpose' Ibid.
'not blatantly mentioned' EM memo, 4 Apr 1943, TNA CAB 154/67.
'Your signature in ink might' JHB to AN, 8 Apr 1943, TNA CAB 154/67.
'General Wilson is referred to' Ibid.
'I referred to him variously' AN to JHB, 14 Apr 1943, TNA CAB 154/67.
'I would never have written' AN to EM, 26 Apr 1954, Montagu Papers.
'P.S. we saw you on the cinema' Ibid.
'Now I hope your friends' AN to JHB, 14 Apr 1943, TNA CAB 154/67.
'a truly magnificent letter' Montagu, *Man*, p. 135.
'It's too velvety-arsed and Rolls-Royce' Atkinson, *Day of Battle*, p. 52.
'laboured' Montagu, *Man*, p. 143.
'I thought that that sort of joke' Ibid.

'Papers actually on the body' CC, memo, 10 Feb 1943, TNA CAB 154/67 p. 229.
'the Chiefs of Staff have approved' TNA CAB 154/67.
'To my surprise I was ushered' JHB handwritten account, undated [15 Apr 1943], TNA CAB 154/67.
'In the higher ranges of Secret Service' Cited in Macintyre, *For Your Eyes Only*, p. 58.
'Of course there's a possibility' From conversation recalled by Randolph Churchill in conversation with JHB, recorded in Martin Gilbert, *Road to Victory* (London, 1981), p. 389.
'Weed-killer goes into the lungs' Ibid.
'took much interest' JHB handwritten account, undated [15 Apr 1943], TNA CAB 154/67.
'I pointed out that there' Ibid.
'In that case, we shall' Ibid.
'General Eisenhower gives full' IZ 1416, received 1620, 17 Apr 1943, Freedom Algiers to Air Ministry, TNA CAB 154/67.

Chapter 10: Table Tennis Traitor

'I get more and more optimistic' EM to IM, 24 Jan 1943, Montagu Letters.
'We ought, by the time' EM to IM, 13 Nov 1942, Montagu Letters.
Mincemeat is in the making' Guy Liddell, *The Guy Liddell Diaries, 1939–1945,* Vol. II (London, 2005), p. 45.
'Plan Mincemeat has been approved' Ibid., p. 67.
'in close touch with many Russians' TNA KV2 599.
'an incurable anti-nationalist' Ibid.
'facilities for sport were far greater' Ibid.
'men of decidedly foreign' Ibid.
'did not think Montagu would get' Ibid.
'his association with the Russians' Ibid.
'an active Fifth Columnist' Ibid.
'he is always very keen' Ibid.
'has a wooden hut' Ibid.
'It does not seem desirable' Ibid.
'whether this refusal is' *Hansard* 357, no 23, 14 Mar 1940.
'I myself have registered' TNA KV2 599.
'most undesirable that he should' Ibid.
'as a criminal conspiracy' Ibid.
'known to be queer in any other way' Ibid.
'The reason for our tentative interest' Ibid.
'Hanno-ball' Ibid.
'certain net-stretchers' Ibid.
'suspected of running an illegal' Ibid.
'be using the channel of international' Ibid.
'I know this all seems very trivial' Ibid.
'I had no great faith in the records' Montagu, *Ultra*, p. 48.
'How is the table tennis going?' Ibid. p. 49.
'That's my communist' Ibid.
'special examiners' History of Operation Mincemeat, 10 Apr 1945, CAB 154/67.
'if the eyelash was gone' Copeiro, *Huelva*, p. 426.
'Mine were used for Major Martin's' Montagu, *Ultra*, p. 149.
'an ordinary black Government' TNA ADM 223/794, p. 449.

'horribly phoney' Montagu, *Man*, p. 145.
'the use of a chain to the bag' CC, memo 10 Feb 1943, TNA CAB 154/67, p. 229.
'little or no wreckage floated' TNA ADM 223/794, p. 445.
'for simplification and for security' Ibid.
'might have been the twin brother' Montagu, *Man*, p. 141.
'far more like' Draft manuscript, *Man*, IWM 97/45/2.
'heartily disliked' Montagu, *Man*, p. 160.
'odd psychological reaction' Ibid.
'told to report to the intelligence' Interview with N. L. A. Jewell, 1991, IWM Sound Archive 12278.
'normal final training' TNA ADM 223/794, p. 445.
'Mincemeat sails 19th April' TNA CAB 154/67.
'enable the operation to be carried' TNA ADM 223/794, p. 445.
'In wartime, any plan that saved' Interview with N. L. A. Jewell, IWM 12278.
'the vital need for secrecy' TNA ADM 223/794, p. 450.
'packed, fully clothed and ready' NLAJ operational orders, TNA ADM 223/464.
'as the steel is made of light gauge' Memo, 31 Mar 1943, TNA ADM 223/464.
'held a super-secret automatic' TNA ADM 223/794, p. 450.
'we suspected the Germans' Ibid.
'Lt Jewell was to impress' Ibid.
'between Portil Pillar and Punta Umbria' Ibid., p. 445.
'Every effort should be made' NLAJ operational orders, TNA ADM 223/464.
'the submarine could probably' TNA ADM 223/794, p. 445.
'the proposed use of a flare was dropped' Ibid.
'on specially prepared slides' NLAJ operational orders, TNA ADM 223/464.
'The container should then be opened' Ibid.
'When the body is removed' Ibid.
'near the body but not too near' Ibid.
'the body and container' Ibid.
'care must be taken that' Ibid.
'Cancel Mincemeat' Ibid.
'Mincemeat completed' Ibid.
'a pleasant time building up' Interview with N. L. A. Jewell, IWM 12278.
'making a life for the Major of Marines' Ibid.
'I had the enjoyment' Ibid.
'Mincemeat sails' 'Chaucer' to Goldbranson, 15 Apr 1943, TNA CAB 154/67.

Chapter 11: Gold Prospector

'Adventure was once a noble' Alan Hillgarth, *Men of War* (London, 1926).
'a young man called Alan Hillgarth' Evelyn Waugh, *Diaries* (London, 1995), 1 Jul 1927.
'that took five hundred men' Daniel Buck, 'Americas', Vol. 52, May 2000.
'squarish man with conspicuously' Ibid.
'men who had had considerable' Report of Sacambaya Company, 23 Apr 1929.
'Sacambaya is a poisonous place' Ibid.
'This was quite an undertaking' Ibid.
'one case containing 200lbs' Ibid.
'100 feet into the hillside proper' Ibid.
'A complete absence of fresh fruit' P. B. P. Mellows, *St Barts Journal*, January 1929, p. 59.

'One of our party awakened' Ibid.
'Claustrophobia brought on by' Ibid.
'He has fallen seriously in love' Edgar Sanders to Alan Hillgarth, 5 Jan 1929, courtesy of Tristan Hillgarth.
'either by the hotel people or the police.' Ibid.
'he doubled up as spy' Burns, *Papa Spy*, p. 22.
'an intense bombardment which' Note on the surrender of Menorca written by Captain Alan Hillgarth, then British Consul in Palma, translated from Catalan by Tristan Hillgarth.
'a decisive German victory over Russia' Alan Hillgarth memo, 13 Jul 1942, TNA ADM 223/478.
'very good' Cited by Denis Smyth, *Oxford Dictionary of National Biography*.
'equipped with a profound knowledge' Ibid.
'privately about anything interesting' Alan Hillgarth memo, TNA ADM 223/490.
'useful petard and a good war-winner' Cited in Andrew Lycett, *Ian Fleming* (London, 1996), p. 158.
'the embodiment of drive' Stafford, *Roosevelt and Churchill*, p. 110.
'secret funds that were made available' Kim Philby, *My Secret War. The Autobiography of a Spy* (London, 1968), p. 54.
'helped to feed the gallant' Ibid.
'local police, dock watchmen and stevedores' Alan Hillgarth Report, TNA ADM 223/490.
'expendable parts of Hitler's war machine' Stafford, *Roosevelt and Churchill*, p. 92.
'took corruption for granted' John Brooks, 'Annals of Finance', *New Yorker*, 21 May 1979.
'the last pirate of the Mediterranean' Ibid.
'It would be a mistake to trust him an inch' Stafford, *Roosevelt and Churchill*, p. 90.
'He has already had two German agents shot' Ibid.
'an amphibious car' 'Spanish help to the Germans', Records of NID12, TNA ADM 223/490.
'There was not a Spaniard who would not' Alan Hillgarth report, TNA ADM 223/490.
'The Cavalry of St George' Stafford, *Roosevelt and Churchill*, p. 93.
'We must not lose them now' Ibid., p. 96.
'his approval can safely be assumed' Ibid., p. 100.
'German victory would mean servitude' Donald McLachlan, *Room 39*: *Naval Intelligence in Action 1939–45* (London, 1968), p. 194.
'the Spaniard is xenophobic and suspicious' Alan Hillgarth report, TNA ADM 223/490.
'I am finding Hillgarth a great prop' Stafford, *Roosevelt and Churchill*, p. 96.
'a natural sympathy' Alan Hillgarth report, TNA ADM 223/490.
'Handling Spaniards is a special' Ibid.
'will be at a very definite' Ibid.
'Even during the worst of the war' Ibid.
'very reliable and well placed' EM report, 21 Aug 1945, TNA ADM 223/794.
'to supply intelligence which' Ibid.
'might compromise a very' Ibid.
'The items were so chosen' Ibid.
'Messig swallowed the stories' Ibid.
'It was a delicate job' Ibid.
'It seemed the listening' Montagu, *Ultra*, p. 121.
'Only by naval ciphers' Alan Hillgarth report, TNA ADM 223/490.

'suborned by a woman in German pay' Ibid.
'kept lists of everyone' Burns, *Papa Spy*, p.190.
'the Germans would have someone' Interview with Tristan Hillgarth, 13 Jan 2009.
'very amateurish and inefficient' Alan Hillgarth report, TNA ADM 223/490.
'Our deportment towards the German' Ibid.
'The circumstances of his release' Rankin, *Churchill's Wizards*, p. 346.
'Wrangal Craker' Terry Crowdy, *Deceiving Hitler: Double Cross and Deception in World War II* (London 2008), p. 142.
'Herewith some photographs' Rankin, *Churchill's Wizards*, p. 349.
'sound in mind' Crowdy, *Deceiving Hitler*, p. 143.
'he is just the type who imagines' Ibid.
'It is time to pass from the defensive' Memo, Alan Hillgarth to Edmund Rushbrooke, TNA ADM 223/490.
'more or less any naval intelligence' Ibid.
'was allowed with little' Ibid.
'I have found a good man' Ibid.
'All operations are, if I may say so' Ibid.
'You and your staff have shown' Rushbrooke to Hillgarth, TNA ADM 223/490.
'undesirable and unnecessary' Ibid.
'James Bond style free-for-all in Spain' Philby, *My Secret War*, pp. 54–5.

Chapter 12: The Spy Who Baked Cakes

'ubiquitous' Harris, *Garbo*, p. 18.
'All classes were represented' 'Spanish help to the Germans', Records of NID12, TNA ADM 223/490.
'In the higher ranks there' Ibid.
'Indeed, the reports went' TNA ADM 223/490.
'particulars on each' Philby, *My Secret War*, pp. 54–5.
'for a very large sum' Ibid.
'precious source' Ibid.
'very high indeed' Ibid.
'I had to fight to get an extra £5' Ibid.
'the cause of death' Colvin, *Unknown Courier*, p. 42.
'examined hundreds of corpses' Ibid., p. 41.
'Nothing happened in the Abwehr station' Interrogation of Hans Joachim Rudolph, Kuhlenthal MI5, TNA KV2/102.
'fleshy, boneless cheeks' Ibid.
'curved hawk-like' Ibid.
'blue piercing eyes' Ibid.
'a dark brown French four-seater' Ibid.
'carefully manicured' Ibid.
'a very efficient, ambitious' Harris, *Garbo*, p. 69.
'contrived to push Leissner' TNA KV2/102.
'became a mere figurehead' Ibid.
'He was an extremely able man' Ibid.
'the esteem and reputation' Ibid.
'by far the best man in Group I' Ibid.
'sent a personal message' Harris, *Garbo*, p. 74.
'extremely busy and that his visit' Ibid., p. 46.
'careful not to underestimate' Ibid., p. 50.

'would be a very long war' Ibid.
'There are people in Glasgow' Ibid., p. 58.
'We have absolute trust in you' Ibid., p. 250.
'My dear friend and comrade' Ibid., p. 257.
'the democratic-Jewish-Masonic' Ibid.
'England must be taken by arms' Ibid., p. 137.
'With a raised arm I end this letter' Ibid.
'His characteristic German lack' Ibid., p. 70.
'the star turn' Ibid., p. 128.
'With good wishes to Odette' Ibid.
'I did the lettering myself' Ibid.
'made cakes which were unpleasant' Ibid.
'extraordinary services' Ibid., p. 261.
'As a keen and efficient officer' Ibid., p. 69.
'We had the satisfaction of knowing' Ibid.
'the many incredible things we ask' Ibid. p. 95.
'the more sensational the reports' Ibid., p. 146.
'In some cases where messages' Ibid.
'Felipe had become our mouthpiece' Ibid., p. 72.
'an invaluable channel' Ibid.
'conviction that the Isle of Man' MSS report, TNA KV2/102.
'invented by Felipe himself' Ibid.
'The information provided' Ibid.
'one of the people who make up' Liddell, Diaries, 10 Mar 1944, p. 179.
'There are officers in Spain' Statement of Josef Ledebur-Wichelin, 25 Nov 1944, at Camp 020, TNA KV2/102.
'leaving a good job as manager' Ibid.
'he could not serve in the Army' Ibid.
'Aryanised' Ibid.
'He has been created an Aryan' Telegram Berlin to Madrid 18 Jul 1941 TNA KV2/102.
'since there appeared to be no' Ibid.
'to let the matter drop' MSS 5.11.41 TNA KV2/102.
'in the pay of British Secret Service' Ibid.
'refused to take the report seriously' Ibid.
'cold and reserved' Ibid.
'Appearance: nervous, uncertain' Ibid.
'Kuhlenthal is trembling to keep' Statement of Josef Ledebur-Wichelin, 25 Nov 1944, at Camp 020, TNA KV2/102.

Chapter 13: Mincemeat Sets Sail

'national importance' Interview with Basil Leverton, 8 Sep 2009.
'I was not to divulge' Ivor Leverton, unpublished diary, courtesy of Andrew Leverton.
'I was still in fairly good shape' Ibid.
'removal coffins' Interview with Andrew Leverton, 27 Jan 2009.
'must have stood 6'4" inches tall' Ivor Leverton, Letter to *Daily Telegraph*, 13 Aug 2002.
'left our passenger' Ivor Leverton, unpublished diary.
'a mortuary-keeper on whom' EM to JG, 19 Sep 1964, Montagu Papers.

'made it as easy as possible' TNA ADM 223/794, p. 450.
'I've got it' Jackson, *Coroner*, p. 149.
'the least pleasant part of our work' Montagu, *Man*, p. 160.
'We decided Bill Martin and Pam' Ibid., p. 162.
'Get an army blanket.' Jackson, *Coroner*, p. 149.
'lightly tied with tape' Ibid.
'reverently' Montagu, *Man*, p. 162.
'a shirt and tie' Ian Girling, *Aston Martin Magazine*, Vol. 33, No. 142, Spring 1999, 'The Horsfall Story: A Tribute'.
'went berserk' Ibid.
'potentially lethal pieces of metal' Ibid.
'The scream that Kath gave' Ibid.
'*I gave her time to start her piddle*' Ibid.
'he claimed to have done 100 mph' John Otter, letter to *Daily Telegraph*, 15 Aug 2002.
'one of us sitting in the window' Draft manuscript of *The Man*, IWM 97/45/2.
'had supper with a corpse parked' John Otter, letter to *Daily Telegraph* 15 Aug 2002.
'much better story' Montagu, *Man*, p. 163.
'partially 'in the know'' TNA ADM 223/794, p. 450.
'being accepted as merely being' Ibid.
'By this time Major Martin' Montagu, *Man*, p. 160.
'We felt that we knew him' Ibid.
'news such as can be written' EM to IM, 24 Apr 1943, Montagu Letters.
'I had to go up to Scotland' Ibid.
'I was to see that this package' David Scott, 'The Man That Never Was: Operation Mincemeat'; Reminiscences of Sir David Scott, Churchill Archives, DKNS II, p. 2.
'It was a real thrill' EM, unpublished account, 7 Oct 1976, Montagu Papers.
'Spring was on the way' Scott, *Reminiscences*, p. 3.
'trim dive' Ibid.
'A final exchange of 'Good Luck'' Ibid.
'Monotony never really set in' Ibid.
'We were never short of meat' Ibid.
'epitome of what a submarine captain' Ibid., p. 4.
'At that time, the chances of returning' Ibid.
'I realised with a bit of a shock' Ibid.
'bashed-in sort of face' John Parker, *SBS: The Story of the Special Boat Service* (London 1997), p. 19.
'Your American gum' Terence Robertson, *The Ship with Two Captains: The Story of the 'Secret Mission Submarine'* (London, 1957), p. 92.
'a happy augury for the future' Ibid.
'a two-fisted fighting man' NLAJ , as told to Cecil Carnes, *Secret Mission Submarine: Action Report of the HMS Seraph* (London, 1944), p. 101.
'We'll fight an army on a dare' Atkinson, *Day of Battle*, p. 82.
'always conspicuously' Citation for Distinguished Service Cross.
'I think we can do it' Robertson, *The Ship with Two Captains*, p. 106.
'sink on sight any vessel' Ibid.
'Put me ashore, give me a gun' Ibid., p. 110.
'constant strain' Ibid., p. 112.
'one grabbed a large' Ibid.
'broken nose' Ibid.

'a lithe, graceful look' Ibid., p. 124.
'We were told that we were not' Interview with N. L. A. Jewell, IWM 12278.
'The unmistakable sounds' Scott, *Reminiscences*, p. 5.
'We knew that at least' Ibid.

Chapter 14: Bill's Farewell

'I rushed home' Interview with JGL, 5 Mar 2008.
'absurd' Montagu, *Man*, p. 167.
'Bill Martin's death' TNA CAB 154/67.
'We were terribly agitated' Interview with JGL, 5 Mar 2008.
'as a joke' Montagu, *Man*, p. 167.
'gathered from every part' John Fisher, *What a Performance: The Life of Sid Field* (London, 1975), p. 85.
'definitely "a find"' Cited in Fisher, *What a Performance*, p. 99.
'the loudest laughter we' Ibid., p. 100.
'all his jokes are clean' Ibid.
'*I'm going to get pickled*' Ibid., p. 96.
'an adequate ration of gin' Ibid., p. 85.
'If an Air Raid Warning' Ibid.
'*When you feel unhappy*' Ibid., p. 103.
'The laughs came like the waves' Ibid., p. 88.
'The weather was warm at last' Scott, *Reminiscences*, p. 3.
'John Brown's Body' Montagu, *Man*, p. 169.
'our pal Charlie' Robertson, *The Ship with Two Captains,* p. 124.
'were such that strangers' *Independent*, Obituary of Michael Luke, 19 Apr 2005.
'mystery suffused with a tender' Ibid.
'very cheerful evening' Montagu, *Man*, p. 167.
'Considering Bill and Pam are engaged' Ibid.
'It would be different' Ibid.
'They kept looking at their watches' Interview with JGL, 5 Mar 2008.
'I had to go and take' EM to IM, 23 Apr 1943, Montagu Letters.
'smitten' Interview with JGL, 5 Mar 2008.
'I am glad Verel' EM to IM, 29 Jun 1943, Montagu Letters.
'the peak of the Deception effort' Holt, *The Deceivers*, p. 366.
'One patriotic Greek managed' Holt, *The Deceivers*, p. 368.
'hygiene in the Balkans' Ibid.
'no major operation could be' Ewen Montagu, unpublished critique of Constantine Fitzgibbon, *Secret Intelligence in the Twentieth Century* (London, 1976), Montagu Papers.
'if they should suspect that the' EM, 31 Mar 1943, TNA W0 106/5921.
'I had to carry the can' EM to 'Ginger', 6 Jul 1943, Montagu Papers.
'Intelligence, like food' Godfrey 'Afterthoughts' TNA ADM 223/619, p. 91.
'with instructions to burn' NLAJ operational orders, TNA ADM 223/464.
Operation known as Mincemeat' Telegram to DSO Gibraltar, 22 Apr 1943, TNA CAB 154/67.
'something of a shock' Scott, *Reminiscences*, p. 4.
'sailors had been sleeping' Ibid.
'the vital need for absolute secrecy' TNA ADM 223/794, p. 451.
'Isn't it pretty unlucky' Montagu, *Man*, p. 170.
'a close-range reconnaissance' Scott, *Reminiscences*, p. 4.

'easy, even enjoyable' Ibid.
'The operation had to be carried' NLAJ operational orders, TNA ADM 223/464.
'an onshore wind' Ibid.
'The next day turned out to be ideal' Scott, *Reminiscences*, p. 4.
'arrange total bombing restrictions' Memo, 15 Apr 1943, IWM 97/45/1 folder #1.
'No known defensive dangers' TNA ADM 223/794, p. 445.
'We were just about to surface' Interview with N. L. A. Jewell, IWM 12278.
'A large number of small fishing boats' NLAJ Report, 30 April 1943, cited in Montagu, *Man*, p. 168.
'landing some pseudo-secret instruments' NLAJ Operation orders, TNA ADM 223/464.
'We crept in a little closer' Scott, *Reminiscences*, p. 4.
'some little stink' Interview with N. L. A. Jewell, IWM 12278.
'I doubt if any of them' Ibid.
'I had seen bodies before' Ibid.
'The blanket was opened up' TNA 223/794.
'We seemed to be practically' Scott, *Reminiscences*, p. 5.
'what I could remember' Interview with N. L. A. Jewell, IWM 12278.
'With some relief' Scott, *Reminiscences*, p. 5.
'He virtually assured success' TNA ADM 223/794, p. 453.
'Because it had been designed' Ibid.
'riddled by fire' Ibid.
'He did this with his usual skill' Scott, *Reminiscences*, p. 5.
'a hell of a time' Interview with N. L. A. Jewell, IWM 12278.
'Daylight was fast approaching' Scott, *Reminiscences*, p. 5.
'It then disappeared, finally' Interview with N. L. A. Jewell, IWM 12278.
'it was seen to sink' NLAJ Report, 30 April 1943, cited in Montagu, *Man*, p. 168.
'We dived and set course for Gibraltar' Scott, *Reminiscences*, p. 5.
'Mincemeat Completed' TNA ADM 223/794.
'Parcel delivered safely' Robertson, *The Ship with Two Captains*, p. 117.

Chapter 15: Dulce et Decorum

'G VI R and the royal crown' IWM, 97/45/1 folder #2.
'which had penetrated the muscles' Ibid.
'should telephone to him at Madrid' TNA ADM 223/794, p. 445.
'would say that he could not talk' Ibid.
'a separate series in his personal cipher' EM to Fitzroy McLean, 30 Mar 1977, IWM 97/45/1 folder #5.
'energetically' TNA ADM 223/794, p. 445.
'Soup Bowl' Copeiro, *Huelva*, p. 411.
'examined the names on the envelopes' Appendix III, in IWM 97/45/1 folder #2.
'react swiftly' Copeiro, *Huelva*, p. 422.
'Well, your superior might not like' Ibid.
'attitude, in refusing the briefcase' Ibid.
'of an English pattern' Telegram to Von Roenne, 22 May 1943, TNA ADM 223/794, p. 207.
'There are clearly two' Ibid.
'On the first incision being made' Edward Smith, former head of Reporting Organisation Section, NID, to EM, 6 May 1969, IWM.
'remarkable presence of mind' Ibid.

'Since it was obvious the heat' Ibid.
'On receiving this assurance' Ibid.
'The young British officer fell in the water' Copeiro, *Huelva*, p. 414.
'nibbling and bites by fish' Ibid.
'The shininess of the hair' Ibid.
'doubt over the nature of the liquid' Ibid.
'He seemed very well dressed' Interview with Isabel Naylor, Huelva, 3 Jun 2009.
'identical' Telegram to Von Roenne, 22 May 1943, TNA ADM 223/794, p. 207.
'that a bald patch on the temples' Ibid.
'either the photograph was taken' Ibid.
'With reference to my phone message' Telegram 012210 sent at 2030 on 1 May TNA ADM 223/794.
'so that the action for suppressing' TNA ADM 223/794, p. 457.
'the suppression of the signal' Ibid.
'taken into naval custody' EM to Cyril Mills, 11 Nov 1983, Montagu Papers.
'The Spanish navy is <u>not</u> in German' EM to C, 21 Jun 1943, IWM 97/45/1/folder #2.
'a rigid disciplinarian' Copeiro, *Huelva*, p. 422.
'suffocating heat' Ibid., p. 414.
'as a mark of respect' Interview with Federico Clauss, 2 Jun 2009.
'W. Martin, aged between thirty-five and forty' Copeiro, *Huelva*, p. 420.
'Class Five' Ibid.

Chapter 16: Spanish Trails

'do everything necessary' Andros report, IWM, 97/45/1 folder #2.
'Notwithstanding his great desire' Ibid.
'These three persons are in command' Ibid.
'intimate friend' Ibid.
'nursed a profound antipathy' Copeiro, *Huelva*, p. 286.
'did not dare to ask this gentleman' Andros report, IWM, 97/45/1 folder #2.
'In Huelva, Don Adolfo' Interview with Federico Clauss, Seville, 2 Jun 2009.
'neither copied nor photographed' Andros report, IWM, 97/45/1 folder #2.
'I am glad to say the naval' Alan Hillgarth to EM, 9 Jun 1943, IWM 97/45/1 folder #1.
'Some papers Major Martin' Telegram 04132, 4 May 1943; Director Naval Intelligence (DNI) to Naval Attaché (NA), 4 May 1943, W0106/5921, p. 32.
'Carry out instructions' Telegram 869, 4 May 1943, IWM 97/45/1 folder #1.
'kept on such a plane' Ewen Montagu, 'Draft proposal for compiler of MI5 history', 24 Jul 1945, IWM 97/45/1 folder #1.
'searching but discreet' Ibid.
'Rumours are extremely easy' Alan Hillgarth report, TNA ADM 223/478.
'select from among his acquaintance' Ibid.
'sincerely anti-war' TNA ADM 223/876.
'I managed to make the Minister' Alan Hillgarth report, TNA ADM 223/490.
'that the Minster of Marine' Alan Hillgarth, 5 May 1943, IWM 97/45/1 folder #2.
'Vice Consul Huelva saw body' NA to DNI, 5 May 1943, 1823, IWM 97/45/1 folder #2.
'Secret papers probably in black' DNI to NA, telegram #071216, 7 May 1943, W0 106/5921, p. 33.
'Normally you would be getting' EM to NA, Madrid, telegram 870, 6 May 1943, IWM 97/45/1 folder #1.

'Understood and acted on throughout' IWM 97/45/1 folder #1.
'promised to obtain copies' Andros report, IWM, 97/45/1 folder #2.
'discreet inquiries whether any' AH Memo, IWM, 97/45/1.
'As the local Germans' Andros report, IWM, 97/45/1 folder #2.
'summoned to Villarreal de San Antonio' Ibid.
'very pro-German and in German pay' Ibid.
'This individual' Ibid.
'to do everything possible to obtain' Ibid.
'Urging him to use the utmost' Ibid.
'accurate information regarding' Ibid.
'either because they were afraid' Ibid.
'Either because of the junior rank' Ibid.
'forwarded, unopened' ABW 2282/43 TNA CAB 154/101.
'only scanty information' JHB memo, 3 May 1943, TNA CAB 154/67.
'Mincemeat was found by' Ibid.
'We sweat away, 11 of us' EM to 'Ginger', 6 Jul 1943, Montagu Papers.
'It is requested that I may' Undated note in Montagu Papers.
'I always was a selfish shit' EM to 'Ginger', 6 Jul 1943, Montagu Papers.
'I have never been able' Ibid.
'If I had made a slip in the preparation' Ibid.
'Official procedure is always' NA to DNI, 5 May 1943, 1823. IWM 97/45/1 folder #2.
'informed that they had not' Andros report, IWM, 97/45/1 folder #2.
'Again they failed' Ibid.
'an official of the [Cadiz] Marine' ABW 2282/43 TNA CAB 154/101.
'did not dare approach' Andros report, IWM, 97/45/1 folder #2.
'an assiduous worker for the Germans' Ibid.
'that he had heard about the body' Ibid.
'many privileges and facilities' Ibid.
'unable to obtain any fresh' Ibid.
'certain high officials in the police' Ibid.
'Great interest was aroused' Ibid.
'Groizar fostered this interest' Ibid.
'One can't imagine' Stanley G. Payne, *Franco and Hitler: Spain, Germany and World War II* (London, 2008), p. 150.
'in the hope that he will come to Spain' Andros report, IWM, 97/45/1 folder #2
'approaches were made by the Germans' Ibid.

Chapter 17: Kuhlenthal's Coup

'Red Indians' Macintyre, *For Your Eyes Only*, p. 32.
'a Spanish Staff Officer' Abw Nr 2282/43, Spain to FHW, 15 May 1943, TNA CAB 154/101, p. 203.
'with whom we have been in contact' Appendix to Operation Mincemeat, TNA ADM 223/794, p. 459.
'my Spanish agent in the General Staff' Colvin, *Unknown Courier*, p. 95.
'case officer' Abw Nr 2282/43, Spain to FHW, 15.5.43., TNA CAB 154/101, p. 203.
'Those seals held the envelopes' TNA ADM 223/794, p. 453.
'It was possible to extract' Report of Special Examiners, 21 May 1943, IWM 97/45/1 folder #5.

'The Spaniards had, very intelligently' Appendix to Operation Mincemeat, TNA ADM 223/794, p. 459.
'They seemed to me to be of the' Colvin, *Unknown Courier*, p. 95.
'A short white-haired man' Ibid., p. 34.
'These letters mentioned' Ibid., p. 95.
'the strategic considerations' Ibid.
'I took them to the basement' Ibid.
'there was no trace whatever' TNA ADM 223/794 p. 453.
'the importance attached to them' Colvin, *Unknown Courier*, p. 96.
'left Madrid hurriedly for Berlin' MSS message 7 Apr 1943, TNA KV2/102.
'all the effects and papers' TNA ADM 223/794, p. 453.
'They are all there' NA Madrid to DNI, Telegram 111925, 12 May 1943, IWM 97/45/1 folder #1.
'From his manner it was obvious' Ibid.
'It is obvious contents of bag' Ibid.
'While I do not believe' Ibid.
'If you concur I will ask' Ibid.
'the genuineness of the report' Atkinson, *Day of Battle*, p. 6.
'All generals lie. All generals are disloyal' Ibid.
'Behind his rimless spectacles' Kahn, *Hitler's Spies*, p. 424.
'The Germans studied each phrase' Ewen Montagu, 'Draft proposal for compiler of MI5 history', 24 Jul 1945, IWM 97/45/1 folder #1.
'Discovery of the English Courier' TNA CAB 154/101, p. 200.
'On the corpse of an English courier' Ibid.
'the Germans studied each phrase' Ewen Montagu, 'Draft proposal for compiler of MI5 history', 24 Jul 1945, IWM 97/45/1 folder #1.
'an experienced specialist' Ibid.
'Large-scale amphibious operations' Ibid.
'A jocular remark in this letter' Ibid.
'The proposed cover operation' Ibid.
'operation could be mounted' Ibid.
'still in action' Ibid.
'must first be rested' Ibid.
'at least two or three weeks' Ibid.
'It is known to the British Staff' Ibid.
'It is, therefore, to be hoped' Ibid.
'initiate a misleading plan' Ibid.
'News of this discovery will' Ibid.
'The circumstances of the discovery' Ibid.
'unless these were clearly' Holt, *The Deceivers*, p. 102.
'wishfulness' Godfrey 'Afterthoughts' TNA ADM 223/619, p. 10.

Chapter 18: Mincemeat Digested

'Hitler had implicit faith' David Alan Johnson, *Righteous Deception: German Officers Against Hitler* (Westport, Connecticut, 2001), p. 77.
'the Western allies would protest' Ibid.
'exactly what Hitler wanted to hear' Ibid.
'Hitler was greatly impressed' Ibid.
'It was his mission to produce' Ibid., p. 78.
'because of their origins' Kahn, *Hitler's Spies*, p. 426.

'if Germany should give in to' Holt, *The Deceivers*, p. 101.
'his way of fighting the Nazi war' Johnson, *Righteous Deception*, p. 126.
'In a moment now I shall be going' Cited in Albert Edward Day, *Dialogue and Destiny* (New York, 1981) p. 91.
'absolutely convincing proof' TNA CAB 154/101, p. 200.
'resounding Abwehr success' Ibid.
'frousty, peevish and petulant' Godfrey, 'Afterthoughts' TNA ADM 223/619, p. 63.
'he had to duck each time he had' TNA ADM 223/792.
'surprising that we only have five' Ibid.
'an enemy landing on a large scale' MSS 2571/T4, cited in TNA ADM 223/794, p. 456.
'a source which may be regarded' Ibid.
'It is very unusual for an intelligence' NID 12 report, 2 Sep 1943, IWM, 97/45/1 folder #2.
'So far as I can recollect' Ibid.
'Everyone jumped up and down' Interview with Pat Davies (née Trehearne), 4 Oct 2009.
'almost certain' MSS 2571/T4, cited in TNA ADM 223/794, p. 456.
'similar details from the letter' Ibid.
'the Germans were reinforcing' Unpublished note, 7 Oct 1976, in IWM 97/45/1 folder #4.
'wonderful days' Ibid.
'the right people and from best' Michael Howard, *Grand Strategy* (London 1972), p. 370.
'You will be pleased to learn' Montagu, *Man,* p. 176.
'Friday was almost too good' EM to IM, 16 May 1943, Montagu Letters.
'proved that we had convinced them' Ewen Montagu, unpublished, undated account, IWM, 97/45/1 folder #2.
'According to information' F. W. Deakin, *The Brutal Friendship: Mussolini, Hitler and the Fall of Italian Fascism* (London, 1962), p. 376.
'in strict confidence' Ibid., p. 377.
'Jordana begged me not to' Ibid.
'especially as he wanted' Ibid.
'Christian, couldn't this be a corpse' David Irving, *Hitler's War* (London, 1977), p. 586.
'It is to be expected that' Deakin, *The Brutal Friendship*, p. 377.
'the original German appreciation' TNA ADM 223/794, p. 457.
'all German commands' Deakin, *The Brutal Friendship,* p. 377.
'Where do we go from Sicily?' Atkinson, *Day of Battle*, p. 14.
'The main task which lies before us' Ibid., p. 15.
'War is full of mysteries and surprises' Ibid., p. 22.
'What [do] you think is going' Ibid., p. 25.
'Appetite unbridled' Ibid.
'to a document that had been' TNA ADM 223/794, p. 457.
'security flap' Ibid.
'Arrangements could then be made' Ibid.
'We earnestly debated' Bennett, *Ultra and Mediterranean Strategy*, p. 227.
'The evaluation office attach special' TNA CAB 154/67.
'The latter immediately despatched' MSS 13 May 1943, 1837, 'Berlin to Madrid No 117 for Samoza. Ref your most secret of 9/5/43' CAB 154/67.
'Oberst Lt. Pardo on the 10th May' ABW 2282/43 TNA CAB 154/101.

'The result of his investigations' Ibid.
'In contrast to the first statement' Ibid.
'He (the Minister for Marine)' Ibid.
'A search for the remains' Ibid.
'The fishermen state' Ibid.
'A medical examination' Ibid.
'Bag not yet arrived' Telegram 877, 18 May 1943, TNA CAB 154/67.
'a small, sealed bag' Ibid.
'Evidence that operation successful' Ibid.
'reported that there was great excitement' AH Memo, undated, IWM 97/45/1 folder #2.
'I naturally asked him to find out' Ibid.
'said that immediately he heard' Part one of telegram 171914, TNA CAB 154/67.
'Why did you go to so much trouble?' Ibid.
'I was anxious no one should have' Ibid.
'He obviously did not know' Telegram 171811, TNA CAB 154/67.
'It can be taken as a certainty' Ibid.
'He told me that all his information' Deakin, *The Brutal Friendship*, pp. 377–8.
'The operation has given conclusive' Ewen Montagu report, 29 May 1943, IWM, 97/45/1 folder #2.
'The seals were photographed' Report of Special Examiners, 21 May 1943, IWM 97/45/1, folder #5.
'Although we can say that there' Ibid.
'sharper than one made in it when' Ibid.
'once symmetrically and secondly' Ibid.
'it was not done on exactly' EM, letter to producer of *The Secret War*, IWM 97/45/1 folder #5.
'as the letter began to dry' Report of Special Examiners, 21 May 1943., IWM 97/45/1, folder #5.
'when the letter is folded up' Ibid.
'Inform Minister of Marine as soon' DNI to NA Madrid, undated notes, TNA CAB 154/67 (possibly not sent).
'letters [were] in fact opened' TNA CAB 154/67.
'likely to pass it on' Ibid.
'Important there should be no' Ibid.

Chapter 19: Hitler Loses Sleep

'consisted of comments' TNA ADM 223/794, p. 459.
'No further doubts remain' Telegrame SSDMBBZ 725, TNA CAB 154/101.
'whether the enemy' Ibid.
'urgent' Ibid.
'reply immediately "since we' Ibid.
'It is the opinion' Ibid.
'since only in this case' Ibid.
'absurd' Ibid.
'This shows how wrong a staff' TNA ADM 223/794, p. 459.
'personal squiggle' Montagu, *Man*, p. 184.
'The Führer does not agree' Deakin, *The Brutal Friendship*, p. 379.
'It is also clear from documents' Ibid., p. 383.
'Within the next few days' Ibid. p. 383.

'It is very unusual and very difficult' Michael I. Handel, *War Strategy and Intelligence* (London 1989), p. 436.
'targets of enemy operation' Deakin, *The Brutal Friendship*, p. 378.
'the Allies wanted to advance' Ibid., p. 379.
'You can forget Sicily' Bennett, *Ultra and Mediterranean Strategy*, p. 227.
'that the Allied attack' TNA CAB 154/67, p. 64.
'Allied submarines had received' Ibid.
'forwarded it to Belgrade and Sofia' Ibid.
'The reports coming from' Ibid., p. 64.
'congenital obsession about the Balkans' Howard, *Grand Strategy*, p. 92.
'In the last few days' Deakin, *The Brutal Friendship*, p. 379.
'the danger is that they will establish' Ibid., p. 380.
'as a precaution to take a further' Ibid.
'natural' Ibid., p. 381.
'If a landing takes place' Ibid.
'I have therefore decided' Ibid.
'Sardinia is particularly threatened' Ibid.
'In the event of the loss' Ibid.
'He foresaw that from Sardinia' Ibid., p. 375.
'through the Spaniards and not directly' IWM, 97/45/1 folder #2.
'The Italian High Command' IWM, 97/45/1 folder #2.
'information from an absolutely' Deakin, *The Brutal Friendship*, p. 386.
'There would be troop and transport' EM to JHB et al, 8 Jun 1943, TNA CAB 154/67 p. 64.
'German circles here have a story' AH to DNI, 1 Jun 1943, TNA CAB 154/67.
'The degree of Spanish complicity' Undated draft letter, IWM, 97/45/1 folder #2.
'adding to our knowledge of German' EM to 'C', 21 Jun 1943, IWM, 97/45/1 folder #2.
'simultaneous landings in Sardinia' Crichton to JHB, 4 Aug 1943, TNA CAB 154/67.
'our refrigerated friend' Ibid.
'had come round to the same view.' Holt, *The Deceivers*, p. 378.
'camouflage' Goebbel *Diaries*, 25 June 1943.
'The truth is whatever helps bring victory,' Irving, *Goebbels*, p. 437.
'Despite all the assertions' Ibid., p. 433.
'resounding' TNA CAB 154/101, p. 200.
'*The Times* has once again sunk' Irving, *Goebbels*, p. 421.
'velvety-arsed and Rolls-Royce' Atkinson, *Day of Battle*, p. 52.
'I had a long discussion with' *The Goebbels Diaries*, 25 Jun 1943 (London, 1948).
'The general outline of English plans' Ibid.
'Try to find out if Greek troops' MSS received 7 Jun 1943, CAB 154/67.
'to investigate the presence' Harris, *Garbo*, p. 135.
'the only serious danger' 'Dowager' (Clarke) to 'Chaucer', 20 May 1943, TNA CAB 154/67.
'legal or illegal exhumation' Ibid.
'By the time that he had been' EM to JHB, 28 May 1943, TNA CAB 154/67.
'Although no one in this world' Ibid.
'Suggest unless unusual' Telegram 878, 21 May 1943, TNA CAB 154/67.
'This to be done unless restrictions' Telegram 879 TNA CAB 154/67.
'Please send me ordinary cipher' Telegram, 23 May 1943 TNA CAB 154/67.
'Suggest Consul place wreath' Telegram 878, 21 May 1943, TNA CAB 154/67.
'as fast as possible' Ibid.
'The purpose of this was not only' TNA ADM 223/794, p. 452.

'Sir, In accordance with instructions' 9 Jun 1943, IWM 97/45/1 folder #1.
'Could you possibly procure' EM to Alan Hillgarth, 26 May 1943, IWM 97/45/1 folder #1.
'A reasonable reward of not more' Telegram 880, 23 May 1943, TNA CAB 154/67.
'No action is to be taken' TNA ADM 223/794, p. 457.
'Insert the following entry' Note to casualty section, 20 May 1943, IWM 97/45/1 folder #1.
'and, if so, where was it?' Montagu, *Man*, p. 178.
'distinguished film and stage actor' *The Times*, 4 Jun 1943.
'severe loss to the British theatre' Ibid.
'The only decent thing they can do.' Ben Macintyre, *The Times*, 30 Dec 2008.
'the first German Panzer Division' DNI notes 31 May 1943, TNA ADM 223/353.
'arrangements for the passage' EM to JHB et al, 8 Jun 1943, TNA CAB 154/67 p. 64.
'strategic position well suited' Ibid.
'completely reequipped' Bennett, *Ultra and Mediterranean Strategy*, p. 224.
'It is now about half way between' EM to JHB et al, 8 Jun 1943, TNA CAB 154/67 p. 64.
'The present situation is summed' Ibid.
'They raised (but did not pursue)' Ibid.
'Mincemeat has already resulted' EM, report 29 May 1943, IWM, 97/45/1 folder #2.
'I think that at this half way stage' EM, 'Draft proposal for compiler of MI5 history', 24 Jul 1945, IWM 97/45/1 folder #1.

Chapter 20: *Seraph* and Husky

'You are to act as guide and beacon' Robertson, *The Ship with Two Captains*, p. 124.
'had delivered his false information' Ibid., p. 126.
'His force was to land in three parts' Ibid., p. 124.
'He was really very short with us' Interview with N. L. A. Jewell, IWM 12278.
'Do as good a job for us' Robertson, *The Ship with Two Captains*, p. 125.
'Discovery' Ibid., p. 127.
'If substantial German ground troops' Dwight Eisenhower to Winston Churchill, 28 Mar 1943, cited in Handel, *War Strategy*, p. 437.
'The submarines would be less' Robertson, *The Ship with Two Captains*, p. 125.
'The American High Command' Jewell, *Secret Mission Submarine*, p. 106.
'a really de luxe experience' Ibid.
'most exclusive spot' Ibid.
'The Wren Trap' Ibid.
'None of the doors opened' Robertson, *The Ship with Two Captains*, p. 139.
'Bloody heap ain't got no springs' Ibid.
'could turn out a meal' Jewell, *Secret Mission Submarine*, p. 100.
'E-boat on port quarter, Sir' Robertson, *The Ship with Two Captains*, p. 126.
'a clearly visible silhouette' Ibid., p. 127.
'It was a ticklish moment' Jewell, *Secret Mission Submarine*, p. 111.
'undecided about her identity' Ibid.
'I knew that would be a recognition' Ibid.
'Down she went in a few seconds' Robertson, *The Ship with Two Captains*, p. 127.
'The captain of the E-boat' Ibid.
'wonderfully conceited' John Follain, *Mussolini's Island: The Untold Story of the Invasion of Italy* (London, 2005), p. 14.

'an exceptionally small head' Atkinson, *Day of Battle*, p. 131.
'His knowledge of how to' Follain, *Mussolini's Island*, p. 13.
'military disaster' Atkinson, *Day of Battle*, p. 53.
'You cannot, you must not, be interesting' Atkinson, *Day of Battle*, p. 34.
'the availability of aircraft and gliders' Wilson to CIGS, 16 May 1943, TNA CAB 154/67.
'gross breach of security' Ibid.
'athletic, middle-aged, of medium height' Crowdy, *Deceiving Hitler*, p. 196.
'an agent of very high class' Holt, *The Deceivers*, p. 360.
'who had promised him an' Harris, *Garbo*, p. 316.
'on account of his linguistic abilities' Ibid., p. 130.
'delighted with their new agent' Ibid.
'speculated that on account' Ibid.
'steal some documents relating' Ibid., p. 131.
'unmarried wife' Ibid.
'officer who had been' Ibid.
'pretend that the agent' Ibid.
'would give the game away altogether' Howard, *Grand Strategy*, p. 91.
'not to be alarmed as the attack' Crowdy, *Deceiving Hitler*, p. 206.
'received increasing reports' Interrogation of Joachim Canaris in Kuhlenthal file, TNA KV2/102.
'was still regarded as the favourite' Howard, *Grand Strategy*, p. 92.
'no measures were taken to reinforce the island' Ibid.
'it was never possible for the Germans' TNA ADM 223/794, p. 455.
'Compared with the forces employed' Bennett, *Ultra and Mediterranean Strategy*. p. 225.
'only half the supplies they needed' Ibid., p. 231.
'well armed and fully organised' Atkinson, *Day of Battle*, p. 53.
'an almost unbelievably' G2 Intelligence notes, No. 18, 1 Aug 1943, WO 204/983.
'hot mustard' Atkinson, *The Day of Battle*, p. 54.
'It will be a hard and very bloody' Follain, *Mussolini's Island*, p. 37.
'If casualties are high' Atkinson, *Day of Battle*, p. 71.
'May God be with you' Ibid.

Chapter 21: A Nice Cup of Tea

'We are about to embark' Follain, *Mussolini's Island*, p. 69.
'all the winds of heaven' Atkinson, *Day of Battle*, p. 67.
'The die was cast' Follain, *Mussolini's Island*, p. 69.
'It doesn't look too good' Atkinson, *Day of Battle*, p. 67.
'breakers and boiling surf' Jewell, *Secret Mission Submarine*, p. 112.
'lay in their hammocks, green' Atkinson, *Day of Battle*, p. 65.
'We are now getting Cadbury's' Derrick Leverton, letter to mother and father, 29 Nov 1943, courtesy of Andrew Leverton.
'It was a most excellent cruise' Ibid.
'He was excellent' Ibid.
'I went up on deck' Ibid.
'The sea had been wickedly rough' Ibid.
'Day Trips to the Continent' Ibid.
'I was standing up on deck' Ibid.
'rather a nice small slam' Ibid.

'There could be no more diving' Robertson, *The Ship with Two Captains*, p. 127.
'three times as difficult' Jewell, *Secret Mission Submarine*, p. 112.
'Unseen planes, hundreds of them' Ibid.
'The invasion of Sicily would be' Ibid., p. 109.
'Many of the men on this ship' Atkinson, *Day of Battle*, p. 36.
'great fires springing up' Jewell, *Secret Mission Submarine*, p. 112.
'the faint throb of approaching' Ibid.
'Their blindingly brilliant beams' Robertson, *The Ship with Two Captains*, p. 128.
'a nerve-tightening, shell-packed' Ibid.
'as much to avoid the cascading' Ibid.
'throbbing beat' Ibid., p. 129.
'a flicker of light from' Jewell, *Secret Mission Submarine*, p. 113.
'dark shapes emerged slowly' Robertson, *The Ship with Two Captains*, p. 129.
'The English language needs' Jewell, *Secret Mission Submarine*, p. 114.
'like footlights on a stage' Robertson, *The Ship with Two Captains*, p. 129.
'Shells whistled high overhead' Ibid., p. 128.
'with different coloured tracer' Ibid.
'With flares, searchlights' Jewell, *Secret Mission Submarine*, p. 114.
'cheering the stubborn little submarine' Robertson, *The Ship with Two Captains*, p. 129.
'Ahoy *Seraph*' Ibid.
'a slightly astonished salute' Ibid.
'You know, those boys' Ibid.
'slide warily back into' Ibid.
'tiny, darting flashes marked the progress Ibid.
'hoped the friendly, ever-joking' Ibid.
'Darby is really a great soldier' Carlo D'Este, *Bitter Victory: The Battle for Sicily 1943* (London 1988), p. 275.
'wished my chaps good luck' Derrick Leverton, letter, 29 Nov 1943.
'As there was still a bit of time' Ibid.
'quite a bit of banging about' Ibid.
'It was getting close to dawn' Ibid.
'slightly premature landings' Ibid.
'The first thing I was conscious' Ibid.
'Occasional mines went off' Ibid.
'tea-sugar-and-milk powder' Ibid.
'Most nourishing, appetising' Ibid.
'added zest to the party' Ibid.
'As the bombs came down' Ibid.
'Another bomb fell in the sea' Ibid.
'little graves about three feet deep' Ibid.
'I had rather an awful sort of dream' Ibid.
'the concussion in my grave' Ibid.
'our chaps are very bucked' Ibid.
'plus quite a lot of "possibles"' Ibid.
'I didn't feel I was suitably dressed' Ibid.
'I therefore designed myself' Ibid.
'Throw them back into the sea' Follain, *Mussolini's Island*, p. 85.
'I'm convinced our men will resist' Ibid., p. 84.
'We must be confident' Ibid.
'Most important' Holt, *The Deceivers*, p. 381
'complete failure of coastal defence' Message Rome to Berlin 2124 11/7/43, TNA ADM 223/147.

'on enemy penetration many' Ibid.
'half-clothed Italian soldiers' Bennett, *Ultra and Mediterranean Strategy*, p. 225.
'At once and with all forces attack' TNA ADM 223/147.
'The counterattack against hostile' Atkinson, *Day of Battle*, p. 103.
'the shortest Blitzkrieg in history' Follain, *Mussolini's Island*, p. 310.
'The German in Sicily is doomed' Atkinson, *Day of Battle*, p. 123.

Chapter 22: Hook, Line and Sinker

'Even if I have once brought off' EM to 'Ginger', 6 Jul 1943, Montagu Papers.
'too keyed-up to read a book' Ibid.
'It is really impossible to describe' Unpublished note, 7 Oct 1976, in IWM 97/45/1 folder #4.
'Joy of joys to anyone' Ibid.
'We fooled those of the Spaniards' Montagu, *Man*, p. 196.
'One specially made canister' Ewen Montagu, unpublished critique of Constantine Fitzgibbon, *Secret Intelligence in the Twentieth Century* (London, 1976), Montagu Papers.
'The most I could do was make' Montagu, *Ultra*, p. 166.
'I do congratulate you most warmly' Dudley Clarke to EM, note dated 14 May 1943, TNA CAB 154/67.
'It is a most interesting story' AN to JHB, note dated 20 Jul 1945, TNA CAB 154/67.
'the greatest achievement' EM to 'Ginger', 6 Jul 1943, Montagu Papers.
'Mincemeat has been' Liddell, *Diaries*, 20 May 1931.
'From evidence at present available' JHB to Inglis, 4 Oct 1943, TNA CAB 154/67.
'was the originator of this ingenious' JHB to Lamplough, 21 Aug 1943, TNA CAB 154/67.
'papers from Sikorski's aircraft' EM to JHB, 10 Jul 1943, TNA CAB 154/6.
'to show that Mincemeat was' Ibid.
'Not worth trying' Note attached to Ewen Montagu, JHB, 10 Jul 1943, TNA CAB 154/6, initials illegible.
'mousetrap for all German' Cited in Follain, *Mussolini's Island*, p. 311.
'Most Immediate' Signal Keitel to C in C Med, 9 Jul 1943, translation accompanying Rushbrooke report 19 Jul 1943, IWM, 97/45/1 folder #2.
'Western assault forces appear' Ibid.
'A subsequent landing' Ibid.
'stating that the High Command' TNA ADM 223/794, p. 456.
'entirely consistent with the' Ibid.
'complaining that the departure' Ibid., pp. 460–1.
'macaroni-eaters' Cited in Irving, *Goebbels*, p. 437.
'Hitler's own reaction was' Howard, *Grand Strategy*, p. 368.
'This report has been proved' Deakin, *Brutal Friendship*, p. 417.
'Undertake a most careful reappraisal' Ribbentrop to Dieckhoff in Madrid: 29 July 1943, Deakin, *Brutal Friendship*, p. 417.
'The documents had been found' Ibid.
'The English and Americans had' Ibid.
'The British Secret Service is quite' Ibid.
'that we should not adopt any' Ibid., p. 418.
'It is practically certain that' Ibid.
'Who originally circulated' Ibid.

'After the invasion of Italy' Interrogation of Joachim Canaris in MI5 Kuhlenthal file, TNA KV2/102.

'at present at any rate' MI 14/522/2 Kurze Feind Beurteilung West, 982 of 25 Jul 1943.

'The only thing certain in this war' Goebbels, *Diaries*, p. 437.

'The sacrifice of my country' Cited in Deakin, *Brutal Friendship*, p. 417.

'inept and cowardly' Ibid.

'We are fighting for a common' Atkinson, *Day of Battle*, p. 140.

'It can't go on any longer' Cited in Follain, *Mussolini's Island*, p. 240.

'Fascism fell, as was fitting' Atkinson, *Day of Battle*, p. 142.

'It is well known that under' OKW/KTB iv. 1797, cited in Bennett, *Ultra and Mediterranean Strategy*, p. 227.

'On no account should we let go' Alan Clark, *Barbarossa: The Russian–German Conflict 1941–45* (London, 1966) p. 337.

'Inescapably faced with the dilemma' Bennett, *Ultra and Mediterranean Strategy*, p. 222.

'With the failure of *Zitadelle*' Christer Bergström, *Kursk: The Air Battle of July 1943* (London, 2007), p. 58.

'a small classic of deception' TNA ADM 223/794, p. 442.

'as widely and thinly as possible' Bennett, *Ultra and Mediterranean Strategy*, p. 227.

'There can be no doubt' TNA ADM 223/794, p. 455.

'Special intelligence enabled us' Ibid., p. 442.

'Sicily has impressed everyone' Stafford, *Roosevelt and Churchill*, p. 107.

'really affected the outcome' Robertson, *The Ship with Two Captains*, p. 132.

'impossible to estimate' Ibid.

'the most spectacular single episode' Foreword to Montagu, *Ultra*, p. 10.

'perhaps the most successful single' Howard, *British Intelligence in The Second World War*, Vol. V: *Strategic Deception*, p. 89.

'Mincemeat swallowed rod' Howard, *Grand Strategy*, p. 370.

Chapter 23: Mincemeat Revealed

'considerable sum' EM to Shinwell, 7 Jan 1951, IWM 97/45/2.

'I am a prejudiced party' EM to Colonel Patavel at War Cabinet Office, 9 Jul 1945, IWM folder #1, 97/45/1.

'It would pay to release Mincemeat' Ibid.

'the Foreign Office would' EM to John Drew, 7 Nov 1950, IWM 97/45/2.

'in case the embargo' Ibid.

'Our intelligence obtained' Radio Monitoring report, 6 Aug 1944, IWM 97/45/1 folder #1.

'I believe this story is the greatest' Ibid.

'Unless some action is taken' TAR to JHB, 31 Aug 1944, TNA CAB 154/67.

'there was in fact some truth' Ibid.

'leave the American authorities' Ibid.

'We should do our utmost to stop' JHB to TAR, 21 Aug 1944, TNA CAB 154/67.

'Dawn had not broken' Alfred Duff Cooper, *Operation Heartbreak* (London, 2007) p. 103.

'Duff Cooper learned of Mincemeat' EM to Roger Morgan, 19 Apr 1982, IWM 97/45/1 folder #5.

'Sir W always wanted to hear this' *After the Battle*, 54, 1986.

'considered the objections' John Julius Norwich, in introduction to Montagu, *Man*, p. xi.

'direct from Churchill if prosecuted' R. V. Jones, *Most Secret War* (London, 1978) p. 217.

'consternation in security quarters' Ewen Montagu 'Postscript', Montagu Papers.

'there could not be one law for' EM to JG, 19 Sep 1964, Montagu Papers.

'wholly contrary to public' Sir Harold Parker to EM, 20 Dec 1950, IWM 97/45/2.

'One would not think even' EM to Sir Harold Parker, 7 Nov 1950, IWM 97/45/2.

'I forced Shinwell to agree that' EM to John Godfrey, 19 Sep 1964, Montagu Papers.

'sympathetically consider advice' EM to Sir Harold Parker, 2 Apr 1951, IWM 97/45/2.

'it would be wrong to publish' Ewen Montagu 'Postscript', Montagu Papers.

'shot off to Spain' EM to JG, 19 Sep 1964, Montagu Papers.

'cabled back in a frenzy' Ibid.

'The Foreign Office's chief worry' Ibid.

'using diplomats to lie' Ibid.

'Further pressure was applied' Ibid.

'the true means by which' Roger Morgan, *Beyond the Battle*, 146, Nov 2009.

'rushed round to the *Sunday Express*' Ibid.

'wholly unexpected' Montagu, *Ultra*, p. 12.

'The request not to publish' Ewen Montagu 'Postscript', Montagu Papers.

'so wildly inaccurate as to be' Ibid.

'controlled version' Morgan, *Beyond the Battle*, 146, Nov 2009.

'someone not under any control' EM to NLAJ, 11 Jan 1953, Montagu Papers.

'The return that the country got' EM to JG, 19 Sep 1964, Montagu Papers.

'The *Express* will submit and get' EM to NLAJ, 11 Jan 1953, Montagu Papers.

'with much black coffee and no' Ewen Montagu 'Postscript', Montagu Papers.

'or should it be "Pam"' EM to JGL, 8 Jan 1953, Montagu Papers.

'The powers that be have decided' Ibid.

'We don't want to alter anything' Ibid.

'a girl working in my section' Ibid.

'Mincemeat is soon going to be' EM to NLAJ, 11 Jan 1953, Montagu Papers.

'My account has been vetted' Ibid.

'I felt that you ought not to be' Ibid.

'I was most interested to hear' JGL to EM, 14 Jan 1954, Montagu Papers.

'merely say that you were working' EM to JGL, 21 Jan 1953, Montagu Papers.

'book, film rights, or other uses' CC to EM, 3 Mar 1954, Montagu Papers.

'As you will recall' Ibid.

'Whilst the general situation' Ibid.

'I do not feel that my own' Ibid.

'The war's most fantastic secret' *Sunday Express*, 1 Feb 1953.

'Although I heartily disapproved' Lord Mountbatten to EM, 31 Aug 1953, Montagu Papers.

'a good deal of persuasion that' AN to EM, 26 Apr 1954, Montagu Papers.

'You and I don't agree' J. C. Masterman to EM, 31 Aug 1954, Montagu Papers.

'Uncle John blitzed me' EM to Margery Boxall, 30 Oct 1950, courtesy of Fiona Mason.

'Your admirable *Man Who Never Was*' JG to EM, 13 Sep 1964, Montagu Papers.

'an exploit more astonishing' *Sunday Express*, 1 Feb 1953.

'managed to give the impression' Holt, *The Deceivers*, p. 370.

'an only son, an officer of' First draft of manuscript, IWM 97/45/1 folder #5.

'His parents were then' Ibid.
'without saying what we proposed' Montagu, *Man*, p. 123.
'I gave a solemn promise never' Montagu, *Ultra*, p. 145.
'My work is such that I will never' EM to 'Ginger', 6 Jul 1943, Montagu Papers.
'thrilling incidents which' EM 'Postscript', Montagu Papers.
'appear to be grudging' Lord Mountbattten to Ronald Neame, 29 Apr 1955, IWM 97/45/1 folder #4.
'I would like to make it clear' Ibid.
'I would have no objection' Ibid.
'There's nothing true in it' Interview with Federico Clauss, 2 Jun 2009.
'a derelict alcoholic found' Cave Brown, *Bodyguard of Lies*, p. 282.
'the wastrel brother of an MP' Ibid.
I have not explored the theory that the body was a victim of the HMS *Daster* explosion, since this is most effectively demolished by Roger Morgan in his essay 'Mincemeat Revisted', *Beyond the Battle*, 146, Nov 2009.

Chapter 24: Aftermath

'absolutely devoted to one another' Interview with Nicholas Jewell, 24 Jun 2008.
'General Mark Wayne Clark' Robertson, *The Ship with Two Captains*, p. 175.
'played a tiny part in ending the war' Ivor Leverton, letter to *Daily Telegraph*, 13 Aug 2002.
'redeemed' Interview with Basil Leverton, 8 Sep 2009.
'developed an intelligence' Denis Smyth, *Oxford Dictionary of National Biography*
'He walked several miles a day' Ibid.
'the most unscrupulous man in Spain' Stafford, *Roosevelt and Churchill*, p. 109.
'quiet, cold-blooded war of brains' Ibid., p. 373.
'The Russians are cleverer than' Ibid., p. 378.
'Thus ends the story' Edwin Sanders to Alan Hillgarth, 28 Jun 1948, collection of Tristan Hillgarth.
'Crazy Nolte is rich' Ibid.
'I am sorry, but I am not free' Colvin, *Unknown Courier*, p. 101.
'His mind was not as it used to be' Jackson, *Coroner*, p. 192.
'Every time I tell a story' Ibid., p. 201.
'His wife was the daughter of' Interview with Federico Clauss, 2 Jun 2009.
'He was always suspicious' Ibid.
'admitted the possibility' Colvin, *Unknown Courier*, p. 96.
'I take off my hat' Ian Colvin, *Sunday Express*, 8 Mar 1953.
'the heroic death of our beloved Führer' Harris, *Garbo*, p. 278.
'News of the death of our dear chief' Ibid., p. 280.
'If you find yourself in any danger' Ibid., p. 277.
'Kuhlenthal was overcome' Ibid., p. 285.
'Kuhlenthal made it abundantly' Ibid., p. 285.
'personally ordered that the medal' Ibid., p. 286.
'remain patiently in his hideout until' Ibid., p. 287.
'he should obey instructions to the letter' Ibid.
'Clandestinely' Ibid., p. 288.
'a melting pot' Dienz Website, http://www.dienz.de/Inhalt/karl-erichkuhlen.html
'he always tried to dress correctly' Ibid.
'De Profundibus' IWM 97/45/2.
'bold man to hounds' Obituary of John Gerard Leigh, *Daily Telegraph*, 1 Oct 2008.

'fought through Italy' Ibid.

'washing up, pottering about' Cited in *Oxford Dictionary of National Biography*.

'somewhat complicated by the fact' Nigel West and Oleg Tsarev, *Triplex: Secrets from the Cambridge Five* (Yale, 2009), p. 288.

'Captain [sic] Montagu is in charge' Ibid., pp. 277–8.

'The German General Staff' Ibid., p. 288.

'When the [invasion] was launched' Ibid.

'intelligent and agreeable' Philby to unnamed recipient MI5, 26 Nov 1946, TNA KV2/598.

'information from secret sources' TNA KV2/600.

'Middle East Anti-Locust Unit' Interview with Tom Cholmondeley, 1 Oct 2007.

'His objective was the destruction' G. F. Walford, *Arabian Locust Hunter* (London 1963) p. 32.

'they are loathsome insects' Ibid., p. 11.

'International Council for the Control' Interview with Tom Cholmondeley, 1 Oct 2007.

'intelligence duties' Ibid.

'wide experience of deception work' Ibid.

'He would not give information' Alison Cholmondeley, letter to the author 8 May 2008.

'He would take a revolver' John Otter, letter to *Daily Telegraph*, 15 Aug 2002.

'invaluable work during the war' EM, letter to *The Times*, 23 Jun 1982.

'The Turbulent Judge' *Sunday Mirror*, 5 Jul 1964.

'Half the scum of England' *Daily Telegraph*, 1 Feb, 1957.

'A boy crook should have' *Sunday Mirror*, 5 Jul 1964.

'discourtesy, even gross discourtesy' *The Times*, 24 Oct 1967.

'If a man can't have a stroke of luck' *Sun*, 2 Aug 1969.

'The public needs protecting from' *The Times*, 26 Sep 1962.

'Few judges have trodden so hard' *Sun*, 2 Aug 1969.

'Perhaps I should have been more' Henry Stenhope, *The Times*, 2 Aug 1969.

'extreme caution and extreme daring' M. R. D. Foot, *Oxford Dictionary of National Biography*.

'Dear "Pam"' EM to JGL, 31 Dec 1980, courtesy of Jean Gerard Leigh.

'one of the buttons I wore' EM to John F. Meek, undated, IWM 97/45/1 folder #5

'Keep a real sense of humour' Ibid.

'There, at the end of the last volume' *Beyond the Battle*, 94, 1995.

'On 28 January there had died' TNA ADM 223/794, p. 442.

'Glyndwr Michael' Inscription on gravestone, Huelva cemetery.

Select Bibliography

Archives

National Archives, Kew (TNA).

Imperial War Museum Archives (IWM).

Bundesarchiv-Militärarchiv, Freiburg.

National Archives, Washington DC.

British Library Newspaper Archive, Colindale.

Churchill Archives Centre (CA).

Mountbatten Papers, University of Southampton.

Labour History Archive and Study Centre (People's History Museum), Manchester (PHM.)

Printed Sources

Andrew, Christopher, *Secret Service: The Making of the British Intelligence Community* (London, 1985).

————*The Defence of the Realm: The Authorized History of MI5* (London, 2009).

Atkinson, Rick, *The Day of Battle: The War in Sicily and Italy 1943–1945* (London, 2007).

Beesly, Patrick, *Very Special Admiral: The Life of Admiral J. H. Godfrey* (London, 1980).

Bennett, Gill, *Churchill's Man of Mystery: Desmond Morton and the World of Intelligence* (London, 2007).

Bennett, Ralph, *Behind the Battle: Intelligence in the War with Germany 1939–45* (London, 1999).

————*Ultra and Mediterranean Strategy 1941–1945* (London, 1989)

Burns, Jimmy, *Papa Spy: Love, Faith and Betrayal in Wartime Spain* (London, 2009).

Cave Brown, Anthony, *Bodyguard of Lies*, Vol. I (London, 1975).

Carter, Miranda, *Anthony Blunt: His Lives* (London, 2001).

Colvin, Ian, *The Unknown Courier* (London, 1953).

Copeiro del Villar, Jesús Ramírez, *Huelva en la II Guerra Mundial* (Huelva, 1996).

Crowdy, Terry, *Deceiving Hitler: Double Cross and Deception in World War II* (London, 2008).

Curry, J., *The Security Service 1908–1945: The Official History* (London, 1999).

Day, Albert Edward, *Dialogue and Destiny* (New York, 1981).

Deakin, F. W., *The Brutal Friendship: Mussolini, Hitler and the Fall of Italian Fascism* (London, 1962).

D'Este, Carlo, *Bitter Victory: The Battle for Sicily 1943* (London, 1988).

Evans, Colin, *The Father of Forensics: How Sir Bernard Spilsbury Invented Modern CSI* (London, 2009).

Farago, Ladislas, *The Game of the Foxes: The Untold Story of German Espionage in the US and Great Britain during World War Two* (New York, London, 1972).

Fisher, John, *What a Performance: A Life of Sid Field* (London, 1975).

Follain, John, *Mussolini's Island: The Untold Story of the Invasion of Italy* (London, 2005).

Foot, M. R. D., *SOE: The Special Operations Executive 1940–1946* (London, 1999).

Gilbert, Martin, *Winston S. Churchill*, Vol. 6: *Finest Hour, 1939–1941* (London, 1983).

Handel, Michael I., *War Strategy and Intelligence* (London, 1989).

Harris, Tomas, *Garbo: The Spy Who Saved D-Day*; Introduction by Mark Seaman (London, 2004).

Hastings, Max, *Finest Years: Churchill as Warlord 1940–45* (London, 2009).

Hinsley, F. H., *British Intelligence in the Second World War: Its Influence on Strategy and Operations*, Vol. I (London, 1979).

Hinsley, F. H. and Simkins, C. A. G., *British Intelligence in the Second World War: Security and Counter-Intelligence*, Vol. IV (London, 1990).

Holmes, Richard, *Churchill's Bunker: The Secret Headquarters at the Heart of Britain's Victory* (London, 2009).

Holt, Thaddeus, *The Deceivers: Allied Military Deception in the Second World War* (London, 2004).

Howard, Michael, *Grand Strategy* (London, 1972).

———— *British Intelligence in the Second World War*, Vol. V: *Strategic Deception* (London 1990).

Irving, David, *Hitler's War* (London, 1977).

Jackson, Robert, *Coroner: The Biography of Sir Bentley Purchase* (London, 1963).

Jewell, Lt N. L. A., as told to Cecil Carnes, *Secret Mission Submarine: Action Report of the HMS Seraph* (London, 1944).

Johnson, David Alan, *Righteous Deception: German Officers Against Hitler* (Westport, Connecticut, 2001).

Kahn, David, *Hitler's Spies: German Military Intelligence in World War II* (New York, 2000).

Knightley, Philip, *The Second Oldest Profession* (London, 1986).

Lawrence, T. E., *Seven Pillars of Wisdom* (London, 1991).

Liddell, Guy, *The Guy Liddell Diaries, 1939–1945,* Vols. I and II; edited by Nigel West (London, 2005).

Lord, John, *Duty, Honour, Empire* (London, 1971).

Macintyre, Ben, *For Your Eyes Only: Ian Fleming and James Bond* (London, 2008).

Masterman, J. C., *The Double Cross System in the War 1939–1945* (London, 1972).

———— *On the Chariot Wheel: An Autobiography* (Oxford, 1975).

McLachlan, Donald, *Room 39: Naval Intelligence in Action 1939–45* (London, 1968).

Miller, Russell, *Codename Tricycle: The True Story of the Second World War's Most Extraordinary Double Agent* (London, 2005).

Montagu, Ewen, *Beyond Top Secret Ultra* (London, 1977).

———— *The Man Who Never Was* (Oxford, 1996).

Montagu, Ivor, *The Youngest Son: Autobiographical Chapters* (London, 1970)

Mure, David, *Practise to Deceive* (London, 1997).

Paine, Lauran, *The Abwehr: German Military Intelligence in World War II* (London, 1984).

Payne, Stanley G., *Franco and Hitler: Spain, Germany and World War II* (London, 2008).

Philby, Kim, *My Silent War: The Autobiography of a Spy* (London, 1968)

Popov, Dusko, *Spy/Counterspy* (New York, 1974).

Rankin, Nicholas, *Churchill's Wizards: The British Genius for Deception 1914–1945* (London, 2008.)

Robertson, Terence, *The Ship with Two Captains: The Story of the 'Secret Mission Submarine'* (London, 1957).

Rose, Andrew, *Lethal Witness: Sir Bernard Spilsbury, the Honorary Pathologist* (London, 2008).

Rose, Kenneth, *Elusive Rothschild: The Life of Victor, Third Baron* (London, 2003).

Sebag-Montefiore, Hugh, *Enigma: The Battle for the Code* (London, 2000).

Smyth, Denis, *Diplomacy and Strategy of Survival: British Policy and Franco's Spain 1940–41* (Cambridge, 1986).

Stafford, David, *Churchill and the Secret Service* (London, 1997).

————*Roosevelt and Churchill: Men of Secrets* (London, 1999).

Stephens, R. 'Tin Eye', *Camp 020: MI5 and the Nazi Spies*; Introduction by Oliver Hoare (London, 2000).

Stephenson, William, *A Man Called Intrepid: the Secret War of 1939–45* (London, 1976).

Thomson, Sir Basil, *The Milliner's Hat Mystery* (London, 1937).

Walford, G. F., *Arabian Locust Hunter* (London, 1963).

Waller, John H., *The Unseen War in Europe: Espionage and Conspiracy in the Second World War* (New York, London, 1996).

West, Nigel, *MI5: British Security Service Operations 1909–45* (London, 1981).

————At Her Majesty's Secret Service: The Chiefs of Britain's Intelligence Agency, MI6 (London, 2006).

————*Mask: MI5's Penetration of the Communist Party of Great Britain* (London, 2005).

————*Venona: The Greatest Secret of the Cold War* (London, 1999)

West, Nigel and Tsarev, Oleg (eds), *Triplex: Secrets from the Cambridge Five* (Yale, 2009).

Wilson, Emily Jane, *The War in the Dark: The Security Service and the Abwehr 1940–1944*, PhD thesis (Cambridge, 2003).

Winterbotham, F. W., *The Ultra Secret* (London, 1974).

Acknowledgments

I am hugely indebted to the scores of people in five countries who have helped me in the writing of this book. In Britain, Germany and Spain, the families of the participants in Operation Mincemeat have been extraordinarily generous with their time, memories and documentary material: Jeremy Montagu, Jennifer Montagu, Rachel Montagu, Sarah Montagu, Tom Cholmondeley, Alison Cholmondeley, Jean Gerard Leigh, John Gerard Leigh, Carolyn Benson, John Michael, Paul Jewell, Nicholas Jewell, Tristan Hillgarth, Jocelyn Hillgarth, Juliette Kuhlenthal, Federico Clauss, Andrew Leverton, Basil Leverton, Yvette Bourguignon and Sir Alan Urwick. Many others, either directly or indirectly involved, willingly contributed additional material: the late Joan Bright-Astley, Gill Drake, Lady Victoire Ridsdale, Peggy Harmer, Patricia Davies, John Julius Norwich, Eve Streatfeild, Nicholas Reed, Isabelle Naylor and Selina Fraser-Smith. Still others offered useful advice and contacts: Annabel Merullo, Sam Merullo, Emma Crichton, Guy Liardet, Jack Baer, James Owen, Jan Dalley, John Scarlett, Ian Brunskill, Robert Hands, Fiona and Peter Mason, Stephen Walker, Sally George, Phil Reed and Robin Hunt. To the other individuals who have asked not to be named: my covert but heartfelt gratitude.

I am grateful to numerous experts in various fields for their advice and guidance: Dr Sacha Kolar on forensic pathology; Neil Cooke on Whitehall geography; Mary Teviot for her genealogical sleuthing; Pedro J. Ramírez, Julio Martín Alarcón and the staff of *El Mundo* in Spain; Jesús Copeiro for sharing his local knowledge and for a fascinating guided tour of Huelva and Punta Umbria; Paul Bryant; Graham Keeley for his work in Spain and Jo Carlill and Paul Bellshaw for their help with pictures.

Numerous historians and writers have also helped me to shape the book: Christopher Andrew, Michael Foot, Frank Stech, Andrew Rose, Roger Morgan, Tim Cottingham, John Follain, Sarah Street, Thomas Boghardt, Andrew Lycett, and Martin Gilbert. I am particularly grateful to Peter Martland, Mark Seaman and Terry Charman for reading the manuscript, and saving me from some toe-curling errors. The remaining mistakes are all my own.

This book has involved many hours of archive research, and I have been helped immeasurably by a number of brilliant and dedicated archivists: Rod Suddaby of the Imperial War Museum; Howard Davies, Hugh Alexander and the staff of the National Archives; James Beckett of the Formula One Archives; Neil F. Murray of the Aston Martin Club; Lesley Hall of the Wellcome Trust; Darren Treadwell of the People's History Museum, and Caroline Herbert of the Churchill Archives Centre.

My friends and colleagues on *The Times* have been, as always, unstinting in their help and advice. I have Duncan Stewart to thank, once again, for the fine maps.

My thanks to Michael Fishwick, Kate Johnson and the team at Bloomsbury for all their enthusiasm, professionalism and patience. Ed Victor has been my rock for each of my last seven books. My thanks and apologies to the friends and family who have put up with me banging on about Operation Mincemeat for three years. And to Kate, as ever, all my love.

Index

Figures in bold refer to illustrations.

ALSO AVAILABLE BY BEN MACINTYRE

AGENT ZIGZAG
THE TRUE WARTIME STORY OF EDDIE CHAPMAN: LOVER, TRAITOR, HERO, SPY

One December night in 1942, a Nazi parachutist landed in a Cambridgeshire field. His mission: to sabotage the British war effort. His name was Eddie Chapman, but he would shortly become MI5's Agent Zigzag. Dashing and louche, courageous and unpredictable, inside the traitor was a hero, inside the villain, a man of conscience: the problem for Chapman, his many lovers and his spymasters, was knowing where one ended and the other began. Ben Macintyre weaves together diaries, letters, photographs, memories and top-secret MI5 files to create the exhilarating account of Britain's most sensational double agent.

'As engrossing as any thriller and more improbable than most'
Daily Telegraph

'For anyone interested in the Second World War, spying, romance, skullduggery or the hidden chambers of the human mind, it would be impossible to recommend it too highly★★★★★'
Mail on Sunday Book of the Week

'Superb'
John le Carré

A SPY AMONG FRIENDS: PHILBY AND THE GREAT BETRAYAL

The No. 1 *Sunday Times* Bestseller

Featuring an afterword by John le Carré

Kim Philby was the most notorious British defector and Soviet mole in history. Agent, double agent, traitor and enigma, he betrayed every secret of Allied operations to the Russians in the early years of the Cold War.

Philby's two closest friends in the intelligence world, Nicholas Elliott of MI6 and James Jesus Angleton, the CIA intelligence chief, thought they knew Philby better than anyone, and then discovered they had not known him at all. This is a story of intimate duplicity; of loyalty, trust and treachery, class and conscience; of an ideological battle waged by men with cut-glass accents and well-made suits in the comfortable clubs and restaurants of London and Washington; of male friendships forged, and then systematically betrayed.

With access to newly released MI5 files and previously unseen family papers, and with the cooperation of former officers of MI6 and the CIA, this definitive biography unlocks what is perhaps the last great secret of the Cold War.

'Thrilling ... I'm not a lover of spy novels, yet I adored this book'
The Times Book of the Week

'Gripping ... Bottomlessly fascinating ... This book consists of 300 pages; I would have been happy had it been three times as long *****'
Mail on Sunday

'Hugely engrossing ... authoritative and enthralling'
William Boyd, *New Statesman*

FOR YOUR EYES ONLY
IAN FLEMING AND JAMES BOND

One morning in February 1952, a journalist called Ian Fleming sat down at his desk and set about creating a fictional secret agent. James Bond was born and would go on to become one of the most successful, enduring and lucrative creations in literature. But Bond's world of glamour and romance, gadgets and cocktails, espionage and villainy wasn't entirely drawn from imagination: Fleming's background and his experiences as an intelligence officer during the Second World War were all formative parts in the creation of the world's most famous spy. *For Your Eyes Only* is the most enlightening, enlivening book on the creator of the spy who not only lived twice, but proved to be immortal.

'A marvellously entertaining and informative book ... deserves to fly off the shelves every bit as quickly as *Devil May Care*' Spectator

'Everything that makes Bond interesting with relation to the real world, in fact, is explored here' *Tom Fleming, Literary Review*

*

DOUBLE CROSS
THE TRUE STORY OF THE D-DAY SPIES

D-Day, 6 June 1944, the turning point of the Second World War, was a victory of arms. But it was also a triumph for a different kind of operation: one of deceit . . .

At the heart of the deception was the 'Double Cross System', a team of double agents whose bravery, treachery, greed and inspiration succeeded in convincing the Nazis that Calais and Norway, not Normandy, were the targets of the 150,000-strong Allied invasion force. These were not conventional warriors, but their masterpiece of deceit saved thousands of lives. Their codenames were Bronx, Brutus, Treasure, Tricycle and Garbo. This is their story.

'I have seldom enjoyed a spy story more than this one, and fiction will make dreary reading hereafter'
Max Hastings, *Sunday Times*

'Addictive and deeply moving'
Independent

'Utterly gripping'
Antony Beevor